'THE TROUBLES TO GREET BEAUTY'

'Von der Mühe die Schönheit zu begrüßen'

The true story about Gretel, a woman of her time.

By Sonja Grossner

THE TROUBLES TO GREET BEAUTY

ISBN: 978-1-907540-31-8

Published January 2011
Reprinted February 2011

Printed and Published by Anchorprint Group Limited
www.anchorprint.co.uk

For my mum.

My thanks and gratitude to my daughter Lorna, friends in Dresden Germany, Mary,

my aunty Dinah and many others for support and

encouragement to write this true story.

Title page; Girl with dove, modelled in terracotta, (approx 1970)

Dedicated to my parents

Gretel Grossner, a sculptress, landscape painter, fighter for peace and antifascist activist.

Peter Klopfleisch, a fighter for peace and antifascist activist.

Here is their story.

In loving memory;

Their daughter and granddaughter,

Sonja Elizabeth Grossner.

Lorna Jane Grossner

England 1986 - 2010

Begging gipsy children, modelled in Prague, about 1935

'THE TROUBLES TO GREET BEAUTY'.

'Von der Mühe, die Schönheit zu begrüßen'.

This is the title of a newspaper article written about my mother's last successful exhibition, one year before she died. At last, after many struggles, the 'Association of Artists in the GDR', 'Verband Bildender Künstler' finally accepted her, and gave her the artistic recognition she deserved.

This last exhibition in Dresden; Gallerie Comenius Orbis Pictus 27, 1981 was organized by the culture league of the GDR, by the city council of Dresden and was a great success.

The hardship and struggles my parents experienced as socialists and anti-Nazi fighters, who were active political dissident during the 1920s and under Hitler, their lives in exile in the Czech republic followed by their escape to Britain is a story that has to be told. Following these experiences they continued to endure life as foreign aliens in postwar Britain and internment camp. Their application to return to Dresden in the 1950's was turned down by the Russian authorities without any reason given. A possible earlier return to the GDR with other émigrés was difficult as they were now the parents of two small children.

A holiday trip 1960 with my mother and sister to Dresden, in the former GDR resulted in permanent residence. There, we witnessed and experienced first-hand the corruption and oppression growing within the state. In 1984 I returned to England with my daughter, then aged 11.

My father was a member of the 'Rot Front Kämpfer Bund', (Red Front Fighters League) and was delegated to represent his area and sent to visit the young Soviet Union. My parents met through their political activities. This is their story, particularly my mother and her fight for artistic recognition. It is also the story of the constant struggles my parents experienced, as anti-fascists, their life in the emigration and the return to the GDR.

Contents.

All poems are written by my mother, (except for two poems, in chapter 7, and two poems in chapter 8 that I wrote as a child).
All photos are of artworks created by my mother Margarete Grossner Klopfleisch, (known as Gretel).

Aquarelle; Autumn landscape, (1939)

Prologue

A friend once said to me, 'You must write it all down,' so here it is;
This is the story of my mother's life and her legacy, her childhood years, fleeing from Nazi oppression, emigration, life in Britain and then the return to the GDR[1]; life behind the 'iron curtain.' My parents went through hell, through the fire of war, to keep their believes and I feel privileged to have been born as their daughter.

Hounded by the Nazis and the Stasi my mother found peace in nature; this is reflected in her artwork.

I have had a wonderful childhood, although there were some dark clouds.
My parents made it possible for me to receive a good education, even private schooling and music lessons. They gave me so much.

When you read this story, of the constant struggles, of the continuous challenges my parents faced and of the repeated persecution from all political sides, fleeing from Nazi occupation, the anguish of internment camp and separation, life as an 'alien,' in post-war Britain, the hope to return to their home, unexplained refusal and when at last they did return the constant mistrust, stalking and spying from the GDR authority and Stasi, it is understandable to grasp the disillusion and disappointment my parents felt when they realized the totalitarian Stalinist state they had eventually returned to. Also, not many tales are told of anti-fascists and their fight for freedom, peace and equality.

Family photo from Maidenhead

---

[1] GDR- German Democratic Republic.

1

The Beginning.

"The events in Keglerheim[2] are for all of us old Dresdner anti-fascists a sad memory, but in spite of everything it gave me a lot of fighting spirit, courage, hope and confidence that the barbaric fascism would not last for ever". Quote from a report Gretel wrote about a demonstration in Dresden 1933.

'Ich mußte Wandern durch die Welt,
konnte nie bleiben wo mirs gefällt,
Ich wurde hin und her getrieben,
So lernte ich Wind und Wetter lieben.'

(Written about 1976)

Translation

'I had to wander through the world,
Could never stay where I liked,
I was thrown to and fro,
And so learned to love wind and weather.'

'Birth'.

'Childhood joyful golden time,
Like a flower, dreaming in sun shine,
Like a happy little whistling bird,
Announcing a better world,
Predestined who remains this childhood
Clean and vivid coloured heart.
That gives a nicer world,
A happier life,
I think that is the root of art.'

(Written 1942)

---

[2] Keglerheim - (house for skittle players). Keglerheim demonstration took place on the 25.1 33. Hitler came to power on 30.1 33.

Introduction.

It was a chilly cold 23rd of November in distant Dresden in 1982. My 9-year-old daughter was with me. It was peaceful and quiet in the chapel, except for the organ and violin music. We were altogether 40 individuals present. I had invited them personally to pay a last tribute to my mother and they all came - the comrades who had looked on us with suspicion and mistrust; - the artists who had never quite wanted to accept mother into their midst; - The various G. D. R. Organizations, S E D (Socialist united Party of the G.D.R.), V D N (organization for victims of Nazism); what were they thinking? - And many faithful true friends.

I had requested violin music for the ceremony - one of her favourite gipsy violin melodies. To begin with, a comrade spoke, praising her as a faithful communist. I thought to myself - how ironical. They were always making life extra hard for us during her lifetime

After that Dr. Dieter Schmidt spoke wonderful comforting words, full of truth and criticism of what should have been done for us: - She had returned to the country and town of her birth, but she was not wanted there. He spoke about her political past - fight against fascism, and artistic development. He stood all the time during the service next to us, a true friend supporting us at this moment of deepest sorrow.

After the ceremony the coffin was carried to her last place of rest, alongside her mother whom she had lost as a 13-year-old child. One could almost imagine my mother's surprise at all those folk trailing after us to her grave, and she trying to get back to life. Then, as the coffin was lowered down into the earth, one of the carriers let the rope slip and the coffin opened. All could see her again dressed in a white garment for that last long sleep.

Now no one can harm her anymore, and it is up to me to protect her heritage and life's work for the world of the future.

It is a very peaceful spot, mother's last place of rest, with many old trees surrounding it and each grave, a tiny, tidy, individual garden with lots of flowers.

Graphic; 'Greeting Death'; (approx 1980).

11

CHAPTER 1.

The Beginning - Childhood, 1911 – 1924.

My mother was a courageous woman and an excellent artist of strong personality. She left me many fine artworks after her death, wonderful sculptures and wonderful paintings. This is her story and also my story.

Gretel was born in Dresden on the 2nd of August 1911. Her father was a cabinet-maker with his own workshop, and her mother an amateur opera singer. At that time the family were relatively prosperous. My grandmother was of delicate health and often seriously ill. The birth was a difficult one, and only through an operation possible, as grandmother was too narrowly built for a natural birth. In spite of this, my mother was her second child and this child fought from the beginning for every breath of life. So grandmother's anxiety that her daughter would not live was blown away in the wind.

My sister and I often asked our mother to tell us her story about her life. On cold winter evenings and before bedtime she told us these tales of her childhood, youth and how she came to Britain. So I am now today, able to recall these stories. Together with these memories and written notes, diary notes and letters, I awaken her once more to life.

In my mother's own words, she writes:
"My father, Richard Grossner came from Bubbendorf, near Leipzig. His father was a farmer and a blacksmith. My father worked hard to become a master cabinet-maker, and in spite of many difficulties always worked independently. He had his own workshop. He died during the Second World War. My mother Sophie Margarete was from birth a 'Tube'. Her father was an independent gardener. His ancestors, 'von Tuba' was resident in Sachsen for centuries. Perhaps this is why my longing for my home Dresden in Sachsen Germany is so immense in spite of the many years that I have been pushed around in foreign countries."

And so lived the cabinet-maker, Richard Grossner together with his wife Sophie, the new born babe Gretel and 6 year old son Johannes, in the midst of the city of Dresden, in Johannstadt on the Lortzing street.

Brother Hans must have been very proud of his baby sister, couldn't wait to see her. Once as mother Sophie went shopping with her two children, she told Hans to take care of baby Gretel and wait quietly and bravely outside the shop. The temptation proved too much for brother Hans. It was an invitation to have an extra peep at the little baby sister. The pram was tall; too big for little Hans and baby Gretel fell out. Fortunately, the bedding and wrappings were thick, as was the fashion of that time and these saved the baby's life.

Father Richard's business was running quite satisfactory. He could even afford an apprentice. The parents were still regular churchgoers and devoted believers in the Christian faith. Years later, this faith is neglected as a result of the enormous hard times and general decline in the standard of living, the war years, the after war years, inflation and hunger.

Little Gretel must have been immensely impressed one Sunday during a church visit, seeing that priest in his long black gown standing high upon the platform, waving his arms around and singing with uplifted glance. The whole congregation listened to him. The temptation was irresistible for little Gretel. She scrambled up on the chair and with childish admiration imitated that high person, waving her hands and singing in the same fashion. The churchwarden must have been very annoyed. How dare that child disturb the church service like this? He took the small child down from her chair and carried her out of the church. The high church doors slammed shut, leaving the small child outside crying.

The next scene is at the day nursery. Mother Sophie was at work and had to leave her small daughter at the kindergarten to play with other children. All were having fun and games, dancing around together in a circle; but not little Gretel. Nothing could move her to change her mind to play with the others. She had her own doll and danced all alone in a corner separately. At that moment, her doll was the most important thing of all

A marriage of a relative caused some distress for the small girl. Little Gretel was now a pretty, proudly dressed bridesmaid. Walking down the isle towards the altar in front of the bride and bridegroom she threw flowers down 'to make the path pretty'. But what was that? Glancing back, she saw all those grownups trampling and squashing her flowers. She ran back between the grownups feet picking up her treasures and trying to save them.

The First World War, and its financially crippling aftermath, was now plunging Germany into a deep depression and was the beginning of a time of considerable privation. Gretel's father has to report for service, but he is lucky. He receives an easy non-dangerous post. On leave for holiday, he returns to visit his family and asks if his 'little doll' has enough to eat. In those days there were still plenty of relatives around, unscarred from the war. Often extended family meetings were arranged.

Grandfather Tube's appearance was particularly unforgettable for little Gretel, with his own poems, drama readings, and tales of century old family legends. These legends and tales handed down from family to family over the centuries still exist today in writing at the museum in Badschandau, further particulars about this later.

In her youth, mother Sophie often sang for an amateur theatre group. But after the birth of her daughter she became too weak and her voice suffered as a result. She did not have the strength to sing as she used to. However, the songs she sang evenings before bedtime awakened the love for music in little Gretel.

My mother wrote in her diary:
"My dear mother died shortly before I left school, before I was 14 years old. Although she died when I was so young, she did not leave me before awakening the love for nature, for art, for freedom and truth. Since earliest childhood the May demonstrations made a deep and everlasting impression on me, then the whole family went and took part on them. I was a member of the youth's working class movement for many years and I had to intersperse my views already at school. I had the ' honour' of being scorned at, hassled and harassed from certain teachers because they had seen me together with my parents at the May demonstrations."

The struggle for daily life was great. The need for food became essential, becoming more urgent as the weeks went by. Father Richards's cabinetmakers business did not bring enough in for the daily needs. Gone were the times of financial security, and plenteousness. The German economy continued to decline, inflation became astronomical, food and other basic necessities grew ever scarcer.

The apprentice had been discharged long ago. Sometimes mother Sophie was able to help out. She worked in a cucumber factory and bought home cucumber juice and seeds not needed for making 'Senft Gorken'[1] so occasionally there was a delicacy together with the dry bread. At other times mother Sophie was able to work at the 'Dresdener Strietzel Market' [2] selling honeycomb. Gretel accompanied her. Watching the shoppers, the Christmas

---

[1] Senft gorken - a certain variety of pickled sour cucumber
[2] Dresdener Striezel Market – Annual Christmas Fair and market

preparations, coloured lights and Christmas merchandise on show and the market dealer's music praising their goods for sale, this created a permanent image in her mind.

It became increasingly financially difficult for father Richard to keep the independent workshop going. The grief, sorrow, daily needs of the after war years, the daily fight for life existence in the city weakened doubly the already delicate health of mother Sophie. Tales of events and scenes during the inflation years are very vivid and strong. There was no food available in the city. In autumn, mother Sophie went with her children to the park to collect acorns. This park 'Grosser Garten' still exists in the middle in the Dresden, a wonderful green paradise in the midst of a large city. In great despair flour was made from acorns. For meals, there was acorn bread, acorn soup, and acorn coffee.

Other variations of urgent indispensable food was made, this included using dandelions All this was the cause of mother Sophie's early death and Gretel's future bad health. Gretel now visits the 'Volksschule', [3](folk's school) on the Durer Street. According to German tradition, the first day at school is celebrated like a special birthday. It is an exceptional day, and children are given presents, plenty of sweets and good things. Family and relatives gather together and celebrate this special day. Children are given 'Zucker Tuten'[4] [bags of sweets]. How different that first day at school is for little Gretel compared with the normal tradition today. Mother Sophie had no resources for a celebration or presents. Instead, little Gretel receives a large bag of sugared carrots. She had asked for them anyway and eats the sugared carrots with great delight on the way to school.

Little Gretel is growing fast, a bubbly and lively child. Mother Sophie is often trouble. She thought she also had a daughter as well as a son, but little Gretel has hardly any thought for girlish behaviour. She scampers around, faster than the boys, often climbing trees competing with the boys and tearing her pretty dresses.

The parent's lack of money and Gretel's urgent desire for sports shoes is the intuitive inspiration of an idea. Father Richard had made some small footstools and so Gretel decides to arrange house visits going from door to door offering them for sale. The parents agree. Brother Hans is supposed to go with, but he is a bit of a coward and leaves the work for the six year younger sister, refusing to go anywhere near the doors. He just peeps round the corner and curiously watches Gretel's movements.

The villas of the rich and wealthier are Gretel's first logical choice to visit, to try to sell her goods, commonsense telling her, that here she could be successful, but she has no luck. Her choice turns out to be quite a dangerous decision, resulting in threatening encounters, being shouted at, and she is even pursued by dangerous dogs. It remains a mystery how the parents eventually find the money for the so long-awaited sport shoes, but Gretel's efforts are rewarded and she joyfully runs to school with her prize.

Amongst the many letters and documents left behind for me after my mother's death, I found following report about an experience she had as a child, here it is in her own words. She wrote this after visiting a performance of Ballet Senegal in Dresden about 1965 and comparing it with an incident from her childhood. A dance company from Africa, called 'Ballet Senegal' gave an unforgettable performance in Dresden. They were on tour around the country.

"With horror and disbelief we read each day in the daily newspapers the cruel reports of other countries constantly fighting for peace and independence. We wish with all our hearts

---

[3] Volksschule– folks school Compulsory eight- year schools system for 6 to 14 years olds.

[4] Zucker Tute-. Pointed cone-shaped bag, all sizes, today filled with all sorts of things, sweets, presents and chocolates for a child's first day at school

that these countries can also overcome their oppressors, start building a better peaceful world with decent acceptable living standards, a life worth living. But the reason I am writing this, is because of an unforgettable episode from my earliest childhood. It proves how far forwards we have ventured, all the good things we have done, even though we must be aware of what still has to be done. I do not know in what year it happened, perhaps 1920. Neither do I know where these people came from; our dark skinned guests that we had in Dresden. But how typical for a government, that was preparing the way for Hitler's fascist regime to display our dark skinned African visitors in the zoo! I went there with my parents and was very saddened to see the gloomy faces of these visitors bitterly and miserably freezing in the cold. They had built themselves open straw huts and their main income consisted of selling peanuts.

What suffering and struggles humankind had to cope with since then. A young man from this group came over to my mother begging; 'Mama would you buy peanuts!' There was no dancing, no singing, the instruments hung idle there, and the cold wind blow over the strings. When one of the men finally started playing the drums, it was more like a death march. How different it is today, how we welcomed our guests. Each drum roll was so clear like the words; freedom, peace and world friendship and we acknowledged this with the most enthusiastic applause.

All of us who saw this ballet clapped so much, our hands hurt. Although this ballet was a completely new experience for us all, and the music was different and strange for us to hear, so was each drum roll unmistakable an expression of the perfect joys of life, to the full. This was so clearly obvious to us all."

This report shows clearly how confident my mother was at first that the GDR government was heading in the right direction, that we were living in a socialist society even though she was already experiencing difficulties within this GDR Stalinist regime. Her great optimism was exceptional and her socialist views unbreakable.

Once, in a time of need and insufficient food rations Gretel encounters a boy apprentice pushing a cart down the road. His cargo was carefully covered. Suddenly the boy slips, the cart topples over, loads of sausages, all sorts and all sizes roll onto the road in front of little Gretel. She cannot remember when had she seen, or even tasted something like this. It must have been a long time ago. The sausages rolled in front of her feet, so easy to reach, so near. It was like looking at paradise. Unable to think much, she turns round and runs home as fast as her little feet carry her. Mother Sophie looked frightened at the breathless daughter, who gasps out the news:
"Sausages are rolling about on the road."
Mother Sophie usually took great care to educate her children to honesty and truthfulness. But desperate times causes her to gasp out in agony, "why didn't you pick some up and bring them home? What have we to eat today?"

Gretel had a pet rabbit, white with red eyes. It was usually her duty to feed it. Every day she used to stroke and cuddle it, but at the same time, because her stomach was rumbling for hunger, unable to control her needs she ate half of the rabbit's food herself. Imagine a child squatting before the rabbit hutch sharing out the potato peels! One for you, one for me!
The day came when father Richard could stand the hunger no longer. This weekend we will have the rabbit. Little Gretel's grief must have been great. My mother never ate rabbit meat for the rest of her life, too deep was the sorrow in that young age. Also imagine the despair of mother Sophie.
"At last, now we can have a decent meal this weekend and you refuse to eat."

Mother Sophie spreads rabbit fat on the bread but Gretel even refuses to eat this. She had already lost her beloved Lordchen, a little white dog because it was too expensive to keep. To comfort Gretel and console her loss, she receives the rabbit skin as a scarf for the cold winter months. This rabbit skin saves her life. Criminal offences at this time were extremely high, (Herman and Denker time)[5]. One day on the way home from school Gretel is attacked by a man. The warm and thick rabbit skin prevents the man from strangling her. A passer-by hearing Gretel's cry for help and seeing her distress, hurries to the scene to assist and aid her and takes her home. The parents have extremely little confidence in the police so this episode remains unreported.

After my uncle died, we found some inflation bank notes among the assets he left behind. These bank notes are a document for themselves, and no one today can even imagine the distress and misery those years must have caused. Inflation rate changed over night. No one knew what would happen the next day. There were long queues for food, (if food was available) and my mother told me of situations where a whole bag full of bank notes was needed to pay for a loaf of bread. The value of money changed so fast that only one side of the bank note was printed on. Image paying 100 billion mark for a loaf of bread, image having to stuff a bag full of these bank notes to pay for a single necessary item!! Next day, these bank notes were of no value and useless. No wonder acorns and dandelions were used as a food supplement. These bank notes are dated between 15th December 1922 and the 5th November 1923. There is a one thousand mark bank note, which has a red stamp put on it, increasing the inflation rate over night to a one billion mark bank note. There were one million bank notes from 15th August 1923 and ten million and one hundred million mark bank notes by 22nd August 1923. By September 1923 there were five hundred million and five billion mark bank notes as well as ten billion, 20 billion mark bank notes, then increasing to 50 billion and 200 billion mark bank notes by October 1923. These documents prove the hardship and enormous suffering the German working class at that time had to deal with.

'Inflation banknotes'

The children accompany the parents on May Day demonstrations from earliest childhood and this experience made profound impressions on them. Attributing both Gretel's appreciation of art and her sense of political justice - both of which were to prove vital to her survival in later years, she recalls the harassment and vilification she received as a schoolgirl from some of her teachers, many of whom were by then being drawn into the National Socialists.

One callous woman teacher waits to seize her chance and uses the occasion when Gretel is preoccupied in a lesson. The teacher calls on her to read aloud. But Gretel does not know

---

[5] Herman and Denker were two murderers who made sausages out of their victims

where to begin. She had been reading ahead. The story was interesting and she did not want to wait, so, in a whispering tone she asks her bench neighbour to show her the place.

Gretel's movements are caught by this heartless teacher's eagle eyes. This is what she had been waiting for, and she gleefully says to Gretel, "sit down, you are stupid."

Gretel's immediate reaction was to reply politely, "thank you, stupid yourself."

This teacher, speechless and her face turning deadly white, rushes out of the classroom. The class is in up roar and excited. After sometime the teacher returns and the lesson continues as if nothing had happened.

Nothing more is ever said, or heard about this event and no punishment given. The teacher had been told that she had no right to say such a thing. This was, for the strict Prussian school system of that time quite an unusual experience.

Shortly after this a new teacher arrives. This teacher recognizes Gretel's growing and developing artistic talents and interests. He is a friendly, thoughtful and sympathetic man completely different from the rest, supporting, praising and encouraging Gretel's ability to draw and reads her imaginative lively essays and stories aloud to the class.

At the school leaving ceremony Gretel is the only one to be alone. No one is with her. During one lesson, the children are told to draw and design various kinds of hats. This was just too boring for Gretel to draw only a variety of hats and the temptation to draw people underneath them irresistible. Gretel tries to hide her imaginative artistic sketches from the teacher and draws the required single hats on the other side of the drawing paper, turning the paper over to continue the figures as soon as the teacher moves away out of eyesight. This kind and thoughtful teacher soon realises Gretel's productive actions, and quietly looking over her shoulder praises Gretel's artistic achievements. Instead of the expected telling of, Gretel finds herself at the centre point of attention and admiration as her work is shown to the whole class. This was the first and only teacher who helped Gretel in this way. Ironically, this particular tutor who first recognized and encouraged her artistic talents was himself a member of the emerging Nazi Party. Maybe he was one of those who let themselves be mislead and were later disappointed.

The time has arrived for the school doctor's annual examination. All he does is to stand yards away, out of their reach and to point to the smaller children, recommending them for the free Quaker dinner, or extra holiday. He keeps well away from the children.

He might catch an illness or something!

Brother Hans is one of the lucky children to obtain a holiday. There was no hope for Gretel to receive one of these priorities. She was one of the tallest in her class and very lively. A girl friend whose parents were better situated gives up her Quaker lunch priority to Gretel. To compensate, a year later, mother Sophie sends Gretel to relatives living in the countryside in the village Bubbendorf. It seems as if this was the only holiday my mother ever had in her childhood. But it was a long holiday, full of happy memories.

Mother Sophie had written to the relatives in Bubbendorf, a small village near Leipzig, requesting help to give her daughter this long overdue vacation.

I don't know now how many brothers and sisters father Richard had, but little Gretel, thinking it best to try to get accommodation with one of the more wealthier relatives finds herself wandering from one to the other, each sending her off to the next. In the end she finds a holiday home with the poorest and less well-off aunt.

Her first impressions were distress and disgust. There was a smelly manure heap right before the kitchen Door. The farm animals wondered free around in the kitchen and everyone ate out of one bowl, which was placed in the middle of the table. At home Gretel was used to the finest furniture and mother Sophie was an extremely tidy and neat little lady, her home was kept accurately spick and span. That first evening finds Gretel writing to her mother.

She wants to go back home because of the foul-smelling manure heap before the kitchen door and because everyone was eating out of one bowl at meal times. This was something totally unacceptable. But next day Gretel changes her mind. The fresh milk, fresh air and play time with her wild romantic cousins compensates for the unusual smells and customs. She visits daily the small new born calf, the little squealing pigs, rides on the ponies back, regardless of the request of poor aunty because the pony was still too young and weak. She gets into lots of mischief, stacks the corn, working with the cousins in the fields, going to the market to sell the farm products and eating the goods on the way there that were meant for sale. In other words she has the time of her life, enjoying every minute of it, and above all, the kind aunt gives Gretel fresh milk every morning - a luxury. The other cousins were not allowed to have milk. It was needed urgently for other things, for making cheese and butter to sell. But Gretel promptly demands her daily milk portions and the dear aunt gives it to her.

School time nears again but Gretel refuses to go home and she is allowed to stay longer. The Second World War has wiped out every single male relative from Bubbendorf. All those wild romantic farmers children became soldiers, food for Hitler's army. Today there are no relatives left in Bubbendorf.

Gretel arrives home with lots of food, happy and bubbling with life. Brother Hans meets his sister at the station, but he has only one thing in mind – food, so Gretel presents him with a portion of the large freshly baked loaf of country bread at the same time anxiously begging him to leave enough for her mother.

City life is still hard and difficult. There is a shortage of everything. Mother Sophie is often ill and has to be sent away to recover. She is sent to a cheap convalescent home outside Dresden to get rest and fresh air. It is more of an inexpensive vacation place.
She has a small room in the village, is able to go for walks, can rest in the park and recreation grounds, and bathe in a nearby swimming pool. Weekends finds Gretel walking all the way through the city of Dresden to be with her mother and even sleeps on the hard floor beside her. There is no money for fares or extra accommodation.
There is still one relative left living in Dresden, Aunt Kate.

The First World War had swallowed all her sons from her first marriage leaving her childless. The second marriage to a widower who has a sweet shop allows aunt Käte to help out sometimes.
Each time Gretel visits aunt Käte she is given a piece of chocolate - a luxury for those times. On her journey to aunt Käte she passes by a café. Often there is music to be heard, entertainment for the wealthier. The magical sound of the violin floating through the door and window of the café pulls Gretel nearer and she squashes her face on the café window to get a glance at the violinist and to hear as much of the music as possible. Here the seeds are sown for Gretel's urge to play the violin.

One day, while walking in 'Grosser Garten' (a large Park in the middle of Dresden) together with her daughter, mother Sophie slips of the small bridge when crossing a pond and falls into the water. Mother Sophie cannot swim and the long dresses, fashionable for that time serve only to pull her further into the depths. Shortly before Gretel had received swimming lessons and had given her mother 'instructions' what to do in an emergency, little realizing that her words would later save her mother's life.
Mother Sophie remembers these words, "don't struggle, straighten your back and you will float up to the surface."
She acts accordingly and Gretel is able to help her out of the water.

Once, about Christmas time, mother Sophie remembers that she had made a large pot of plum jam and had put it aside for emergency cases. Hans was instructed to fetch the pot, which was on a shelf in his bedroom. Again it was a time of need and starvation. How the parents reacted, mother never told me, because the pot of plum jam was empty! Brother Hans couldn't resist the temptation of having something so delicious in his room and had 'licked a little bit' and again 'a little bit' until there was nothing left.

A short while before, Gretel had entered his room for something, only to find him scratching out the last bits. Brother Hans, wide-eyed and feeling uncomfortable at being discovered quickly pops a spoonful into Gretel's astonished opened mouth. Mother Sophie was always aware of the needs for her son. Following episode reminds me strongly of a graphic from Käte Kollwitz, a well-known artist who drew graphic portraits of working class people. This particular artwork shows a starving mother with two children. She has a small piece of bread in her hands, only enough for one child. She gives this piece of bread to the older child; the younger sister pulling on her mother's dress and crying receives nothing.

Brother Hans often received an extra sandwich for the way to school. She tried to hide this from Gretel but not always succeeded. This caused much questioning, why the brother should get more! Then Gretel was just as hungry.

It is perhaps one comfort that in the year of mother Sophie's death, Gretel has at least, for the first time a friendly understanding teacher. Until this time, the teachers were of a typical old fashioned Prussian German style, always provoking and hurting the working-class children, making school life difficult for them, picking on those especially who had been at any sort of demonstration.

Mother Sophie spends more and more time in hospitals. Gretel has a girl friend, an adopted child from the neighbour. She is very pretty and has long curly hair, also a wonderful voice. Together, at Christmas time they go round from hospital to hospital acting, playing and singing. Gretel was Father Christmas and her friend a Christmas angel. Their performance for the sick people in mother Sophie's ward was such a success that they were requested to repeat it in other wards and hospitals, especially for the sick children.

Mother Sophie returns home, still extremely ill. There is the story about Gretel returning home one day after school and bumping into a neighbour.

The woman asks Gretel, "how is your mother? I am told she is dying."
Gretel rushes home to her beloved mother to find her walking around the room desperately supporting herself with a stick, and saying, "I must live for my child, she is so young and needs me."
Gretel replies, "you must rest and lie down to get better."
Mother Sophie dies; leaving her daughter, still a child, 13 years, but well prepared for later life. My mother's memories of her mother were so vivid and real that she was able to pass on this picture to me, so that I can say today; 'I know my grandmother', in spite of the fact that I have never seen her personally. My grandmother was a kind, loving, tidy and righteous woman and above all a mother thinking first for her children. There is also this last picture of grandmother's burial, Gretel only 13 years old and during the ceremony she holds her mother's hands for the last time, no one daring to take away this last privilege. Years later on returning to Dresden, my mother's first thoughts and her visit were to grandmother's grave, where she now also lies. (Grandmother's birthday is on the 29th February).

Shortly after the death of mother Sophie a far related great aunt travels down from Berlin to visit the family. She is a spiritualist and Gretel is disgusted at the great aunt's efforts to 'speak to the dead' in a ritual at their home. Gretel wants her beloved mother to rest in peace and she goes out of the sitting room to hide in her corner in sadness and disgust at the great aunt's efforts. Also this Great Aunt including her whole family were Nazis!!

At school, after mother Sophie's death, the friendly and understanding teacher continues to help Gretel, giving her extra lessons, inviting Gretel to his daughter's own birthday party and there are school outings. He is concerned to cheer Gretel up and to do his best to give her some happy moments. He continues to read out her essays to the whole class, especially about her holiday memories. Her imaginative, lively and extensive ability to write entertains everyone. She writes about the farm animals and other country incidents. How the cows have gloating eyes and the piglets squeal. At that time city children had hardly any chance financially to go out into the countryside. Some of them hadn't even seen farm animals.

It is a contradiction that this teacher should have been a Nazi. In this last year there is also confirmation or 'Jugend Weihe [6]'. In spite of her proletarian life, Gretel chooses confirmation. She goes to the religious lessons instead of the nature and life studies with her teacher. Perhaps this choice is the result of little bits of religious believes left and her mother's death? Or perhaps because that last teacher, in spite of his friendliness was a Nazi? I leave this question open.
Alone and sad she often visits her mother's grave.

Hans and mother Sophie   Gretel and Hans   Gretel's parents

---

[6] "Jugend Weihe"- ceremony for boys and girls coming up to the age of grown ups.
   Later also traditional custom in the GDR

CHAPTER 2.

Awakening - Youth, 1924 – 1933.

'Wild klammert sich eine Kiefer am nackten Felsen Stein,
In Moos gefelsenrisse da bohrt sie ihre Wurzel hinein,
Und höhnend schaut sie in den Abgrund, reckt die Wipfel stolz und frei,
Lieber will ich kämpfen um Erde mit Stein,
Lieber vom Sturm gebrochen sein,
Als unten im Walde ein krüppel.'

Translation

'Wild clings a pine to the naked rocks,
In the moss filled rock cracks she bores her roots,
And scornfully she gazes in the abyss, stretching her treetop proudly and free,
I'd prefer to fight for earth with stone,
Rather be broken from the storm,
Than down in the woods be a cripple.'

(Written in her youth time).

'I was thirteen'

"As a mother my heart is especially open towards children and youth. I always watch with pleasure how the kindergarten teachers take the little ones for a walk. Clean and carefully guarded, they hold each other's hands. It wasn't always like this. I remember a little boy living in our house, whose father and mother were lucky enough to have work. The child played all day alone in the dirt in the backyard, by the ash pit, often hungry and cold. I was 13 years old and had just lost my mother. I felt pity and sorrow for the little boy, so when I came home from school I took him into our flat. I washed him, combed him and gave him my playthings. Today the youngest member of our great family is well guarded and taken care of, today, the time for which we have fought."

Written 1965 in Dresden. My mother still believed in a successful future for a socialist GDR and describes the contrast between her teenage years and our first five years spent in the GDR. On the one side, this little boy was neglected because the parents were lucky enough to have work, then, in the GDR, children from parents at work were given nursery school places free of charge, and carefully looked after, but everything was monitored and all was not as perfect as it seemed. Individuality was not acceptable and everyone had to 'fit in' a certain dictated system from the Stalinist state.

1.Teenager.

I want everyone to laugh and cry when reading this story. I want everyone to know my mother. The early death of mother Sophie forced the child to grow up quickly, rather like the wild animals in the jungle, like the young wild deer. It is vital that the fawns learn to move, to walk and run as soon as possible otherwise wild beasts will feast on them.

Gretel must learn quickly. It is the same old story. Only the strong, intelligent and clever have a chance to survive in the time of growing fascism. Either, you are weak and strong gusts of wind carry you away in its predetermined path, or, you are as strong as the pine tree clasping onto the bare rocks, as described in my mother's poem.

Times are hard for Gretel. Although she is still at school after her mother's early death, the two men at home have high expectations, requesting Gretel to do her utmost best in the household, to do the entire house keeping, cooking, cleaning and all the household washing. The washing tubs are too heavy for her and she is often obliged to ask her neighbour for advice, for help, and how to do certain things.

Her father was no exception to the general opinion in those days that a girl belonged in the house and so Gretel works in various households as a maid, as a children's nanny and in between she also continues house keeping for her father and brother.

A better and higher school education was unaffordable. Father Richard cannot afford to offer his daughter this possibility, so Gretel attends evening classes. She combats the lack of hope to obtain more knowledge through determination in order to realize her plans and special wishes and years later in the emigration, in Prague Gretel's dreams become reality.

The year 1926 finds Gretel helping in a household of a lady who owns a coffee, tea and chocolate shop. Another time, 1928 Gretel is a children's nanny for a lady with three small children. The time arrives when Gretel takes her place as one of the vast masses of unemployed. She joins the Socialist Workers Youth Organization, continuing to attend evening classes and begins with her music studies.

Sometimes she has the chance to earn a little extra money as model for the art students. She attends modelling classes herself, and stood as model for Otto Dix's life drawing classes at the art school in Dresden. She asks him for advice about her desire and longing to study art, and he tells her to just start painting and sketching, to do what her heart tells her to. She takes his advice and even goes without food to purchase the essential material necessary to begin. The art students notice her determination and give her some of their sandwiches, as Gretel has nothing to eat. These collected impressions and influences are later off great importance.

Her own words report:

"With about 17 years, I began to take an interest in the arts, for music and especially for sculpture. Because of my occasional modelling lessons I decided to do some modelling myself and later to study at the art school. In the meantime I carried on with my music studies. I found an excellent violin teacher, Mr.Heine from Dresden Reisiger Street 39, who lived in the same house where my father had his workshop. Mr. Heine was a professional musician. He said: Lass! I'll make a musician out of you. But as the Nazis came to power, I had to flee away from Dresden and my music studies were at an end. He gave me violin lessons without taking any payment. These experiences inspired me, to use my talents and wishes to form socialist ideas artistically."

How was it possible for a proletarian girl to learn to play the violin and to have such 'high dreams' of studying? Only because of Gretel' s strong personality, courage and optimism to continue with her plans, at all costs. She never forgot the musicians in the café and the magical sounds of the violin that had sown the seeds for her love for music.

Gretel saves money from her work as children's nanny and household help. Then, together with a friend, buys a violin in a second hand shop. What now? Gretel knew that she could not appear at home with a violin. Father Richard had told her that he was against it and that she would never learn to play it. Mother Sophie wasn't there anymore. Gretel was alone. Without any help or lessons just with nature's talent, Gretel learns to play her father's favourite melody in secret. She leaves the violin at a friend's places. Takes it out with her on wanderings in the Dresden Heide (woodlands surrounding Dresden) and begins to practice her violin studies alone. Then, when Gretel thinks she can risk it, she steals one night quietly with her violin under her arm before the door of her father's apartment. Father Richard is inside, sitting in the kitchen together with brother Hans after a days work. Carefully Gretel begins to play. The sound of her father's favourite melody floats through the door, at first a little hesitant, then getting stronger and louder. Father Richard is astonished. He opens the door and is even more amazed. There stands Gretel playing her father's favourite melody on her violin. Father Richard had no idea of Gretel's plans.

"Come in, come in Gretel, play it again, I never thought you would be able to do something like that. How wonderful" are father Richards' joyous words.

Now at last Gretel is allowed to take her violin home with her and to practice, for the moment, until the arrival of the stepmother.

Gretel begins her music studies with Mr Heine. Wishful dreams slip within reaching distance. But Gretel's financial means are limited. All her saved money is spent. So one-day after a further lesson with Mr Heine, Gretel thanks him for everything he had done for her, apologises and says she cannot come any more, as she has no more money to pay for lessons. Mr Heine is totally distressed. He believed that father Richard had paid for her lessons. He says to Gretel;

"Lass, this is impossible, you are so talented, we have just begun. I'll make a musician out of you. I'll help you get a position in the woman's orchestra in Berlin. No, you cannot give up now. I will speak with your father. Come next week again and don't worry about the payment."

Mr Heine visits father Richard in his workshop and speaks with him;

"Mr Grossner, your daughter is very talented. I would like to help her with her music studies. She can't give up now. Don't worry about the money. Instead make me a shelf."

And so, Gretel's violin lessons were paid in this way, with making shelves, foot- stools and the like. As soon as one item was used up for her violin lessons, Mr Heine ordered another item.

My mother must have been quite talented. To start violin playing late with 15 or 16 years and to reach a high standard such as the Kreuzer violin studies in such a very short time is only possible for someone with exceptional qualities and a strong will to learn.

From this time onwards the violin was always a true and faithful companion for Gretel for the rest of her life and accompanied her through all her travels across Europe as an anti-fascist refugee. Gretel plays the violin in the proletarian 'agit-prop' youth group - and in the workers' orchestra (1931).

Some years later, the violin is used as a disguise for illegal political work: the case was successfully employed to carry anti-fascist leaflets to contacts. Later, in the emigration in Czechoslovakia Gretel plays her violin in the emigrant's orchestral band.

About this time, (1928) Gretel becomes acquainted with the composer and communist Peter Klopfleisch, They were both members of the workers youth movement and this is where they met each other. Once, when all were sitting outside in the open on the lawn, having a meeting, Peter whispered to Gretel:

"You are just the sort of girl I want to marry."

Gretel answers the nine-year older companion: "You are much too old for me."

Peter replies; "I am going to Russia. Don't you want to know about it, when I come back?"

This encounter was brief. Both could hardly know how involved each other would become in each other's lives. The young Soviet Russia was something like a wonder for the young socialists, a land in paradise, free from approaching fascism, and a world of the future. Peter was to go to a party schooling course, and so his words made Gretel quite curious.

Both Gretel and Peter were conscious during this period of the sharp division, and absence of co-operation, between the socialist and communist parties across Germany, there is not much unity and friendship between them, each working separately to counter the Nazi threat. They have too many different opinions and arguments. Both would also later come to regard that as a crucial mistake by the left.

Later, after the war, the two parties unite, and become the S.E.D. in the previous G.D.R. (Socialists United Party in East Germany). My mother often told me about this crucial mistake made at that time.

It is the year 1929, and again Gretel is working in households of various rich people, as house help, maid or children's nanny, but she then returns home to her father to take care of him and to do his house keeping.

Not all treat Gretel badly. Sometimes her employers behave decently and regard Gretel as a human- being, but the bad experiences outweigh these by far.

There are various incidents and pictures appearing before my eyes as Gretel searches for work. She discovers that she has more freedom when she has a day job and a room elsewhere. I am not sure in what year following happened, if it is before or after father Richards's second marriage, and before or after Gretel's dangerous accident. In any case it happened some time between 1928 and 1931:

Gretel is pleased, she feels lucky because she found cheap accommodation. She pays for the room and goes off to look for work. Late evenings she arrives only to find that someone else is also sleeping in that hired room - a man. The Landlady refuses to give Gretel her money back, and so Gretel is again without accommodation. At home the future stepmother is already beginning to take possession of the place and Gretel is not wanted.

Another time, Gretel still under-age and thinking that she has had luck with finding accommodation and work in a villa, awakes the next day only to find that she has been tricked. It is a home for homeless adolescent girls. Everything happens under the eagle eyes of strict matrons. The whole place was more like a prison with no freedom. The adolescent girls were forced to do kitchen work, often forced to do silly senseless things, like polishing the same knives and forks which already had been cleaned each day before, and sewing initials on hangers and tea-towels. The girls were all dressed in grey. Some had been there already for years. For nature and freedom-loving Gretel this was a terrible ordeal, a nightmarish incident.

The only fresh-air allowed were on the walks in rows of two's down to town, the strict matrons guarding the girls carefully. Gretel writes a letter to her father. She has to do this in secret and begs her father to take her home. She threatens to off travelling and tramping around the world, like her brother Hans. This was quite customary for young men in those days. Her brother Hans was already off on one of these journeys and father Richard lived in fear that his lively daughter would do the same. It would have been a disgrace for a young lady at that time.

The letter is written, and a plan is made. Gretel's companions try to convince her that her plan is useless. The girls are too well guarded by these strict and harsh matrons. Gretel is optimistic and laughs saying: "We shall see."

Again it is time to go on one of those dreary walks into town, in rows of two's. All set off. Gretel is armed with her letter. On the other side of the road is a letterbox and quick as a weasel, before any of the matrons could close their astonished opened mouths, Gretel had stepped out of the row, ran across the road and put the letter in the letterbox.

Gretel waited in vain for a reply. She did not give up hope. It was uncertain whether father Richard received the letter. The days dragged on. No reply came.
On the next occasion during one of those outings Gretel escapes and runs off home to her father, as far away from that prison as possible.

Had the future stepmother picked up the letter and prevented father Richard receiving it? One can only guess.

Life finds Gretel again in need. Due to unemployment Gretel can't pay the landlady the rent for her accommodation. This landlady visits Gretel's father without her knowledge and demands the missing money. Father Richard gives the landlady Gretel's beloved violin as payment.

When Gretel arrives home to fetch her violin, it is not there, nowhere to be seen. It is not easy to convince her father that this is not the way to deal with the problem. She again threatens to go off wandering and travelling around the world. Her dismay at the loss of her violin is so great that father Richard reluctantly trots of to fetch the instrument back. He did not realise that his daughter loved the violin so much. In his opinion, Gretel was responsible for the payment of the room herself, but Gretel was still under age at this time.

'**Und wenn ich streich die Fiedel,**
Dann ists um mich geschehen,
Dann hör ich nur das Liedel
Und möcht vor Freud vergehen.'

Translation;

'**And when I play the fiddle,**
Then that's it with me,
I hear only the song,
And melt away for pleasure.'

Gretel is relieved to get her beloved violin back and all is well again, for the moment. Another time, once sitting in her room, a hand appears at the window, leaving a bar of chocolate and a greeting behind on the window- sill. She then realises that it is the 2nd August - her birthday. Her brother just had delivered the birthday greeting. No one is with her. She is alone in her room on this special day when she should be with her family celebrating.

But she is not always alone. Gretel has many friends in the youth movement and they nickname her 'Piepmatz' [1.]

Between employments, Gretel takes time of to go wandering in the beautiful Sächsische Schweiz, (Saxon Switzerland) the Sandstone Mountains on the Bohemian border and to continue with her art and music studies. In winter she accompanies her friends on skiing trips in the Erzgebirge, (surrounding hillsides,) and on walks in the Heide, a beautiful woodland surrounding Dresden. The dazzling white woods look like a scene from fairyland. There is peace and joy between the hardships of daily life. It is no wonder that Gretel later, living far away in foreign countries, distant from this beautiful place cannot find peace and has to return to her place of birth.

Gretel's grandad, Theodor Tube.   Map of Saxon Switzerlan

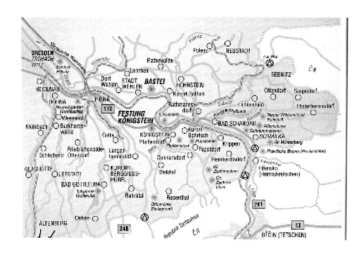

[1.] Piepmatz – My mother's nickname meaning little bird.

The legend, part 1.

Many legends and tales surround Saxon Switzerland. The roots of our ancestor's are embedded in these myths and tales. The district of Schandau is undoubtedly very old. The time of its foundation is not exactly known. Much has been alleged about the name 'Schandau'. Historians have expressed various opinions. Dividing the word Schandau into Schand (shame) and Aue, (place) meaning 'place of shame', is the most used and known explanation. There were hostilities between these early Lords, von Duba and King Ottokar from Bohemia.

Once a fierce battle raged between the bohemian King Ottokar and the Knight Witigo von Duba in the Kirnitzsch valley. The Knight Witigo von Duba is a descendant from an old family, the 'Birken von Duba,' and owner of an estate. A feud broke out between them.

Nearby the mineral spring that was discovered later and from whom the spa today has its name, the Count Bernhard, from Camenz, whilst leading a group of knights and mounted troops against Lord Duba from Hohnstein, came upon the Knight Raubold from Niemanitz, who was also an enemy of the Dubas, but secretly had made a pact with the Dubas and wanted to use this opportunity to destroy the enemy army troops.

The knight in anger hurls the count out of the horse's saddle and lifting a heavy stone throws it at him, crushing his chest, whereby the Count from Camenz in deadly combat throws him down. The latter, provoked and enraged by the disloyalty of the knight, with his last breath of life curses, calling out: "Death and shame! Place of shame." (Tod und schande - Schandaue - Bad Schandau). So reports the myth.

In the history of the town Freiberg there is the belief that in remembrance of the surrounding area called Sandua, or Zandau by the town Leipa, Lord Birken built the new castle Zandau. We can read about a possible existence of a castle on the Kiefericht in an old book. This castle was used as a place of sanctuary and refuge against possible local disputes and quarrels. The builders considered this possibility and at first thought of the area by Meissen and the rather narrow valley. They then built a stronghold, 'Zandau an der Elbe' by the less significant Kalmitz River. A similar structure now stood on the top of the mountain. The town and market place runs parallel to it, by the so-called place Kiefericht. Signs of the old walls and ditches can still be seen today. Sebnitz, Hohenstein and Zandau form a triangle so that each of these communities can help each other in case of urgent need and emergency. Houses were built in the valley around the castle Zandau. The name of the town changed from Zandua to the softer sounding name Schandau.

Millions of tourists visit these Sandstone Mountains each year, admiring this unique landscape with its deep valleys set in between the rocks, gorges and precipitous cliffs with the river Elbe flowing between them. It is a paradise for rock climbers and the deep dark forests beckon and invite nature-loving wanderers. These old tales and legends of past historical events of the Bohemian aristocracy linger in and between these Sandstones Mountains and castle ruins. These knights became robber knights in the 15th century.

The 'von Duba' name from the twelfth, thirteenth century was later changed to 'von Tuba'. Later still, they sold their 'von' title and change the name to 'Tube' as our great great great grand parents were ashamed of the 'robber knights' history in our family ancestry. My grandmother's maiden name was Tube.

But let us now return to the 20th century. The noises of these old battles disappear into nothingness. At the moment the place is peaceful, but soon new battle sounds will be heard over this beauty spot.

2. Peter Klopfleisch.

The acquaintance with Kurt, Gretel's first love, had an important influence on her artistic interests. Kurt was an artist. He worked in a cheese factory and went to evening classes at the art school. The mutual interest and love for art and nature brought the two together. It is a very romantic time for Gretel. They go on wanderings and on holidays together, painting and discussing problems. Gretel's artistic qualities are only just beginning to form. Kurt had already achieved quite a high standard in the arts.

Kurt's mother is a very understanding and sympathetic lady and Gretel finds a motherly friend in her. If anyone could have taken mother Sophie's place to some extent, then, it was she. This friendly lady continues to visit Gretel long after the end of her friendship with Kurt She brings her sometimes a cake and other things, they talk together and Gretel has a motherly friend.

Kurt has a sister who is mentally handicapped. In winter, as a young child, she had fallen over on the ice and hurt her head. The result was disastrous. She is often in hospital and Gretel helps to take care of her like a sister. Later, as the Nazis came to power, they put the sister aside; this sort of thing was a common usual occurrence in the time of fascist terror. It is highly likely that the Nazis helped end her life.

An everlasting memory is the holiday they have together in the Luneburger Heide. Kurt and his Piepmatz wander from youth hostel to youth hostel. Sometimes they are the only visitors there. Time stands still for the two lovers. Life is full of sunshine and joy. They paint landscapes and write romantic poems and if historical events had been kinder, they might have spent the rest of their lives together. But Kurt is not interested in politics; he is not concerned with the escalating political restlessness around them. His only interest is in his art and he is politically very short sighted. His opinion was, "let Hitler come, he won't stay long." For the wide-awake and lively Gretel this opinion was unthinkable. Regrettably, this was a common opinion of many politically shortsighted Germans at this insecure restless time.

The Socialists youth movements' motto was; "they who vote for Hitler, votes for war." This was the beginning of the end of the friendship. Then after Gretel's accident, from which she was scarred for life, Gretel is not fine enough for Kurt any more.
We all met Kurt years later in Dresden. He often came to visit us. He never forgot my mother and deeply regretted his decision. If the wheel of time could have been turned back, nothing would have stopped him from marrying his 'Piepmatz.'

From the artist in the 1930's, developed a night watchman in the 1960's. From the young household maid in the 1930's, developed an artist and sculptress of great personality in the 1960's.

I must not forget to mention other youth friends. There is a girl friend from brother Hans, who played the guitar and carved figures out of ivory. There are the friends in the Nature Friends Movement to whom Gretel also belonged. We met several of them again years later and for all, my mother was still 'Piepmatz'.

Peter keeps up his interest for Gretel. The more powerful the fascist terror grows, the more intensive becomes the political antifascist front. Together, Peter and Gretel work for peace, and their friendship deepens.

Peter's father was a lace maker from profession. He came from a weaver's family and since 1910 he worked as a health insurance officer.

My father was born on 6th April 1902 in Düsseldorf on the Rhein. He had six younger sisters and a Polish mother. My father never spoke much about his childhood. His parents had little money to buy extra things for their only son. It was more worthwhile to buy something for the six girls, so in a way, my poor father was a little neglected. This was not due to ignorance from his parents but was the result of financial restrictions and escalating hard financial times.

His school days were spent during the First World War in a time of strict military order. The old-fashioned teachers were only interested in militaristic conduct and discipline as was accustomed at that time. Father suffered greatly under it. Perhaps his political antifascist awareness arose from his tough and harsh school days.

He was a very intelligent child, excellent at mathematics and top of his class. At an early age he was exposed to the injustices of the economic system, when he was denied the possibility of a higher education scholarship in favour of a less academic, but financially superior pupil in his class. Although Peter was by far the more intelligent and best, the pupil with the better financial situated parents received the scholarship.

In June 1916, because of his excellent school results, Peter is offered an apprenticeship as compositor in the printing trade with the Düsseldorfer newspaper.
Peter completes his apprenticeship in February 1920. Now he has a proper profession, quite an achievement for a proletarian boy at this time. The amount of time his father had spent searching for a suitable apprenticeship for his only son had been well worthwhile.

Highly politically aware from earliest youth (1918), Peter joins the socialist workers youth movement. 1920, after his successfully completed apprenticeship Peter travels around the country collecting experiences and looking for work.

1925 finds Peter in Tübingen near Stuttgart; there he enrolled in both the German Communist Party, (KPD) and the Rot Front Kämpfer Bund, (RFB) (Red Front Fighter's League)[2] and was sent to a party schooling course in Russia, an experience which reinforced his faith in Marxist ideas. The years 1925 and 26, finds Peter visiting Moscow in the young Soviet Russia for the first time. The huge differences between growing fascist Germany and the young optimistic Soviet Russia, leaves a powerful influence on Peter for the rest of his life.

Peter travels around Germany. In these years he also visits Munchen, Altenburg, Frankfurt and Berlin. In 1927 he is in France and then in Leipzig. 1928 Peter arrives at last in Dresden, where he meets Gretel for the first time. In the summer of 1928 Peter is of again on his journeys; visiting Sweden, Stockholm, then back to Düsseldorf and Dresden.

Nothing is mentioned in papers and documents left behind for me about my father's second visit to Soviet Russia that he made during these years. For some reason they remain silent about this second visit!

1929 Peter is in Hamburg, then he returns back to Dresden. On his journeys he is sometimes full employed, part- time employed and at other times unemployed.

My father was extremely active at this time of growing fascist terror and whenever possible spoke openly, in public, at meetings and on demonstrations against fascism.

By 1929, he had become a popular and renowned anti-fascist speaker, who was also active in the production and distribution of anti – fascist propaganda. He uses his knowledge in the

---

[2] RFB- founded on the 31st May 1924.
Rot Front Kämpfer Bund, (Red Front fighters League). Class-conscious workers belonged to this organisation. This proletarian organisation was founded as a safeguard against reactionary associations of the German monopole capitalism and against the danger of a new imperialistic world war. The RFB developed within a short time to a strong democratic antimilitaristic organisation with 150000 members. This organisation fulfilled an intensive collective work, together with the action unit of the working class, against the politic militarists and war preparation politics of the German Imperialism.

printing trade to help print illegal leaflets – including the drawings of political caricatures for the anti-fascist newspaper, and becoming ever further involved as German unrest and Hitler's party swelled.

From 1929 to 1930 onwards Peter disappears further in the anti-fascist underground movement, becoming even more and deeper involved in the fight against growing fascist terror. From this time onwards he is registered as unemployed. Peter is also an enthusiastic Esperantist, using this world language also for his political activities.

Gretel and Peter, by 1931, were now working together in the Anti-Fascist Front, renewing and strengthening their friendship, and known to their comrades as "The Two Blues" (each activist being primarily referred to by their assigned nickname, for security reasons). Gretel produced artistic propaganda by singing and playing her violin in the proletarian youth group, in addition organising collections for the Red Trade Union Organisation and publicly leafleting against Hitler, whilst Peter continued his writing and speaking in the same vein.

My father was active in the printing trade, printing newspapers and leaflets for the party, especially in the last days before Hitler…possibly when Hitler was coming to power. The illegal material and small press had to be moved regularly. It was important to change the position frequently. One day the following incident happened. It was again time to move the illegal press. The case was so heavy and Peter was struggling to carry all this illegal material to the tram station. Peter waited to board a tram. The tram arrived and Peter struggled to lift the heavy case with all this illegal material into the tram. A young Nazi in SS uniform saw Peter struggling. He came up to him. Imagine how my father felt, his heart pounding in fearful excitement and thinking that his illegal act had been discovered! He was at this time already a wanted man. Imagine the anxiety of the young anti-fascist that the case, which was very heavy, heavy with illegal material and heavy physically would not break open and betray him! But all this young Nazi wanted, was to offer his help and to help my father lift the case onto the tram!

Peter and Gretel work together in the 'anti-fascist front' helping each other in many ways. Because Peter had been so active in public and was so well known in certain groups for his anti-fascist activities, not only because of his schooling in Russia, but also because of his RFB membership he was a much wanted and searched for anti-fascist. The Nazis were after him.

After the fall of the Berlin wall I applied for copies of Stasi [3.] files that had been made and kept on my parents from the East German Stalinist state. I am still waiting for copies of files made during the GDR time, but I have received something about my father's activities before he had to flee Nazi Germany. These papers describe how several anti-fascist comrades had been arrested and were obviously subject to brutal detailed investigations forcing them to betray friends, colleagues and comrades in order to try to stay alive.

These copies of reports written by the Nazis describe how important it was for them to find the authors of certain illegal articles that had been published in the illegal 'Rote Frontkämpfer', (Red Front Fighter) newspaper. The Nazis forced their prisoners to tell them how many papers they had distributed and to whom they had contact, how much money they had and where meeting were held. These documents state that these prisoners supposedly made these statements out of their own 'free will' but it is highly likely that they were obviously under extreme pressure. These documents were taken between March and November 1933. It seems, that after the RFB and other anti-fascist organisations were forbidden by the Nazis, the comrades decided to meet up to decide what can be done. The

---

[3.] Stasi – East German secret police.

Nazis wanted to know everything about these illegal meetings. Many of these prisoners had families and were obviously anxious about their safety. Obviously my father was the person responsible for certain articles that had appeared in these newspapers and this had upset the Nazis enormously. Especially one particular newspaper, 'Die Rote Faust', (The Red Fist), seems to have upset the Nazis the most and my father's name is betrayed.

Another prisoner reports that comrades within the KPD were apparently in disagreement with each other because of political differences and that the organization split. This fatal mistake made, was to cost many innocent people their lives during the coming years of Nazi terror.

During these months the decision was made to inform Peter to flee to safety and so my father had to flee over the border into Czechoslovakia, in the emigration, already in May 1933. Luckily he was not at home on the 15th May when the Nazis entered his flat to arrest him. The next day Peter fled over the border.

The only 'weapon' my father ever used were his speeches against fascism, against Hitler, against war, for peace and a better world. The only 'military' uniform he ever dressed himself in, was the uniform of the 'Red Front Fighter's League' (RFB).

It took many years before Peter can return to his home country at last and can visit the graves of his parents.

In Maidenhead 1946 after the war, my father asks the Red Cross to search for his parents. The message he receives is very sad. His father had died 1944, it is said of a chronicle heart complaint. Peter was very bitter and quiet when speaking about his father's death. It is highly likely that the Nazis had made life difficult for his father. Occasional remarks made confirm this suspicion. Father Klopfleisch takes the first possible opportunity to visit his only son in Prague in the emigration some time between 1935 and 1938. It is the last time Peter sees his father and the first and only time Gretel meets her future father-in-law. Peter's mother dies November 1950 in Düsseldorf. Her longing and last wish to see her only son remains once more unfulfilled. Peter was now living in England, in the emigration and there was no money for a home journey.

A few weeks before my father died in Dresden 1976, he received a special medal and recognition for his active part 1918 - 1945 in the fight against Nazi terror. It gave him much comfort and peace.

But we must now leave Peter and returned to Gretel's life.

'**Friendship is like a song**
That helps you along.
Friendship is like an everlasting flower
That comforts you in darkest hour.
Friendship is like a happy whistling bird in May,
I dance with you through life
And in my memory you stay.'

(Written in England, about 1950).

3. Cinderella.

When I think of this part of my mother's life, when pictures of the stepmother appear before my eyes, I cannot help to think about the old well-known fairy tale of Cinderella. Here is also a cruel stepmother. This one blinded from Nazism and greed. The time 1930 - 1933 could resemble the stepsisters, (growing fascist terror in her home town). The memories of Mother Sophie and the visits to her grave resembled the fairy godmother. Peter is the prince who carries Gretel off to a world of 'wealth and riches'. The lost shoe is the common interest for peace and a better world. The prince is a poor emigrant who had to flee from Nazi terror. The emigration is the horse, on whose back the two rode away. The awaking artistic talents, Gretel's future pictures, drawings and her wonderful sculptures represents the world of wealth and riches.

Self portrait; Prague; (approx , 1933).

'Ich bin ein Lump ein Bettlerscheich
Hab nichts und doch hab ich ein ganzes Königreich
Die Vögel sind meine Musikanten
Die singen für mich im grünen Hag.
Die Blümchen auf der grünen Wiese,
Die lachen fur mich den ganzen Tag.
Und Nachts schlaf ich in einen Bette
Mit hunderttausend Edelstein
Das grosse Himmelszelt ich wette
Ist schöner als dem König seins
Und hab ich auf den Heustock keinen Raum
Dann schlaf ich eben auf einen Baum.
Bis mich früh Morgens die Sonne weckt,
Und meine Vogelmusikanten singen
Dann ist mein Frühstückstisch mit Tauperlen bestickt,
Und Glockenblumen für mich ringen,
So kannst das Lied du weiter singen.
Von forne und von hinten,
Wer Freude, Friede, Schönheit sucht,
Der wird sie immer finden.
Wenn er ein Stück des Herzens nur
Kann öffnen der Natur'.

'I am a scamp a beggar sheikh, (King)
I have nothing and yet I have a whole kingdom.
The birds are my musicians.
They sing for me in the green bushes.
The flowers on the green meadows
They laugh for me the whole day.
At night, I sleep on a bed with hundred thousand precious gems,
This huge heavenly tent I wager, is better than the King's own.
And if there is no room on the haystack
Then I sleep just in a tree.
Until the sun awakens me early morning
And my bird musicians sing.
Then my breakfast table is decorated with dew pearls
And bellflowers ring for me.
And so this song can be sung
From beginning and from the end.
Who searches for pleasure, peace and beauty,
They will always find it,
If he allows a piece of his heart
Be opened from nature.'

(Written in the youth time).

Once again Gretel is a housemaid. She lives at home and works during the day for the wife of a doctor (1930 from February until June). Gertrud, the future stepmother often visits father Richard. Hans and Gretel sit in the kitchen, leaving the best room for their visitor. Hans often complains about 'that woman.' He is extremely unhappy at first about their father's new lady friend, but Gretel tries to convince Hans that it is good for father Richard to have a companion. He is often lonely and already had been living too long by himself. He needs someone of his own age, but Hans never stops complaining and grumbling. It is Gretel who gives Gertrud a warm welcome.

Again, between one post and the next employment Gretel gives herself some freedom. It is the only way for Gretel to get time off to go for wanderings, or to carry on with her studies. She finds another post in July 1930 in a private household. Then one fine day when Gretel is free she takes her bicycle and goes off for a ride in the Dresden Heide, (wonderful woodlands surrounding Dresden). The weather is fine; the sun burns hot on the thirsty dry earth.

It had been a beautiful enjoyable day out in the woods; of into Gretel's much loved nature, away from the noisy streets, away from the noise and dirt of a large city. It is the 17th of August 1930. Time was passing by quickly and Gretel must hurry to get back home in time. Her bicycle is an old faulty second hand one. She did not have enough money to get a better and safer one. But Gretel is young and happy to have been able to afford the one she has. It was enough to get out of the town on free days and to be independent from the town trams. Optimistic, free and happy she cycles home. She comes now to the Körner Street. It is a very steeply downhill road with many curves. The Körner Street leads into an extremely busy main road junction, full of shops, people and traffic. Gretel speeds down the road, at first, without a thought of the oncoming danger. She races on and on. Suddenly she realises that she has lost control over the bike. The brakes are not working, the bike's speed is increasing, and the road is getting even steeper. There is no hope; the brakes just refuse to work. She manages to turn one corner, then the next curve, and on and on, round the next bend. There is the main road and a tram comes in sight. She rings her bike bell, all the way - hoping that this might help, warning everyone to get out of her way; there is no stopping. Perhaps Gretel can make it, round that bend - but that tram is quicker and - - - - - -. Gretel loses consciousness.

Onlookers gasped in shock thinking that Gretel can't possibly be alive any more. The tram conductor tries to help, passengers and passer-byes rush to the scene to try to help, but it is not possible. Gretel's bicycle was too fast and she lands exactly beneath the tram. She had raced down that road in such a tempo that no one could help her. The tram must be lifted with a crane before anyone can reach her.

Gretel awakes in hospital with a broken jaw and concussion. Gretel has a good doctor in the hospital, but he is a rough and hard man. Gretel's teeth are sticking out Her teeth have to be pushed into place and tied together. For many weeks, Gretel is only able to suck soup between her teeth. Her life is in danger and often only hanging on a thread.

There are times of unconscious nothingness and times of painful consciousness. But the doctor is excellent, she did not lose any of her teeth, and her jaw healed good, but it left a scar which she carried all through her life. The doctor was quite a rough man, but he understood his handy work. Gretel had to swallow down the pain when he treated her. But then the doctors argued, because each of them had different opinions. They wanted to try some kind of new experiment on Gretel. Instead of the usual flesh transplant they decide to use some sort of new chemical stuff, and Gretel seemed to be a good subject for this experiment. Of course it doesn't work. The wound breaks open again, and also Gretel's health worsens.

On 25th September 1930 father Richard marries a second time. He visits Gretel in hospital together with his newly wed wife. Father Richard informs Gretel that she can now call Gertrude mother. Gertrude does not seem to have many kind words for the ill Gretel. No one can take the place of mother Sophie. Her father's second marriage to this vehemently Hitlerite stepmother eventually forces Gretel out of home and house. But just now Gretel desperately needs kindness, comforting words and friendship, but her desires are ignored. Kurt also visits her, but he soon loses interest. He does not like the scar on the side of her jaw. All this worries Gretel; the new stepmother who has no friendly words for her and the ignorant friend. She worries more than is necessary about her face. But a friend from the youth movement comes to visit her and cheers her up.

He says; "that face is just as sweet as ever. Lass, I'll still kiss you any time."
These comforting words from this nameless friend from the youth group have never been forgotten.

It takes Gretel an awfully long time to recover. The ward is big and there are many patients. She has already spent many months in hospital. She urgently requires peaceful surroundings with less noise in order to recover fully, so the doctors decide to send her home. They believe she would have more peace and rest in her own room at home! Gretel is still very shaky and nervous after her long illness. She leaves the hospital on 17th March 1931. (Perhaps now the reader may understand why I compare this part of mother's life with Cinderella!) The stepmother greets Gretel coldly and without any friendly words. The two men are busy working. In the meantime Gertrude had become quite good friends with Hans. He was so much easier to influence than Gretel.

Father Richard is convinced that all is well, he has a new wife and he believes Gretel has now a new mother! But Gretel needs a lot of rest and she is still not fit. She is still weak and struggling to deal with normal everyday requirements. The next day on 18th March in the morning, the stepmother greets Gretel with the words:
"When are you are going to get up. You lazy thing! You have been so lazy these last nine months. When are you going back to work?"

There is no room for Gretel at home. Cruel Gertrude proves to be an uncaring and heartless stepmother. She tries to persuade Gretel to join the Hitler Youth. She says, that Gretel would have an easier and more comfortable life if she would join them.

Only one day after leaving the hospital, still weak and shaky Gretel decides to look for work. She does not want to stand in the way of her father's happiness and new marriage. She finds a position by good understanding people and works again as a household maid. Gretel leaves home for this new job, but she is not allowed to take anything with her. Gertrude says she needs everything for her own two men. In spite of all this, Gretel is pleased for her father, as he seems happy and content with his life. He is getting old and has now a companion.

We met the stepmother 1960 in Dresden. By then she had been paralysed for many years and was confined to her own room. She died in 1964, but she gave Gretel the little hut on that so wonderful property where we were to spend so many happy hours later during the GDR years. This property belonged to my uncle and grandfather, which they had at first rented and then later bought during the first GDR years. They survived the bombing of Dresden at the end of the war by living up there. It was a beautiful place on the outskirts of Dresden, on the edge of the woodlands, high upon the hillside of what used to be an old vineyard, with breathtaking views over the whole of Dresden, the river Elbe, the Elbe Sandstone Mountains and reaching far into the distance over to the 'Erzgebirge' (ore mountains). Did Gertrude have a bad conscience? Was she feeling guilty as she gave it to us?

Gretel's visits to mother Sophie's grave are many. The place is well looked after. It is a peaceful place, that little piece of earth under the birch tree.

The kind and friendly employers, a family Hähnel, try to help and support Gretel, as she is still too weak to work as a housemaid. She does her best although she is still very shaky and nervous. Mr Hähnel writes a letter to Gretel's doctor asking him to help and informing him that Gretel is in urgent need of a convalescent place. The slightest physical effort is too great a strain for Gretel and after a few weeks she is ill again, a result of the accident and too early back to work.

The friendly words and letters supporting Gretel facilitate some kind of help from the doctors and the state health service. She is on sick leave from 28th April 1931 until 22nd June 1931.

About this time Gretel leaves her father's home for good. Fascism is on the increase. The stepmother continuously tries to persuade Gretel to join the Nazi youth and is appalled that she has no success in converting her stepdaughter to her own fascist ideas.

On the 26th June Gretel resigns from her membership with the evangelic and Lutheran church. About this time Gretel also joins the German Communist Party.

Again Gretel is in financial need and must look for work. She moves out to the countryside hoping that the fresh air, and away from the city noises and smells might help her to recover completely. On The 27th June she finds work in a youth hostel in the Saxonian Switzerland, but not for long. Then she moves on to her next job.

The darkest years in the history of Germany are nearing. Life is bitter and hard. Let my mother now report in her own words about the next events. A 'cold and icy' wind blows slowly over the whole of Germany.

'Grau und klitschig wie der Leib einer Schlange kriecht die Gasse
Baufällige Häuserreihen wie gebeugte Gestalten.
Hier schleicht umher das Elend mit seinen dunklen Gewalten..
Kein Sonnenstrahl spiegelt sich hier in Fenstern,
Kein Sonnenstrahl balgt sich hier lüstig mit Schatten.
Was ist Sonne? Das kennen nur die Satten,
Dunkel sind die Fenster der Häuserreihen
Und blicken in die Gasse hinein
Wie Augen aus einem Toten- Schädel.
Gebeugt schleichen die Menschen umher,
Am Not und Sorge tragen sie schwer,.
Not und Sorge will sie nicht verlassen.
Ich möchte Ihnen in die Gesichter schreien
Verständigt Euch Arbeiter massen!
Vom Kapitalismus müßt Ihr euch befreien.
Dann wird ein Plätzchen an der Sonne für jeden sein.
Grau und klitschig wie der Leib einer Schlange kriecht die Gasse.'

Translation;

'Grey and slippery like the body of a snake creeps the alley,
Ruinous house rows like bent distorted figures.
Here creeps poverty around with its dark forces
No Sunbeam reflects here in the windows
No Sunbeam wrestles playfully with the shadows.
What is sunshine? Only the satisfied know it.
The house row windows are dark,
And glance down in the alley
Like eyes from a death skull.
People creep around bent.
They carry heavily in need and worry,
Suffering and grief will not leave them.
I'd like to scream in their faces
Come to an agreement worker crowds,
Free yourselves from Capitalism!
Understand each other!
Then there will be a place for everyone on the sun.
Grey and slippery like the body of a snake creeps the alley.'

(Written in the youth time before 1933).

" An episode in the life of a proletarian girl"

Experienced 1931 in the county by Freiberg in Sachen.

"I had to do some shopping in the next town. The shopping took longer than expected and I had to wait quite a while at the counter. I knew that Frau Gutsbesitzer[4], by whom I was in service, would count the minuets until I returned. I stepped hurriedly down the small pathway between the waving fields to the large farmyard, which was situated further away from the village. The dog came barking and tail wagging out of his hut. Although I was only two weeks here, I had made good friends with him.

My employer was a very obnoxious nasty woman who called me; "That Thing – Lazy messy piece." This was the name and greeting she regularly gave me.

I had hardly entered the kitchen, when Frau Gutsbesitzer came bustling through the door; "Now comes that lazy Thing!" She screamed. "Lazy Mist Stück![5] Where have you been loafing around again? That Thing goes for a walk and we do the work." I answered quietly that I had hurried but I had to wait longer than expected. I came back as fast as I could.

"Hurried? – You call that quick! That Thing is only quick with grub. You've only come to the farmer's to feed yourself full!" screamed the Frau Gutsbesitzer even louder.

I went out to do my work and met my colleague, Miss Friedel Scholarin behind the kitchen door. She had listened gleefully with eagerness, with a scornful smile on her face. She had not noticed that I had seen her. Her expression changes as she caught sight of me and she whispers in my ear; "You came back so quickly."

Class differences between house maids.

My colleague was 16 years old. She was the trustee and advisor for Madam. Madam often shouted: "You have got to do what Miss Friedel tells you. You know Friedel has the higher position. You are only an employee. You dirty thing."
In this way, Madam succeeded to pay Miss Scholarin only a pocket money. She was false like a snake and felt heavenly uplifted. But I had made out a proper income, which I had obtained for the first two weeks. Because of this, my colleague was jealous. We both had to work 16 hours daily, from early morning, 4 o'clock until evening, 8 o'clock, usually it was 8.30 pm. Working hours were only interrupted by meal times. Very occasionally we had 10 minutes at dinnertime; it was never longer.

Sleep is the only recreation.

Then I crept up to my chamber and threw myself onto the bed. Was it a wonder that I was always so dead tired and broken by those long exhausting working hours without a decent break? Apart from the fact that I had just overcome a serious illness, Miss Scholarin also often commented that she could hardly stand straight.

We both could hardly wait for the Sunday to come round. In the afternoon we could throw ourselves onto our beds. Then the objects in the room seemed to dance around, I was so exhausted. With fearful wild heartbeats I counted unconsciously the minuets I was allowed to rest.

[4.] Frau Gutsbesitzer - Madam-Mrs Estate Owner; it was custom to call the ladies like this after their property, or after the title of their husband, e.g. Frau Doctor, Frau Professor.

[5.] Mist Stuck – translated means messy piece, this is a swearword, an offensive expression.

Loss of consciousness is only theatre.

It often happened that I couldn't think clearly any more, and so it was one day. I was busy in the kitchen when the floor seemed to disappear under my feet. For a short time I knew nothing. I had lost consciousness. Then I heard the hissing hard laugh of Madam and her screaming voice. She called; "Now Friedel, just look here and see what a theatre that Thing is doing."

I found myself lying on the stony cold kitchen floor and all my limbs were shaking.

"We won't let ourselves be fooled from a stupid person from town." scorned Madam.

I was not able to speak a word. Madam stood over me, looked down at me laughing. Miss Scholarin stood at the kitchen door watching this scenario alert and frightened.

I felt as if I was carrying a heavy stone on my head. It was like a holiday when I was without a headache for one single day. This headache was a result of my accident and I had already recovered and got over it, but here it began again. I was glad when the kitchen work was completed and the Frau Gutsbesitzer said to me that I should carry on working in the garden. "And Friedel, go out as well. Otherwise that Thing will stroll around and eat all the raspberries. She thinks she is only here to stroll around and feed herself. We must always urge and drag that Thing with us."

This was the usual tone spoken to me, and at the same time it was a successful method to stimulate Miss Scholarin to do more work.

Miss Scholarin begins to recognise her position.

As we worked in the garden together Friedel said to me with a tense solemn face, "she does that with all of them. The one who worked here before you, also fell over unconsciously a few times. All my predecessors were not longer here than 3 to 4 weeks." This was new. I had not heard Friedel speak of Madam like this before. Friedel said;

" One toils so hard for those few marks, you never have free. I haven't been home for 6 weeks. I have such a longing to go home. I am going to tell my mother about this treatment and I'm not going to accept it any more. In the end, I'll be in the same position as you." Friedel's home village was quite a distance away from the farm; a long 6-hour walk by foot. Suddenly she remembered her 'position of authority', stopped talking and was still. We worked silently together. My back ached from bending. I straitened myself and glanced over the fields. Over there, the woods sang their own melody. How I would have liked to find some strength and happiness on a free Sunday to go for a walk over those fields and into the peaceful deep dark woods that were inviting and beckoning to me to come. But like all everything during my employment with Madam this secret wish was immediately killed by the only one torturing me; Sleep! Sleep! Sleep!

"Come, get on with the work!" shouted Miss Scholarin to me, how extremely lazy, to allow myself to straighten up, for just half a minute. Then we took a basket with weeds to the compost heap.

Insult and abusiveness as daily bread

O' unlucky victim, I had slipped and put my foot into the manure hole. I went back to the house, into my room to put another pair of stockings on. I hadn't reached my room yet, when I heard downstairs Madam's screaming voice;

"What is there to look for upstairs? Stinking beast! The lass works outside, and that Thing lay's in bed, hey?"

As I came down and explained the case to her, she meant, that she would refuse to pay me 30 marks wages, no way was she going to do this. 'The diligent lass' working outside is so busy, she is something better than I am and gets much less wages.

Many more, cheaper and better workers are around. She would yet show me how to work, other wise she would throw me out.

And then she added; "Actually I'll give you notice!"

I was boiling with anger. In spite of these remarks, I asked politely;

"Please Madam, what does Frau Gutsbesitzer mean at all with a Thing? You always speak about a Thing."

She laughed scornfully; " I don't intent to have conversation with you. Get back to work!"

As I went, she called sneering: "I don't know, That Thing is not able to move from the spot with her deformed crippled legs."

Until then, I didn't know I was supposed to have deformed, crippled legs. It was the first and last time I have heard this comment from Frau Gutsbesitzer.

Frau Gutsbesitzer provokes, in order to save my wages.

My colleague confessed to me, but only through an accidental slip of her tongue, that Madam wanted me to run away, so that she does not need to pay my wages. But I did not run away, as much as I was looking forward for the end of the month, in spite of the fact that I was dreading it. Horrified of what was to happen, unemployed, and the certainty that I would get no financial support as I had been ill for one year and because of this I had not fulfilled the claim time necessary. It is vital that I find work again at all costs, and I must try to live as long as possible from my last earned wages.

With this thought in my mind the last day of that month came creeping on at last.

Cheated out of my hard earned wages.

I had packed my case and went to fetch my papers and wages. Frau Gutsbesitzer stood up and called out of the window:

"Friedel, come in!" as she appeared Madam said,:

"You see here, that I now give this person 18 marks and 71 pennies wages." I hesitated.

Madam pushed a piece of paper to me and said: "Here sign!"

"No please, I get 30 marks wages" is my answer.

She laughs and says: "I have told you, you will not get 30 marks wages. 25 marks wages, and from that 6 marks, 29 pennies for expenses are taken of it. Haven't you learned to count in the city?"

I protested: "This is against our contract!"

I was upset and shocked about this meanness. I put my hands balled to fists in my pockets, and swallowed down the words that wanted to press themselves over my lips.

I repeated: " I get according to our contract 30 marks cash money."

Miss Scholarin stood next to Madam, her hands on her hips, shaking her head and shocked about my cheekiness to ask for my correct wages.

Madam declared: "You do not need to take the money! But I have no wish to talk to that Thing. OUT! Other wise I'll throw you out!"

My latest illness and the bad treatment I had received here made me feel so sick, that I was not able to do anything. Shaking on all limbs, I picked up the 18 marks, 71 pennies.

<u>Farewell to the "strengthening and healthy" country work.</u>

Madam opened the door, pushed me roughly out, and with a sneering laugh banged the door on me. I took my case and went. My only friend, the dog, howled a last greeting. My case seemed far heavier than usual. Something hurt in my breast and I felt as if a few strings had broken, but I knew where to go. Slowly I went down the pathway, between the waving ripe cornfields. On the hilltop I threw myself down onto the grass. I needed a few minutes to calm down and compose myself. The property stood in full glance of the midday sun surrounded by rich fields and flowering meadows. The large udders of the chewing cows on the fields were heavy and rich with milk.

Everything, as far as I could see belonged to those farmers who had so shamefully betrayed me of my money. For which unemployed person, is 11 marks 29 pennies a small amount?

Labour, Court and Justice

I took my things to a woman who also worked at the farmyard and had whispered to me only that morning:
"If you don't know where to go, then come today to me and sleep a night at my place."
Then I took the bus into the next larger town, Freiberg and searched for the Labour Court.
The Officer at the Labour Court listened to my story, took up my complaint and said that I was right and that I should get my money. An appointment was made for 6 days later. One day before this appointment I received a letter from the Labour Court in Freiberg informing me that the appointment was cancelled. There was also a copy of a letter from Frau Gutsbesitzer, directed to the Labour Court. She had twisted everything as needed, to suit her.

The Labour Court also informed me that firstly I must show them my competence to complain because I was not yet 21 years old. I had complained three time independently, in spite of my under age because I had entered this employment service alone."

Was this the convalescent and holiday Gretel needed after her long and serious illness? Why was there no room at home for Gretel?

'Der Arbeiter.'

'Die Räder surren die Hämmer dröhnen,
Das Brühlen der Maschinen verschluckt manch stöhnen,
Der Arbeiter vom Lärm halb taub,
An den Lungen frisst der Staub,
Ein Wettrennen zwischen Mensch und Maschine,
Tempo, Tempo, Tempo,
Ohne Ende und ohne Ziel.'

Translation;

'The Worker.'

'The buzzing wheels the thunderous hammers,
The deafening noise of machines swallows most groans,
The worker from noise half deaf,
His lungs eaten from dust,
A race between man and machine,
Tempo, Tempo, Tempo,
Endless and aimless'.

Gretel returned to Dresden, and recovered fully from her illness. I do not know if she finds work after this, but in October she has a position again as housemaid. Gretel is now not only an active member of the German communist party; she also joins the 'Rote Gewerkschaft organisation'– R.G.O. – (the red trade union organisation) for the latter she is cashier. Gretel becomes further more involved in political activities. She plays her violin in the proletarians agitprop (Agitation -Propaganda) group and works together with Peter in the 'Antifascist front.'

The political illegal fight brings the two antifascists closer together. They were both of two completely different natures, the mathematical inartistic and unmusical young man and the romantic young woman, an artist and musician, but at this time, the antifascist fight was a daily necessity for both and this political activity brought them closer together.

Daily, fascism is growing, daily, the fight becomes harder and bitter. Hand written notes from this time are scarce and very little remains for me to read.

Gretel has to take care of herself, as there is little help to expect from home, from the stepmother. Her brother and father are far too involved in their own daily problems. If Gretel is hungry then she stays hungry. If it is her birthday, then she is alone, or with Peter.

The winter months are cold and Gretel has a chilly chamber. She has not got enough blankets. Gretel remembers what her mother had said:

"When I go, there is enough household goods, blankets, bedding and other equipment for both of my children later when they get married, and live their own lives, I am so glad and thankful for this."

During a visit to her father and stepmother, Gretel asks if she could have one of the spare blankets. But the stepmother is very reluctant and refuses.

One extra cold night as Gretel sits in her hired room freezing and thinking of happy times when mother Sophie was alive, she remembers to have seen a blanket, old dirty and ragged, used to protect a car parked outside on the street. She goes out and looks anxiously around. There is the car, a thing protected from the freezing frost. A few streets away, is her home, with mother Sophie's well kept bedding for her children and the reluctant stepmother! Gretel quickly takes the old ragged blanket and runs away with it as fast as she can! It is the only time she ever took anything away from anyone.

Once, a fair is in Dresden. Gretel goes there together with her friends, not that they have much money to spend, but they all visit a gipsy – a fortune-teller. The gipsy tells Gretel that she will travel far, in other countries. Gretel is pleased about this, what romantic youth would not look forward joyfully to an adventure, to see other countries? But the gipsy is serious and says:

" No, you will not be happy. You will have to come back to Dresden and you will then have enough money! But it will take a very long time!"

4. In the Underground.

'Sie litten und starben für kommendes Recht,
Sie kämpften für ein besseres Menschengeschlecht,
Nun wollen wir schützen und behüten,
Zur Pracht und Fruchtbarkeit bringen die Blüten,
Keine Mühe zu groß, es wird sich lohnen,
Für Brüderlichkeit mit allen Nationen.'

<u>Translation</u>

'They suffered and died for future justice,
They fought for a better world,
Now we need to protect and take care,
Blossoms growing to splendour and fruitfulness,
No troubles too much, it's all worthwhile,
For friendship with all nations.'

Gretel's increased involvement in the illegal political fight against fascism makes it impossible for her to visit her father, brother and stepmother regularly. There is less chance to see them and she has to keep away in order not to endanger them.

Brother Hans is not so active at first. Once, when Gretel asks him if he would also join the K.P.D, he replies:

"Well they did invite me once. I went, but then they did not invite me again, so I did not go."
But a short time later brother Hans is just as heroic in his activities as Gretel and Peter.

This time, the stepmother has no influence either on Hans. Hans becomes politically involved in other antifascist groups and so it is best for both, brother and sister to keep apart.

Hans and his friends decide to collect some weapons and to hide them, in order to have weapons ready for the resistance to fight against fascism, when time has ripened for action. The workshop seems a suitable place for their plans. Hans has no idea what Gretel's activities are. Gretel has no idea what Hans is up to, also father Richard and the stepmother haven't the faintest knowledge of the activities of their children.

One night, Hans and his friends go to the workshop, pull down a wall and resourcefully stockpile these weapons, hiding them inside the walls of his father's workshop, then building the wall up new again. This was in the time of growing Nazi terror a most dangerous enterprise.

Apart from this, Hans is much loved by his stepmother, has protection, a home and can work in his father's workshop. He also becomes a cabinetmaker, and can help the ageing father in his business. He was also a great nature friend and rock climber. Later he joined the 'Roter Bergsteiger' league, ('the 'Red Mountain Climbers league') an antifascist rock climber's group that was also actively working against Hitler's approaching terror reign. But one day, about 1934, the Nazis discover his antifascist militant activities and he is arrested. He is caught up in a large process at the time when Gretel is already living in Prague in the emigration. During the court procedure he stands up true and faithful as an antifascist and socialist, his life now hanging in the balance and risking execution. His life is spared and he is given a prison sentence and serves about two years, the exact time is not known, before he was sent to Greece with the 999 punishment battalion, and whilst risking his own life again, refused to take part in any executions of partisans. My uncle suffered greatly during this time.

I never knew my grandfather, but I met my uncle again when we went over to Dresden 1960 for that 'holiday of no return'. He had managed to visit us over in England about 1953.

He told us many stories of his adventures and how he helped partisans escape and avoid being arrested by the Nazis. His cabinetmaker skills were obviously in great demand by the officers, helping him avoid certain unbearable orders and saved his life many times. He also received recognition by the GDR authorities as a victim of the Nazis, as well as my parents.

There are two episodes I will mention here. Once my uncle was ordered to attend an execution of partisans. In great frustration he wondered how he could avoid this. Refusal could cost him his life. Lucky for him he had been asked to make some furniture for a higher commandant. The next day he arrived as ordered, but dressed only in his working cloths, wooden shoes and armed only with his hammer, saw and box of nails and material for his work.

"I have a very important job to do for 'Herr officer'… It has to be completed by the end of today," was my uncle's comment.

The officer replied, "I should have you executed as well," but because a higher commander had ordered the furniture, the officer allows him go. My uncle was unable to help those poor partisans, but another time he was ordered to search a house and could help warn them of the oncoming danger. He entered the house as ordered and pretended to search intensively. Instead he helped to hide them. He then managed to persuade the officers that the house was empty. Another time he manages to get kitchen duties peeling potatoes. His, is a different story than my parents, but he had put himself just as much in danger.

These are only three of the many episodes he told us about.

Gretel is happy to find more and more employment as a model at the art school. It was about this time when Gretel met the well-known artist Otto Dix as a model for his class. Somewhere there exists a painting of my mother from Otto Dix. Gretel's longing to become a painter is growing rapidly. She asks the artists again for advise and help.

One artist informs her: "Lass I can see you are already painting with your eyes, all you need to do is to go to a shop and buy a paint box, brushes and paper. Use your eyes. For the beginning the cheapest materials will do."

This time, Gretel's earnings as a model at the art school is sufficient to help her buy material and she uses this possibility to get more acquainted with art and artists.

The year before Hitler comes to power, Gretel is working with the 'Anti-fascist Front', together with Peter, the purpose and aims of this organisation to stop and prevent the spreading and widening of 'National socialism' (Nazism). She is also active singing and playing her violin in the proletarian youth group, using their artistic possibilities as propaganda against fascism. This 1931 founded music group fulfilled valuable agitprop work. They called themselves 'Die Rote Raketen' (the red rockets).

The two, Gretel and Peter unite as a team, corresponding and helping each other. Sometimes Peter calls round to Gretel and they have a 'delicious' meal. Peter had bought some cut of sausage ends at the butchers. These sausage ends were usually thrown away, but young unemployed Peter is sometimes able to purchase these delicatessens cheap.

Peter talks at public meetings, he writes articles and draws caricatures for the anti-fascist newspaper, and before it was prohibited wears his RFB uniform.

In the midst of this political anti-fascist front, the friendship between the two deepens rapidly. Gretel is also leafleting pamphlets:

" Who votes for Hitler, votes for War!"

She collects money for the Red Trade Union Organisation. Their whole lives are now spent trying to prevent Hitler coming to power and warning as many people as possible what would happen if Hitler should succeed. It is an extremely busy and dangerous time. Neither Gretel, Peter or Hans, saved one ounce of their breath for themselves in this fight. Neither of them thought once for themselves and risked everything. They risked their lives, endangering themselves to highest degrees, for a better world.

On 25th January 1933, a mass anti-fascist demonstration was held in the Dresden 'Keglerheim',[6.] incorporating civilians, workers and anti-Nazis along with active politicians. This mighty demonstration against growing fascism, against the danger of Hitler coming to power had an ever-lasting impression on Gretel and gave all anti-fascists strength, courage and hope. During the huge protest meeting, at which both Peter and Gretel were present, Nazi police stormed the building, shooting many demonstrators dead in the crush.

As the hall was fully packed it was difficult for anyone to get away. Many innocent citizens, workers and anti-fascists lost their lives at this protest meeting.

The Nazis had come to suppress this revolt that had been organized against them
Merely days later, Hitler was ensconced in power - yet the corpses of the victims were borne aloft in honour to their graves by their comrades, amidst a second even mightier demonstration, so foreboding that even the Nazi Police ('Sipo') hesitated at first to charge in.

Gretel recalled the powerful inspiration of that day:

About the sad events in Dresden Keglerheim 1933.

"The events in Keglerheim are for all of us old Dresdner anti-fascists a sad memory, but in spite of everything it gave me a lot of fighting spirit, courage, hope and confidence that the barbaric fascism would not last for ever.

As the victims were carried to their graves there was unity between the workers of Dresden, and the solidarity was so powerful that the fascist police dared not interfere.

12 years![7.] For so many, years of anguish, many are not with us any more, but the fighting spirit, the will for peace and unity has not been wiped out. It is good and right that we tell the youth something about the past, in honour of the first victims who died on the long and difficult path to peace and freedom, and to educate our young friends to a conscious activity for their happy future. Sadly, the heavily armed police hesitated for only so long.

We were a group of youth with bicycles. We marched quietly and disciplined but determined to 'fight'. The Sipo[8.] were heavily armed, their faces flaming with anger.

I heard amongst the noise and screams of the Sipo police the order, "bicycles out!" But I did not want to withdraw so quietly. As I finally looked around, I saw that I was the only one left with a bike. I first became conscious of the immediate danger when the Sipo came crashing towards me with uplifted truncheons. A pair of young boys next to me said;

"For heavens sake lass, disappear, get out, quickly!"

These two young lads unceremoniously bundled me away from the crowd down a side alley, along with my bicycle. They closed their ranks quietly and disciplined. I have to be thankful to my young unknown revolutionary comrades. Their quick action saved me.

After I had taken my bike back home and returned to the neighbourhood of the Keglerheim, the devil was already loose.

This is for us now past history but it cannot be a completed chapter as long as similar and even worse things happen in other countries."

Written 1965 in Dresden after an annual peaceful memorial demonstration in Dresden held in honour for the victims of this event. This annual peace demonstration was a yearly tradition in Dresden in the former German Democratic Republic.

[6.] Keglerheim - (house for skittle players). Keglerheim demonstration took place on the 25.1 33.
Hitler came to power on 30.1 33.
[7.] 12 years - Here is meant the years 1933 to 1945, 12 years of Nazi Power.
[8.] The Sipo - Nazi police.

'Wir gehen durch den wilden Wald, der Majestätisch rauschet,
Die Sonne scheint, Vöglein singen und wir mit Freuden lauschet.
Sonnenlichter spielen mit dem Schatten in der Stille!
Und überem Weg, da springt das scheue Wild!
Am Wege, da stehen Baumreisen
Zeugen aus vergangenner Zeit,
Sie trotzten Kampf und Sturm und grüßen
Uns in des Waldes Einsamkeit!
Wir schreiten vorwärts froh und frei,
Und wollten garnicht trauern,
Da fällt ein Schatten vom Hügel mit mosigen Stein
Und uns befällt ein Schaudern!
Hier im graußiger Zeit, verflossen,
Hier wurden sie erschossen,
Hier noch ein Hügel, da noch einer,
Was anderes als Friede und Freiheit wollte keiner!
Die hier geschlagen und geknechtet starben;
Sie kannten nur noch Not und Darben;
Vergeßt es nie! "Es darf nie mehr geschehen,
Das geloben wir euch Kameraden,
Die ihr nie mehr mit uns könnt gehen!'

Translation

'We wander through the wild roaring majestic woods,
The sun is shining, birds are singing, and we listen with delight.
Sunlight plays with the shadows in the stillness,
Timid wild come bouncing over the path.

Giant trees stand in our way,
Witnesses from the past.
In defiance they stand up against the storm and send greetings
To us in the forests loneliness.
We stride forward, happy and free,
We do not want to be sad,
There falls a shadow from the moss stone hill
And we tremble and shiver!
Here in cruel times past,
Here they were shot,
Here is a hill and there is another,
They wanted only peace and freedom!
Here they suffered, fell and died.
They only knew want and starvation.
Never forget, it must never happen again,
Comrades, we pledge
To you, who can never be with us once more.'

(Written in convalescent home in Karnzow 5.6. 64 in GDR).

Hitler had now come to power. Peter is in great danger because of his political activities; 'Rot Front Kämpfer Bund' (Red Front Fighters league) membership and his work with the illegal press.

He is one of the first to disappear in the underground. The position of the illegal press must be changed often. At this time the incident happens, mentioned earlier about the young Nazi helping Peter to carry the heavy case into the tram. What would have happened if he had known that he had helped transport the illegal press! Peter and Gretel have to hide because of their anti-Nazi political activities. There is a warrant out for their arrest.

Peter's comrades had warned him that the Nazis were searching for him. With his life now directly in danger, Peter is forced to flee, Gretel assisting him in crossing the German border over to the Czech Republic in May 1933.

Whilst continuing her political anti - fascist activities, leafleting illegally, collecting subscriptions from reliable members, delivering messages and illegal declared publications, prints and illegal hand written notes, she manages to remain in sporadic contact with Peter. The illegal trip over to the Czech Republic leads along the river Elbe into the beautiful Saxon Switzerland. The trip into illegality is a difficult one, the path often steep leading over the Sandstone Mountains and through the deep dark forests. Gretel makes this journey several times, each time taking with her something for Peter, some of his belongings, his bike, some necessary things needed for daily life, and at the same time she helps with this activity to keep the contact between the antifascists in the emigration and the antifascists already living in the illegality at home in Dresden.

The Nazis, now they had the power to reign, searched for all well-known communists, and antifascists. They want Peter he had been so active. They were furious about his anti-fascist activities, his public speeches and writings that he had edited in the anti fascist leaflets. If Peter had not escaped he would have landed in prison and then sent to one of those already growing concentration camps.

Gretel wonders what to do with the rest of Peter's personal belongings and hides the remainder of his possessions left behind in Dresden, placing them in storage with sympathetic friends. Everyone hoped that this situation would last only for a short time and that fascism would soon be defeated. No one dared think that it would be years before a return to Dresden would be possible.

Gretel had still kept the friendship up with Kurt's mother. As Kurt was not involved in any anti-fascist activities and was an un-political person, Gretel hopes that it will be safe to hide some of Peter's possessions at their home and so she takes Peter's diary notes of his journey to Soviet Russia, some illegal material and Peter's Red Front Fighter's League uniform with to Kurt's mother and hides all these things up in their attic.

She sees Kurt's mother for the last time. Gretel never forgot this friendly motherly lady who was able to take mother Sophie's place in her life. Gretel hopes to be able to collect these things in due time. But the Nazi terror is growing and also the daily arrests of antifascists. Reluctantly Kurt and his mother decide to destroy this dangerous evidence for fear of the implications should the Nazis discover them. It is too risky to keep all these things. All these personal belongings from Peter are burnt.

It must have been a great disappointment and painful for my father to lose these things. All his youth and childhood memories were contained in them, his personal diaries and his proudest possession, his Red Front Fighter's League uniform. But he had escaped. He was, for the moment safe.

After the events in Keglerheim it is only safe to live with reliable friends and comrades. For some time Gretel lives at a house in the Reissiger street in Dresden by a Mr Stoklas who has sympathy with the anti nazi movement. Gretel's political activities do not stop her from going out on wanderings and walks in her beloved Saxonian Switzerland.

In our family there has always been a longing to walk through those deep forest paths, and to breath the air on those rocky sandstone mountains of that part of Germany where our ancestors are so deeply rooted and trod along life's path. Still today, living so far away from Dresden I feel pain and longing to walk regularly over that glamorous wonderful piece of earth, and this feeling grows stronger when looking at the paintings, pictures and photos of the Saxonian Switzerland.

One of Gretel's girl friends fiancé is imprisoned for some activities against the Nazi movement up there in Castle Hohnstein. The two girls decide to set out, and to go wandering into the Saxonian Switzerland and to see if Gretel's girl friend can visit her fiancé. This enterprise is not without danger.

Early one morning the two girls set off. They take the train; pass through Heidenau – Pirna – Wehlen. They leave the train and cross over the river Elbe. This river like a silver ribbon divides the landscape. On one side are many hilly plains. A bit further on is Königstein and the forest rocky terrains surrounding it. In the distance are the hills of the Erzgebirge and like a waving beckoning hand in the far distance, Czechoslovakia, the emigration and Peter. On the other side of the Elbe are tall steep rocks of sand stone, small valleys and paths leading through them to the villages on the other side. The two girls cross the river Elbe. There is, and has always been a ferry service connecting the two riverbanks.

Wehlen is a small village on the banks of the Elbe. It seems as if the old village cottages have never changed their style through the centuries. They still have thatched roofs and the ceilings of the rooms inside are low. In front of the cottages are tiny, tidy, neat little pretty gardens. The windows are like small little holes. The path leads the girls through this village, soon leaving it behind, to climb up the steep slopes into the rocky sandstone mountains. They wander through the deep pinewoods and along small paths like caverns between the sandstone rocks. Leaving the village Wehlen and Rathen behind them, they soon, after wandering over the famous Bastei (strong rock formation) come to 'Polenz Tal', (valley). This long path, which leads the way through the tall rocky sandstone mountains and forests, is situated next to a stream, which fervently flows accompanying the path on its way. Our ancestors used to look down from their castle in Hohnstein, watching out for carriages and horsemen. It is along this path that the two girls have to wander. Their aim is Hohnstein. They leave that long Polenz Tal path behind them and crossing the small bridge over the stream, wander up the steep slopes through the woods and rocks leading up to the Castle Hohnstein. The Polenz Tal is not an isolated place as a few farmers live next to this stream in picturesque little farmhouses.

We have wandered many times along this path. It was one of our most loved wanderings. Castle Hohnstein has changed its face several times during its long existence, changing with the history of time, between - castle - prison - youth hostel - prison- KZ - youth hostel and memorial for the victims of the past.

Now, in our story the Nazis use it is a prison and KZ. The two girls arrive at Hohnstein after their long wandering, but Gretel does not go inside the castle, she stays outside. Gretel does not agree with her friend's behaviour, because she flirts with one of the soldiers in order to get some priority for her fiancé

.

Back in Dresden the situation is worsening rapidly, daily getting tougher. Luckily Gretel manages to get a passport, just in time so that she can travel abroad if necessary. The date of the official stamp in her passport is the 23rd of May 1933, most probably the time of Peter's escape in the emigration.

Gretel's anti-fascist activities bring her in various critical situations. My mother's notes report of following incident;

How Hitler influenced normal people is clearly apparent in following description of an episode when Gretel uses her violin to take anti-fascist material to a comrade living outside Dresden.

"This is only a small episode that I would like to report about, but it is so characteristic for this point in time, when the Nazis blinded so many people with great promises. It was in summer 1933. Our anti-fascist working class groups and organisations were broken and smashed. Many comrades had to hide themselves. I was given the task to take up contact with a young comrade. He lived in a lonely house at the edge of the Dresden Heide. I packed my violin and a bunch of music notes under my arm as I intended to present myself as a music friend, then I knew that the comrade played the mandolin.
    I arrived and knocked on the door of this lonely house. An elderly proletarian woman opened the door. I asked if I could see the comrade.
    She answered: "come in and wait, he will be home soon."
She showed me in, but on entering the front room I received a great shock. I looked and saw in sheer disbelief a large portrait of Hitler hanging there, decorated and surrounded with fresh green oak tree branches. I had to be careful I could not show my true feelings. I asked myself, was this a trap? I was so taken by this nasty surprise, it was difficult to hide my anxiety, but I managed to laugh and said that I had an excellent piece of music that I wanted to give to her son. I was sure he would like it and he could give me another piece in exchange for it. Whilst thinking to myself, that running away would only make me look suspicious, make things worse and endanger everything I followed the woman into the living room. Oh shock! It was even worse there. I could hardly believe what I saw and with great effort I kept control over myself. On each wall hung Hitler pictures, decorated with little flags and flowers. I felt like sitting on hot glowing coals, with burning embers under my feet. If only I could run away, but I couldn't.
    The woman began to speak about Hitler.
    She said; " He is a good man. He will give us work and bread."
    She went over to one of the portraits, and folded her hands in prayer. I looked at her bent back, her hands used and rough from hard work and I looked at her troubled face. I thought to myself, if only one could speak openly and talk to her, what a dreadful mistake she is making, her judgment of the situation is so wrong. Is the man I am waiting for really a comrade? Is he her son? How is this possible?

    In fear of being betrayed I picked up my music notes and whilst turning the pages spoke to her about the wonderful folks music! As the doorbell rang, a hot wave shot through my head. I hoped no one would notice my anxiety. What if an SA[9] man should come through that door and take a look inside my violin box! He would find something that would cost me dearly; my life, imprisonment, KZ! An elderly man stepped into the room, his hand held high in Hitler salute position. Obviously the father, I thought. I was so glad that I could not stand up. I held

9. SA - Nazi police.

48

my violin case between my knees and my hands were filled with the music notes so that I could not perform the compulsory Hitler salute. I kept on talking about the wonderful folks music and repeating myself in fear that my real motivation for my visit would be revealed.

Again the door opened and a young girl came in with a bunch of flowers. She placed the freshly cut flowers in a vase before one the Hitler portraits. The mother was enraptured and the father with a stern look on his face, tried to take on a military posture. I praised the pretty flowers.

At last the comrade came. I had waited so long. I had seen him once at our red sports group, before Hitler's time. Bewildered I searched in his face and thought; no he cannot be a traitor, impossible. As I gave him my music notes, he smiled consciously knowingly and sympathetic. Quickly he accompanied me out of the room. I opened my mouth several times, speechless, unable to talk and looked at him questioning and challenging. He had understood what I wanted to ask him, and said;
"I am so sorry, surly you had a shock, but my foster parents believe in Hitler."
Only after receiving this explanation could I dare to give up the materials that were meant for him. Then I swiftly departed, hurrying away as quickly as possible. I have never forgotten that evening.

These poor working class people were so deceived by Hitler's men, declaring him as a good man giving workers employment, the work being no other than building roads, which were then used to march into and occupy Czechoslovakia. We anti-fascist's could see clearly in advance the path Hitler was going. The work he had, was for war preparation and with this it was to be the last piece of bread for many."

(Written 1965, in Dresden).

Years later back in Dresden in the 1960's, my mother found a book dedicated in honour for the victims of Nazism. The stories and photos of anti- fascists, who were executed, gassed, tortured or who had disappeared during the Nazi time is printed in this book for everyone to read. She found the portrait of this young man in this book!

By this point, Gretel was essentially living in a form of hiding, passing from one comrade's room to another, not daring to make contact with her father and stepmother or her brother Hans, for fear of endangering them. As her brother Hans was also politically active in the anti-fascist movement it is crucial for Gretel to change her address frequently; the Nazi police were already searching for her. Gretel must leave her accommodation and room she had by Mr Stoklas in the Reiniger Street. The political situation is worsening rapidly. The Nazis search the house of Mr Stoklas and keep strict watch on it. They also keep a firm eye on her father's house, so the militant anti-fascist activities from brother Hans and his friends, hiding those weapons in the walls of the workshop create an even more precariously dangerous situation, resulting in his arrest and imprisonment.

5. The Escape.

‘**Das kleine Blümchen, es macht mich froh**.
Noch weiß ich nicht warum, wieso.
Ein Blümchen so rot wie das Blut.
Es atmet, es läßt mich träumen.
Es grüßt die Vögel auf den Bäumen.
Ein Blümchen so rot wie das Blut.
Die Blume hat eine Zaubermacht.
Mit ihrem leuchtenden Rot.
Ein Blümchen so rot wie das Blut
Wie die Fahne der Arbeiterschaft.
Die leuchtet fur Freiheit und Brot.
Eine Fahne rot wie das Blut.’

Translation

‘**That tiny flower, it makes me so glad,**
Still I don’t know how and why.
A little flower, as red as blood.
It breathes it lets me dream,
It greets the birds on the trees.
A little flower, as red as blood.
The flower has a magic power,
With it’s sparkling red.
A little flower, as red as blood.
Like the flag of the working class,
That shines for freedom and bread.
A flag as red as blood.’

(Written 1960 in Dresden).

Gretel is very optimistic, even in these difficult times, like in her poems. The comrades help each other, but it is getting increasingly difficult. Daily the houses of friends are watched; daily the houses are searched for illegal materials and anti-fascists in hiding and arrests for anti-Nazi activities continue to increase wildly.

My mother told me about a tragic incident of a family, where the father is forced to go into hiding because of his anti-fascist activities. For his wife and son, life is sad and lonely without him and the situation is a dangerous and difficult one.

The father visits his wife and son regularly in spite of the perilous risk of being caught. On those evenings and nights, when visiting his family, he lives in the garden shed. Somehow the father is able to manage it, without being seen. But the Nazi police keep firm surveillance over the activities going on in the house. They even go so far as to make enquiries at the boy’s school. The parents are unable to speak openly to their child. They have to look on in silence and see how their child receives a Nazi education. Each spoken word could endanger the father’s life. And so it happens, in school, the Nazi teacher asks the boy about his father and the boy without wanting to, in childish simplicity, not realizing the results, gives away the place where his father hides at night, when visiting the family. The result is devastating; the father is arrested and executed!

'Gedanken zu zwei Bilder'.

'Nie wieder soll geschehen,
Das grauen der faschistischen Barbarei.
Nie wieder hören und sehen,
Der Kriegesopfer röchelndes Totes geschrei.
Den fleisigen und mütigen Kämpfern wir geloben.
Beim Blick auf unsere neu erbaute Stadt von oben
Zu erhalten das friedliche und frei pulsierende Leben.
Weiter zu wirken zu bauen, zu schaffen und streben.
Das Mädchen da, dem das Leben gefällt,
Wie der Kelch einer Blume am Fenster der Welt.
Mit sonnigen Lachen und Zukunfts frohen sein
So müßten die Menschen wohl überall sein.'

Translation

'Thoughts about two pictures'

'It should never again happen,
The horror of barbaric fascism,
Never again hear and see
The war victims rattling death cry.
The diligent and courageous fighter, we solemnly promise
While looking at our newly build city from above.
To keep that peaceful free pulsating life.
Further to work, to build, to create and aim
That lass there, who loves life,
Like a goblet of a flower at the world's window,
With a sunny smile and happy future looks.
So should be all people, everywhere.'

(Written in Dresden 1.2.65)

Gretel uses her passport to go over the border to visit Peter. She becomes an important contact for the comrades left behind in Dresden and for those comrades already living in Czechoslovakia in the emigration. Everyone hopes that the situation will not last long and that there will be an end soon to the threatening fascist dictatorship. The dates in her passport are, 2nd June, then 6th June, 8th June, and 11th June 1933. At Snezniku is passport control. She also went over the frontier at other times, illegally avoiding the officials at the border. This part of the story is difficult to write, as my mother seldom spoke about this particular hard time.

It is as if this illegal time was to stay illegal and silent forever. The Nazi's are furious that Peter has escaped them. In their anger, they hunt for Gretel. She is now wanted as a hostage. By now the Nazis had issued a warrant for Gretel's arrest in the hope that through her they might seize Peter.

By now it has become nearly impossible for Gretel to hide by comrades or anti-fascists. Everyone, who worked against Hitler, even those with the smallest revolutionary anti-fascist action must expect arrest. In order not to endanger anyone Gretel responds to this by retiring into even more solitary hiding. She finds an empty factory, taking up residence in this abandoned building, and tries to keep going, living in this isolated place as long as possible, relying on other comrades to pass messages and food to her.

From the distance she glances at her father's home. She can see him going in and out of his workshop and from afar she can see her brother Hans. But she cannot go and greet them. The home of her childhood, where she was so happy with her mother Sophie is carefully and rigorously watched day and night.

The Nazi's even keep vigilance over friend's houses. The situation worsens daily. The comrades help her – they keep contact and bring Gretel food. The connection with brother Hans has now totally broken down. But Hans himself is also in danger. In the workshop, hidden in the walls are still the weapons! For Gretel the time for parting from her so loved hometown Dresden is nearing rapidly. She does not want to leave Dresden, and hopes to hold out in the empty factory. But the fascistic terror is growing daily.

'Du meine Stadt, Dich möchte ich nicht missen,
Wärst Du mein Liebste, würde ich Dich küssen,
So manche schlaflose Nacht.
Habe ich in Gedanken an Dich zu gebracht,
Als ich weit fort in der Fremde weilte,
Und nur in die Errinerung zu Dir eilte,
Errinnerung an Freud und Leid,
Errinnerung an schwere Zeit,
Wo faschistische Bestien
In Menschen antlitze gespien.'

Translation

'You my town I would not like to miss you,
If you would be my dearest I would kiss you,
So many sleepless nights
Have I spent in thoughts of you.
As I was far away,
Living in foreign countries,
And only in memory could hasten to you,
Memories of pleasures and sorrows,
Memories of hard times.
Where fascistic beasts.
Spat in peoples faces.'

Gretel loves her hometown. Although Dresden never seems to have treated her kindly; in times of barbaric fascism, hunting her like a criminal, in peace times causing her unnecessary difficulties and grief, she remains true and faithful to her beloved hometown, a fighter for peace, for humanity and for a better life.

'Die Einsamkeit.'

'So weit wie das Meer, so weit
So gross ist meine Einsamkeit,
So teif wie das Meer unendlich
Wie der Fisch im Wasser unständlich,
Dünkler Felsstein, Du am Meeresstrand,
Irgend wie bist Du mir verwand.'

Translation

'Loneliness.'

'So wide as the sea, so far
So great is my loneliness,
So deep like the sea, immense endless
Like the fish in the water indistinguishable,
Dark rock stone on the sea beach
Some how you are related to me.'

(Written in England in internment camp Isle of Man 1940).

Finally, the decision is made that the risk for her is too great, and she is instructed by her comrades to leave Dresden to flee, to emigrate - and, with it, Germany.
Life is now too dangerous, too difficult. The only personal possessions she can save is her much loved violin. The Nazis have ruined all her plans she had in Dresden for her future. She must now begin a new life and live among people in a foreign country as a foreigner, in a place, new and strange to her, and learn to speak another language. There are two more dates in her passport, the 8th July and the 20th July!
And so Gretel leaves Dresden behind her and wanders off over the beautiful Saxon Switzerland, through the deep forests into the emigration, wondering how long she will be away. She leaves Dresden heavy hearted and sad, already pining to return home. It is very difficult to turn away from this beautiful place, where the old ancestors have their roots and the old legends of the Duba's ghost around.

The Bastei, Saxon Switzerland.

The Legend, part 2.

The oldest landowners from whom one finds actually historical notes were, the 'Berken von Duba'. Their forefather Berkowitz in the year 1004 was promoted to highest country Lord from Bohemia because of his faithful service. The sign on the shield from the 'Berken von Duba' are two oak branches crossing each other on a yellow background.

The name Duba came from the castle Dub that they owned, which was situated in the district of Bunzlau. The name of the first owner of the castles Hohnstein and Schandau was 'Hinke von Berken', Freiherr [10] von Duba (1330).

The names of the proprietors are not chronologically in exact order. A document from the master of Lüttichau and the author of the topographical office from Hohnstein mentions the masters von Tuba, " Anno 1490. Father Johanne Episcopo Misnensi gave the honourable master Birk von der Taube, master in Hohnstein, the ordinance as vicar to Sebnitz. There came many other Lords of 'von Tuba's', various owners of the Castle Hohnstein, each with their own special problems, concerning their Priests and properties.

Heinrich Birken, (1430) sold the 'Leite an der Elbe,[11] which was opposite Schandau to his brother 'Hans Birken von Duba' for 5 pieces of Groschen.[12]

There is mention of a Hinko Berka von der Tuba as owner of Hohnstein, and 1361 Heinrich Berka von der Tuba also completed a written statement that Hohnstein belonged to Bohemia.

In 1381 a certain Hinko owner of Hohnstein and Schandau erected the high alter in the chapel by 'Lieben Frauen' in Leipa. Also in the little town under the castle Hohnstein was an endless early mass subscribed in the priest's church.

Meanwhile the Lords 'Birken from Hohnstein' had to suffer under various changes. The priest of Pirna announced expenses, which changed their lives and the character of their possessions. They were very sensitive about this. The power over their possessions and status was further restricted. In the year 1452 the electorate prince 'Friedrich des Sanftmütigen', (meaning Friedrich the Soft- hearted), gave Hohnstein over to a representative of the prince. Also at the headquarters in Schandau, prince Ernst and the Duke Albrecht were mentioned as officers to Hohnstein. The Dubas had to step back, further and further. They fell into bad repute, as thieves and plagiarists. Centuries later the ancestors changed their name from Duda, to Tuba and then to Tube and whilst feeling ashamed of the past bad reputation sold their 'von' title. German aristocracy used the word 'von' before a surname.

My uncle Hans had some kind of documentary proof about this ancestry. It was hidden away in a large box with the marquetry pattern of the Duba's coat of arms on it.

When my uncle died, my mother went to his apartment to sort things out. She found it in this box. Regrettably she left it there, waiting for the final settlement from the solicitors concerning his assets. Then a little latter, when everything was sorted, this documentary proof was missing; stolen! As is known the Stasi were everywhere and no locked doors helped to keep things safe. My uncle's death happened also under certain strange circumstances, why were so many syringes laying around his apartment? We never found out. He had no illness to justify this haul of syringes. But that was centuries ago. Now back in the 20th century, Gretel, the daughter of the last offspring of Sophie Tube, was to leave her home country to become a poor emigrant and she was an active anti-fascist.

---

[10] Freiherr – Lord or baron.

[11] 'Leite an der Elbe' – Piece of land with rock formation.

[12] 'Groschen '– pennies.

If you ask yourselves: why I bring up this old story here, partly medieval history, partly legend? Then my answer is; to show how the two world wars disturbed families, uprooting people out of their elements, where they had lived, not only all their life's, but generations of that particular family had trodden along life's path in that particular part of the world; to show how the war had scattered families apart – blowing them far away from their original stem.

Gretel is very unhappy in the emigration and her optimistic belief that a return is possible keeps her going. Although her passport is valid for several years, the visa can only be used until 23rd of November 1933. Gretel, feeling very restless decides to try to return, having this date very much in mind. But things are even more difficult in Dresden. It is only a very short visit that she can make. The last date in her passport is 14th November 1933. This return means again living isolated in the illegality, in the empty factory building. Life is one endless hardship. There is no chance and possibility for Gretel to stay. Watch is kept on every suspicious person or building. She cannot visit anyone. It is a lonely, sad and heart breaking enterprise – this experiment to try to return and stay in Dresden.

The Nazis still keep watch over father Richards's workshop. A little later, after Gretel then lives finally in Prague, the Nazis search the workshop and find the hidden weapons. Hans had been betrayed. He was arrested and kept 2 years in prison. And so, Gretel fled over the border into the Czech Republic, a fleeting last glance at her beloved Dresden, escaping into the unknown. It is not to be the last time she has to travel off into an uncertain future. She does not know how long it will take until she can return. She does not know how many years will pass by before she can walk again on that piece of earth she so loved!

We went over to Dresden, summer 1960, for a holiday, and this holiday was to change my whole life.

After this cold short unfriendly November visit in 1933, Gretel leaves and walks off into the emigration away from her much loved Sachische schweiz, through those deep pine woods and over those giant rocky sand stone formations. But she has a good and faithful friend waiting for her, Peter, her fiancé. Reunited with Peter in Prague, the two survive for months in a ramshackle hut. The time in Prague, in spite of all extreme hardships, bad insufficient food and starvation, was to be a happy and prosperous one.

In this box was originally some kind of documentary proof of the Duba ancestry.
Later missing due to Stasi interference.

'Es gibt ein Wort wie Glocken klingen,
Ein Wort das jedes Herz läßt singen.
Voll Freud und Fröhlichkeit so Rein,
Es kann nur das Wörtlich Frieden sein.
Es fällt auf fruchtbare Erde
Es blüht im Sonnenschein
Dem Menschen Freud und Ehre
Der Frieden kanns nur sein
Es kann nur Frieden sein.'

Translation

'There is a word that is like bell ringing.
A word that sets each heart singing.
Full of pleasure and happiness, so clear.
Peace can only be that word,
It falls on fruitful earth.
It flourishes in sunshine.
For mankind, joy and honour,
It can only be peace
It is only peace.'

(Written about 1962 in Dresden).

Saxon Switzerland.

CHAPTER 3

First Emigration – The artist awakes.
1933 – 1939

'Das Gewitter.'

'In sommerlicher Reife und Früchte schwer
Brütende Hitze liegt auf der heissen Erde,
Kein Lüftchen regt sich, alles still.
Ferne am Himmel türmen sich Wolkengebilde
Leises verhaltenes stöhnen,
Wächst heran zu grollen und dröhnen
Die Blitze zucken wie feurige Schlangen
Die Erde in Zittern und Bangen,
Bis auf die dampfende Erde wie Segen
Ströhnt hernieder erlösender Regen.'

Translation

'The Storm.'

'In the ripe summer, heavy with fruit
Brooding heat lies on the hot earth.
No air movement, all is silent.
Far in the heavens, cloud formations are towering.
Faint restrained groans,
Grow nearer to rumblings and roaring,
The lightning flashes like fiery snakes
The earth is shaky and anxious.
Until, comes on the steaming earth like mercy,
Pouring down free releasing rain.'

(Written 3rd October 1948).

Oil painting;
Beggar in Prague;
(approx 1930-33)

1. The Two Blues.

Have you seen Prague? It is a wonderful city, very romantic with plenty of sculptures everywhere. Especially the beautiful statutes on the 'Karls Brücke', (bridge over the Moldau), provide an everlasting impression – unforgettable. Years later, on a holiday, I stood together with my dear mother on that bridge, looking down at the Moldau. She showed me the places where she had been during the emigration years. We visited 'Prager Vennedig', and stood on the bridge by the canal, looking over to the view I recognised from my mother's watercolour painting. This romantic place resembles the picturesque waterways in Vienna and so was given this name. We visited other places as well and searched for several old addresses of friends from the time when my mother used to live there, but today Prague is a different place and passing years have brought many changes. We could not find them; they had just disappeared, as if they had never been there before. I would have loved to find my mother's early sculpture work that she had to leave behind in Prague. I would have so liked to see them, but the address of the lady who bought them does not appear to exist any more. Instead, while searching, we bumped into a police station.

Gretel was now living in a strange country as an emigrant. Life was difficult and living conditions extremely bad, their shabby accommodation, the ramshackle hut providing at least a roof over their head, but Gretel and her fiancé Peter were now reunited and they both were young and optimistic.

The Nazis were left behind, gone the anxiety, of being caught and having to hide in empty factory ruins, at least, for the moment. But they both stood before an emptiness – a nothingness. They had to learn a new language, and Czech is a very difficult one to learn. They had to get used to new customs and find new connections. It was very difficult to obtain a firm foothold in life. The refugee committee in Prague accepted and helped the two fugitives. But before they could receive any sort of financial help, any money they had brought with them had to be used up first.

Gretel had earned reasonably well as a model during the last year in Dresden and both refugees still hoped that they could return home soon.

The two decide not to stay in Prague, in the midst of the city noises, confronted with the constant worry and tension of the political situation and uncertain future, but to use the hard earned money wisely for a holiday – a journey through the beautiful Czech countryside. So the 'Two Blues',[1] (as they were now nicknamed) set off with rucksack, violin and bikes, on an everlasting memorable trip.

My mother's diary notes begin on the 21st of July 1933.
It is a happy and joyous holiday. The Two Blues travel off along the country roads, through towns and villages. Perhaps it was their honeymoon? My parents are only years later able to marry in England. But the time in Prague was the beginning of their life together and so I allow myself to declare this holiday journey as a sort of unofficial honeymoon.

My mother writes: "Most probably I would have married Peter Klopfleisch already in Prague. The home of my parents was full of finest furniture, as my father was an independent master cabinetmaker. I would have had the finest trousseau. Today my best sculptures are carved out of wood. How much more and better could I have worked in my fathers workshop if destiny had allowed it."

But the two are unable to marry, neither in Nazi Germany, nor in Prague. In Nazi Germany they would have been arrested. In Prague it would have meant visiting the German embassy.

---

[1] 'The Two Blues' Due to the political situation, every antifascist in the underground movement was firstly known by their nickname. My parents were known as 'The Two Blues'.

This would have had the same result, ending in arrest and then sent off to concentration camp. So, as the situation is now, the 'Two Blues' manage without a marriage ceremony. Gretel plays her own wedding march on her violin accompanied by the wild birds in the woods. Peter collects the wedding feast from nature herself. The woods are full of mushrooms and wild berries, and the wedding sermon is spoken by the blue sky and hot summer sunshine. Everything is exactly like in Gretel's poems. The two are King and Queen, and a whole kingdom is laid out before their feet. Although they have nothing – only each other, they are young, prosperous and powerful in courage.

The weather is good. It is high summer. Sometimes the two just sleep wild in the woods. The moose builds a soft bed, the stars shine like far of lighted candles for our honeymooners, and above all, the two are now (for the moment) free from Nazi terror. Free to walk open in the fresh air and enjoy what life has in store for them.

Peter has sufficient knowledge of the Czech language and is able to talk to the local people; also many farmers can speak german quite fluently, so there is no problem with conversation.

Once while camping in some deep pine forests the two lovers meet some gypsies. They exchange some friendly words with each other and the gypsies try to sell some of their goods to them. The 'Two Blues' then continue their journey, but later during that day, Gretel discovers that her beloved violin is missing. Where was it? Where had she left it? The woods are deep and they had not kept to the path, wandering along carefree and happy.

Slowly but surely Gretel finds her way back to their camping place from that night. Would she find her violin? Or had the gypsies taken it? No there it was, nice and safe, still under the trees where she had tucked it away.

Sometimes the two sleep on haystacks. Some farmers are friendly, and helpful, but some are also hostile. One friendly farmer offers our two honeymooners the opportunity to sleep in his barn on the hay. The next night the friendly farmers barn is burnt down. Luckily Gretel and Peter had decided not to sleep there that night. They had found something else.

Now it is time to think about a more comfortable accommodation for a few nights after sleeping rough out in the open. Gretel and Peter arrive one day at a village called Zilina. Today Zilina is a modern little town, quite different from the village of that time. Gretel and Peter are glad to get a cheap room and at last a comfortable bed. Unsuspecting they settle down for the night. But what is that, something is biting, crawling and pinching them. The bed is full of fleas! The whole room is full of fleas – its even worse the whole village is full of the little beasts. Later my mother always spoke of 'Zilina the flea town'. They spent an extremely uncomfortable night, trying to catch these tiny unpleasant biting insects and made a vain attempt to get some rest between the spaces of time of scratching and hunting these obnoxious insects. The farmer next day is surprised at our two honeymooners distress and answers, "It doesn't matter, it doesn't matter" and shakes some flea powder down his neck!!

The two escape as quickly as they can away from Zilina the flea town, away into the safety and cleanliness of the open countryside.

Perhaps the Nazis had taken the fleas away with them, then, today the fleas have disappeared! Perhaps it had done the Nazis some good!

Gretel's 22nd birthday is spent together with Peter on this happy journey. At least for the moment, our two lovers are able to leave all worries behind them. Mother Nature takes good care of them and they enjoy life to the full. One of the many places Peter and Gretel visit on their trip is the Mazoka Caves.

Years later, whilst on our holiday revisiting those places of the emigration years, we also went to see the Mazoka Caves. It was amazing to see those wonderful stone formations and large stalagmites, an unforgettable experience. My mother had told me so much about this place and I was curious to see them myself.

We met a group of English tourists at the entrance and on hearing the English language spoken by this tourist group I became quite excited. I hadn't seen England for so long, it was now 12 years since that memorable holiday of no return! The tourists were very friendly, especially when they heard that I had been born and grew up in the UK. It was wonderful to hear some people speak English after such a long time, and I realized how I longed to see the places of my childhood again. It also helped me to understand and made me aware how my mother must have felt, to flee from her beloved Dresden, to safety, away from Nazi terror.

The English tourists invited us to accompany them into the caves. Our dog Bella was just as welcome. The caves are partly under water, and in some places, a boat had to be used to see the stalagmites. Afterwards the tourists invited us into their bus and we even had a meal with them at their hotel. We had been camping and we were not so finely dressed as the tourists travelling with their stylish bus and elegant hotel accommodation, but it didn't seem to matter. Everyone was so friendly. GDR tourists would have behaved completely different.

But now back in 1933 Peter and Gretel are still enjoying their long holiday. They visit the Tatra, those wonderful Czech Mountains between Czechoslovakia and Polen. The beautiful scenery inspires Gretel to use her artistic talent to paint and to write poems. One day, the two decide to climb to the top one of those mountains. Our two honeymooners plan to spend the night in the mountain hut, high upon the heights. But each visitor has to carry up a log of wood in order to get something to drink and to be able to sleep the night at the mountain hut. The climb up the mountain is hard, exhausting, and very tiring due to the heavy load they are carrying, but in the end they succeed. They arrive safely at the mountain hut, are able to enjoy the magnificent panorama of the Tatra Mountains a hot drink and a warm bed for the night.

Back in Prague, life is again serious and bitter. Memories of the enjoyable holiday and the adventures they had, visiting the Czech countryside, the Mazoka caves and the Tatra Mountains are overshadowed by the need to find accommodation, food and other daily necessary things. The hope to return to Dresden soon, is unthinkable, and Peter and Gretel are not happy living in the large common wards of the emigration hostel crammed full of emigrants of all walks of life. They find a wooden hut, cold, damp and draughty and here, the two live together. It is cold in winter and there is no heating. In spite of this, Gretel and Peter prefer to live in their 'dog's hut', to be alone with each other and to sleep on straw sacks on the hard cold floor as they had no furniture. These impossible appalling hard living conditions, that all emigrants faced, resulted in Gretel's rheumatic illness later on.

Mother's own words report:
"Because of the extreme urgent need, lack of provisions, lack of food, we had no money to buy the most necessary things for daily needs, and for the first time I had stomach complaints."

The German emigrants were not allowed to work. It was a daily fight against starvation. Peter was able to earn something sometimes, whilst giving private lessons and he received often food at the pupil's parent's home.

Good political courses are held in the hostel enabling the refugees to see clearer what was happening in Nazi Germany. But the hard life and starvation has its results. Gretel has for the first time heart trouble (pericardium inflammation). Later, Gretel receives treatment for headache (migraine) and giddiness (vertigo). Is this a wonder with the hard life she leads?

'Weg Gefährten.'

'Du siehst sie wie Steine am Strand,
Du trifst sie in jeden Sand,
Weggefährten.
Einige sind bunt und lebendig,
Sind interessant.
Einige sind kühn und gespickt,
Andere sind scheußlich und schrecklich.
Und immer wohin der Strom des Lebens auch fließt,
Immer wieder sind es neue Weggefährten,
Die mann grüßt.
Laßt uns zusammen stehen,
Für Friede und Freiheit im Land.
Ihr alle die tatkräftig drehen,
Das Rad der Geschichte,
In schwieliger Hand.
Weggefährten, so fern wir uns sind,
Oder unbekannt.
Zusammen stehen wir Hand in Hand,
Und Arbeiten und Bauen für unser sozialistisches Land.'

Translation

'Path Companions.'

'You see them like stones on the beach,
You meet them on all sands,
Path Companion.
Some are coloured and lively,
Are interesting.
Some are brave and keen,
Others are malicious and frightful.
And always where the torrent of life flows,
And always its new path companions,
That one greets.
Let us stand together,
For peace and freedom in our land.
All of you who turn the wheel,
Of history energetically,
With worn workers hands.
Path companion, so far apart from each other,
Or unknown.
Together we stand hand in hand,
And work and form our socialist land.'

(Written 1965 in Dresden).

61

Now I am too sitting in a strange place, even if it is the country where I was born and grew up. But I have been too long away – 24 years! I have longed to see those places where I lived as a child. I tried to flee into the past and tried to forget the pain of those last ten years spent in Dresden under that Stalinist regime.

I long to see Maidenhead, my birth town, I long to walk along those paths I trod together with my dear mother. I long to recall dearest childhood memories, the thicket, Boulders Lock, the river Thames, the golf course and Bray park. Only once have I managed to get back, for two days! I would love to have at least a holiday, there, where we used to live – as a family, together with my mother, my father and sister!

I feel like the poem at the beginning of my story, then, destiny planted me in a little town in Britain, strange and far away from my longings and desires. Yes, I did find new friends; but all of them have new faces, and most of them were only curios to see and hear about that strange woman who came over from East Germany. My daughter and I were alone in a strange new world! And, still I wonder, where are the known faces of the past?

My mother must have felt similar, as she decided to try to go back for that cold short November visit described in the previous chapter.

In spite of the extreme conditions, the two were happy with each other's company. Peter and Gretel's 'Villa' (the wooden 'dogs hut') was situated next to a factory and there was no rest, no peace at night, always the humming and thumping noise of the machines, and the factory smells crept through the thin wooden walls – so little comfort for my dear parents! At one time Gretel and Peter have a little kitten. I'm quite astonished about this then, later, Peter begins to hate all cats. But in the wooden hut the little kitten brings some life and pleasure to both of them.

'The big sister', Modelled in terracotta,   'Mother with children' (approx. 1935- 1936)

These two sculptures were modelled in Prague.
Influenced by the artworks from Käthe Kollwitz and as a member of the Oska Kokoschka club.

2. The Artist.

Gretel wanders through the strange city looking for a violin teacher. Everything is new – the language, the people. She stands before emptiness, but it is also at the same time a new beginning. It is difficult for Gretel walking through Prague, a new strange place, knowing no one to brush away the past and begin anew – and at the same time to be optimistic and to look straight forward positive, but into an uncertain future! Her long search is successful and extremely important for all future events in her life.

Gretel's search for suitable continuation for her violin studies is unsuccessful, instead, she finds a sympathetic and encouraging art teacher, Käte Schäffner who was a personal friend of Käte Kollwitz. She recognizes Gretel's talents, informing her, 'you are a born sculptress'. Gretel is sceptic about this, knowing that she would have to leave all work behind when the time comes to move on. For sculpture work you need room, and material, and what would happen to her work when she is either able to return to Dresden, or would have to flee again? In spite of these thoughts Gretel is delighted with this prospect and her work develops a strongly aesthetic, yet distinctively political style of socialist art.

The meeting with Käte Schäffner [2] is the turning point in her life, the destine finger point for Gretel, showing her the way she has to go. The art teacher recognises Gretel's hidden talents and helps to bring them to life.

My mother reports in her own words:
" In Prague, in search of a music teacher I found an art teacher, Käte Schäffner. She accepted me as a pupil. She was a personal friend and colleague from Käte Kollwitz. Under her amiable artistic instructions I began to work not only in painting and drawing but also in sculpture techniques. It was a hard fight for technical knowledge, work, materials and tools. The acquaintance with Käte Schäffner was of great importance for my whole life. She also gave me private lessons in anatomy, sent me to life study classes and also sent me to a sculptor, [3] for extra lessons. He then took me to the large stone sculpture workshop in Prague where he worked. Käte Schäffner's efforts to try to get me into the academy in Prague failed because they only accepted Czech citizens. However, all my efforts to learn in spite of all difficulties were successful.

It seemed as if I could reflect the souls of normal people in my work. Then my sculptures were well liked and admired and often folks came over to me and said, 'I like that very much. Oh I must have that figure!'

Käte Schäffner was very energetic in her efforts to prove to me that I was talented for sculpture work. She told us so much about her colleague and friend Käte Kollwitz and also explained to us her techniques and how she worked.

I have seen and learnt a great deal in Prague in the stone workshop. If one is hungry to learn and has the desire to create then you learn quickly. I was also member of the Oskar Kokoschka emigrants artist club. The unity and harmony of all emigrant artists in Prague was excellent, and this important experience of working together and helping each other was very useful and beneficial for me. To my acquaintances belonged the Dresden author Max Zimmering."

So in the end, the long search in Prague was successful, and Gretel had found a wonderful encouraging teacher and good friend in this lady, Käte Schäffner, a personal friend of Käte

---

[2] Käte Schäffner was a south German art teacher living in Prague, personal friend from Käte Kollwitz
[3] Prof. Grund was the sculptor tutor .
Life studies were made possible for emigrant German artists who were members of the Oskar Kokoschkar club 1937.

Kollwitz. Gretel does not forget her violin and she continues to play. There is an excellent and influential Agitprop group in Prague with Hedda Zinner, of which Gretel is also an active member with her violin, but in everything she does, her sculpture talents dominates.

It is always with regret that my mother mentions the unsuccessful search for a violin teacher. But as destiny decides, the sleeping artist awakens. Under the influence and instructions of Käte Schäffner the artistic personality Greta Grossner, like a budding tree branch bursting into bloom, develops rapidly to full strength.

Käte Schäffner has always a friendly word, good advice and a quick eye for the needs of her pupil. Gretel's portraits and drawings show a very strong character and Gretel enjoys forming with her pencils the figures and objects she has in mind to create, to life.
As reward for good and successful work, Käte Schäffner regularly presents some urgently needed material for the poor emigrant artist. One day it is a pencil, or several pencils, charcoal, paper, paints or even a watercolour box. But, very time before Gretel receives the paint box, Käte Schäffner throws the black paint demonstratively out of the open window with the remark, how bad it is to use black.

There is also Gretel's little student colleague, Eva Schwarz, a Jewish girl. Later she dies through Nazis hands. The two students are good friends. They work hard, solving artistic problems together. Eva has a brother who slips more and more into bad company and Eva often speaks of the worries her parents have because of this.

One day as Gretel arrives at Käte Schäffner's house for her art lessons; she is extremely astonished to find her place full of tools and materials needed for modelling. Whilst the other pupils carry on with their drawings and study sketches, Käte Schäffner orders Gretel to begin modelling. Gretel stands there open mouthed and confused, "What is happening here today." Käte Schäffner replies, "Miss Grossner, you know you are a born sculptress. You must begin here now and today."

Gretel replies, "But what is going to happen with my Sculptures? I am only a poor emigrant. I will have to wander further and I can't take them with me!"

Käte Schäffner is very persistent. No 'buts' and 'ifs' are accepted. She persuades Gretel to put aside any arguments that might prevent her from beginning to model and create her sculpture work. Käte Schäffner does even more. Persuasion is not enough. She does everything in her power to put Gretel on the right path for life. She not only instructs Gretel in anatomy, but also sends Gretel to life study classes, ignoring all costs. She does her utmost to support Gretel and manages to send her for lessons in a stone sculpture workshop. It is quite a large place, only men are working there and she is the only female.

A sculptor Mr Grund (later Professor) leads the business and schooling courses. But it takes some time to win the sympathy of the men around. No one believes one minute that the young girl will keep up in strength, and that she will soon give up after having knocked her fingers sore. But no one knows Gretel. The men had seen several girls have a try, but not one had succeeded. Gretel is completely different; she struggles, and knocks and works determined and stubbornly on and on, hardly pausing for a breath. Her life's blood flows through her hands into her sculptures, forming, reflecting the thoughts and spirits of the souls of the people around her.

Only after Gretel had proved that she would not run away whimpering, only after she had hurt her fingers and they were sore and bloody, only then after the men realized that she is different does she receive help, lessons and instructions. Käte Schäffner had recognized the sculptress in Gretel. It is thanks to the knowing and 'seeing eye' of the experienced art teacher that Gretel becomes what she is today. Gretel is refused admission into the art academy in Prague because she is a foreigner, but life itself proves to be a far better high school.

There are many artists in the emigration. Among them are many well-known names like Max Zimmering, Kuba. Balden, R. Graets, J Heartfield, Oska Kokoschka, H Warner and many others. These anti-fascist artists in Prague form a group, and work with their art against fascism.
Gretel becomes a part of this important part of history. Together with these artists Gretel not only learns and studies as one of them, but together they work for peace and a better world.

This part of history; the past, the role these emigrant artists play is so important that the future GDR artists cannot, (as much as they would like to) ignore Gretel's part of it all. Later, together with these artists, Gretel's name is also mentioned in books, an everlasting convincing document.

In the summer to autumn of 1937 in Prague, these artists build a group, calling themselves the Oskar Kokoschka Bund, (League). Within these few years since 1933, Gretel has developed into an enthusiastic and talented young artist accepted and respected from her colleagues – a full member of their society, a member of the renowned Oska Kokoschka league.

Most of the emigrants live in the emigration hostels in Strasnice, where important activities took place. Two artists' festivals were organised in the year of 1937 that found a strong resonance in the public's eye. The second festival was especially successful. Many German and Czech antifascists worked collective together. Not only exhibitions of artworks but also culture programs were shown.

In the midst of all these artistic activities Gretel's health worsens and she must pay a heavy price for the insufficient and bad food. She suffers under headaches and giddiness, signs of starvation. Gretel receives treatment from Dr Altschul. He orders a salt less diet. Gretel has also stomach trouble and must stay in hospital, but she soon has to leave because she has nothing to eat as relatives were expected to bring in food each day for the patience's. The hospitals did not provide any food. So it was customary that time, in pre-war Prague.

As much as Peter would like to help, there is nothing, practically every little, or no food available to bring into the hospital. Through the initiative of the young Dr Hans Kalmus working at this hospital Gretel underwent some examinations that resulted in the young doctor's questioning, " Just tell me, what do you eat?" This doctor writes a note to his wife, gives Gretel the address and says, " Go to this address, give this note to my wife and get some food." Gretel leaves the doctor, with note and address in her hands. She makes her way through the busy per-war city of Prague. Again Gretel finds sympathetic and helpful people who help her. The doctor's wife after reading the note goes into the kitchen and comes back with a plate full of good food and a hot drink. So, for a short time Gretel receives employment by his wife as a children's nanny. With the earned money Gretel is able to buy herself some food, which she needs so urgently.

Dr Hans Kalmus was the oldest son of Sanitätsrat [4] Dr Kalmus and who had a leading position in the hospital in Prague. Later, during the Nazi occupation, Sanitätsrat Dr Kalmus together with his kind amiable and helpful wife Elsa, die in the Ghettos of Prague, murdered by the Nazis. In Dr Kalmus' house, Gretel finds friends, work and admirers of her sculptures.

One day, as Gretel arrives to take care of the children, Frau Elsa takes Gretel into the room of her son Carl. She is determined to help Gretel in a special way. Before the astonished Gretel can say anything, Frau Kalmus orders her son Carl to clear various shelves and drawers in his room.

---

[4] Sanitätsrat – German honorary title for distinguished doctors.

"Carlchen," she say's, "Gretel needs urgently some shelves for her wonderful sculptures. They must be kept in a safe place. And Carlchen you really can do without those drawers. You have enough other cupboards, Gretel needs somewhere for her drawings and pictures. That drawer will be excellent for this purpose."

Carlchen is obedient. At once he puts his study books to one side and clears the required shelves and drawers. Gretel is speechless, she does not know what to say, but Frau Elsa is very much concerned and insists that Gretel should have these things for her artworks. Carlchen even helps to transport the shelves and drawers to the wooden hut where the two, Peter and Gretel live

Why must such good people suffer and die through Nazi hands? Let these words become an everlasting tribute of thanks to these kind people who helped my mother and others in need at this time of growing unrest.

1938 finds Gretel again ill with stomach trouble; she has ulcers. Is this a wonder? The emigrants are often able to get something to eat at the emigrant's kitchen in the hostel.

One day, following incident happens; Gretel is so hungry. The emigrant's kitchen cook, with a very serious look on his face, gives Gretel a bowl of food, a one-dish meal. Hungrily Gretel eats every little bit of it. The kitchen cook looks on wide-eyed and does not dare to say a word. With the last spoon – Gretel realizes that the food was full of maggots!! The cook says it is nearly too impossible to cook anything for the emigrants. The food they get is from the beginning always bad. "It really isn't fun to cook for you and to see how you starve", is the cooks comment.

Aquarelle painting of Prague, 1936.

'Der Landschaftsmaler.'

'Was eigentümlich ist es mit Farben
Du brauchst nicht zu sprechen. Sie sprechen für Dich.
Sie singen und schwingen und lächeln warm,
Und Du kannst ruhen in ihren Arm.
Doch mußt du beherrschen Schatten und Licht,
Schatten und Licht – zwei Dinge.
Und beide mußt du zwingen,
Mit kühnen Pinselstrich auf ödes Papier.
Und Du wirst finden sie sprechen zu Dir.
Doch mußt Du Augen haben zu sehen,
Der Sonnenstrahlen golden tropfenden Regen,
Wie lustig die Wölkchen schwimmen in des Himmelsblau,
Die Blumen ein buntes Völkchen,
Tanzen auf tauperlen bestickter grüner Aue.
Des Herbst bunten schimmer,
Des Wassers unstetiges geflimmer.
Nun los mal los,
Da liegt ein Sonnenstrahl auf grünen Moos.
Kommt und laßt uns fangen ihn ein,
Dann wird er der Zauber des Bildes sein.'

Translation

'The Landscape Painter.'

'There is something peculiar with colour,
You don't need to speak, they speak for you.
They sing and swing and smile warmly,
And you can rest in their arms.
However you must master shadow and light,
Shadow and light – two things.
And both you must compel,
With bold brush strokes on deserted paper.
And you will find they speak to you.
Yet you must have eyes to see,
The sunshine's golden drops of rain,
How jolly the little clouds swim in the skies blue,
The flowers, a coloured little folk,
Dance on dew pearl embroidered green fields.
The autumn's coloured shine,
The waters unsteady glitter.
Now come, begin,
There lays a sunshine beam on the green moss.
Come and let us catch him,
Then he will become the magic in the picture.'

(Written on October 16th 1948).

Gretel not only forms sculptures with her hands and watches the movement of the folk and nature around her, she also formulates her feelings and thoughts in her words. Many times have we sat together somewhere outside in the countryside looking at the landscape in front of us. Sometimes she would sit there for half an hour or even longer before beginning to paint, absorbing the scene in front of her in smallest detail. I have seen her create her artworks from earliest childhood. On empty paper appeared a picture, a landscape, a drawing. Out of a wet bundle of clay was formed a figure that had feelings of its own, it would laugh or cry. Even more, later, her wooden sculptures, rather like a fairy tale, were born under her hands.

She used to look long at a piece of wood. Sometimes for days, sometimes for weeks, months or even a year, then, suddenly, it was as if the wood had spoken to her, and told her what it was that the wooden cover was hiding; that noble, that branch, that sticking out end, everything meant something. Only then would my mother take her tools and work and form and create the sculptures she left for us all, for the world behind.

Woodcarving; 'Cat and kittens', (Approx, 1947)

67

'Die stürmischen Wellen brausen,
Es funkelt und glitzert das Meer.
Ein Boot segelt weit da drausen,
Ich sende Euch grüße von hier.

Die Sonne bricht durch die Wolken,
Dem Flüge des Sturmvogels folgen.
Meine Gedanken,
Frei, ohne Schranken,
Wie Vögel fliegen über stürmische Meere.
So die Gedanken besiegen
Die schwere Erde.'

Translation

'The stormy waves rage,
The sea sparkles and glitters.
A boat sails far outside,
I send you greetings from here.

The sun breaks through the clouds,
Following the flight of the storm birds.
My thoughts,
Free without barriers,
Like birds flying over stormy seas,
So the thoughts overcome
The heavy earth.'

(Written about 1945).

After modelling her clay figures, Gretel takes them to the art school to be burnt. Sitting in the tram with her figures on her lap, holding them carefully often causes some sensation to the on looking Czech working-class people. They often come over to Gretel, speak to her and admire her works. One particular figure caused even action.

Gretel had modelled a group of gipsy children; a young gipsy boy standing proud and upright holds a cap out in his hand, and behind him his little brother dressed only in a shirt, that just about covered him up to his waist, leaving the rest showing naked. On the other side stands his sister. All three are raggedly dressed and without shoes. The impression must have been great, then, on seeing this figure the immediate reaction of the workers in the tram take out their purses and even put money into the held out cap of the young gipsy boy.
I have only a photograph of this figure. I would so like to know where it is, if it is safe! Another time, a Czech citizen asks Gretel to model several Indian figures for his country weekend hut. Sometime later Gretel finds copies of one of her sculptures she had sold to a man on the market place. Profit had been made out of her talent. Gretel would so like to try to paint with oil colours, but it is too expensive. Now, how to solve this problem?

On one of her walks, whilst passing an antique shop, she sees some oil paintings, or rather attempted efforts on display in the shop window. This gives Gretel ideas, and she returns a little later with some of her work to try to sell them. The shop owner, looking at her work and recognizing her talent has another idea and asks Gretel to paint the oil pictures he had attempted. So now, Gretel has the possibility to work with oils. At the same time she learns how to use these colours and receives material for her efforts. She does not earn anything for painting these pictures for this man, but she collects valuable experience. The owner from the antique shop is very pleased, Gretel's oil pictures are sold and he asks Gretel to paint more. So now Gretel has oil painting materials. This was for the young enthusiastic artist worth more than money.

Gretel has one success after the other with her artwork. It is a very active life in the emigration; there are meetings and discussions about politics, culture programmes and exhibitions, an endless row of activities. Once, during a culture programme that combined gymnastics, music and speeches, Gretel's mistaken inaccuracy of doing the gymnastic movements in the opposite direction to the other performers, moving downwards when the rest move upwards, causes great amusement among the public and livens up the situation.

My mother mentioned only once the following to me. Life in Prague was hard, the daily struggle against starvation and the threat of a second world war growing rapidly and a doubtful secure future very vague and uncertain. Peter and Gretel live together as husband and wife. They need each other's company in this situation, living in a strange country, working for peace and a better world. Gretel loves children. Her desire and yearning for children of her own and a normal life is immense, and so the day arrives when she expects a child. This event should be a joyful one, but it is instead, a great worry. Our 'two blues' are concerned about the insecure future and the threat of war. It was already clear that they would soon have to emigrate again, almost certainly for a second time. To give birth and to bring up a child in this situation, living in a wooden cold, damp and noisy hut? As a result of these worries and the extreme difficult living conditions Gretel has a miscarriage. My mother's pains remain unwritten, unsaid, but known!
Later, my Mother told me of many tales about mothers with small children who were hunted and chased around from country to country. She didn't want her child to suffer like that. I will report of these tales later.

Somehow, Peter's father succeeds to come to Prague to visit the two, little knowing and realizing that it will be last time father and son see each other. Peter never sees his father again. Gretel would so like to be a good host, to serve her 'father-in-law' a decent meal and give him proper accommodation, instead of the primitive and insufficient 'dogs hut' but Gretel hasn't even a tablecloth to put on the boxes which served as a table.
Oh poor emigrant life! Is this the reward for anti- fascist fight!

'Dresden.'

1902 – 1933   'O Du mein Dresden an der Elbe, Heimat stadt wie bist Du schön,
So wie Du warst mit dunklen Gassen, Palästen und die Höhen,
Doch immer dacht ich Heimatstadt wie bist Du schön,
Jedoch es wurden mehr und mehr der Frühlingsmorgen,
Da wir erwachten voller schwerer Sorgen,
Es schallten unsere Arbeiter Lieder,
In dampfen Gassen unserer Schritt,
Wir riefen komm doch Brüder kämpfe mit,
Kampf den Faschismus nieder.

1933 – 1945	Doch unsere kräfte waren nicht vereint, Nur zu bald manche Mutter weint, Um einen der mit folter Qualen, Den Kampf für Frieheit mußt bezahlen, O Dresden Du, wie hast Du doch gelitten, Manche und manche mutig haben sie gestritten, Auch die, die wegen dieser Schmach und Schande, Fliehen mußten in ferne Lande.
1945	Im Bombenregen mußtest Du untergehen, Dresden Stadt an der Elbe, warst Du doch so schön, Ich war im fernen Lande, Sah und fühlte den Schmerz die Brande, In manch einen unser Emigranten Lieder, Hatten wir gesungen, wir kommen wieder, Wie lang der Weg, wie lang der Zeit, Wir sind Erbauer von Frieden, Sozialismus und Einigkeit.
1946	Wie lang die Nacht die Schmach, Doch endlich kamm der Morgen der Tag, An den über Dresden die roten Fahnen wehen, Mein Dresden Du, nie zuvor hab ich gesehen Dich so schön.
1950	In harter Arbeit mit ehrlichen fleiß, Die Trümmer verschwinden mußten, Dank einen jeden, Dank und Preis, Erbauer des Sozialismus.
1960	Die riesigen Kränne so kühn und frei, Wie die Ideen ihrer Erbauer, Zum fröhlichen Schaffen ist jeder bereit, Zu ende Unterdrückung und Trauer, Die Maschinen summen ein friedlichen Lied, Der kollektive Bauer auf dem Traktor seine furchen zieht, Und alle singen wir nur ein Lied, Über lernen, und friedliche Arbeit, Kommt und singt und seid bereit, Was ihr geschafft haben zu Schützen.'

Translation

'Dresden.'

1902-1933	'Oh you my Dresden on the Elbe home city, how beautiful you are, So as you were, with dark alleys, palaces and the heights, Still, I always thought, home city, how beautiful you are, However the spring morning came when more and more, We awoke full of heavy worries, Our songs of the working class rang in stuffy alleys our steps, We called, come on brother, fight with us, fight fascism dead.

1933-45	But our strength was not united,
	Only too soon, some mothers cried,
	For one, who under torture and suffering,
	Had to pay the fight for freedom,
	O Dresden, you, how you had to suffer,
	Some and others of courage had to dispute,
	Also those, who because of this insult and shame,
	Had to flee to far countries.

1945	In rains of bombs you had to sink,
	Dresden, city on the Elbe*, you were so wonderful,
	I was in foreign countries,
	Saw and felt the pain of the fire,
	In some of our emigrant songs,
	We sang we will come again,
	How far the way, how long the time,
	We are the builders of peace, socialism and unity.

1946	How long the night of disgrace,
	But at last dawned the day,
	When over Dresden the red flag fluttered,
	My Dresden, You, never before have I seen you so fine.

1950	In hard work with honest labour,
	The ruins had disappeared,
	Thanks to all, Thanks and praise,
	Builders of socialism.

1960	The giant cranes, so bold and free,
	Like the ideas of their builders,
	For happy creation is everyone ready,
	To end oppression and sadness,
	The machines hum a peaceful song,
	The collective farmer on the tractor turns his furrows,
	And we all sing one song,
	About learning and peaceful work,
	Come and sing, and be prepared,
	To safeguard your creation.'

(*Elbe - River running through Dresden. Written in Dresden 1960).

How obvious it is, when reading this poem to grasp and apprehend my mother's happiness and delight to see and live in her much-treasured Dresden again. But her return to Dresden 1960 was also to be shadowed by a chain of gloomy political circumstances.

3. Again Escape.

The dreadful thunder of the Second World War is nearing. A second time, Gretel must be prepared together with Peter to flee, to leave again everything behind; friends, teachers, study possibilities, and many good artworks!

My mother reports:
"Our artist group had taken up connection with the English Artist International Association, who helped many others, and myself to flee further on to England as the Hitler troops marched into Czechoslovakia.

Whilst living abroad, it became particularly clear to see what was happening in our homeland and it was sad and deeply moving to experience this again and again.

As the intense situation increased and war was expect between Nazi-Germany and Czechoslovakia, I succeeded in taking up a nursing course and completed an exam to join the red-cross sisters, so now, I was fully prepared to stand together with my Czech friends in one action front. But then, everything changed. In the meantime, March 1939 the Nazis erected the protectorate Bohemia and Moravia. I had to flee again with my fiancé out of Prague leaving everything behind and to break up my studies."

The Kokoschka League existed until 1938. The ending of this artist group became at the same time the beginning of the Foundation of the Free German League of Culture in London and the once exiled Czech artists belonged to the most active members.

But back to my story - Peter and Gretel are still struggling in Prague. Both are prepared to fight together with their Czech friends against Hitler. All emigrants were prepared to help defend Czechoslovakia, either with the weapon in hand or as Red Cross nurses. So, as Hitler began the invasion of Czechoslovakia, and the onset of hostilities that would become the Second World War loom perilously close Gretel takes up this Red Cross course, and is prepared to work as a frontier nurse should that be necessary. This Red Cross course giving Gretel some knowledge in the medical profession would have enabled her to work as a nurse if Prague had become a frontier in the case of the approaching war. But then parts of Czechoslovakia are 'given away' and it is clear that Peter and Gretel will have to emigrate once more. Where to go? Russia seems the most appropriate place for both of them, but they do not receive permission.

About this time Peter and Gretel are asked to support a man with accommodation for a night. He is also an emigrant. But he had obtained the permission to emigrate to Russia. Peter is out, somewhere else on an important mission and Gretel is alone with this man. He is a very unsympathetic and rough looking character. Gretel feels extremely uncomfortable with this man. She is alone and senses that there is something wrong, something is not right.

They talk together about politics and about war.
He says, "It is no trouble to kill people if there is a necessity to do it".

Gretel shudders and is relieved when Peter returns. Later they find out that this man, who then eventually did immigrate to Russia, was a spy!

Peter and Gretel even think about emigrating to Hondoras, painting happy romantic pictures in the air, about taking care of herds of sheep, from pictures of undisturbed nature, deep woods and animals. But the reality is different.

The Oska Kokoschka league had forged a connection with the British Artist International Association, the A.I.A and they assist many of the members to travel and take refuge in England. Pre-guaranteed employment being a condition of the artists' entry into Britain,

Gretel has luck and is offered the post of kitchen maid and house-help to the well known British surrealist painter Roland Penrose, in Hampstead, London who was a personal friend of Picasso. Roland Penrose wanted to help refugees escape and later, once my mother was resident in the UK he also helped pay for her art studies. He had many Picasso works on display in his house. Because marriage was impossible living in Prague, Peter has to stay behind, but they both agree that Gretel should accept this possibility to flee to safety, away from the approaching fascist terror. Agreeing that Peter would follow her as soon as possible, the two make their farewells, and Gretel embarks upon the journey to Britain.

Again this means learning a new language, to live again under long-term conditions as a foreigner - an emigrant. Another émigré woman artist refuses to accept work as a house-help. She says that her hands are not made for kitchen work! Years later, my mother discovers that this lady, because of her fussy attitude is taken to a Nazi concentration camp.

Only those emigrants who had obtained employment were allowed to leave Czechoslovakia with the last possible transport.

Before the artists leave Prague, their artworks were put together in a folder. This was presented as a gift to the Czech President Edvard Benes as thanks for the friendliness and hospitality the Czech people had offered the refugees. Gretel's artworks from this most important time in Prague have to stay behind. Fortunately she is able to sell most of her artworks to a lady who is an art historian and art collector. So hopefully these artworks were given into good hands. Have these wonderful artworks survived the war? I wish I knew where they were. Is this art historian still alive today? And what was her name?
What has become of her sculpture work; the group of begging gypsy children, the refugee family, and the fairy story teller? Do these wonderful artworks still exist?

But now, at this moment Gretel has to consider herself particularly lucky. She has found an excellent place for her work. She is still young, and can create many more sculptures later! She manages to take a few pictures and drawings with her, and these artworks, portraits and pictures are so powerful that they find many admirers today. The money from the sale of the sculptures was used to buy important things needed for the long journey that lay ahead.

Solid thick travel cases are bought; an English dictionary and a book about English cookery take their place in the luggage.

Gretel has not the slightest idea about the English language and cannot speak a word of it. What about English cookery? She is supposed to help out in the kitchen, how different will the English cooking customs be to what she is used to? She is again about to embark on a new adventure, into a strange new world far away from her home, her dearly loved Dresden!

The diminutive time left for Gretel before arrival in the new foreign country is used to learn the most necessary vocabulary and basic principles needed for British cooking and catering traditions.

I do not know the exact date when my mother left Prague and Peter behind, but according to two words written in Peter's diary from 1939, the 4th March could be accepted as the date for the beginning of the journey to England.

Not a word was ever mentioned about the farewell scene, the parting embraces and farewell words, unfulfilled desires and longings to return home, this can only be imagined. But I know that many fine emigrants, and artists had to stay behind in Prague. One of them was my father. When would the 'Two Blues' be together again!

Not all emigrants left behind would survive the approaching war, and many tragic events happened in the effort to escape. Would Peter be among those who managed to escape?

And so Gretel is able to leave on the last transport for women and children out of Czechoslovakia to 'safe' nations (that included Britain) before the Hitler troops arrive. This transport took them through the Czech Republic, up north a long way round - Norway,

Finland, Scandinavia. The Nazis are closing in, nearing from all sides. It is an extremely dangerous journey. The train is packed full, overloaded with women and children. Sometimes the train can only just manage to slip through the last free available narrow passage, hardly an hour's journey away from the Hitler soldiers.

I do not know how many days this train journey took, until the refugees could board the ship awaiting them at a harbour in Sweden, but it was a tremendous round about way.

The tiring train journey seems endless. In normal times this journey would have been a pleasant one, full of enjoyable excitement, travelling through strange foreign countries. But so, it was a fearful and frightening journey. The air is heavy with anxious talk, children crying, tired worried mothers with babies in their arms, and the heavy breath of the older emigrants. In the midst of this scene is Gretel, her thoughts fly back to Peter and the next thoughts fly ahead to that new strange country - England! In her lap are the two books; the English dictionary and the book about English cookery. At last at a harbour in Sweden the refugees can leave the train and ascend the waiting boat.

I know for certain that this refugee transport went through Sweden, then my mother told me of following tragic incident. A child, a small girl was dangerously ill with a high fever. The mother is extremely worried and in despair. It looks as if the child is dying. Red Cross nurses try to help. In Sweden the child's health worsens. The mother is advised to leave her small daughter behind. A couple in Sweden offer to take the child and care for her as their own until times are safer, or even until the war is over. The mother has no choice. Her daughter's life is at risk. Sad and heavy-hearted she leaves her daughter behind in Sweden with this friendly couple whom she had never seen before. This mother remains hopeful and maintains positive thoughts throughout long the war years, hoping and believing that one day she will be reunited with her daughter again. But after the war, the child refuses to accept her real mother. She wants to stay with her Swedish foster parents at all costs. She had been too small to remember her mother.

There were many such tragic stories of women leaving their children behind. There is the tale about a young couple fleeing from country to country with a small boy in a pushchair. This restless life proves too much for the small child and as a result, he becomes ill with a brain fever. He never recovers from this illness.

Another story is of a mother, after managing to arrive at last in France is separated from her husband and child after being hunted from Nazis with blood thirsty hounds. Then there is the tale of a mother who leaves her child for safety in a Closter and is never seen again.

My mother told me of many such tales from this time; sad tales about lost children, lost husbands and wives, from tragic separations of loved ones and dear relatives!

The weather is awful. The ship takes the refugees around Skargarak to Britain. This is usually always a stormy corner, the weather does not improve, the stormy sea, howling wind and rain worsens and Gretel is seasick. The ship is loaded with refugee passengers. Every corner is used. Gretel is one of the lucky ones. Just think! The poor anti-fascist refugee travels comfortably as a first class passenger! But during the sea journey Gretel is so seasick that she loses her way on deck and finally lands in the captain's own cabin. She doesn't know where to go and is distraught, but the captain is friendly and understanding. He leaves Gretel where she is and orders the doctor to help her.

Gretel arrives in England, safe at last, carrying a little luggage, a few of her Prague paintings and her beloved violin on the 9th of March, 1939- one day before Hitler arrives in Prague. Czechoslovakia had become Gretel's second home. In spite of all difficulties and hunger, the time in Prague was of great importance.

‘Herbst im Walde.’

‘Kahl ist das zarte geflecht der Birkenzweige,
Doch scheinen die Birken vom Frühling zu träumen,
Und auch der Himmel scheint ein sonniges lächeln zu zeigen.
Doch Raben krächzen von kahlen knorigen Eichenbäumen.
In die immer frich grünen Wipfel der Kiefern, fallen
Spielende matte Sonnenstrahlen.
Und ruhen auf moosbewachsenen Waldboden,
Auf rot leuchteten Blättern auf toten.
Durch das köstliche Waldes schweigen,
Tönt des munteren Waldvögleins Lied,
Und das muntere Farben spiel tanzt einen Frühlingsreigen.
Meine Seele jauchzt wie Geigen,
Wieder bin ich ein Kind, das da fand im Schoß
Der Mutter Nature, eine Freude so groß.
Ob Frühling, ob Sommer, ob Herbst oder Winter,
Sucht sie nur, überall sind sie versteckt,
Der Freude herzliebe Kinder.’

Translation

‘Autumn in the Woods.’

‘Barren is the tender wreathe of the birch tree branches,
Yet the birches seem to dream from spring,
And the sky also seems to show a sunny smile.
Yet crows croak, from barren gnarled oak trees.
In the ever fresh green tops of the pines, falls
Playfully dim sunbeams.
And rests on the mossy forest floor,
On red shining leaves, on dead ones.
Through the charming quietness of the woods,
Sounds the song of the merry little forest bird,
And the bright playful colours, dances a spring song.
My soul revels like violins,
Again I am a child, that found in the lap
Of Mother Nature a joy so great.
If it's Spring, Summer, Autumn or Winter,
Search for them, they are hidden everywhere,
Happy sweet dear children.’

(Written in her youth time).

The connection with Dresden is broken, and remains silent for a long time. How is Brother Hans, and her father? What does the stepmother think now? And mother Sophie's grave? Is someone caring for it? Gretel's beloved Dresden is so far away. The longing to wander in the rocky mountains of the Sächsishe Schweiz[5] remains unfulfilled for many years to come, but the memory and tales are alive and real.

---

[5] Sächsische Schweiz – Saxon Switzerland.

75

'Dresden, Du, Heimatstadt,
Wie muß ich wieder Dich sehen,
Perle an der Elbe,
Aus Ruinen mußtest Du erstehen,
Wie hast Du doch gelitten,
Wie hast Du doch gestritten,
In flammenbrunst mußtest Du untergehen,
Und wie im frühlings Morgen,
Die Sonne steigt glitzernd im frischen Tau,
So steigst Du noch im Kampf und Sorgen,
Herauf, Prachtvoll neu erbaut.'

Translation

'Dresden, my hometown,
When will I see you again,
Pearl on the Elbe,
Out of ruins reborn,
How you have suffered,
How you have fought,
Through bursts of flames you had to perish,
And one early spring morning,
The rising sun shining through fresh dew,
Out of fight and struggles,
You arise, magnificent and new.'

Graphic; 'Old man.' Prague,
(1936)

76

The Legend, part 3.

The village Rathmannsdorf belonged to the parish of Schandau. George Birken from Hohnstein gave up this part to Schandau, in the year 1467. The whole population of the little town Schandau and the village Rathmannsdorf were now put under the care of the council of Hohnstein.

Under oath, 12 frantic men reported how they spoke to George Birken and persuaded him to help them. Humbly, these villagers begged him to make improvements for a good and better town; with humble and active request through events, and in writing, also of faithful service they had completed for all at that time, and for the future; and what they would like to do. And because of this, they requested to be given to the village of George Birken, so that the whole population of the little town of Schandau and all descendants with their inheritance, and further descendants for all times should serve as mounted armed marksmen.

Also, how often and seldom that would be, and they asked and called the officers on duty at Hohnstein to defend and protect them from all danger.

At this time, great troubles were eagerly taken to enrich the churches with gifts, and to establish many requiems. So founded in 1381 Hinko Birken von Duba, together with Tenczel von Frauenstein and Gunther von Grieslau from Stürza a perpetual early mass in the little town underneath the castle Hohnstein.

At the time of the Hussite changes, the churches also split their paths, then the Birken von Duba were keen members of the Hussites. Wenzel von Duba accompanied Johann von Chlumen Huß to the council at Canstanz, and Andreas Duba even married the commander in chief, Zizka's daughter, Balbins.

Gretel is far far away from the place of these scenes. This time she is alone waiting, hoping, will Peter make it? Will Peter manage to escape?

Mother protecting her child, terracotta Prague, (1935)

4. Peter's Story.

My father never told me much about himself, about his experiences and adventures.
Back in Prague Peter had to go into hiding again. Gone were the times of freedom. The past situation from1933 in Dresden had caught up with the present. That dreaded atmosphere to go around carefully, always on the alert - is someone following me? Why is that person over there in the tram staring at me all the time? Is he a Nazi? Is someone watching our room?

There it was again; 1933; Dresden; Nazis, arrests; and now war. My father wasn't allowed on the train with Gretel, he again became a fugitive - hunted with dogs. Peter flees on foot, away from Prague. He has to make his way over to Poland before being able to board a boatload of refugees fleeing to Britain. He must reach a certain address in Poland. Then he would be safe for the moment, and would be able to apply for permission to enter Britain to be reunited with his Gretel.

How many days or weeks was Peter's journey to freedom? How long did it take him to reach that certain address in Poland? He never spoke about it, but once my mother mentioned that several times Peter was hunted with trained blood hounds!

Peter succeeds to reach that certain address. He arrives safely, he is lucky, but how many others had been caught and were unsuccessful in the struggle to flee to freedom and safety? Back in Prague, the Nazis were using their power to erect their 'thousand year reign'. They erected also ghettos and in one of the Prague ghettos the family Kalmus and Gretel's friend Eva were suffering the fate of so many millions of Jews. After my father's death I found several letters, which he had written to Gretel in May 1939 from Poland.

"My dear Gretel,

Now I am still here. This time things seem to improve. Yes, that was an extremely difficult and dangerous damned adventure. Hopefully now at last I have overcome it. You cannot imagine how I felt, and how I am feeling now.
Sorry I have little time at the moment. That's why I write now only a few words to you, at least to your relief as I haven't written since the 12th of March. In the meantime you will have got the message from K. in Pr. (supposedly this means Kalmus in Prague,) that I was there on the 15th March, and received your post and also 500 Kronen. I really needed this money damned desperately. Even now I am sitting here again, absolutely broke."

"My dear beloved Gretel, excuse please the perhaps somewhat dry tone from this my first letter, which I am writing in a hurry. I hope to send you a proper longer and detailed one within the next days. Temporarily, put up with these short words. I am so glad that at last the moment has arrived when I can write freely at least these words to you. You can perhaps imagine what this means to me, and of course also for you, - after what I have had to leave behind this is already a great achievement!
At least, from now on we two can keep in contact through writing - hopefully undisturbed - until - we both have each other again! And that this may happen soon hopes and wishes as well as you.
        Yours Peter."

"P.S I have only been able to write a short card greeting to my mother from here for certain particular reasons. I will be able to write more to her, later on, from the next stage of my journey. You know how to contact her and you can always write a few words about me in your letters until I am safe, in another country, hopefully in England with you. I know extremely little about my future destiny. Everything seems to be a great muddily mess here, because of the vast amount of Jewish economic emigrants."

One can only read behind the words and between the lines of this letter to realize and understand the adventures my father had

The next letter is written on the 5th May 1939 from Katovici.

He writes;

"Now l am one day in Katovic and already registered with the English consulate. At the moment I do not know when I will get my visa, or when the journey will continue, but hopefully very soon, then the 'caring' emigration department have accommodated us, and treat us worse than dirty pigs. The bedding on which I am sleeping is three weeks old and a different person has slept on it every second or third day. The air in the sleeping ward is worse than pestilence. There are supposed to be louse here as well as bugs and fleas. You are only allowed to write postcards and these are to be given up at the culture municipal for further transport. That I am able to write this letter, is only possible thanks to our 'Paula'.

"We arrived here absolutely empty handed and quite without money. We had to give up everything we had before we crossed the frontier. Instead, we were supposed to get 10 zloty each at the other side. We received nothing.

I gave up 150 Kronen - here- for that, they took away the rest of the small change, which we had kept. The only person we can trust and who tries to ease our situation, if possible, is our 'Paula'. The food in the dining hall is completely insufficient. I had to apply this morning extra for a postcard in order to write to you from here. I had to wait nearly 2 hours, only to find out that perhaps we may get some postcards this afternoon.

I left my luggage in Prague, from where perhaps it could be sent on to London. I left Prague only with a brief case containing a few most necessary things. And I had to give up the briefcase. I am sitting here with no shirt to change, no towel, no pyjamas or track suit – nothing, only my razor and toothbrush in my pocket. We were supposed to get the most necessary things new." …….

"l am so glad that this is only a transition stage. That the joy at last to be out of hell should be so spoilt is of course very unpleasant. But, when you just wander over the road, and when you go to your lodgings and you do not need to look around anymore, if no disagreeable person is following you, and you don't need to be afraid of meeting any awkward acquaintances, and the "good friends" in the black and brown and green and grey cloths are nowhere to be seen, so this consciousness alone helps to make the present situation bearable."

Peter complains about the unclean conditions in the sleeping ward. He complains about the smells and the dirt. The sleeping wards are overcrowded with all sorts of people from all walks of life, and of course, there are also some unpleasant characters around. He complains that bath tickets are only available on doctor's orders. "Now I will stop complaining. I am happy to have been able to get a piece of paper to unburden my heart. And, at last, I am even happier that I can send you, my darling, this piece of paper, and that I can speak openly and freely. How nice it was, we two together, in our primitive room in Prague! When we are together again, then we will make things as pleasant as possible. I wait with longing for this moment. Then hopefully, we can organize everything ourselves, as we want it, and as is right and comfortable for us both."

"I hope that we can marry as soon as possible after my arrival, then I don't want us to be torn apart again….. That was awful, I was alone…and what then happened. But it was indeed good, that you were already in safety. That experience was a cursed strain on the nerves!
    Katovice 5.v.39"

"Dear Little mouse!
"Have you dreamt about me last night as I about you?
We are starving, getting dirtier and getting fleas in this place!"

    The longings, hopes and struggles for survival are clearly visible in these words. The fugitives are squashed together, scrambling and struggling over and on top of each other in the effort to escape the spreading advancing war.

    On the 9th May Peter is still In Katovic, but the situation is more positive. He had received some money from Gretel, which enable him to buy some necessary things, and food. Poor Peter was starving for something decent to eat. His visa for Britain had already arrived and he hoped that the journey would continue within the next days.

    "I cannot inform you with what ship I will arrive and when, . …Then usually we are told very little about things. We will travel as a collective transport, without passports. Most probably we will get some sort of paper in England. Also I don't know where we will live in London. Hopefully, nothing will stand in our way, so that no one can tear us apart anymore, then I would like to live our private lives for ourselves."

    Over the channel Gretel is waiting for her fiancé! Peter had lived one week in Katovice. Looking through my parent's papers, I found a small green coloured diary notebook from 1939. Pages were torn out, and it had been much used. If this little notebook could talk, what story would it tell? It looks as if it had been thrust into a pocket, and had once been wet! It is my father's notebook. This notebook had accompanied my father in 1939 from Prague as he fled to Poland, and on over the channel to Britain. 1940, this same notebook accompanies him on his journeys to the internment camp in Australia!

    Peter leaves Katovic on the 11th May 1939 one minute before midnight. He seems to have been in good spirit, and happy at last to be on the way to Gretel.

    Peter's notebook reports;

"On the 12th of May over Kastelholm, Göteburg through Sweden, Golynia". On Saturday the 13th May, he arrives at the harbour Kalmar. He continues to makes notes of the places he passes through: Emmaboda, Alvestoc, Värnamo, Grimsas - 96 kilometers.
"Limmarad, Boras, Göteborg - 125 kilometers, wonderful lakes between wooded mountains and islands. Then 6.30 on board the 'Succia', 4500 tons heavy, and off to sea".

"On the 15th May 7.30 Tilbury. Then on the train, 11 o'clock arrival in London St Pancras station." Here Peter waits in vain, inside then outside the station, and then at last off to the hostel. Obviously Gretel had no idea that Peter had arrived. He had emigrated a second time, again into a foreign country, to live as a foreigner, not knowing when or how he will be able to return to his home country. He had to leave his luggage behind in Prague. I know my parents tried to organize to get the luggage sent over to London, but I do not know if they succeeded. Peter had fled with only a brief case, which he then had to give up.

Thanks to the money Gretel had sent him, he had been able to buy some things for the journey: a suitcase, a pair of sandals and some other necessities. The emigrants in London awaited impatiently each new arrival; who had managed to escape this time? Then one day on the 15th May 1939 Peter is among the newly arrived, a few months before Britain was plunged into the Second World War. The 'Two Blues' are together again in safety.
What sort of life will they lead in England? What does the future hold for them?

All this happened in 1939 - the outbreak of the Second World War. My parents fled from Nazi terror into an uncertain future. In 1984 I returned to Britain. Have I also been fleeing? From what? And why? Where in the world is peace?
I tried to flee back into the times and places of happy childhood.

'Two sisters', modelled in terracotta (approx 1933)

'Sorgen tropfen von meinen Herzen
Wird tropfen wie Blut in den weissen Schnee.

Sorgen sind Schmerzen,
Sorgen tuhen weh.
Ein Vöglein flog im Sonnen schein,
In die weite Welt hinein.

Es flog durch Sturm und Donnerbraus,
Es flog Tag ein, Tag aus.

Nun ist es ein bischen müde geworden,
Es brauchte ein Heim, ein Nest.
Ein bischen Ruhe und Friede.

Da ist keine Ruhe in dieser Welt,
Alle Baume sind gefällt.

Unbedeckt von Schnee ist ein kleines bischen grünes Moos.
Da setzt sich unser Vöglein nieder,
Aber einsam und Heimatlos.

Einsamkeit frißt an den Herzen,
Und ist wie die Sorge so gross.
Fast wünscht ich könnte die verfallenden Wände vertauschen
Mit des Vöglein grüner Moos.

Verloren die Hoffnung das ich fände
Eine Seele mit der ich zusammen singen konnte.

Es sind die Kinderstimmen
Die ich da höre sagen,
Komm Mutter du darfst nicht klagen,
Du mußt weiter fliegen
Den Sturm und die Wolken besiegen.'

Translation;

'Drops of sorrow from my heart
Become drops of blood in the white snow.

Sorrows are pain,
Sorrows hurt.
A little bird flew out into the sunshine,
Out into the wide world.

It flew through storm and thunder,
It flew day in, day out.

Now it has grown tired.
It needs a home, a nest.
A little peace and quiet.

There is no peace in this world,
All trees have fallen.

A little spot of green moss is uncovered from snow.
There our little bird rests,
But lonely and homeless.

Loneliness eats the heart,
And is as large as the sorrow.
Nearly, I wish I could exchange the fallen walls
With the little birds green moss.

The hope I found is lost
A soul with whom I could sing together.

It is the voices of the children
I hear them calling,
Come mother you must not complain,
You must continue to fly
And conquer the storm and clouds.'

(Written during the emigration years).

Early sculpture work.

Begging gypsy with monkey'   Self Portrait; watercolour

Early sculpture work.

'Father with son'   ' Old man with walking stick'

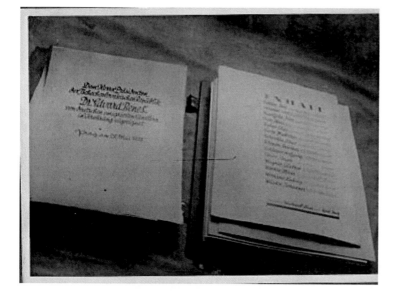

Before the artists leave Prague, their artworks were put together in a folder. This was presented as a gift to the Czech President Edvard Benes as thanks for the friendliness and hospitality the Czech people had offered the refugees.

Interlude

"As I fled from the Hitler fascists and had to leave Germany I swore that I would return one day. My heart and thoughts were always in my home country." Quote from a letter my mother wrote to the GDR authorities confirming her longing to return home.

Woodcarving; 'Vagabond'

This section is a reflection on past events and the uncertain future facing the 'Two Blue's'. A new stage in Peter and Gretel's life was about to begin. Gone were the dreams of a soon return to Dresden. What must have been Gretel's thoughts on her journey over to Britain? Hitler's army were marching into the Czech Republic, Peter fleeing again from fascist terror, their whole world falling apart. The time in Czechoslovakia had been a happy and successful one for Gretel. She was now an artist with recognition, was a member of an important organization, 'The Oska Kokoschka League. She had studied with Käte Schäffner, a personal friend of Käte Kollwitz and she had sold many of her early sculptures. Prague is a beautiful city and its here that formed Gretel's future artistic abilities.

If Peter and Gretel had been able to stay in Prague, their future would have been a happier one. Never again would they be as happy as they were in Prague. Although life was hard, starvation, lack of money and no real home, only that ram shackle hut they had lived in, it had been for both a very successful time. Approaching Nazi terror destroyed again their lives causing more hardship and adversity. The harsh conditions in which Gretel had lived in, did not deter her strong will to learn. She had had many positive experiences, encouragement from other artists and help to continue her artistic work. Would she receive the same positive response and support in Britain?

What must have been her thoughts on the ship, on the stormy ocean around Scargarak, an English dictionary and a book on English cookery in her hands? Her thoughts wondering back to happy times, and Peter, where is he?

Imagine Gretel whilst on the ship looking through her luggage and taking her diary in her hands. It's the diary she wrote Summer1933. How happy they were. Opening it up she reads, and memories come flowing back;

"On the highway.

<u>Thursday 17th August;</u>

The mountains set in wonderful morning light, butterflies tumble over the field, drinking the silver dewdrops, forest birds whistle in the shrubs. The whole world around is full of sun and spirit. I wash myself in the rousing babbling mountain stream; the sun is shining warm, silver waves dancing, wild and cheerfully bouncing over the stones. A little sunbathing still, it's the last time we saw the Tatra so near. Then we packed up our tent and strolled further down the high way. Over there, a couple of deer grazing peer confidently over to us with their soft brown eyes, behind us the wonderful panorama of the Tatra Mountains. We strolled further along the Strebsko Pleso Sea, the powerful and majestic mountains towering behind. Then we came to the forest path where we had been before stumbled over mushrooms and blue berries. As we arrived at the railway station Strba where we had left our bicycles black clouds appeared. The mountains disappeared in the clouds, it was getting even darker, and a strong shower of rain fell. We had hardly travelled a little when Peter had a puncture again. Something got into my eye, it hurt and again Peter had to pump his wheel up. We were looking forward to the downhill descend. Instead we were now going uphill, but in the direction of the station Strba. So our return trip was a bit of a muddle. It stopped raining behind the village Strba, and the mountains appeared again as blurred silhouettes.

Then again on the highway a puncture and we had to push our bicycles to the next café and that was eight km, Peter complaining all the way going uphill and his broken bike. Patches of Rain fell, soon here, soon there and it looked as if the clouds wore large slippers that reached down to earth. Grey, red, and blue ribbons covered the mountains that partly appeared again. It was like miraculous magic, and then the mountains disappeared completely. Over the Karparten lay heavy black thunderclouds, in the distance thunder, sounding like the hollow wild groans of a giant, piercing lightning flashes in the sky, a red cloud came sailing along, lit up from the sun. The sky lighted up blue-green, the mountains appeared as shadows and disappeared again, like an apparition. So wonderful is everything. I am so full of joy, pleasure and life, but Peter complains.

At last we reach the village that consists 70% of half fallen ruins, farmers like gypsies, brown, coloured, clothed in rags. Girls, small and tall with their long wide coloured skirts, curios large children's eyes appear under the big folds of the headscarves. A real Slovakian village, no one could speech German, nowhere could we find anywhere to stay the night. We were sent to one ' hostinez'[1] to another, to one private place after the other. It was too cold to camp. It was now quite late; small clouds were still sailing in the skies and stars twinkling between them. We bought a new tyre for the bike at Bata and wanted to travel through the night. Half of the village population came running along and curiously stared at the strangers, a big invasion.

Busily discussing, there they stood in front of the shop window. Peter repaired his bicycle wheel in the shop, a boy sunburned brown helped him. Then a better-dressed farmer came, someone had fetched him. He alone could speak German, 'You can sleep at my place,' he said. He had Russian boots on, white woolly trousers with red stripes, a vest with wide sleeves, red embroidered band and collar and a green felt cap. Then we strolled along until the

---

[1] <u>Hostinez; hostel.</u>

end of the village as the farmer had told us. Everyone had gone to bed already. A sleepy boy led us into a room, put a small candle stump on the table and disappeared. I looked around; 'looks damned empty here,' a pair of wood blocks, and wooden planks over it, there was nothing else in the room. 'Genuine Slovakian night accommodation,' said Peter, as I was about to ask, 'Where are we going to sleep?' I was distressed for pleasure about this proficient bed. Then I discovered a pair of bricks and a slanting plank over it that was supposed to serve as a cushion. Nice, how beautiful, we did not sleep 'so soft and comfy' for the rest of our journey.

Friday 18th August.

Our joints aching and stiff we got up, the farmer stuck his head round the door and said, 'Good morning, slept well?'; 'Hard' we said, 'tak tak' (yes yes) he said smiling. Then we wandered on, happy to be on the road again eating dust clouds. An extra gust of wind in front of us caused difficulty, wiped sand and dust into our faces. But the sun shone hot, white clouds floating in the sky, the Tatra Mountains sank in the distance like a beautiful dream. At Mikulas Peter had to repair his front wheel, it was now the front wheels time for repair.

Under willow bushes, the wind blowing through the branches above us we had our midday rest. First I had to clean the mushrooms, got rid of the frustrating maggots, and then I cooked the mushrooms. A large herd of cows and sheep came strolling by. We continued our journey along the Waztal (Waz valley), through Slovakian villages along the Waz River flowing soon on our right side, and then on the left side of the road. The view was beautiful, all around us rocky mountains.

Now the road went a little downhill, but the wind prevented us to move forward, we had to peddle as if we were going uphill. The sun disappeared behind red glowing clouds, small red clouds like streaks of fire floating everywhere in the sky. Soon the mountains lost their red shine, the night spread out, stubbornly the stars kept peering through the clouds again and again. We could not find a camping site, the valley was so narrow, rocks ascending steep on both sides. We left the road. We wanted to sleep in the woods, but discovered a gypsy camp on the other side of the path. If we had slept here we would surely not have any bicycles and violin any more. We returned to the village and slept in the hostel for Czech tourists. I was so hungry, and would have preferred to spend the 12 kronen[2] on food but Peter was pleased to sleep in a proper bed.

The sun seemed to smile as it shone through the window, looking out onto a pleasant valley before us. We had oncoming wind again today and we travelled 10 km before we had breakfast. On the other side of the bank of the river rose a loreley rock formation. Thick white clouds covered the mountains. We continued our journey along spectacular Slovakian roads covered with dust clouds, and through Slovakian villages that often looked like gypsy communities. The Slovakians are a mixed population of different types of people and gypsy folk. Everywhere on the wayside were wild looking begging gypsies. Peter was ahead. I called after him that I was thirsty and wanted to get a drink of water. Children, mostly clothed in rags looked at me curiously. The half collapsing wooden huts were called living accommodation. In a wooden shed, starving farmers were grinding their small harvest by hand. That's how it looks here everywhere. Yesterday I met a farmer whose trousers existed only from holes and sewn on patches. Peter obviously had travelled ahead. I hurried on, but could not catch him up.

Before a level crossing I had to wait quite a long time for a train to pass by, then a herd of cows blocked my path. Why didn't Peter wait for me? Then a car drove by and the driver

[2] Kronen; Czech money.

asked me in broken German if I was looking for a civilian. I said yes, although I was not quite sure what he meant with civilian. He said I should wait, and how right he was, I had missed Peter, I was now 10 km ahead of him. Peter had asked the driver to tell the girl in the blue dress to wait.

The valley was beautiful; the wide bed of the river Wag, on both sides steep mountains. Our path continued along the slope, winding around the mountains, how wonderful this is. When I can wander through the world, or race with my bicycle around the world, yes, then I am in my element, hunger, tiredness, dusty roads, cold weather, hard sleeping quarters, nothing matters. The pleasure that is in me, above all the happiness that controls my thoughts, the birds that fly in the sunny sky cannot feel any different, they are free, like I feel free, then the wind could not disturb us in this narrow valley, and the descending downhill roads. In spite that I already had a terrible lesson by cycling, it can't be wild enough for me; a steep hill, a sharp bend, and a pair of those well-known Slovakian potholes, there you go Grete, laying there, farmer and cows staring. Luckily nothing happened, I scraped my arm and bent the pedals.
In Zilina we were able to get the bike repaired."

Gretel stops reading for a moment, looking out over the ocean she remembers the good times and wonders what will happen to these Slovakian people, and the gypsies they met on their trip. She smiles when she remembers what happened in Zilina.

"We stopped by the side of the road and thought, thick rain clouds wandered over the sky, camping is critical, it was only five thirty, should we travel on or look for night quarters here? What should we do? There came a man over the road, 'Ahoy' he said greeting us, and asked, 'where are you going?' That was the good question so many had asked us already, so many times, and we would answer; 'going to Egypt!' Then they would stare at us with open mouth. Did they understand what we had said? We asked this lively friendly chatty man who spoke to us in Czech and German, where can we find somewhere cheap to sleep the night. 'Come with me, at my place' he said. 'How much', asked Peter. 'Na, nothing,' he said. Oh well, lets go early to bed tonight we said to each other. Then, when we arrived in his place we discovered that his wife was exactly the opposite than her lively guest friendly husband. 'You will remember Zilina,' she said. But the meaning of these words became regrettably clear to us only during the night, otherwise we would have hurried away that minuet!
It began to rain outside. We sat on the straw sack beds, inside the small hut given to us for that night. 'Ha, ha' said Peter, 'here it's clean and warm and does not cost us anything; here we are in good hands.'

I had cooked macaroni for supper. During our evening meal Peter said, 'seems I've got a flea.' Before he went to sleep he shook his things outside the window, then we crept comfortably into our beds hoping to have got rid of this nice little animal. But Peter discovered the opposite. But damn, something bit me as well. How can that flea bite you and me at the same time? Then began an extensive hunt for fleas. Heavens above, what is that on my back, legs, stomach, head, biting me everywhere. ' Me as well,' said Peter as he put the light on. 'Of course its fleas' he said, ' here I have one of these beasts.' At once, the death sentence was proclaimed over that little animal and immediately carried out. We shook our blankets out of the window and wrapped ourselves up tightly. Within a few minuets, it began again, this horrible plague, on twenty places biting all at once. Sweating, we sat on the edge of our beds and looked at each other angrily. What to do? That good man, he has a flea circus, damn! Then Peter had an idea. Fuel, fuel from the cooker, we could rub ourselves in with it. We stood naked by the window; it was still raining. We shook our cloths and rubbed ourselves with fuel. For a few minutes it was all right, but then this cruel game began again.

We began to accept our fate, tossing and turning grumbling in bed. A whole army of fleas tormented us.

I had an idea. I thought, perhaps the king of the fleas has ordered his servants to stay in our beds, and so I laid myself down onto the floor. I don't know if it was the tiredness or if these little biting beasts were so kind as to leave me in peace for about five minuets so that at last I fell asleep. But then, they all came back to their feeding bowl. How cruel, I complained and swore, (I had learned that so good from Peter). Nothing helped, oh the agony, my body was now covered with boils. Peter was also tossing and turning and swearing in bed. Every two minutes he put the light on, again and again mumbling, ' another one and another one' and furiously he squashed it throwing it onto the floor. It was a dreadful night, our only desire, longing and craving for this night to end. If our bicycles had not been locked up, we would have fled swearing in the night in spite of the rain away from Zilina.

In the next room some Czech road workers were sleeping. We asked them how could they sleep here. They laughed, pulled a little bag with powder out of their pockets and rubbed it onto the places on their bodies where the fleas have bitten. They always carry this powder around with them.

How happy we were as the morning dawned, that the hunt for fleas would soon end. Rain, rain nothing but rain. In spite of the rain, we dragged the rest of our flea bitten bodies as quickly as possible away, only when the flea town Zilina was behind us, were we relieved. It was still raining, the mountains sunk in mist and my arm hurt.
We had to ride through thick mud, today we did not need to 'eat' dust clouds, instead we got covered in mud. In a farm guesthouse that was at the same time shop and hairdresser we had breakfast at dinnertime. Meanwhile it stopped raining. We travelled on through a small town, then we cycled over the Jablin pass. Here, years ago heavy fighting with Hungary took place. Now we are in Moravia. The sun came peeping from behind the clouds, only to disappear again. Instead of mountainous landscape the countryside was hilly and more cultivated. Instead of the poor rundown farm huts we had seen in Slovakia, we saw the usual farmhouses, for us now like palaces.

In Postzika we looked for a small farmhouse, a place to sleep on straw as rain clouds again appeared in the sky. Here three languages were spoken, Czech, German and mainly Polish. The farmers here were so nice and friendly. Evenings I played my violin in front of the house and Peter told tales of his adventures. The house owner who could speak German had to translate for the others listening. We then made ourselves comfortable on our straw beds, but the fleas started biting again. Those dear little beasts had crept into our things, but it was not as bad as the night before. Compared with the previous night we slept quite well.

Monday 21st August.
A bright clear starry night sky looked down on us that evening, but as we rolled out of our straw beds early in the morning everything looked grey and dreary. The streets were damp. Today, the dust clouds by the Chau lakes could not bother us. My right knee and arm hurt. The wind was blowing against us again, so we could not progress as quickly as before. We now arrived at regions of Czechoslovakia that spoke mostly German. These parts were scattered in the middle of country. We came to Fridek-Mistek, which was also a pure German speaking little town. It was dull the whole day, but shortly before sunset, the sun cheekily came out for a second with golden eyes peering through the clouds. In Klopsdorf, [3] by Freiberg we asked a German farmer if we could sleep in his barn. He was very friendly, gave us eight kronen, each of us a pot of milk and bread with butter, but he could not let us sleep in

---

[3] Klopsdorf; dorf translated means village.

89

his barn. Its full and they have just begun to harvest the crop. A visiting relative of the farmer gave us ten kronen. 'Here take, I am a countryman,' he said. The farmer sent a young boy with us to show us the way to the neighbouring village, Mühle where we left our bicycles. There, we found somewhere to sleep and given bread and milk. We told the farmer that we were on a long journey and our money was running out."

Gretel's thoughts return to the present situation. The sea around Skargarak is stormy. Huge waves crash against the side of the ship. Gretel is seasick. She loses her way on deck and ends up in the captain's own cabin. The friendly captain asks the ships doctor to help her and soon Gretel is recovering. Her thoughts wander back to happy times.

"Tuesday 22nd August.

As the morning dawned it became lively around us. In one corner of the barn were little chirping chicks and the mother hen clucking, in the other corner young cockerels practising their crowing, at the door a cat and dog sleeping, cuddled peacefully together. As the dog awoke and saw that something was moving in the straw he began to bark loudly. By breakfast I was pleased to spread pflaumenmus[4] thick onto my bread, and oh how awful, the bread nearly walked away, it was full of maggots. I went to the village shop where I had bought it. It was the same shopkeeper who had given me the address in Klopsdorf. He looked at me wordless and took the populated pflaumenmus back. At the market we bought various things and walked contentedly with our bicycles along the streets in Klopsdorf. There, the farmer, whom we had talked to yesterday, asking if we could sleep in his barn came running towards us and said, 'just think, how lucky you both are that you did not sleep in my barn. It burnt down within five minuets. You both would have been completely lost in my crammed full barn, everything is lost, the harvest, the tractor, all destroyed.' Fear and horror griped us. If we had stayed there, we would have suffered such a horrific death, the end of our happy voyage! This was something we could hardly believe.

Now that we left the Slovakian territory the roads were improving, no more 'eating dust clouds.' Although this area had only gentle hills like coloured waves, the road was dreadfully hilly, going up and down. Often we met begging gypsies clothed in rags with their horse and wagon. On a lawn next to a gurgling stream we had our lunch and eat some apples we had picked on our way. Then we continued our journey. The whole day was dull, all lost in hopeless grey. Rain clouds forced us to sleep in a hostines[5], a small room, two beds costing fifteen kronen and a night without fleabites.

Wednesday 23rd August.

It rained the whole night and still rained as we set of in the morning. It is 80 km to Brünn and Peter would like to be there by midday. We struggled onwards again, cycling against the winds coming towards us from the west. Again the road was bad. My leg hurt. We had to push our bikes for long distances and I tried to ride as quick as a passing by motorcar. The sun came out amidst white clouds floating in the sky. At the roadside a quick lunch and of on the road again, passing a team of oxen, holy icons, gypsy wagons, coloured field and the country roads. At 4 o'clock that afternoon we reached Brünn. Peter went to the 'verband'[6] and came back with 50 kronen.

We slept at the hostel of the Czech tourist club, but first, we had some fine warm soup. Then something pinched me. Mostly evenings, since Zilina something begins to bite me. I don't know if it is the nasty memory or if a dear little beastie wanted to keep us company!"

---

[4] Pflaumenmus; a kind of plum jam.

[5] Hostines; is a Czech hostel.

[6] Verband; obviously here is meant either bank or union where Peter was able to get some money.

Awaken from her dreams of past happy times the reality of her present situation comes back to her in full force. Has it only been six years since she left Dresden 1933? Now again Gretel is on a journey into uncertainty, what is going to happen?
That wonderful trip, those happy days, soon Gretel will arrive in England, a new country, and a new life? When will she be able to go back home? I will end this section with a last quote from her diary;

" <u>Saturday 28th August.</u>

Its 76 km still to Prague, we can get there comfortably today by this afternoon. Lovely sunshine again, also the wind is not quite so wild. We had our lunch by some young birch trees amongst flowering blue berries. In my mind I imagined nice sun bathing, but how horrible, the whole of the morning was so beautiful sunshine, also so warm whilst we were cycling. Just as we had our midday rest, thick clouds covered the sun. We were now travelling in an area we knew well. We are still on the country road. We stood on a hill in the sun and glanced back down that country road. We have been rambling around on these country roads now for three weeks and spent a week climbing up steep mountain paths. It had been four sunny unforgettable weeks.

It seemed as if the country road was suddenly winding through wonderful mountainous countryside with forests, and ruins on the mountains along rustling rivers, gypsies on the wayside, farmers in rags, derelict farm huts, here and over there a smiling face from some dear person that we had met and then the road was lost in the stunning mountainous landscape of the Karparten, mountains as far as you could see, disappearing on the horizon. Then the mountains seem to grow to giants, high towering up to the sky, rocks and ice. Nervously bits of snow clasp on the steep rocks, a wild mountain stream tumbles down over them and over there smiles peaceful a mountain lake. -' Come Gretel' said Peter, he had sorted out something on his bike and wanted to continue. With this I awoke from my wonderful dream. - Dream? No, it is true. Am I pleased to be back again in Prague, that we are now here again? Peter meant the strenuous journey, camping and so many things we experienced what was not pleasant was now at an end. But I would like to roam through the world forever, take everything as it is and find everywhere everything as a wonderful experience. But we are in agreement with each other about one point; we had a wonderful time, a great journey it was. Nearly four weeks we have been travelling along those country roads."

2.

Life as an Alien

"How lucky are those who can live all their lives in their home country with their families."
Quote from a letter Gretel wrote to her brother 1946.

'Ich sende Euch grüße zum Scherzen.
Aber die Sehnsucht brennt mir im Herzen.
Meine Heimat möcht ich mal wiedersehen,
Mit dem Mönch auf den Mönchstein im Sturme stehen,
Gern würde ich die Burg mit der Hütten vertauschen,
Und den flustern der Vergangenen Kindheit lauschen,
Hier in der Fremde entwurzelt, verloren,
Zum Kampf für die Freiheit war ich geboren,
Da erwacht der Träumer von seinen Traum.
Ein säufzer fliegt in den Weltenraum'

Translation.

I send you greetings in pleasure.
But yearning burns in my heart.
My homeland I want to see again,
And stand with the monk on the Monk stone [1.] in storm,
Gladly I would like to exchange the castle with the huts,
And listen to the whispering past of childhood,
Here in foreign country uprooted, lost,
To fight for freedom I was born,
There awakened the dreamer from his dream.
A sigh flies up into the heavens.

(Written in England living at Hareshoots).

Oil; 'Woods and Boulders'

---

[1] Mönchstein', Monk stone; Here is meant a certain rock stone that my uncle Hans and his rock climbing group climbed up regularly in the Saxon Switzerland mountains outside Dresden.

CHAPTER 4.

The Second emigration, 1939.

The Legend, part 4.

The oldest part of the town Schandau is called 'Zauka' or 'Dzauka' meaning 'maid' in Wendic. Wendic is a minority language or dialect spoken in that part of Bohemia. It has its name from the same named village, to be found nearby on the west side of the town by the ferry. Alongside the houses in the valley, between two mountains that lead to Altendorf is the churchyard.

Nearby, on the mountain above the market place called 'the Kieferich' was once supposed to have stood a castle that belonged to the 'Birken von Dubas'. Today, not only are ruins to be seen, but also sometimes the ghost of a young white lady. She harms no one.

Once upon a time, every night at the twelfth hour in the valley that runs between the Zauken valley that goes through the town to the Kirnitzsch valley and from there back to the castle ruins a jet black matted hound with fiery eyes could be seen haunting this place.

Folk say that this was the ghost of the baron von Duba. He was well known for his brutal and barbarous lust and desire to plunder, rob and greed. A poor hungry peasant once begged him for a piece of bread. The baron set his dogs on him, chasing him from his castle. The baron suddenly died and was transformed into this hound with fiery eyes and condemned to wander restlessly through this valley forever. Then it happened, after so many years, centuries later, about 1700 – 1710 that a certain Anna Büttner whose father had just died, (she was his beloved only child) went to the churchyard towards evening to pray next to the fresh grave of her dearest departed father, and for sorrow and grief downhearted did not realize how late it was and dark it had become. So it was that the hour of midnight found her still crying and pining next to the grave of her dearest departed. Then look! There appeared suddenly the fiery hound, not threatening and frightening as usual, but silent and sad. It sat down on the neighbouring grave mound and the innocent naïve maid, who felt that this poor cursed condemned creature must have a far heavier heart ache than she herself could feel, did not flee, instead she went to him and stroked him gently, speaking words of comfort and reassurance. And look! The hound became quite friendly, sprang up to her wagging its tail, licking her hands and its eyes were not so wild and fiery anymore. It appeared to want to say that her comforting thoughts, words and sympathy had brought him the hour of deliverance and salvation.

So much is certain, then since that day the hound has not been seen again. So is the legend.

In London 1939.

How would you feel, being hunted and chased around from country to country, in search for peace? Imagine, at last, although far, so far away from the place of your birth, you think, 'at last, now we are safe, and can begin to live'.

How wrong this thought proved to be, how false. Little did my parents realize that their awful adventures were only just beginning! I am not just writing a biography about an artist, but the history and time when all this happened is so important for everyone on earth. There are many moving tragic true tales unwritten and forgotten. This is one I know of, and can report about, so that no one needs to forget what happened 1939, so that it may never happen again.

Through the connection with the Oska Kokoschka league[2.] and the Artist International Association, emigration was made possible for the émigré artists. The majority of the emigrants were of course Jews from all walks of life fleeing not because of their political views but for racial reasons. My parents fled because of their political anti-fascist activities.

20th January 1939; this is the date of a letter of confirmation for Gretel to come over to England. She came alone on the boat, over Skargarak. Imagine, arriving in a strange country alone, unable to speak the language and not knowing what the immediate future holds! I don't think anyone can even anticipate what it was like. The ship took Gretel further and further away from her place of birth. I still have the English dictionary she brought with. My mother told me how she only had time during the journey over the channel to Britain to learn a little English as well as time to learn the basics of English cookery, as she was to work in the kitchen. With these two books in her hand, an English dictionary and a book about English cookery she prepared herself for her future post, not knowing what to expect and not knowing what the future would hold for her. Where was Peter? Would he be able to join her soon? And all those left behind in Prague, now living in the Prague ghettos? And so Gretel arrives in Britain, one day before Hitler marches into Prague, 9.3.1939 with a letter sent to her from the Co-ordinating Committee for Refugees, London.

'Co-ordinating Committee for Refugees. Domestic Bureau,
5 Mecklemburgh Square, (off Guilford Street), London WC 1.
'Concerning your position by Mr Penrose Esq., London.
Herewith we send you your identity card and your work permit for a household post. We ask you to call upon the British consulate with this card to apply for the application for the visa and to show it to the British authorities. Keep this card safely and by entry into England show it to the officer.
When you have arrived, would you then please contact your future employer straight away and inform him of the date of your entry.
If your train arrives too late in London for you to continue your journey to your future place of employment so please contact the administrator of the Jewish shelter, 63 Mansell Street London E1 who will be waiting for each train and will give you accommodation for a night. If you should not need your permit card then please send it back with the reasons why?'

If Gretel's train arrived too late for her to continue her journey, if she had to stay the night at the Jewish shelter, and how she felt arriving in England I do not know. She never talked about this. This is left to the reader's imagination.

Gretel was lucky. Roland Penrose, a well-known artist living in London wanting to help refugees offered Gretel a position in his household. There, she works as a house help and general help in the kitchen. Mr Penrose, a very social sensed helpful man tells Gretel that he mainly wanted to help emigrants. Gretel's first impressions on entering Mr Penrose's house must have been filled with amazement and awe then he had many original Picasso pictures hanging there in his home. Admiring these artworks alone must have been sufficient encouragement for her to continue her own work.

With his help, Gretel is able to continue her studies for her profession as a sculptress. He helps Gretel with contact to the art school and pays for further studies, enabling Gretel to attend art and sculpture classes with Professor Carter at the Reading University, studying part

---

[2.] Oska Kokoschka league; This organisation of anti-fascists artists living in Prague helped émigrés to find refuge in Britain.

time. One more contact should be mentioned here, Mr Padley from Reading who was working at the University and also helped Gretel.

How is Gretel coping with learning a new language, after speaking Czech and now English? Apparently, sometime during the first months at a dinner party Gretel tries hard to say something. She wanted to say that 'the food is a new thing', meaning that what was given to them was different to what she was used to. But to her dismay her words are wrongly misinterpreted and her new friends think she said instead, 'the food is a nuisance'. Gretel asks for 'paper for the soup' meaning pepper for the soup. However, she soon learns to speak English perfectly.

Peter arrives in England at last 15th May 1939. His immigration regulation landing card informs the English officials that the 'number of souls on ticket, one, 1 ss Largs Bay-passenger no 391'. Now at last thinking they are safe here in Britain, Peter and Gretel get married in London on the 19th June 1939. What sort of celebration did they have? My mother told me that they asked a stranger from the street to be a witness to their marriage.
They lived in London, in Hampstead for one year before moving to Maidenhead.

Many of Gretel's artworks, were left behind in Prague, but they must still be somewhere as they were given to an art historian. We tried to find this lady later, without success. These early sculptures are mentioned in the catalogue, 'Kunst im Exil' 1938.

Four sculptures; 'Mother with child,' 'Fairy story teller,' ' Comedian,' and 'Gypsy Children' were sold to a woman doctor, an art historian in Prague 1939 before Gretel left the Czech republic for Britain. Her name is regrettably unknown to me, but they should still be in this private collection wherever they are.

In Prague, 1937 the Oska Kokoschka League organized exhibitions and two Art Festivals took place in the emigrants hostel Strasnice. Many exhibitions and activities are organized through the 'Free German League' on culture in Great Britain.

How different it was, when Gretel returned to Dresden 1960, and she was told by the GDR artist organization that her artwork was insufficient and that she should wait before she could get her recognition, that she did not have enough with to prove her ability! That time 1939 her work in Prague, her Oska Kokoschka League membership was sufficient to help her further with her artwork.

Aquarelle; 'Dark Woods'

The Legend, part 5.

The origin of the name 'Birk von der Duba'.

The house of Berka, whose coat of arms consists of two oak branches crossed over each other, belonged to the related house of Howora the oldest aristocratic family of Bohemia. An ancestor of the latter was hunting master to duke Jaromir in the year 1085.

Once, whilst hunting they both were separated from their attendants and fell into the hands of the Werschowoczer who were robbers by trade. They tied the duke and his hunting master naked onto an oak. As the robbers were about to shoot them both with arrows, Howora begged the leader of the robber band for mercy and asked for permission to blow three times his hunting call on his horn. Alone the tones of this specific tune that Howora played on his horn showed the scattered servants not only the place where their master was, but also that they were both in danger. They hurried to help them, and so both were saved from certain death.

For gratitude and thankfulness the duke showered his faithful servant with rewards and gave him the title ' von Duba', (meaning oak).

1140, due to this relationship and in connection with the life saving action from Howora, Friedrich Berke inherited the castle Duba. The Benedictine monastery that duke Jaromir built at the place where all this happened, stood until King Wenzel's time. Then it was destroyed.

Aquarelle; 'Woodland'

'The Little Weed.'

'I heard the little weed whisper,
Someone trod down my brothers and sister,
So as the wind did blow
I decided to grow,
Just on a house wall
And I grew better,
I grew fine and tall.

One day there came an artist along,
He did not do what other people would have done,
He did not pull me out,
He looked at me,
Took pencil and sketch book out,
He made me happy and proud.

He wrote a poem about me,
About the sun beams playing on the red brick wall,
About the tender green weed,
His poem gave me wings to fly,
High up in the sunny blue sky.

I just wanted to say, how nice it would be
If everyone of us could see
All the nice little things happening everywhere
Happening around us always there,
To see the finer and deeper sense
That brightens up our existence'.

(September 1948)

Many exhibitions and activities are organized by the 'Free German League' (FDKB; Freie Deutsche Kultur Bund).

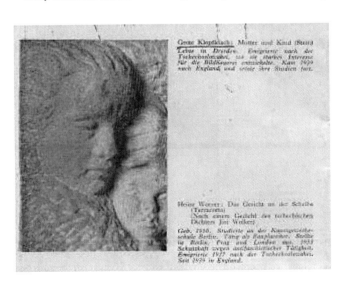

97

CHAPTER 5.

Internment Camp.

Watercolour; 'Hampstead' 1940.

Gretel and Peter were now living in Maidenhead. What a year it must have been for them. No one can even imagine the experiences of that year alone that 'The Two Blues' had to suffer. Fleeing again from approaching Nazi terror, thinking they were now safe, life in a new country, speaking a different language, different customs, their marriage, moving to the emigrant home in Bray court, by Maidenhead, Berkshire, and now internment, imprisonment, life behind barbed wire!!

Britain 1939 – 1960 should have treated my parents differently, made them feel more at home, - not regarded as aliens – not interned, then perhaps our lives might have been different and we might have stayed in Maidenhead - not returned, perhaps gone back to Dresden just for a holiday as originally planned!

My poor parents fled from Dresden from Nazi Germany and then fled from the Czech republic as Nazi invasion began, then thinking they were safe were interned, my mother sent to Isle of Man and left ill without help for months, practically dying, my father sent to Australia deported as a dangerous person. It is no excuse to say that there was no proof that my parents were innocent of any criminal offences and were perhaps Nazi spies!

The British feared anyone coming from Germany and irrespectively interned them, what ever their background.

My father's diary that he wrote of his experiences as an internee sent to Australia describes the hardship, suffering, despair and longing for freedom. This diary is a book in itself describing the harsh treatment and bad conditions they were subject to. It did not count why they had to flee from Nazi Germany.

Even when they were released and freed, they were still regarded suspiciously from certain officials. They were still 'Germans' and lived in Britain as stateless persons.

I want everyone reading this to try to imagine the huge stress, anxiety and struggles my parents felt and experienced. The dates alone show how fast these dramatic events followed each other. At the beginning of that year 1939, they were both still in Prague, Gretel's flight on the last possible transport out of the Czech Republic, her arrival in Britain 9th March 1939, and her job as house help by Ronald Penrose. I do not know the date when Gretel leaves Prague on that last refugee transport.

Peter was left behind. He was still in Prague on the 12th March that year. Imagine Peter's flight on foot, chased by hounds, his arrival in Katovici on the 5th May that year and at last his arrival in London 15th May. In June my parents married, at last hoping that they were safe and then they moved to the emigrants home in Bray court by Maidenhead. Now what happened; Peter's arrest, internment, sent to Australia, life behind barred wire, and then Gretel's arrest and internment on the Isle of Man.

1. Gretel's Plight.

Peter and Gretel moved to the emigrant's home in Bray court by Maidenhead, Berkshire on the 23rd October 1939. At last they thought they were safe and hopefully could live here until a return home was possible. When would that be? A Dresden comrade; Arno Schönherr was the leader of the home. Their peace is short lived. Although Peter and Gretel were registered as refugees fleeing from Nazi Germany, the authorities could not accept their reason for exile. They were greeted with mistrust and suspicion.

In spite of the fact that both had been accepted as refugees and allowed to enter Britain they now faced further difficulties and problems. No one trusted them, and it seemed that the authorities were particularly doubtful about my father. Still at first the two seemed to be safe for the moment and Gretel became pregnant. Obviously hoping for some kind of normal life the two began to make plans for the immediate future, including wishful thinking of having their own family. Gretel's visit to a doctor ended in disaster. It seems that this careless doctor, instead of helping her, made some sort of examination that harmed her and caused her to start bleeding, a short while later she was interned.

Something my mother mentioned once gave me the impression to confirm this. Perhaps it was not carelessness from this doctor, but hatred because of Gretel's German nationality. The result of this doctor's ignorance and heartless behaviour had tragic results. About this time, Peter was arrested and interned. He was to be sent to Australia. It seems that panic was on the agenda, fear and anxiety on the daily menu. Then, a short time later Gretel was arrested, also with the intention to be interned and to be sent to the Isle of Man.

Although Gretel was pregnant at the time no consideration whatsoever was taken. Other internees were given different treatment, and sent to Scotland, to help in the forests cutting wood. In contrast to Peter who kept a diary of his experiences, Gretel spoke little about what happened to her, but certain incidents are known. Her arrest must have been quick and no time given for any sorting out then she told me of following episode;

Gretel must have been transported to the police station in Maidenhead at very short notice and obviously questioned. She was very concerned about her few belongings that she and Peter had been able to save on their flight from the approaching Nazis.

It seems that not all internees at the home could be trusted. In such situations as my father describes in his diary notes, all sort of people from all walks of life were thrown together. Gretel is extremely concerned about the safety for her violin that had accompanied her since she had left Dresden. She informs the policeman that had arrested her that her violin is an extremely valuable instrument and worth a large amount of money. "If it gets lost, or broken you will be personally responsible for it" she tells him. Somehow Gretel manages to convince this policeman and he sends his constable immediately back all the way to the emigrants home in Bray Court to fetch it. This constable has no choice but to hurry as fast as he can and bring it back to the police station for safety. Obviously he had to make his way back by bicycle. Now what? On arrival back at the police station in Maidenhead with the violin, the policeman is puzzled what to do with it. After discussions he has to make his way back again to the emigrants home to deposit the violin in safe keeping with some official. Gretel is not allowed to take it with her. Some time later, her violin was sent over to her on the Isle of Man.

We still have this violin, and it now belongs to my daughter. If this violin could talk, it would tell many tales; how Gretel learned to play it, how it was used to hide illegal anti-fascist material way back in Dresden, how Gretel played in the Agitprop group in Prague and many other tales. But now her violin was for the moment safe. Sometime later it seems, her violin was sent to Reading to Mr Padley for safety. He worked at the University where Gretel had already started to attend art classes.

Gretel and Peter have no knowledge of each other's fate. Where is Peter now? Gretel is sent to the Isle of Man to be interned. Little is know about her journey, but my mother, with other internees was sent to Holloway prison before being interned.

What crime have my parents committed to be treated like this? It seems that Gretel was amongst one of the first groups to have been sent over to the IOM, the number on her registration card shown as 898. Gretel arrived on the 30th May 1940; the first internees arrived on the 27th May. It seems, according to records, that the internees were taken onto the ship from Liverpool. Were there hostile crowds to greet these poor emigrants that had fled from Nazi terror?

The journey over to the Isle of Man must have been under extreme cramped conditions. There are mothers with babies and small children on the boat and there is a lack of nappies and underwear for the children. Some of the women in despair pinch clothing and underwear out of the other internee's luggage. The anxiety and repeated experience of mistrust has a disastrous effect on Gretel's health. Her arrest, imprisonment at Holloway prison and then the journey over to the Isle of Man, squashed in the overcrowded boat, not knowing what has happened to Peter only contributed further to her ill health and miscarriage. Gretel was sent to the Rushden Internment camp on the island where a whole area was sealed of for the women with their children. This was no holiday camp for Gretel, but uncertainty, restlessness and full of anxiety, a life behind bared wire and progressing illness, only 6 months later, after her miscarriage did she receive medical help on the island. It was a very hard time and no help from doctors.

She reports in her own words;

"Difficult hunger years during the war and inflation in earliest childhood times could not deter my strong nature. I was able to cope with homelessness and I silently accepted this restless life, but on the Isle of Man my health was neglected, destroyed and ruined forever".
What happened next is something no one should have had to experience.

21st June 1940 Gretel receives a letter from Mr Padley. He hopes Gretel had received certain goods, her clothing and her violin that had been sent to her.

Graphic; 'End'

100

'Nächte.'

'Nächte traumlose Nächte, schwebende Stunden,
Ihr seid wie balsam auf brennenden Wunden.
Nächte, in deinen Armen selige sekunden.
Nächte vom Glück umwunden
Nächte, mein Leben zerstörenden zerfressende Nächte,
Wie ein Gefangener in dunklen Schachten,
Und heulend höre ich im Wind,
Das ungeborene Kind,
Dunkelheit ohne Licht,
Nächte ohne Dich'

Translation.

'Nights.'

'Nights dreamless nights, floating suspended hours,
You are like ointment on burning wounds.
Endless nights, in your arms blissful seconds.
Nights from luck surrounded
Nights, my life disturbing consuming nights,
Like a prisoner in dark shafts,
And crying I hear in the wind,
That unborn child,
Darkness without light,
Nights without you'.

(Most probably written in internment camp).

This poem and the artworks created on the Isle of Man tell enough about the suffering and pain Gretel experienced. No words can express her feelings. The poem about the dark endless nights, and her sculpture of a mother, her arms wanting to hold her unborn child says enough.

Despair; modelled on IOM in internment camp

Isle of Man, Internment camp, 1941. Watercolour

Gretel's registration card on Isle of Man.

Gretel suffered severely on the IOM[1], left bleeding of months without any help and practically dying.

Following notes have been found in the Manx National Heritage records;

'**Margarete Klopfleisch** (Klopfleisch, Margarete (on list) Marketa (on R.C. & Police Permit) Guelo (on signature): Rushen Camp c/o Bradda Glen, Port Erin. Date of Birth 2.8.1911 in Dresden. Occupation Domestic. Last address outside of the UK, Prague. Married. Cert. of Identity 714 Prague 27.10.38. 9.3.39 Conditional landing at London. 2.11.39 Exempt internment until further order. Tri. Bucks. Refugee from Nazi oppression. Name deleted from Police Permit to proceed out of Rushen Internment Camp Area for the purpose of proceeding to Douglas Court House, in order to appear before the Home Office Advisory Committee. Dated Tuesday 8th April 1941. (Box IOMC Movement Permits) 20.5.41 Leaving IoM for Bray Court, Maidenhead, Berks.

A sculptress and artist. She even managed to exhibit some of her work in the camp. A clay figurine of hers from this time "Woman in Despair" testifies to her unhappiness at the internment experience. A watercolour she produced in 1941 features a large barbed wire fence dominating the foreground, with bleak hills beyond in an unapproachable and unpopulated landscape. A committed Communist Party member (From *Politics and Culture in TwentiethCentury Germany*, B115/79) Returned to Eastern Germany after the war (From *The Internment of Aliens in Twentieth Century Britain*, B115/18). Died 1982 in Dresden (From *Art in Exile in Great Britain 193345*, B115/84). 715315 issued 10.3.39 at Bow Street, London (AKAM 291/5).'

I have to make following comments to this record; concerning the remark that Gretel returned to Eastern Germany after the war; this is not correct. We went 1960 for a 'holiday of no return.' The war ended 1945. Concerning the comment that her artwork 'testifies to her unhappiness at the internment experience'! Can anyone imagine how Gretel must have felt, so ill and desperate for help and no one there to help her! Her child lost through the miscarriage and no doctor, just her art, her enormous will to survive and her incredible talent to express her feelings in her work. As the months pasted by Gretel became so ill that she was unable to get up and spent most of her time in bed. My mother told me how her internee companions were very worried about her, how they bought art material to her bedside for her to use and how they discussed how to help her and encouraged her to continue. An exhibition of works from the internees was organized to welcome a new senior camp officer. Her friends decided to place Gretel's artwork so, that the new senior camp officer when entering the room would see them straight away. They hoped that the sight of Gretel's artwork would help her get the urgent medical help she needed.

Gretel had now been seriously ill for months without medical help. Peter believed that Gretel was still expecting their first child. It was supposed to be a happy occasion; the birth of their child. He had no knowledge what was happening and the uncertainty must have been very distressing.

---

[1] IOM; Isle of Man.

Landscape, painting, IOM.

Crucified; modelled from clay in internment camp IOM

This exhibition of handcraft and artworks made by internees for the new senior camp officer saved Gretel's life. The fact, that her friends had put her sculptures right at the front of the table hoping this would help highlight her plight, particularly this one sculpture modelled in clay of a woman in despair about the loss of a child caught the new senior camp officer's eye.

It worked. This lady saw the pain and desperation in my mother's artwork and ordered immediate medical help. 'This lady needs urgent help' she immediately informs the IOM officials. There was not much time left. Gretel had been left bleeding for months without help. Her sculpture, 'Despair ' had saved her life. The symbolic portrait of a despairing mother holding her arms without a child in them informs the new camp senior officer of the dangerous life-threatening situation Gretel is in and she is transported to a hospital on the island. Only a difficult operation can save her, but the doctors tell her she can never have children, this happened Christmas 1940.

Gretel writes on a slip of paper that she wants to have children and holds this note tightly in her hands as she is put on the operating table. She manages to keep conscious for a short while before the operation to make sure the doctors get her note. She holds on long enough to hear them say that her wish for children will never become reality. According to doctors opinion help had come too late. Because of the too late help Gretel received, she has to suffer many years of ill health. That life saving operation was done in the very last minuet.

Gretel and Peter had no idea what was happening to each other. The internees sent to Australia were made to believe that their loved ones, and wives were in the second boat also destined for Australia and that they would all soon be together again. From the two boatloads of internees sent to Australia one went down hit by an enemy torpedo. Only one internee from this boat survived this attack.

August 1940 the Artist refugee committee write to Gretel; "It is dreadful to think that your husband has been sent to Australia. We all very much hope that it will be possible for wives to join their husbands. Your pictures are quite safe and the committee will look after them for you". This letter just confirms the belief given that they were supposed to follow their husbands in the second boat.

The British Artist International Association helped free Gretel and Peter. They send Gretel financial help and art material. A year later she is allowed to leave the internment camp but her health is ruined. The sadness that she has now been told that she will never have children is devastating, her wish to become a mother now uncertain. A friendly sympathetic older

103

English lady offers Gretel help and sends her to her own personal doctor, even paying for special treatment needed.

The Artists refugee committee write a letter to Gretel, 8th March 1941 informing her that "Theo Balden and Heinz Worner have now got back safely from Canada, so you see it is possible to bring them back from deportation, even when it seems quite impossible."

Gretel was released from internment camp 20th May 1941 and then sent to Bretthouse in London, a convalescent home for refugees. In June, she receives a letter from a friend who is still on the IOM. She hopes Gretel is enjoying her liberty and that she misses Gretel's company. She enjoyed walking with her and now only women who knit are left behind. She does not want to lose contact with Gretel; her name is Lilo Ullman

2nd October 1941; Gretel receives a letter from the home office informing her that the secretary of state has given instructions for Peter's release. He had now returned from Australia, was back on the IOM. After his release, they both move back to Maidenhead to the emigrant's home.

Watercolour; 'Farewell Isle of Man' 1941

2. Concerning Peter's compulsory journey on the ship to Australia.

I found these notes somewhere in my father's diary about the compulsory journey he had to make. From these notes and letters, it is clear that he was counting the days of his return journey back to Britain. The longing for peace and a happier life, the longing to be reunited with Gretel is obvious. The journey apparently took 58 days and it seems that there was no direct way to get to their destination.

I am not sure about the correct spelling of these places, as now, the hand written notes are not clear to read;

Sydney – Wellington – 5 days.
Soujonon – Wellington – 1 day.
Wellington to Panama – 21 days.
In Panama – 1 day.
Panama – Curogao – 3 days.
In Curogao – 1 day.
Curogao – Halifax – 6 days.
Halifax – Soujonon – 5 days
Halifax – Glasgow – 15 days

Drawing, charcoal of Isle of Man

Peter's experiences in the internment camp, the journey to Australia and his life over there is a book in itself. It would be too much to write it all here so I will translate extracts from his diary and letters. Before he was transported to Australia he was taken to the Isle of Man. The address from the internment camp was;

"p'- camp, house 40
c/o Chief postal Censor, Liverpool.

A year after Peter arrived in Britain thinking now he is safe and can be reunited with Gretel he is arrested and interned. 17th May 1940 he writes a letter to Gretel, hoping that this episode is only a short one and that soon things will be sorted out. It must be a mistake! It is hard to believe what then happened. Ten days later, Monday 27th May the women were interned. On the 30th May 1940 at a time when Britain was reckoning with landing of Nazi troops on British shores Gretel was interned in spite of the fact that a court hearing committee from the tribunal hearing in Berkshire district registered and recognized her as a refugee from Nazi oppression and as such from internment camp not to be interned. Peter had been arrested some time earlier and was already interned waiting to be sent to Australia. Peter and Gretel heard nothing and knew nothing about each other for months. Examiners opened all letters and much of it was blanked out.

There are two dates noted in his small notebook; Saturday 1st June, the journey to the camp and Saturday 15th June, transfer to Isle of Man. Later, when the internees were on the ship to Australia they were led to believe that their wives were following on the second ship. The internees on each ship were led to think, 'our women are over there', but then, the second ship is no longer in sight and the internees have no knowledge of the fate of the second ship, that it went down and all expect a single man drowned. Luckily Peter was not on that ship. What must the internees have gone through, not knowing what was happening to their loved ones and the constant uncertainty!

Peter sends Gretel a letter 25th June 1940. He is wondering what is happening, no sign, what is happening to their baby, and he is worried. This letter was sent to Gretel from the county Barracks in Reading where Peter was kept. He asks Gretel to bring him some clothing when she comes to visit him. He does not know why she cannot come then he was arrested and interned before Gretel.

Friday 27th June Peter writes a letter to the chief constable asking for Gretel's address as he had received an answer confirming that Gretel was now also interned.

Saturday 29th June Peter writes in his notebook; "for the first time since weeks I was able to read a newspaper. The newspaper was a week old. Concerning the front; the German army has now marched deep into France, Italy is at war, there are fights in Africa, and Paris is occupied."

Sunday 30th June Peter was again able to read a newspaper. He writes in his notebook; "German – Italy – France, armistice, cease-fire settlement, taken into effect since midnight".

6th July 1940 in Douglas on the Isle of Man Peter writes; "I am still waiting for letters and for my belongings. This year we have missed the anniversary of our wedding."

8th July 1940, a letter to Gretel from Douglas inform her that; "I have just announced myself voluntary for Canada. We were promised that our wives, who are also on this island, would travel with us over to Canada. Gretel, will you come to?" Rest of the letter is blanked out.

Peter reports in his diary how they were told that their wives were to follow in another ship and that they would be together when they arrive in Canada. On arrival at the harbour they were made to believe that their wives were already on another ship.

The first part of my father's diary, of his experiences concerns the situation and circumstances of his journey on the 'Dunera'. He writes; "the journey on the 'Dunera'[2] was the most awful experience and one of the worst times of my life. Only a German concentration camp can be worse. We had to wait a very long time at the harbour before we were allowed onto the ship. Already the 'welcoming' from the guards as we stepped on board prepared us for what we were to expect.

That first evening, Wednesday 10th July 1940 as we arrived in Liverpool from the IOM we were greeted with a bleak picture of devastation. Various utensils, papers and a mixture of personal belongings that you usually take on journeys, mixed with bags, suitcases, rucksacks and small opened cases were laying on a nearly mans high heap wildly thrown together in the rain on the side. On board the ship, the officers and crew shouted and swore at us horribly. Everything we carried on us, or held in our hands had to be thrown on deck onto one of the many large piles of belongings and luggage. Those who did not throw their belongings onto these piles, or were not quick enough, were stripped regardless and their belongings confiscated. Even coats and spectacles were taken and thrown onto these piles. Music instruments flew high somewhere onto the deck. The internees were kicked and hit with clubs, and had to suffer a downpour of this treatment.

Even bayonets were used. Then we were bundled down into the rooms below where we had to experience a thorough body search. There everything we had in our pockets had to be emptied onto the tables; the sergeants threw pens, pocketknives, shaving-kit and tobacco into buckets. Unceremoniously they put special good pieces into their own pockets. I was able to hide and save my new expensive pen and my good pocketknife that I was allowed to keep legally before my departure. Up on deck the armed forces even tore up all letters and documents throwing them in large sacks or buckets. Many of us walked around with completely empty pockets.

Later that night, the buckets and sacks with our belongings were returned to us and we were allowed to search and pick out our things, but of course the most valuable assets were missing. Most probably some of the other internees who were able to rummage around first in those buckets also stole some things. It was dreadful to see how people tried to look and search through those piles of torn paper for their documents and passports etc. Each regarded their own things as most import, and the squabbles and arguments were harsh and ruthless. Amongst the torn papers were passports, birth certificates, and other important irreplaceable documents. It was a complete senseless and ridiculous destruction, purposely done to create damage. That was our first evening. The supposed journey to Canada was to take 10 to 14 days. No one knew that our journey was to take two months.
Towards midnight, at last we received something warm to eat, then we had nothing the whole day. For the moment we had no sleeping arrangements. We spent the night sitting at the tables and lying on the hard floor."

My father goes on to report how only the next afternoon, hammocks were given out for sleeping and how squashed they all were together in that far too small room that was meant for 124 people and now 200 internees were squeezed together. There was not enough room for everyone to put up their hammocks. Nighttime, every spot on the floor and tables were occupied and above them hung the hammocks, so tightly and packed together that there was insufficient room to walk or stand up straight. If you had to go out nighttime you stumbled over internees sleeping squashed together on the floor and knocking your head on those sleeping in the hammocks. Peter slept on the floor under a table and was constantly knocked on the head from those trying to creep past him.

---

[2] 'Dunera' is the name of the ship my father was on, when he was sent to Australia .

106

Peter continues to report about the food often not properly cooked and insufficient causing stomach complaints. Some foods such as fresh fruits were sold illegally for money. He writes about the various types interned, the philosophical talks and discussions held.

It took some time before the internees got used to the sea, seasickness becoming something they all experienced. The internees were often ill with diarrhoea because of bad food and help from a doctor was hard to get.

Friday 12th July finds Peter seasick; the rocking of the ship in the stormy waves takes some getting used to.

Saturday 13th July, Peter takes his first walk on deck and wonders what has happened to the other ship on which their women are supposed to be. It cannot be seen anymore.

Tuesday 16th July, the day is very hot. The ship is going on a southeast course. It does not look like going to Canada. Looks more like going to Africa. Where are they going? It's not at all clear and Peter hopes that the authorities are not sending their women to Australia while they are sent to Canada!

"Wednesday 17th July, officially we are going to Australia and the women most probably are being sent to Canada. For Gods sake Gretel, what is going to happen to us?"

Wednesday 24th July, the ship arrives at Freetown, Sierra, but Peter is glad when the journey continues because the porthole windows are opened again.

Saturday 27th July, now the ship has arrived in Africa at the harbour from Akra, Gold coast? The internees are locked down under deck and can only peep through the closed portholes to the world outside.

Peter writes; "if one would have been able to lay down comfortably in a bed or been able to sit at ease in a chair, then in my opinion this whole seasickness is only a problem for the first couple of days. On the 'Dunera' we have all had to experience the most impossible situations, there was no such thing as comfort, nothing at all. The whole circumstances of our accommodation and treatment reminded me of the tales of transport of the slaves in the middle ages!"

As they reached the equator the heat became unbearable. They were not even given cold drinks, just the warmed up water that was called tea and had no real resemblance with tea. Peter writes that these two weeks were the worst of the whole journey. The internees were locked in the rooms below as they reached the harbours in the tropical zone; the small windows were locked allowing no fresh air into their sleeping quarters. The hygiene was something unknown and the men grew beards because their shaving equipment had been taken away from them. The internees received a small piece of soap twice a week pro table, insufficient for all, only enabling them to wash their faces. Towels were not available, some managed to steal a tablecloth somehow, Peter had only his handkerchief or toilet paper. Some who had money were able to 'buy' themselves something.

Concerning safety regulations in case of emergency, Peter reports in his diary; "There were no safety and rescue possibilities for us in case of a disaster. We were locked up. The exits were woven thick with barbed wire and only two very small and narrow passages left free. There were no lifebelts prepared for us. If the ship had been torpedoed or would have hit a mine, all of us, about 3000 prisoners would have sunk miserably with the ship to the bottom of the ocean. Only a few would have been able to get on deck. Thousands of us would have been stuck in the rooms below and sunk with the ship to the bottom of the ocean. Everything said later by the officers in charge about organized safety and rescue plans and that there were sufficient lifebelts is not true, does not correspond to the real facts. Only when we arrived at Capetown were large boxes with lifebelts presented and 'put on show'. Before that, nothing was seen at all." Peter writes that the soldiers slept above on deck, had their kit bag with them and they would have been able to save themselves.

Concerning investigations and searches in the luggage from internee's, Peter reports; "On Monday 15th July during our walk on deck some of the sergeants suddenly started to rummage around in the rooms and took anything they could away with them; bags, money, pens, watches, rings, purses and pencils, medicine from the sick, spectacles, tobacco, cigarettes, matches, everything possible and impossible. The next day we were filtered as we went back to the rooms after our walk on deck. Thereby my good purse was taken away from me and thrown into a large sack with all the other confiscated goods. Luckily I had safely hidden my bag, pen, watch and pocket knife."

Peter reports about the so-called walks on deck of the 'Dunera'. These so-called exercises took place once each day. It was the only time the internees had the possibility to get fresh air. He writes that; "This 'exercise' consisted of several hundred internees being chased around the ship's deck, also up and down the stairs, for about a quarter of an hour several times briskly trotting about. Then we were driven down to our smelly 'caves' beneath the deck. That was our recreation!

Six machineguns were set up and directed at us. The guards, sergeants and officers always screaming and shouting; 'Come on! Hurry up! Get a move on! Their language accompanied by cruel swear words. Several times one or the other officer or sergeant was drunk. Then it was especially bad."

" In the south seas, albatross accompanied us instead of seagulls. But we could not even admire these undisturbed for a few minutes. When you dared to start daydreaming, admiring the flight of an albatross and envied the birds freedom, then you were suddenly ripped out of your dreams by the screaming officers; 'will you get a move on, you…!'
There was no 'exercise' on Sundays, and when we were in the harbours. We then stayed down under deck locked up. We could only see land for seconds through the toilet portholes. The washroom portholes were always shut. You had to queue up in order to see something of the world outside from these toilet portholes. This was something we organized ourselves so that at least each of us saw something of the outside world and not one person occupied the view the whole time. But we still had to be very careful, then if the guards had noticed this they would have shut these two portholes as well."

"Our space under deck was 20m by 12m and about 2.50m high, in this room, about 200 people were squashed together."

"The most depressing situation was so many people being awfully squashed together in the smallest of spaces. Even by certain intimate things we were not alone, always someone there to make sure everything went according to regulations! The uncertainty of our destiny, no news from the outside world, was impossible to tolerate. There is no possibility to hear from you Gretel, or to know how you are, not the slightest chance for any news from you, or to send you a life sign from me. What must you, my Gretel also be going through, how endless and alarming this time must be, also for you …now is end of September, and I still know nothing how you are?"

Peter describes the various different types of people on board the ship. There were many religious internees, orthodox Jews and other religious groups as well as Catholics. It seems there was also a priest and a rabbi present. Also quite a few authors and actors who helped organize some sort of entertainment for the internees. Anyone who had money could 'buy' themselves certain goods like chocolate, biscuits, fruit and tobacco that otherwise was not available. Peter had no money so he could not obtain these delicacies. Clothing was a problem. Their belongings were confiscated and only much later, and only partly were the internees belongings returned to them. During the time on the 'Dunera' the internees only had what they had on and hardly anything else. Peter writes that, "what a delight it was as I at last was able to use soap, a towel and a toothbrush."

Thursday 8th August 1940, arrival in the harbour Cape Town. Peter writes; "By chance, I have washing up and food fetching duty, so I can admire the panorama from Cape Town from the kitchen window. That is quite a different view than that from the toilet porthole. The town offered a wonderful unforgettable view in the evening light. It was the first town I saw since the beginning of the war without blackout."

"Friday 9th August evenings we continued our journey. Wonderful weather. After our departure we opened up the portholes in the washroom ourselves and so we could admire a little the wonderful mountainous landscape, the south coast of Africa. If only we could leave this swimming stinking prison and climb up those mountains! Where is Gretel? Luckily the guards have not noticed the opened portholes in the washroom."

Saturday 17th August 1940, Peter is quite ill again. The next day, 18th August he writes a letter to Gretel; "Now we have got this new letter page. We have to use it although it is designated for prisoners of war only and we are but interned refugees from Nazi oppression." Peter also had received a message about Gretel's dangerous illness.

Tuesday 27th August 1940, arrival at the first Australian harbour." We have all had to undergo a medical examination. Luckily I'm all right."

Wednesday 28th, after breakfast the journey continues. Peter is longing to be free. "Outside is wonderful weather. The sun is shinning. The air outside is so wonderful fresh! Through the porthole you can even see sometimes green. If I only could be free outside, in the fresh air, in daylight, in the sun!! and with you, my Gretel !!!"

"Tuesday 3rd September 1940, arrived in harbour Melbourne . Outside is wonderful weather. But we down here we cannot feel any of it."

" Wednesday 4th September. Wonderful cold morning. We are freezing down here, especially at night."

"Friday 6th September, Good weather. Arrived in Sidney. Fine landscape - rocky coast. From the train we see at last a town without blackout, we see people, gardens, women, children, after two months at last. At last its over. We are on land again. Those guards who terrorised us for two long months stayed behind."

Saturday 7th September; after a cold night the internees continue their journey by train, now through Australian bush country. They are all so glad that they are no longer on the 'Dunera'. The 'Dunera' nightmare is no longer. Each of the internees receive a good breakfast, plenty of fruit and six sandwiches. The soldiers accompanying them are friendlier. Peter writes," These soldiers were so different than the 'Dunera' bandits; Royal Norfolk, Royal Suffolk and A.M.P.C. were the 'Dunera' crew. None of us will ever forget that. How different and comforting it is here… Gretel when will I hear something from you! And when will we see each other again?"

"Sunday 8th September; At last for the first time since two months I have not had to sleep on the hard floor. The night is cold."

"Monday 9th September 1940; At last we can view the stars in the sky at night and admire the star constellation the 'Southern Cross' in the night sky"

"Tuesday 10th September; I am so hungry. Again there is less to eat. Certain individuals get the biggest and best portions for themselves. The wind stirs up sand clouds. The camp is sandy and dusty. It's a place at the end of the train line."

"Sunday 14th September; Again, insufficient food. Lots of telegrams have arrived but there is nothing from Gretel. Where is she? The outside world knows where we are. I hope Gretel knows where I am." Peter does not know if Gretel is still on the IOM. He is wondering about his luggage, when is he going to get it. Some internees have received their belongings.

"Wednesday 18th September; Rich people can send telegrams, costs about one pound. The rest of us cannot even send letters. Those who have money can buy cigarettes and chocolates. Those who have no money get a small beggar portion. I refuse, not worthwhile to bother about. Handkerchiefs and teeth brushes are still not available. Perhaps later, possible for those with money."

"Thursday 19th September; Today I got my small case back again. Nothing important is missing. At last I can brush my teeth, dry myself with a towel and shave myself with my own shaving equipment. My case is only slightly squashed, in comparison to others still in relatively good condition. Today, for the first time since two and a half months I have been able to brush my teeth and dry myself with a proper towel. What an extraordinary unbelievable luxury."

"Desperation"; Modeled in internment camp, Isle of Man.
(Approx 1940-41?) Later used as model for a wood carving of the same idea

3. Continuation of Peter's diary.

Peter started writing his diary on the 26th September 1940 in Australia in internment camp. The diary notes are written as a letter to my mother who was by this time also interned on the Isle of Man.

He writes; "My dear Gretelchen, I write this letter to you from internment camp in Australia. I begin writing on the 14th September. It is a sort of backwards working diary since I wrote my last letter to you 9th July 1940. On the 10th July began the long and unexpected journey. Since Saturday 7th September I am in internment camp HAY in the Australian out back about 18 hours train journey from Sydney." He then describes the camp and the accommodation, the uncomfortable sleeping arrangements, mattresses consisting of wire netting that constantly creaks by every movement, the thin straw sacks and the two blankets allowed. He writes about the cold freezing nights, that he has no coat, pyjama or jumper, no warm underwear but the days are warm. He writes that now is the end of winter, the landscape is desert like and there are many sandstorms the wind blowing the sand through the 30cm open gaps covered with wire netting between the walls and ceilings in all the barracks. On such occasions the air, food and clothing is covered with sand. "All food soiled from sand in a few seconds, the sand scrapes between your teeth, plates and spoons are covered with it." He is happy that the food is better and at last can enjoy his meals. At last, after that terrible time on the 'Dunera' now he can walk in daylight and enjoy walking in sunshine. The camp is surrounded by threefold bared wire, but in spite of this he is glad that now there is a little more 'freedom'. He can walk around the camp alone, the walk taking about fifteen minutes, he can look up to the night sky and undisturbed admire the stars. They have even been given their own piece of soap, and soon are to get towels, toothbrush, toothpaste, and clothing. They haven't had these things now for two months.

About the return of the luggage and cases with the belongings of the internees Peter writes; "Today, 29th September the return delivery of our luggage is still not complete. This will take some weeks to sort out although we need our things. Many will never see their belongings again. Many cases are empty, half empty, and nearly all cases, with a few exceptions show signs of having been broken into, contents robed, and partly severely damaged. Some cases show an appalling picture of senseless destruction. By some cases the lid was simply cut off with the bayonet or completely pulled off. By other cases the locks were broken off.

Only now, when we saw our luggage again, we could see how the guards had treated the harmless luggage from defenceless internee refugees in such a senseless and ridiculous manner. Many lost all their possessions" Shoes were another problem reports Peter, many cases had different sized shoes tied together, any good and new shoes were mostly missing and in some cases were only single shoes. Peter writes that he was lucky to get most of his belongings back and that "the Australian officers here in the camp admit that it cannot be denied what has happened."

He is worried that he has not heard anything from Gretel, how is she? But Peter is now feeling much better, in spite of the lack of freedom and being surrounded by bared wire. Even the guards and officers are friendlier and there were no more military personal with guns directed at them, as was the case on the 'Dunera'.

There are many types of different people in the camp and the internees can 'rule' themselves, but as Peter reports; "no one can however ignore the fact that we all are equally interned, who ever we are, and at the moment no one has any positive prospect of freedom, even when he thinks he has a right and some sort of priority to it."

Peter writes a letter to Gretel wondering how she is. He has no knowledge of her whereabouts, he is curious to know if they are now going to have a child, as Gretel was pregnant before he was interned. He has no change of clothing, and hopes he can get something sent. He hopes it is possible that he will be sent back to IOM. His address is;

From Peter Klopfleisch c/o address; Aliens Internment Camp
5 Strepton road.
Huyton, near Liverpool.
To Margarete Klopfleisch c/o address; Women's Internment Camp
Isle of Man.

My comment about this; I did not know that my mother had married an 'alien from outer space'!

I found sound further notes about his stay in Australia. October 1940, he writes; "On our way over to Australia on the ship, I slept on the floor or in a hammock. Fruits are available in the canteen, but of course only for those who have money. There is a scandalous difference in internment camps between those who have money and those who are penniless. The rich ones can have all they want for money and we can't even get a little thread or garn to repair our last few rags, in which we are walking about."

Peter wonders if Gretel has received any information about his transfer to Australia and he often dreams about Gretel. "There are rumours that many of the women in Port Erin are released. Other rumours report that the women are on the voyage following their husbands. Some people believe that our wives are in Canada." Peter knows nothing about Gretel, where is she? What is true? He is desperate to know. "It is a heavy burden to be so far away and to know nothing of each other."

My father's diary continues on the 8th November. By now he was already two months in internment camp. He writes; "I have joined a working party for road work. We work two hours in the morning and two in the afternoon. At last my shoes are repaired. Now I can wear shoes again. It was high time, as I had to wear a bandage on my left foot. I have been walking around to long, nearly two months without shoes."

10th November; Peter writes how glad he was to see trees, woods and a river where the internees on the working party were allowed to bathe. "That was a special delight after those two months in that dreary, sandy, dusty, bare internment camp in the desert." That evening Peter felt for the first time so much better. He had clean cloths to put on and they all were given a good meal. "Today is like Sunday" he comments in his diary.

Friday 15th November; The newspapers report that 212 women whose husbands have been sent to Australia are to be sent over as well. Peter wonders if this is true.

On the 20th November 1940 the Artist refugee committee report of a scheme for sending 220 of the IOM women to join their husbands in Australia. Also according to these letters, other internees were released earlier than my parents. Peter still has no news about Gretel. A postcard from Gretel dated 28th June is at last delivered to Peter on the 23rd November. He has no idea how ill Gretel was and December finds him worried about Gretel's health and her illness. His voyage to Australia was so completely unexpected. Peter reports about his life in the camp. Obviously those with money are able to purchase special things; "Yesterday evening the premier of 'Snow White' was shown, for those who bought tickets, so only for 'account holders'. After the performance, about 11 pm began again peace disturbing noise. Now we know who these people are that walk around outside the huts talking loud unceremoniously until 1am keeping us awake. Yesterday evening we found out that they are mostly, without exception, well off people. The noise started after the theatre performance. Here is a real class divide on a small scale. There are welfare receivers, (regrettably I am one of them), then 'workers' who work for a laughable sum, (1.. for hard, and -/6 for light work in kitchen and toilet etc), then small account holders and then finally the 'capitalists with large accounts. And then there is the 'parliament', a right stupid old lot that talk too much."

Peter writes about his feeling on New Years Eve, how sad he is, living behind three-fold barbed wire, so alone amongst selfish and unpleasant people. He keeps thinking of Gretel and wondering how she is.

1st January 1941; Peter describes a beautiful tropical sunset view, the wonderful colours, that he had never seen anything like it before and wishes Gretel could paint it. He writes a letter to Gretel; "Why don't you write." The separation is devastating and Peter's longing great. He does not know that Gretel is so ill. He does not know if Gretel was informed about his transfer to Australia and about his two months voyage on the ship. At least he is feeling better and healthier now.

Friday 3rd January; Peter describes how hot it is in this part of Australia, and how he longs for Gretel, "we will be together again someday. It poured with rain the whole night and day, lots of floods and so much dirt in the camp, but these last days have been better than the big heat previously. At least I now have proper shoes." His concern that he still has not heard from Gretel continues, "if only I would get post from her! I have already written to her eight time from here, before yesterday the last letter. Why do others get post regularly and others noticeably nothing for long time? It seems that any letters took about three months to arrive.

Tuesday 28th January; Peter describes a comet that can be seen in the south up in the night sky, how beautiful it is; "a star, large with a tail that has a length of three moons."

Saturday 8th February; The Trust fund sends money, and Peter receives one pound. The internees organise to send a collection of letters and Peter sends a message for Gretel; "she should write to me at last."

Tuesday 11th February 1941;Peter receives a telegram; he now finds out that Gretel was seriously ill. The telegram was sent on the10th February;

Telegram to detainee Peter Klopfleisch, HAY Internment camp.
"PENROSE JUST RECEIVED YOUR LETTER GRETE RECOVERING ILLNESS COMMITTEE GIVES HER HELP AND SYMPATHY APPEALING RELEASE BOTH OF YOU ALSO MWHLMANN FORESTRY WORKER STOPHERROTH RECOMMENDED BY ACADEMY CATEGORY 20
ROEDER ARTISTS COMMITTEE.
4 52PM.T."

Wednesday 12th February 1941 is Peter's father's birthday. He is now 65 years old and Peter wonders when and if he will see his father again.

Saturday 22nd February; "Yesterday Mr Penrose sent six pounds and five shillings by telegram, that is five English pounds. The telegram that came a few days ago and now this money, seem to show that now at last, my first letters (from September) are beginning to bear fruit." A few days later Peter receives a message from the Artist's committee informing him that Gretel was very ill. He is grateful to Mr Penrose, and believes he arranged appeal for her release.

March 1941; it seems that my father did not even have his spectacles, only now was he able to get a new pair. He is informed from the Trust fund group that he is now on a list as married with a wife in England to be allowed to return. Because of various confusing contradicting messages Peter is not sure what is going to happen. He receives at last two letters from Gretel and is still not sure what had happened with her. One letter informs him that she was not sure if she was going to come over to Australia. Peter has no idea how ill she is.

6th April 1941, my father's birthday, and this year it's on Palm Sunday. He writes about the past unhappy year, forced separation, loss of child, and internment camp. He has a dream; "I was aloft in the air. Was I a bird? I don't know, but I was flying somehow. Below was a lovely landscape, like in May. Many large trees, bright and green, and some birch trees in typical yellowy green, the colour of spring. A large green forest in the background and before it a large blue lake with lovely islands, and a meadow with really fresh green grass, and heather and a blue sky above the scene. A girl was lying in the heather, and I saw you." "Can one believe in dreams? Perhaps this dream means that a new spring is approaching? My birthday on the same day when I was born; on Palm Sunday! Ah how wonderful it would be to experience again all the wonders and pleasures of life and not be forced to suffer all the unhappy and unpleasant events of this past year! This last year of my life was so bad; internment, forced separation from my Gretelchen who was expecting our child. This enforced separation is the reason why we have lost our child! Then the deportation to Australia and the journey on the 'Dunera' with all that horrible treatment we had to endure.

A reunion as soon as possible with my Gretelchen and a quiet civil life, that is my birthday wish, and of course together with all guarantied circumstances." Peter again complains about lack of contact and that post is so slow. He writes; "Some friends whose wives were not interned have received post over the 'Trust Fund' as a prize, and as punishment, because my Gretelchen is locked up I have now not heard from her for two months. The last letter is from 18th December. Why am I such a stepchild in respect of post? Why?"

14th April 1941 Thinking of Gretel, Peter declares by signature his wish to go back to England, but the transport back could take some time. He is a non-smoker, and complains about exposure to smokers! My father was very particular about these things. He longs for walks and wanderings in the mountains and forests and thinks back on happy times when they both lived together in the Czech republic.

Monday 5th May; at last Peter finds out how ill Gretel was. He wishes he could have been there with her and perhaps she would not have suffered so much. His letter to her 7th May 1941 from Australia confirms he loves Gretel as always, as before and that the consequence of the operation does not change anything, unjust internment and forced separation is the reason for their suffering. He writes; " Don't believe all the 'nice' stories that are probably told to you about the 'nice' lucky life of the internees in Australia."
Life behind barbed wire, living in primitive conditions, disgusting manners of some of the other internees, so many restrictions and unpleasantness makes life unbearable.

Saturday 17th May, Peter's diary reports that Major Layton was again in the camp and that all married men have signed a document wishing to return to England. The journey is supposed to begin soon. He hopes to be back for Gretel's birthday.

Thursday 22nd May; Peter, together with the last of the 200 internees leave the camp and begin the return journey. Now the empty camp was to be filled with Italian prisoners of war.

Thursday 27th May; Peter is happy. He receives a message from Gretel; "Gretel is free! Evenings I received a telegram from her sent 21st May. She is in Bray court again. Thank God, she is out of that dammed internment camp. Hopefully I will soon be with her. Our journey on the ship will begin soon."

Peter's return journey on the ship; S.S. Largs Bay. 14182 t. starts on the 4th of June. How different this return journey is. "Major Layton kept his promise; we travel as proper passengers and we are completely free on the ship like all the others, without any restrictions and differences. We are four in our cabin." Peter describes his return journey. This time it is more of a pleasant adventure; he can walk around free to enjoy the views. He can socialise and talk with his companions and the sailors, enjoy a drink at the bar and has a proper bed to sleep in.

Monday 9th June; Peter describes the beautiful scene, travelling between the Islands of New Zealand. "That was wonderful, mountains and forests, the mountains rising out of the sea. The highest summit, (3 - 4000 m high) was covered in snow. It looked like the Alps. If only we could stay here. How beautiful the morning sun shines on the summits of the snow covered mountains on the horizon."

Wednesday 11th June 1941;this is the date when Peter 'relives' the same day twice! It's called 'antipodes day'. "That means we have crossed the time zone. We have travelled over the world where the 11th June ends just as the 12th June begins and the longitude where the day begins that had just ended." A warship accompanied the ship where Peter was on; "the accompanying warship sent a message over to us. Mornings was a lifebelt safety practice and we were given certain instructions in case of emergency."

"Thursday 12th June; my mother's birthday. She is 66 years old today. I have not heard from her and she has not heard from me since nearly two years. There was a breathtaking clear starry sky that evening. I cannot remember to have ever seen such a beautiful starry sky! If only Gretelchen would be standing next to me. I made acquaintance with an Australian sailor, Jack. His wife and child are back in Australia. He bought me a glass of rum and gave me a postcard from New Zealand."

Peter is happy to be able to walk around the ship free, to be able to enjoy his compulsory trip round the world, the stormy waves and to observe the shining stars in the clear night sky. He makes friends with his fellow travellers, has a drink with them at the ships bar, there is even a boxing match organized. He can have a bath and wear clean cloths, sit in the deck chair up on deck and there is help if he is seasick.

Friday 27th June; Peter describes the scenery; "The ocean illuminated stronger yesterday than the evening before, and the lively game of the flying fish is so wonderful to see, Gretel could study their movements. We also saw a few birds, not seagulls or albatrosses, gliding in the wind, hardly using their wings." That afternoon Peter went to see the semi-finals of the boxing match and that evening he admires the wonderful clear starry sky. He can admire the star constellations; 'the great bear', 'the southern cross' and the brightness in the water; "or rather the foam lights up so bright, and everywhere lights, like hundreds of dashing bright diamonds, an amazing view! I had to write it down this evening so I can tell Gretel how wonderful this experience is. She is not here with me to admire this incredible experience of nature."

Saturday 28th June; that evening the equator is reached, the ship nears the Panama Canal and then the dangerous Atlantic Ocean. Sharks are swimming around. That night, the sailors celebrate crossing the equator till early morning.

The next day land is in sight, a lonely rocky island that gives an uncanny eerie impression. It seems to be unpopulated. "A strange peaceful picture. I sat on deck, the sun was sinking behind the horizon and I looked at that serene rock island. Some people were sketching and I thought what a wonderful keepsake Gretel would have to take back with her if she were here. Suddenly, at about 6pm, dreadful banging and lightning from explosions came from the back of the ship. It was the ships weapons. Four shots were fired. It was a military exercise. In the radio we heard the news that in the Atlantic an American ship had been torpedoed." The next day they arrive in America and Peter can admire the wonderful view.

"Tuesday 1st July; In the harbour of Panama. Now by daylight we can see how breathtaking the view is here. Everywhere, all around us, mountains and luscious green parks with palm trees and special trees you see only otherwise in botanic gardens, birds flying around that you see only in zoos."

Peter is so glad to be able to observe these wonders of nature. He cannot forget that it would be great if his Gretel was there with him and the circumstances of this journey had been under better conditions. They are all told to make preparations just in case of emergency, as danger zone will soon be reached. The lifeboats are ready and all passengers have to prepare their own bags, just in case. He is fed up with endless travelling around the world and longs to be back with Gretel, often he thinks of home so far away.

They reach Canada; they see many warships and many different kinds of travellers come on board. He wonders if he will soon be released when they arrive in England.

"18th July; from today onwards, daily ten thirty am, we have to go to the lifeboats with our lifejackets. We have to carry them around with us all the time now. We are to get gasmasks as well. I have made myself a bag in which I can put some other things in as well."

19th July, Peter again admires the fascinating views, how the red glowing sun ball sinks direct into the ocean undisturbed from any mist on the horizon and then the clear starry night sky. He is concerned about certain narrow-minded traders now on board, and their senseless talk. "The war between Nazi Germany and the Soviet Union has made them quite mad." He wonders if Gretel has any idea that he is now only one week away from Europe! He is so glad that he now has decent and good meals.

"Saturday, 26th July; sometimes early morning an aeroplane could be seen searching the ocean before us. One was supposed to be there yesterday evening as well. I went bathing and then went to bed. Late afternoon five to six large warships (destroyers) came towards us and strengthened the safety of the convoy. We are now and for the next days direct until England in the most dangerous zone. But we are well guarded and can hope that nothing will happen."

" Sunday, 27th July; On board a few more M-G's have been put up and from today the guards wear steel helmets and carry guns." Obviously some on board were getting quite nervous, especially those traders that kept annoying Peter with their ridiculous talk. Any bumps, noises or gunfire contributed to their anxiety. But the journey continued safely without any incidents. It's Gretel's birthday soon and Peter is *allowed* to write her a letter. The best birthday present would be if he were there with her.

Tuesday, 29th July; we might have only two more nights on this ship. "The view is beautiful, mountainous land and mountainous islands, everywhere steep cliffs, glisten green when the ship nears the beach. This is not North Ireland as I first thought, its Scotland and the Hebrides. We are already in England."

"Wednesday 30th July; now the lifeboats have been put away, hardly anyone carries their lifejackets around with them. This is much better and now the voyage is fun and enjoyable. The good weather, the realization that the journey is coming to an end, we are safe, the stunning views and the nearing mountainous green coast, but to this comes the tension what is going to happen to us after our arrival."

Thursday 31st July; the ship passes a factory where they see the first ruins, but no other sign of war and bombers. After breakfast official are supposed to come on board. Then the internees will find out what is going to happen with them. Lunchtime arrives and they still have no idea what is going to happen. Their luggage is already taken of the ship and the first three groups of passengers leave. It looks as if they will have to spend another night on board. It seems that all passengers had left by teatime. The internees were then called into the customs sheds. There, the names of fifteen people were called out who were given permission and allowed to travel home. The rest, about 125, had only their names called out. They were not told what was going to happen, or where they were going to be sent. No one knew anything. The hope for freedom seemed something of a dream for the internees. New officials were now dealing with things and it looked as if there was no hope for freedom. Peter is in despair, what again life behind barbed wire? He can hardly stand it any more. His thoughts are with Gretel and he longs to be free and with her.

Friday 1st August; the internees luggage is already sent ahead somewhere, they no not where. It is believed that the journey will continue to the Isle of Man. They are happily surprised and glad that the guards are now friendlier with them. "What a difference to last time when we left. This last year in England feelings and attitude must have changed a lot."

The internees are sent back to the Isle of Man, still no freedom. Peter is given a job in the kitchen and can earn something, but he wants his freedom and to be with Gretel. Post as before, take a long time to get anywhere and leaves Peter wondering how his Gretel is.

19th August 1941; Peter hopes that the artist's committee's application for release will be successful. He had to return to England, as there is no release in Australia for civil internees. Over in Australia, living inside triple barbed wire, cut of from the outside world was very difficult. Outside you could see kangaroos and parrots. They were free! He sends thanks to Gretel's new lady friend, Julie Reich who had helped her so much in hard and lonely hours when she was so ill. He hopes to get Gretel back as she was. It is clear from this letter that the continuous strain of struggles and fleeing has already a negative effect on their relationship.

Thursday, 28th August; Peter writes in his diary; "Today I was outside by the intelligence officer regarding questioning for my tribunal hearing tomorrow." The next day this hearing takes place with an advisory committee. On the 2nd September Peter is allowed to see Gretel who came over to the IOM to visit him. He writes; "After one and a quarter years I could see my Gretel again. At last, but only for a few hours and a military person was always present." The next day he can see his Gretel again for an hour before she has to leave.

Douglas 13th September 1941; Peter is still on the IOM. He longs for freedom. He writes; "My studies of mathematics are interrupted. There are too many troublesome people around. I can only do mathematics when I am alone. Gretel is the only person whose presence does not disturb me. I urgently need slippers and Mrs Smith kindly sent me a parcel." My father was very keen on maths. If he had given the chance, he would have become a maths teacher.

The Artists committee was obviously helping to get my parents released from internment camp but Peter knew nothing yet of this.

"I don't know anything about my case. That's so sad, having been brought back from Australia to England for the purpose of being reunited with my wife. This is an odd reunion, if even to get a letter from my wife I have to wait longer than a fortnight"

"Tuesday, 7th October; towards five o' clock evenings, the runner from the internment office came to congratulate me. Tomorrow morning, nine o' clock I am to go to the internment department outside. That means RELEASE! I can hardly believe it, is it really true?"

"Wednesday, 8th October 1941; at last its nine o' clock after a nearly sleepless night. It's raining. I am going out. It is true! I a released! On category 19!..

At two o' clock afternoon took luggage out. The investigation went smoothly. Nothing is taken away; therefore I have nothing that I am not allowed to take with me. I have had to pack up extra carefully some wet washing. Doesn't matter, better than taking it with dirty. The journey is not that far. Yesterday evening I made myself some sandwiches so as not to have to much to do in the morning."

"Thursday, 9th October 1941; That morning, 7.15 am, left the barbed wired behind.

In the office we were given our stuff and behaviour instructions, then down to the harbour and on to the ship.

Departure at nine o' clock, slowly the Isle of Man disappears in the mist behind us. We arrive at Fleetwood at 12.30. In a shed at the side of the harbour our papers are stamped and then each of us go on our individual way to the train. Departure at two o' clock. How strange this all is. Eight o'clock evening arrival in London.

I am afraid that Gretel is not there any more but already at Bray Court. After some difficulties, a stranger in the Blackout, till at last 9.30 evenings I am by Gretel!..."

Amongst my father's papers is a certificate dated 9th October 1941 from the camp commander from Douglas Isle of Man. This certificate states that Peter will be issued with 26 English clothing coupons.

This story about my parents, their struggles and difficulties, their courageous fight again Nazi terror and the following events are so important. It must be told. Why did they have to suffer so much? If my parents had not experienced internment, my father not sent to Australia on the 'Dunera', that senseless dramatic journey, the bad treatment the internees received on their journey up to Australia and my mother's illness, lack of medical help, not treated as 'aliens', then my parents might have been able to settle down in England and felt more at home.

These are only extracts from my father's extensive diary and letters, but it does give some idea how he suffered and the longing for a peaceful happier life, for freedom away from bared wire.

As far as I know, no apologies have been given to my parents from the British authorities for their suffering in internment camp. They both were released after a year. So with recognized that they both were not Nazis. In fact they were given refugee status on arrival in Britain.

Europe in Chains, wood carving. (1942)

CHAPTER 6.

Motherhood 1942 – 1946.

Gretel with baby Sonja.

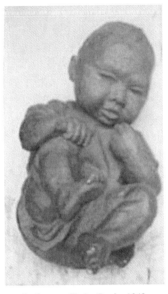

Sculpture of baby Sonja, 1943

Gretel and Peter are now living in Maidenhead. They receive a small one roomed flat, very insufficient, but at least they are together. The dramatic events of the internment camp, although not forgotten and forever in their memory slipping into the past. Both were now living far away from their home country, the second time in a strange land, different language and customs. Peter had not seen his parents or sisters now for many years. They were still living back in Düsseldorf. Neither had Gretel seen her brother Hans since her hurried departure fleeing from Nazi Germany. Both longed to return home to a peaceful world. Life had to continue, somehow. How was life back in Dresden? Contact was limited.

I found a letter my father wrote to uncle Hans dated 12th May 1942. He writes, 'nowhere is a country where 'Milk and Honey flows', the dirt has been mixed, thrown by the fascists, and the majority of the Germans have followed the Nazis, and through this inactivity helped the Nazis. Now we all have to suffer.'

The quote from this letter says enough, and informs us of the pain and anguish my parents suffered.

Peter was now working and earning good, a little over the average wage. He had a job in his profession in the printing trade. Gretel continues her studies at the Reading University and she is also one of the founders of the Maidenhead Art Club. She is registered as a student at the university from 1941 to 1942 for two days a week as a part time student and from January 1944 to June 1945, one day a week. She could not afford to become a full time student. There are also further exhibitions in Maidenhead, in Cookham and also in London.

About this time Peter and Gretel become acquainted with a lady who becomes my adopted aunty, my aunty Dinah. I believe she belonged to a group of English people who were dedicated to help and support refugees. We kept contact with each other or the rest of her life. She came to visit us in Maidenhead many times and took us children out. She was always my aunty, the only aunty I ever knew and on my return to Britain became also an aunty for my daughter.

Gretel's wish to become a mother is at last fulfilled December 1942 when I was born. Here are her thoughts in her own words;

'Christmas Memories'

"The memories swing like the strings on a harp plucked strongly
What was the best Christmas ever? There is no need to ask, there is no need to think, and the answer is just bursting to come out.
But it is not fair to paint all the other years in grey, a good portrait needs a pleasant coloured background.

Looking back into the past, I feel like standing on a mountain, following the winding path to the place where the journey started. Sitting on my mother's lap, I felt very puzzled about that Father Christmas. I had just kissed him, saying thank you for the presents. There was a really nice long white beard growing on him. But why was my elder brother so very naughty to Father Christmas, and my mother could not help laughing. He crawled under the table. He pulled hairs out of his beard. Father Christmas only pretended to smack him, and he got his presents after all. And why did my father go out just before that Father Christmas came? I soon found out the story behind that.

Not many years later I was playing Father Christmas myself together with my little friend who had beautiful blonde curly hair and a wonderful voice. She was the Christmas angel.

We went to see the younger children in the house opposite and our friends across the road. We soon got invitations to come and play in the children's hospital, for the sick children, and that was the best we could think of – to give a little pleasure and comfort to sick children.

I am still standing on top of that mountain, following the path that led me there from one Christmas to the other, up to the best of all and for ever.

I am determined not to write a sad story and often my thoughts are flying too fast to pass by quickly.

But my thoughts cannot fly past that group of young people on skis in the snowy mountains. Speeding down the hills like the wind, sliding through the deep quiet woods, all trees wrapped in a thick cover of white glittering snow, like in fairyland, each tree taking a different shape. Yes, I still hope to celebrate Christmas like that once more.

And now I am nearly on top of that mountain, from where the warm breeze of memory guides me to tell that tale. I cannot stop and dream of the past anymore. I have to look down the other side, into the future. I have to guide my child along the rough, difficult and often dangerous path through life.

Yes, the child that was born just at Christmas, a very old story had come to life again, and the star that shone in mother's heart is just as bright and true, like a painter stepping back from his easel looking at his picture.

Some very important features are still missing, the face of that night nurse with the features of an ugly bulldog. Her words proved that. Her words, spoken to a person in agony, to a mother's fearful heart;
"Will my baby live – it is only eight months?"
Her words; "Some babies live, some babies die," came like a stroke of a whip to the wounded.

It was obvious that the stars above showed more mercy and understanding than human eyes.

The world was turning round and round in the wide empty space, and all the other worlds, clear and bright, far and near, each anchored in its own way, yet somewhere so near. If I could only reach out I would touch them, the world was so small.

And then the miracle happened. A new star appeared, more beautiful and nearer to me than all the others. It came nearer and nearer to me. It's sparkling light fell into my heart.

Oh, that beautiful star is so near now that I can touch it – and there was the newborn baby's first cry!"

I do not know when my mother wrote this, perhaps 1942 – 43? It shows how she was longing to be a mother and for a normal life.

I was born too early, I should have been born in January, but my mother said I was in a hurry to be there in time for Christmas. Her fear that her first-born might not survive was unfounded and somehow in spite of that first cold cruel nurse, Gretel held on until the nurse on duty changed. The next nurse on duty was a very friendly lady, different to the one before. She came into the room with me in her arms singing that well-known song; 'you are my sunshine', that was it; Gretel named her first-born Sonja, that's me.

Woodcarving, 'Mother and Child'. (approx.1943 – 48)
Now in Halle Moritzburg Gallery since 1965

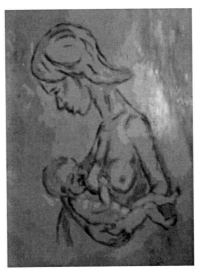

Graphic; 'Mother Breastfeeding baby'.
(Approx 1942 - 44?)

This woodcarving, 'Mother and Child' is now in the Gallery Halle Moritzburg by Leipzig. They bought it 1965, and at that time, the VBK[1] still did not want to accept her in their midst.

This graphic,' Mother Breastfeeding Baby,' is one of the artworks that have been damaged by Stasi interference 1972. My mother recreated it to its original state.

Gretel continues to exhibit in London with the Free German League[2]. There are further exhibitions with the Maidenhead and Cookham art clubs.

1945 Gretel keeps up her membership with the International Artist Association, but I do not know for how long, as things were becoming too expensive. One letter reports that membership costs 10 shillings and 6 pence.

1946; contact with Dresden is kept under observation. All letters sent to her from brother Hans arrived opened by examiners. Various letters to her brother Hans reports of her life now in Maidenhead; 'We are now living in the country, in a little town called Maidenhead quite isolated from the other emigrants. Most of them are still in London; the only contact with them is by post. This is a disadvantage for us both, but it was lucky for us to live here in

---

[1] VBK; Verband Bildender Kunstler, - Professional artists organisation from the GDR.
[2] Free German League' (FDKB; Freie Deutsche Kultur Bund).

Maidenhead when the bombers came. Most of them flew past us. The artist emigrant group stayed in London. That is why I did not really take it seriously about the publication of the booklet with pictures of our work. Now I have received the message that they have used the photos from my relief 'Caring Mother with Child' in stone that I carved in Prague. I have only a photo of this'

Another letter 6th April 1946 reports of Gretel's worries that she has not heard anything from Dresden for sometime. Her child is now three years old and Peter would like to return as soon as possible, but Gretel would like a life sign from someone from Dresden first. It is a worrying time

One letter from her brother informs Gretel that her father had died. In a letter; 14th May 1946, Gretel writes; "I can follow the events happening in Dresden better than you think, I have no illusions and was prepared for the worse. I was really very worried about you. It is so sad that father had to go during such a dreadful time. Please write more to me about him, was he still angry with me. Were you with him as he died? What were his last wishes and thoughts?"

She writes that she would like to carve a stone sculpture for her mother's grave and that she had worked half a year in the stone sculpture workshop in Prague.

She reports; "Now things are so much easier, we have enough to eat, and a second room for Sonja, two years we struggled, living in only one room. Every night I sit here repairing things because everything is so expensive.

None of us had the peace and rest we needed. Hans, do not give in to the depression. Fight it. Things will get better. I have had such a difficult time and these past years were so hard. I was seriously ill when interned on the Isle of Man and heard nothing from Peter. Sonja is really my masterpiece after all the illnesses and operations I have had. I was seriously depressed as I thought I would never have children. Now I am expecting a second child. Sonja is big and strong, an intelligent lively and jolly child, such a chatterbox so that one has to laugh a lot. Sonja is English and speaks perfect English, only a few words German. She has here the full rights as any other English born child. That is an excellent law here.
When I return to Dresden we will work together.

Whilst in internment camp I worked with the most primitive tools and was able to create some good artworks. This has helped me greatly but nothing can be done artistically in Britain, can't earn anything with it here. Can you earn anything with art in Germany? In Prague, people were more interested in art."

Gretel writes that her brother Hans was depressed after having been forced to serve in Hitler's punishment army, but proud that he never shot anyone and risked his life in doing so. Gretel was proud of her brother.

She writes that this gave her something back of her lost confidence in humanity, and tells him that; "we are living here as foreigners and have to keep strict to the rules. Peter is so impatient to return, but back into a city in ruins and the poison from the Nazi?"

"How lucky are those who can live all their lives in their home country with their families."

In a letter to Hans, 30th June 1946 Peter asks about friends, Erich Glaser, Franz Fillinger, and asks about Rudolf Szepansky, what has happened to him? He tells Hans that he is now living 13 years in exile and about his 'forced' journey around the world when he was interned; South Africa, Australia, New Zeeland, Panama Canal, how he lived behind barbed wire and now back in England since summer 1941. He tells Hans that Gretel knew nothing about him for the first six months and that now they have Sonja. Since October 1941 they are living again in Maidenhead, that he has work as a compositor. His mother is now 71 years. Peter was looking forward to returning to Dresden and wants to return as soon as possible. Their second baby is now on its way and Peter hopes to return as soon as their second baby is ready to take with.

The birth of Gretel's second child is difficult, the uncaring nurses do not give Gretel and her second child the care and attention needed. Her second child is fed with cold milk, not cleaned properly and so Gretel has to leave hospital after the birth of her second child and return home with the new borne babe far to early. Also through neglect, her breasts become seriously infected. She has to undergo a further operation. All this proves too much for her. The results of her past life, hardship, starvation and internment camp, the previous years of struggle have a disastrous result. Her second child is only nine months when Gretel becomes ill again, her strength gone. This time she is in hospital for five months.

At this time the other emigrants applied to return to Germany to the GDR[3]. But my parents cannot return. My sister a newly born babe and my mother too ill to think of a journey back home; a result of the after effects of her traumatic experiences and the disastrous effects of her time in the internment camp on the Isle of Man. My father never fully forgave my mother for this illness. He did not mean it, but unconsciously it was for him a disaster, he so wanted to return to Dresden with the other emigrants.

Gretel and Peter now receive a second room but it is very damp and later proves fatal for my sister's health.

Further letters from Gretel to her brother Hans report of their life now in Maidenhead and her desire to be able to work together with him;

"I hear that there are now exhibitions in Dresden. I am looking forward to the day when we can work together. I know it is difficult to work as an artist, but here in this village and as a foreigner there is little hope, but I also have less time because of my two children. The birth of my second child was very difficult for me, and has left me quite ill. Is it possible for you to visit us? Peter said they did not want to stamp the parcel I sent to you and he had to take out the cigarettes. It was obviously only by chance that the first parcel with the cigarettes got through. I understand your wish for a home. I am also homeless, yet I have to create a home for my two children."

"I know that when I come home I will feel even more homeless.
I regrettably cannot share Peter's dreams of a democratic society, that is so far in the future and I see only lots of dirt. But we must try to do the best. I am so pleased that you have recovered and begin to have some peace and rest. I have had my legs in the grave several times, two miscarriages, a very difficulty stomach operation and a breast operation. We will have lots to talk about when we see each other at last."

Gretel's brother Hans also sculpted. I have only a few of them. Where the rest are, I do not know.

Gretel writes; "You have lost 30 sculptures. You have been busy. I have hardly a dozen sculptures here and I guess that I have made at least 200 sculptures back in Prague. I have had to leave them behind everywhere. I was extremely lucky in Prague to have been able to sell them cheap before I left, the same has happened with my pictures. Now I have no time to work. I would like to send you a picture but I am not sure if I can. I am so glad I can send you something to eat, even if it's only a small amount."

Obviously their home in Dresden was bombed and now in ruins, then Gretel comments that; "I could cry about father's books. I was a child as I was thrown out of the house from Trudy, (the step mother). How I would have liked to poke my nose in that cupboard. I urgently needed some education and knowledge. Little Röschen[4] is quite like Peter, and Sonja is quite like me. She would like a mouth organ to play. It's such a shame that the wooden hut (mountain hut property) is so neglected and over grown, we could enjoy it and have a party up there later. Perhaps Peter and I can live there?"

---

[3] GDR; German Democratic Republic.
[4] Röschen - My sister Lindy's real name is Rosalinde. We called her later Lindy.

A letter that Peter sent to Gretel's brother Hans August 1946 confirms the seriousness of her illness on the Isle of Man during her internment and that it is; "thanks to Dr Frank that Gretel is still alive. Thanks for her intervention that the responsible persons, the authorities on the IOM began to look into Gretel's illness and to help her and that she then had that life saving operation. Gretel is still ill after her current operation and can hardly walk.
Sonja is a little 'wild fang' very lively. Here we have no relatives to help care for such a lively child. In a few weeks the first emigrants will return to the Russian zone. Honesty I regret so much not being able to be with them. I could be over there more helpful than here."

The quote from this letter explains so much the desire to return to somewhere where they could feel they belong, to return to a place where they could feel at home and help build up a new peaceful world. The constant fleeing and disastrous events of the experience of internment has left them both vulnerable and stressed.

2nd October 1946 Gretel writes to her brother Hans;
"Sonja is so proud of her little sister and copies everything I do with her dolls. Just to mention her doll is bigger than her baby sister. I made her the doll last Christmas. We have just heard on the radio of the death sentence in the Nürnberg case. It is a great shame that the greatest criminal is not there, not present."

On the 20th October that year Gretel writes;
"Because I had to get up too early after the birth of my second child, my legs are bad. They hurt, are swollen and blue. Hans, keep this under us, the memory of Trudy gives me a little bitter taste. If only Trudy would have behaved a little friendlier and understanding in my early youth years, then many hardships I had to experience as a result would have been spared. Here we do not starve, but I cannot send you anything, its not allowed."

Gretel was proud of her two children and wrote that, "Sonja has fairy eyes and Röschen is a sunny godly picture. I have received a commission from the lady doctor who treated me to carve her a Madonna in wood. It has to be a good clothed figure. My own idea would be a proletarian Madonna. It is not going to be an easy job; I am still physically very weak."

Trudy was the stepmother who practically threw Gretel out of the house when she married her father.

I believe this might be the sculpture my mother
carved for the lady doctor who helped her. (approx 1946)

On the 28th Dec 1946 Peter received a very distressing letter from his mother. In this letter she informs her son of the sad fate his father experienced by the Nazis. He was arrested and sentenced to hard labour. The Hitler government took his pension away, and by forcing him to do hard labour in spite of his delicate health contributed to his death. The Nazis had forced him to transport heavy loads. He died March 1944, five weeks after his 68th birthday.

It seems that during the time when Peter and Gretel were living in Prague as political emigrants and starving, the relatives in Düsseldorf were better off and had sufficient food. This letter was opened by the English censors.

Woodland watercolour

'The Goldfish.'

'In the glass the goldfish swim,
Easy floating, like feathers in the wind,
Beautiful colours,
Colours of golden sunshine,
Happy colours,
Colours of golden wine.
Beautiful movements,
Like born acrobats.
Blowing silver bubbles,
Magic looks like that!
Cool clear water,
That's all they wish.
I wonder if I'd like to be a fish?'

The Legend, part 6.

The Legend of Jutta von Duba

The castle ruins of Altrathen can still be seen above the village of Rathen near the Bastei rocky stand stone mountains in Saxony.

In the tenth and eleventh century, the Germans occupied the Wendic[5] territory. During a stormy battle and in the heat of a fight that took place there, many fell into the nearby abyss called 'the Martertelle', (martyrdom) and lost their lives.

In recent years, skeletons, skulls and human remains, as well as arrowheads and swords were found there.

Later, this castle belonged to the duke of the castle Dohna. The family 'von Duba' became owners of this castle through marriage. At that time the castle was called Riesenstein[6].

One duke 'von Duba' named Witigo had a beautiful daughter named Jutta. He wanted his daughter to marry the young Bohemian King Premislaus Ottokar. He ordered an artist to come to paint her portrait so that he could send the portrait to the young Bohemian king. The artist was young and handsome, and so inevitably, a love affair developed between them. Against all expectations this relationship found a happy ending, because the artist under danger of his own life saved the maid from a sudden bolt of lightning during a storm. A fire broke out as a result of this unexpected bolt of lightning whilst the young maid Jutta von Duba was praying in the castle chapel. The young artist without a thought for his own safety hastened to the scene and saved her life. The father was so thankful that the young man had saved his precious daughter that he did not hesitate to allow him to marry her.

Woodcarving, (approx 1945)

'Twisted Bushes.' Crayon. IOM (approx 1940)

---

[5] Wendic is an ethnic minority group.

[6] Riesenstein translated means giant rock.

CHAPTER 7.

Gretel's Children 1947 - 1953

'Mother bear'

'Die Sonne küsst die braune Erde,
Ich liege im grünen Gras und schau
In das unendliche Himmels blau.
Davon fliegt alle schwere,
Und jubeln höre ich Chöre,
Ich bin ein Blümchen auf grüner Aue.

Ganz lustig zirpen die Grillen
Ganz leise weht der Wind,
Ganz nahe das glückliche stimmchen,
Von mein herzigen Kind.

Das bringt mir zurück die sonnige Tage,
Wo ich noch nicht kannte das leid.
Wo ich noch nicht hörte das Klagen,
Aus den Grab der Dunkelheit.
Das bringt mir zurück Sonne und Freud ,
Die Stimme meines Kindes liebes Glockengeleut'.

<u>Translation.</u>

'The Sun kissed the brown earth.
I lay in the green grass and look
Up into the endless blue sky.
All difficulties floating away,
And joyful I hear the choir,
I am a flower on the green lawn.

Quite cheerfully the grasshoppers chirp
And softly blows the wind,
Nearby the happy little voice,
Of my dearest child.

That brings back the sunny days,
When I knew not the sorrow.
When I knew not the lamenting,
Out of the grave of darkness.
That brings me back the sun and happiness,
My child's dear voice like bell ringing'.

(Written 1948)

Graphic;' Self Portrait with children'1949

1. Memories of Childhood.

My childhood was a very happy one. But the letters from my parents show a completely different world. Their story is nothing like my memory of my childhood; their desire to return to Dresden was always constantly present and their optimistic belief in a better and peaceful world so obvious. My parents protected us from their worries. Although we only lived in a very bad and damp flat, consisting of only two rooms and in extreme cramped conditions I was an optimistic and lively child. My earliest memories are of my mother playing the violin to me, singing songs her mother sang to her.

I remember my aunty Dinah came often to visit us. This lady was to become my adopted aunt. She was helping refugees from Nazi occupation and she was a very good friend of my parents.

How happy I was when my little sister arrived. Now we could play together, but then something happened and my mother became ill.

My mother told me how I took her round to a neighbour, trying to support her before she collapsed. She said I tried to support her with my small hands. The next episode I remember is being in a children's home playing with a new friend. I cannot say it was a nice place, but my father came to visit me as often as he could and above all my aunty Dinah came and I introduced her to my new friend. When I returned home my aunty Dinah continued to visit my friend I had left behind at the children's home and eventually my aunty Dinah adopted her.

It is no wonder that Gretel became so seriously ill after all she had gone through, but it is not exactly known what was really wrong with her. My little sister Lindy was only nine months old when Gretel fell ill. She was in hospital for nearly five months. A letter dated 3rd September 1947 that Peter wrote to Gretel's brother Hans reports that Gretel is still in hospital and that it costs him quite a bit of money, but its manageable. The costs are made according to his wages. Peter hopes that his unmarried sister from Düsseldorf will come over to help care for the children. Nearly everything is prepared. But aunty Trudy, Peter's sister, never came. My father reports how he only now found out that Gretel was in a half conscious state and had to be artificially fed for some time. Gretel looks now much better, but is still very weak.

It was a special delight when my mother played her violin to us and I continued to beg her to learn to play the violin also. When I found out that my mother wrote poems. That was it. I had to do the same. My mother's poems were of course mostly written in German and I think she tried to get us children to speak German as well, so that we would become bilingual and be able to speak both languages equally. Regrettably this plan did not work out. We went out playing with other children, muddling up the two languages and started to speak German instead of English. The result was disastrous, then the kids started taunting us as Germans, Nazis. After this, my parents concentrated on us speaking as perfect English as possible. The effect was amazing; the neighbours came up to my mother and said how beautifully we spoke English, better than their own children and asking how come, how did she manage it? Then my parents were very strict with us and we were not allowed to speak in the Berkshire dialect. Our English pronunciation had to be perfect.

Today, when anyone tells me I am German, they are wrong. I never have regarded myself other than English having been born here, lived here for the most part of my life. Over in Germany we were always regarded as English.

I remember 'Father Christmas' coming to visit us and I wondered why he sounded so like my mum! Sitting on his lap, listening to his stories was perfect and I was very happy.

I remember going out with dad, a trip to London and the visits to London zoo. He took us down to the allotment where he grew fresh vegetables and we had our own small tiny bit of earth to grow our own seeds.

Then there was the 'Tiger Hunter', an amazing interesting lady artist friend of my mother's. The friendship was mainly based on artistic interests only. Politically my mother and Mrs Moore were of completely different positions. This lady was a very talented excellent artist, and her wonderful paintings are still vivid in my memory today. I often wonder where her incredible beautiful paintings are today. What has happened to this lady's artwork? I think her name was Mrs Elsa Moore. When we went to her house we were always astonished at the loads of tiger skins she had; decorating the floor instead of carpets, and hanging over the settees and chairs.

The stories the Tiger hunter told, of her time with her husband in India, of her adventures in the Indian jungle were interesting and exciting to listen to. She stressed that she only hunted down man-eating tigers. She obviously was asked to do this from the residents who felt threatened by these dangerous animals. She said she only shot those tigers that had killed and hurt the civilians living in the villages near the jungle. She told us she went out alone to do this. She was a very rich lady, extremely well off with loads of money. It was an interesting friendship; the two, my mother and the 'Tiger Hunter'. For some reasons this friendship ended about 1957. I do not know the reasons, but I think the friendship ended due to political differences.

Out painting with the 'Tiger hunter'

They both, Gretel and Elsa learned from each other and went out together on painting trips. They both were members of the Maidenhead art club, and both exhibited in the same exhibitions with Stanley Spencer and the Cookham art club. This friendship, between the very rich wealthy Mrs Moore and the poor emigrant, my mother was remarkable and while it lasted, a happy one.

I will never forget the years 1950 – 1952; our living conditions were very bad, the rooms damp and wet. My parents always lived that time with thoughts of going back to the socialist German Democratic Republic. Apart from the bad living conditions we were not bad of. My father had work and my mother had sometimes part-time work. All house hold goods and other necessary acquirements for the household were reduced to a minimum. Everything pointed to a return to the GDR.

At first, when Gretel and Peter moved to 19 York Road in Maidenhead, they only had a one-room apartment. Later they receive a further room that was extremely damp. Living in this damp apartment caused my little sister to become ill with asthma. My parents were very protective and did everything to keep any of their worries away from us children.

Gretel's two children; Sonja and Lindy

I knew parents wanted to return back to Dresden and increasingly argued a lot about things. My childhood was a safer environment than my mother's. My parents were both concerned that we would grow up in a safer and more secure environment than they both had experienced. We knew they had made an application to return to East Germany about 1950. Their sadness and distress at the refusal for permission to return without any reason given was something they could not hide from us. I remember well those last years at the old damp flat, before we moved to the new council house, living among packed boxes. When at last the refusal came after years of waiting, both parents were very upset, especially my father, he then gave up all hope, my mother never gave up, but continued to believe and hope, her longing to return home dominated all else.

My years at the primary school were good happy years. I went to the 'Brownies' and Brown Owl was a good friend of my mother. I loved acting, and the last year at the primary school. I was given the opportunity to take part in a pantomime, ' Snow white'. I was given the main part as the witch. In this version, the witch a good witch, the queen was the bad one. I cannot remember the exact story line, but one scene is still vivid in my memory, the witch's desire to have beautiful long blond hair was to become reality if she could have the heart of a beautiful lady who had just died. She was to get this heart but not knowing that it was to be Snow White's heart. Instead, she was given the heart of a pig. After making the spell and sticking her head into the cauldron she came out with a head full of curly pig tails and looking into the mirror she said, 'Oh well, it's quite becoming!' Of course this scene brought laughter from the audience.

We went on holidays at the seaside, went walking in the Maidenhead thicket, along the River Thames and Chiltern Hills, we went with mum and the Tiger Hunter on painting trips, we went with dad to the allotment and when my sister was in convalescent home at the seaside because of her asthma, we went to visit her. The fact that we sat on packed boxes for about two years did not really worry me, then mum had told me lots of tales about our fairy tale uncle Hans. I was looking forward to meeting him.

For a while, mum worked at a garden nursery. Once my sister was selected to play the fairy queen in a play at the town hall. She was very pretty. Mum made the stage decorations.
One day a teacher came into our classroom to collect pupils for their violin lesson. That was it! I put my hand up and wanted to join in but the teacher refused. After all, my mum played to us regularly on her violin and I wanted to play the violin also. That day after school I ran home as fast as I could. Somehow I lost my hat somewhere; it 'flew' over a wall.
I arrived home breathless and mum very concerned asked; "What is wrong?"

I told her panting not waiting to catch my breath; "The tea..teacher would no..ot let me jo..oin in with the vio..violin lessons.."

The very next day mum went into town and bought me my own three-quarter-size violin, and so, eight years old, I started to learn the violin and joined in with the violin music lessons at school.

My mother was my first teacher. I learned to play extremely quickly and was soon top of the class. The violin lessons in school were very basic, but useful, and I very soon 'grew out of them' found them insufficient. I also could draw well at an early age. My mother told me that she recognized my artistic talents and said that she was concerned then an artist's life is not an easy one!

Another photo of Gretel's two children; Sonja and Lindy

Goat's head, terracotta, (approx 1950)

This inherited love and urge to play and write music and to creative art, is something I have inherited from my mother. Her incredible hard life, how she learnt to play the violin, as a 13 year old after losing her mother, pressing her nose on the windows of the cafes to hear and see the café musicians play, how she bought her own violin with the money she earned by baby sitting, how she was unable to bring the violin home as it was not acceptable to her father, not fashionable for girls that time and how she became an artist, a sculptress has had an impact on my own life.

My parents were very supportive. My mother prepared me for the audition to get into the Berkshire junior music school in Reading. At the audition the examiners just did not want to believe that my mother was my teacher. She had done such an excellent good job and prepared me well. They thought I must have had private lessons. That my mum was my teacher was something unbelievable. Those violin lessons at that primary school were definitely not enough, far too slow. That school had also a good art teacher that I found encouraging. I drew lots of pictures, composed many own little tunes as soon as I started learning. Regrettably, many years later these very early compositions were stolen, and lost; ruined by the Stasi[1] in East Germany during the raid in our flat in Dresden 1972 -1973. What sense the destruction of these pieces have, is a mystery, who would want to do this?

A little later, my mother paid extra for me to attend private lessons. My violin teacher was a good friend who played the violin in the Burham orchestra. This lady was a professional musician who used to play in a professional orchestra and now gave private music lessons. So now I not only went every Saturday morning during term time to the Berkshire junior music school in Reading, I also had these very supportive private lessons with my mother's friend

---

[1] Stasi; Secret police in East Germany.

from the Burnham orchestra. My mother played also in this orchestra and later took me on trips and on music courses. It was great fun and I was very happy.

It was only natural for me to copy my mother and also have a go at writing poems. Here are two of them. These two poems were inspired by my acting and my journeys to Reading to the music school.

Lady Godiver' Woodcarving

'The Witch' (aged 10)

'Through the dark night,
A witch came in sight,
With a nose,
From her head to her toes,
With red and green hair,
A head shaped like a pear,
All through the night,
The witch came in sight.'

'The Train to Reading,'(aged 12)

'The train to Reading ,
Goes rushing past.
Rushing along,
So very fast.
Field and hills,
Housed and mills,
The cows and sheep,
Of little Bo-peep,
Go rushing past,
So very fast.
The train to Reading,
At last does stop,
And out of the doors,
The people pop.'

From 1946 –1960 there were many exhibition possibilities for Gretel organized by the Maidenhead and Cookham art clubs. There were also exhibitions with the Artists International Association in London at the Hampstead Festival, also other exhibitions in London, Reading, and Eaton College.

Aquarelle; 'Boat on the Thames'

2. My parents never gave up.

The story from point of view from my parents, show a different picture. These extracts from letters express their longing to return, daily struggles and also the feeling of alienation living as a foreigner in Britain.

The restless life Gretel and Peter led, living in hiding, constant fleeing from Nazi terror, and after their arrival in Britain, thinking 'now we are safe' only to be interned by the British as aliens, all this had a disastrous effect on Gretel's health. She was not strong enough to return immediately after the war. Gretel and Peter had now two small children to look after, and this was given priority over everything else. Severe shortage of food and other daily necessities prevented a return to Germany straight away after the war. Dresden was in ruins. The occupying Russian authorities some years later, turned down the application for return to Dresden.

Woodcarving; 'Eve' 1945

16th November 1947, letter to uncle Hans informing him of the shortage and rationing of food and that we had a little garden where we grew our own vegetables. Gretel was now out of hospital since October. Little Lindy came out of the children's home with lots of sores and wounds on her body and during the four months in hospital she had hardly put on any weight. Peter desperately wants to return to Dresden to help build up a new and better world.

He writes that; "Here in England we are only the bothersome stepchildren!
In the first instant I must care for my two children. Here in England away from Germany, we can see clearly how the Nazis mislead the German folk."

It was a special treat whilst living still at that old small damp flat, when my mother went out painting with the 'Tiger Hunter' to enjoy the nice roast dinners my father made and the outings to the allotment. We were too small to go painting with mum and the 'Tiger Hunter'.

2nd December 1948 Gretel informs her brother that; "we are growing more and more out of this small flat. We are now on the list for better council accommodation, but I feel that I will become a grandmother before this happens.

Sonja is learning well at school, and she brings back home good drawings. Today she made more work than her smaller sister, pushing her little sister accidentally into the tub with the soaked washing. This made a lot of extra work in the small kitchen, cries and tears, but it was so funny and jolly."

She writes that she has started to model the two heads of her children.

Modelled in terracotta; 'Gretel's two girls'

1949; a letter to her brother Hans informs him that;

"We have good connections with the English comrades and people from the labour party. I am longing to see Dresden, I long to be home again. I lost my home with the death of my mother. At least here in England the children have their home, are happy and have enough to eat. That is the most important thing." She writes about the good critics of her artwork in the newspapers, about the Maidenhead art club and that she goes regularly to meetings and discussions as well as evenings where they paint, sketch and model.

She writes; "I am recognized as a professional, but many hearts in England want to see only modern art. It is very difficult here in England to get somewhere, especially as a socialist. I always thought I could help build up a socialist country in Dresden. Now you write that there is no workers art club in Dresden. Maidenhead is so small we have one here. Dresden is so big. I am sure I would get the support from the authorities to help build up something similar like we had in Prague back home in Dresden."

Gretel is so confident that she could sort something out, but that she is also aware that everywhere posh and nosey people would be around.

Another letter from Peter to Gretel's brother Hans informs him that since 1947 they have lost all contact with the other emigrants. He does not know who is still in England and who has left. He also tells him that it was Gretel's doctors that had advised him to postpone the return. He regrets and is sad that he has not enough money to visit his now 73-year-old mother once more. Travel would cost a week's wages.

He writes; "If you have children then there is nothing much left to save. Main thing we do not hunger and have enough to eat. The children do not hunger, but there is not enough variety of food, too much the same. But the children do not understand this."

He informs Hans that not everything is ok; "The other people in the house often make us understand that we are not wanted and should return to our own country. They would be pleased to see us go. They treat us like certain Germans, like certain people who came from Ostpreussen or Oberschlesien and were called Pollaken. It is mostly the children that upset them and go on their nerves but we cannot change that and they cannot do anything."

Gretel and Peter had to wait until 1950 to apply to return to the GDR. By now things were a 'little' different over there and it was not easy. They waited unsuccessfully for permission to return. Finally the long awaited decision came, a refusal without any reason given, after a two and a half year wait! Peter became bitter and cross, not understanding why he had been refused permission to return. He felt inclined to give up any further attempts. After all why, why should they, the East German authorities not trust him? He had done so much, he had fought in the underground movement, and he had stood up and talked against fascism and warned publicly at meetings about the dangers of the approaching Nazi terror. There had been a warrant out for his arrest and he suffered emigration and internment camp! He was so angry. This had also a disastrous effect on their marriage. Gretel on the other hand never lost hope. Her determination, optimism, courage and belief were exceptional. The Stalinist dictatorship in East Germany was not something my parents were aware of whilst living in England. This was not so obvious.

Throughout the next years Gretel continues to work artistically. New sculptures are created and she continues to go to the Maidenhead art club and she attends the university in Reading and Maidenhead as a part time student.

She has further exhibitions of her artwork together with other artists in London, Glasgow, Windsor, Eaton College and Reading as well as in Maidenhead and Cookham together with artists like Stanley Spencer. She also has commissions to sculpt garden sculptures and children's portraits as well as other work. She gains her professional recognition through her membership with the AIA[2] and has further exhibitions in London, Glasgow, Windsor, Eaton College, and Reading University.

She has work as a gardener, house help and other extra jobs in order to earn the necessary household money and continues her violin studies and plays in the Burnham orchestra.

She keeps up her hope to see her hometown Dresden again through connections with her artist friends, amongst them the Dresden sculptor Heinz Worner and Franz Fillinger, a well-known communist from Dresden. The contact with her brother Hans and her youth friend Ruth Altmann gives her support to keep up her positive views. 2nd November 1950, her brother Hans informs her that he now has completed his master exam as a cabinetmaker.

In another letter 1950 to her brother, she informs him;
"The children have lots of good food here more than we had as children. I play in Burham orchestra, made many new artworks and have painted loads of watercolour pictures". "The children are more rooted here more than you think, more than Peter believes. The disunion conflict of split and torn Germany is also our conflict. If you could hear the hateful talk here you would think twice about a return to a place that's like a second Korea."

Gretel's doctor is a Jewish emigrant from Austria and understands Gretel's worries. He treats her for all sorts of things, eye tests, hormone treatment etc. She models his son's head for him.

Gretel writes; "Peter says it is not my fault and I also say it's not my fault that we have not returned earlier, so it is possibly little Lindy's fault that she just came into the world that time, but in the end, isn't it the hospital's fault that they did not give my child the treatment she needed, she was given cold milk to drink and they refused to treat my sore breast. That was the beginning of my illness."

"I went to Sonja's school and told the teacher off that she must not hit my children. The teacher hit Sonja with the ruler on her head. She practically apologised. Sonja came home today because she is fed up with school meals. She says I am the best cook in the world and the best loveliest mother. Lindy just smiles silently."

In a letter 28th May 1950, Gretel reports to brother Hans of Peter's enthusiasm for Esperanto. She writes that there is no employment possibility in Maidenhead and that things were different in Prague.
"In Prague I was only a beginner. Now my work is so much better, but my sculpture work is ignored. I do not like living in Maidenhead. The children have so much better food than we had as children. This is their home. My feelings to return at this stage are completely split. I am not feeling well, have glandular problems".

16th December 1950, Peter receives a letter from his sister Martha from Düsseldorf with the sad news that his mother had died. She was 76 years old. Her last wish remained unfulfilled, to see her only son once more. When was it the last time she saw him. The letter also informs Peter about his brother in law complaining about Nazis at his work place.

Through letters I found out something I never knew as my father hardly ever spoke about his childhood. His parents were socialists and had suffered under the nationalists, the Nazis. Together with her husband they both educated their children to be good peace loving people. She could not see her only son again because he had to leave because of the political situation.

---

[2] AIA; Artist International Association in London.

1950 – 51; Gretel writes to Hans that the King of the UK had died, and now is time to write a letter. 'Lindy needs lots of milk; she is not so strong as Sonja. Here she can have sufficient milk. In spite of this I want to return. Peter does not seem to want to, or has second thoughts about going to the German consulate in London. I do not want to send things to the German consulate because of old Nazis being around. My children hardly speak any German'.

We were obviously living on packed boxes and cases, had hardly any own furniture. Gretel informs Hans about the too expensive price of furniture.

Obviously a newspaper wrote an article about one of the art exhibitions where my mother exhibited. Her artworks were given excellent good critics, but they wrote that the head teacher of the art school made the sculptures. Gretel complained about this mistake hoping it would be corrected. This head teacher had no artworks exhibited at this exhibition. Her works were given a different name under them.

Gretel writes; "Lindy cries when I speak about returning to Dresden. She is frightened to travel over the sea. But Sonja is different. She says it will be a great adventure and is pleased."

February 1951, a letter from Peter to Hans;
"We came here practically empty handed. Gretel had two cases and I came with only the cloths on my body. Everything was left behind in Prague. I never got back the cases I left behind with friends hoping for better times. Now it is too late and my belongings are lost. Now we have two children and a household as well as the artworks from Gretel. I want to prepare for the return but Gretel does not want to return to a ' second Korea'. I quite understand this opinion." "We need new things, warm clothing for the children and bed mattresses. Sonja often brings her breakfast sandwiches back home with her. She says she has no time to eat because she wants to play with the other children, or is it perhaps she dares not eat as the other children might take the food away from her? Today she was hit on the head with a ruler because she could not read quick enough. Luckily my wages are ok, not to bad."

This letter shows clearly the differences and hardships of the emigration years.
"In March this year, it will be nearly twenty years, for twenty years we took it for granted that we would one day be able to return. If it were for me personally, I would have returned long ago, I would not be living here anymore. Here things are getting more and more expensive. I am thinking about returning to Düsseldorf. But there also is no room, lack of housing and living space everywhere."

Peter's earnings were not bad but he has to work overtime to make ends meet.

April 1951; Gretel writes to her brother Hans; "Sonja is top of class playing the violin. Our hands are tied because of the children. It would be dreadful if they said to us, 'Why didn't you leave us in England. I am looking for work, but as a foreigner refused, not given any employment. It was not my idea to learn Sonja two instruments. Lindy does not like the violin. She says she wants to become a singer. Peter is not interested in a return. He believes that they will make him accusations that he did not return earlier. Lindy is ill again. Nosey Maidenhead orchestra does not want foreigners in their orchestra. I travel with the bus to another little town. There no one knows us and no one asks where we come from. These people are really friendly. I am not sure how we can finance the return journey. Please keep that little kitten for us then the children already cry about leaving their cat and goldfish behind."

Obviously I was already going to the Berkshire Junior music school in Reading where it was also a requirement to learn to play the piano.

A letter July 1951 from brother Hans informs Gretel that he now has full recognition as VDN[3]. Peter replies by telling him how extremely disappointed he is about the refusal to be allowed to return to Dresden. It seems he just gave up hope. Gretel was not willing to give up. This letter also reports about the death of his mother and that he saw his mother the last time 1928. He writes that he had hoped to get his sister over to England to help look after his children when Gretel was in hospital but his sister was refused permission to enter the UK. When the other emigrants returned he could not. He had two children to look after. He was worried that the authorities in the GDR[4] would not understand that he in the first instant wanted to look after his children. He thought that the authorities would take it badly, and not understand. After all they had now refused permission for them to return. He so wanted to be part of that new world and help rebuilding up socialism.

16th March 1952, again a letter questioning about how to finance the return to Dresden and on the 5th May 1952 Peter and Gretel were still waiting for a positive answer to be allowed to return. In the meantime they continued living at 19 York Road. The house was falling to pieces and extremely damp

22nd June 1952 finds both of them still waiting. Money is put aside for the return journey, but this is difficulty because of rising living costs.

June 1952;

"We have to give up ever getting a council house. Only childless couples and people with one child get it. What is wrong in Berlin, Why do we not get any answers?"

Obviously, about this time something happened in the GDR, revolt against the Stalinist regime.

Gretel writes to her brother;

"We also have followed the events from the last week in fear, and listened to the angry cries from the bloodthirsty war hyena in anxiety. We have had to hear these words quietly. It is sickening. I could give the answer with my artwork, but here this is lost endeavour."

3rd July 1952, a further letter to brother Hans tells him that;

"I am not giving up hope, one day I will knock on your door. Dresden is my home. I believe that in Dresden I will be on the better side. But I am condemned to rot here."

From these letters it is so obvious and clear the hard life and hardship my parents as well as my uncle Hans was suffering under, lack of strength to continue and to be optimistic.

A letter from brother Hans tells Gretel that;

"I believe your tired and broken frame of mind is the same as what is happening to us all over here as well. It is as if we are uprooted. That generation whose childhood had suffered during the First World War, whose youth was worn out by the years of the Second World War and now a time of fruitful happy creativity is made impossible due to the thoughts of a third world war!"

Concerning the application to return, a letter 5th August 1952 reports that;

"We have now sent of the proper forms that we received at last. They are now three months on their way. I wish so much to have a happy weekend up on the apple mountain[5]."

---

[3] VDN; Recognition as victims of Nazi oppression by the East German government.

[4] GDR; German Democratic Republic

[5] Apple mountain; Here is meant the mountain hut property. At that time many apple trees grew up there.

30th August 1952; "this miserable flat has a bad effect on Lindy's health. My large sculpture, a woodcarving is on a journey in an exhibition that is travelling around for months, from place to place. I am looking for work, but there is no hope. There are lots of sculptures in the park at Windsor in need of repair. As you may have heard we are going towards 'wonderful times'." Peter reports how his old bicycle was stolen and got it returned in pieces, also of an accident where a car drove over Gretel's bicycle. Police say they want to find the persons responsible but because they are 'foreigners are not taken seriously.

"Dear brother, when will we see each other again, if only for a few days? I have heard that here people buy the return tickets for their relatives, but that seems to be for those living in West Germany. The permission to come would then be so much easier to obtain."
Gretel's wish to see her brother that time 1952, as impossible as it seems was more realistic than my wish today, 2010 to see my sister again, thanks to Stasi interference.
I wish so much, if only for a day, to be able to see her again, to talk to her personally, but this will never happen, and I am so sad about this.

21st September 1952 finds my parents still waiting for permission to return.
"Which way should we travel, over Poland? As long as we get the visa to enter the GDR there is no problem to travel over Poland".
Obviously this question arose because of border problems.
"According to newspapers here, there must be loads of empty houses and flats because of thousands leaving daily, fleeing from East to West. I wonder if there is anyone left?"
This remark was written to brother Hans and proves the strong belief my parents had in a socialist society over in the GDR.

Peter wrote; "Here in England there are enough idiots that believe everything that is said in the newspapers. Lindy is ill again and now in convalescent home. She has asthma."
He mentions names of friends with whom there is no more contact;
"-Arno Schönherr, he was until 1933 chauffeur in the' Workers voice', (Arbeiterstimme).
-Max Schneider with whom Peter was in Australia in internment camp. He was from Chemnitz.
- Karl Becker was before 1933 'Reichstagabgeordneter',(member of the house of representatives; like house of parliament)
-Ilse Kroner; she came to visit us in Maidenhead 1945. She was from Berlin. She was with Gretel in internment camp on the Isle of Man. She helped Gretel when she was so seriously ill.
-Franz Fillinger;1933 – 1939 from Prague from the emigration years".

September 1952, as Gretel and Peter had heard nothing from the GDR authorities about the longed for return, Hans wrote to the GDR authorities asking how long it would take and informing them that; "its concerning the return from emigrants." By now, all contact with friends that have already returned was lost. Gretel and Peter were obviously isolated, there was no more contact with the other emigrants, we were still living at 19 York Road and waiting.
October 1952 finds both still waiting and wondering why it is taking so long for permission to enter the GDR, to return to Dresden. The Russian authorities did not trust my parents. Others, Polish emigrants received permission to return within a few weeks and they even got free travel papers, but my parents had to wait and wait so long. Peter fears that this pulling out could have negative effects. If he talks about this in England then this would be propaganda for the opposition. He fears he would have to keep quiet about this here and there.

Gretel writes to her brother about the price increases and the rationing. She writes how much her children enjoyed the meal, asking for more. She is distressed and finds it very disturbing about hearing that the old Nazi generals should go free and that they are supposed to be honest people! She is offended that Peter obviously wrote that he stayed in England because of her. She states in her letter that she had told Peter to get the return sorted out already one and a half years ago.

This was the start of arguments and disagreements between my parents, the unhappiness and unsettling life, living in a foreign country, not being able to return earlier.

Peter wrote to uncle Hans informing him;
"We now have an offer for a council house. We have hardly enough money to buy a bed. We need to keep what we have for our return. This is the main reason why I have not accepted the offer from my employers. If we do not accept this offer we will have to stay in this one. The only way out is to get an answer as soon as possible. I have filled in the forms and sent them of. When will we get an answer?"

8th March 1953 found Gretel and Peter with their children still living at 19 York road. A move was now inevitable. The house owner wanted to sell the house. How to afford a move with furniture and also keep something for the pending return and little Lindy constantly coughing ill with asthma was a constant worry.

Gretel informs her brother about the general political condition in England;
"If I tell the political opposition the truth, then I get the answer it is free for me to go back if I want and they tell me I am better of here. As we are still waiting for an answer about our application to return, this is food for them."

15th March 1953 finds Gretel again writing to her brother;
"Last night I dreamt of you. The return to Dresden seems impossible. It is so offensive to see how easy it is for others to travel to Germany, but we are as good as denationalised, deprived of civil rights as punishment because we are anti-fascists. Thanks for your letter. It is strange that it took so long to get here. We are feeling extremely bitter that they, the Russians, treat us so incorrectly and give us no answer. If Peter had returned with the others, he would have had to leave me ill behind with two small children. How can they regard that as the correct thing to have done! Lindy is now 14 days in hospital with pneumonia. Why can't those in Berlin understand that we at last want to live-in peace and rest? Or is it only possible for them to understand only old previous Nazis and excuse them?"

20th April 1953;
"We found our names in the local newspaper that we are to get a new council house. That is all we know at present. That is custom here. They start to build the house after your name appears in the newspaper. We have to move out of this damp flat. Now we have a council house. It costs slightly more than a week's wages. I never could believe that we would get such a house. We have as good as no furniture and no money to buy any with. For the children, you are their fairytale uncle. They saw a man in town and said, our uncle could look like that."

How my parents suffered and how they longed to return, to belong somewhere, to be part of a new peaceful world. This is so obvious in their letters, yet they made it possible for us to have such a happy childhood and kept these worries away from us as much as possible.

Then at last it came, the long awaited answer, but the permission to return was refused without any explanation, a return denied. My parents who had suffered so much were told that they were not wanted in the GDR. No one can even imagine their disappointment and my father's anger at this refusal. He was so bitter and angry. A short while later, Peter had a serious accident, was ill for some time. It took him a while with difficulty to recover.

Aquarelle; The river Thames by Maidenhead

Our window at our new council house

Three sculptures on this photo are now lost. These three sculptures must still be somewhere, left behind in Maidenhead. On my return 1984 I never got back home to Maidenhead. Instead I landed in Leicestershire.

CHAPTER 8.

Pining to Return 1953- 1960

'Out with dad'

1. Family life.

Life in the old damp flat was becoming increasingly difficult. The dampness affected Lindy badly, causing her ill health, asthma and bronchitis. The move over to Dresden, years later proved to be good for her. She never suffered from asthma again as long as I knew her. But at this time, it was not easy. Are we going over to Dresden? Are we going to stay? Are we going to move to another house? The future seemed so uncertain. I remember collecting addresses from my friends because of the constant talk of returning to Dresden. It was an unsettling time. I knew my mother wanted to go back home so badly.

A letter Gretel wrote to her brother Hans tells of the sadness, feeling of alienation and her yearning to return home after living for such a long time away from her place of birth. After all, she had been driven out of home, had to escape from approaching Nazi terror. At first, her flight to the Czech republic was supposed to be only temporary and Prague was not that far away from her beloved Dresden. Her time spent in Prague, in spite of the hardship of emigration was one of the happiest times in her life, giving her study opportunities and experience as an artist.

In her letter to her brother, she wrote; "When will we see each other again. I am so sad. Why do we not get an answer about our application to return? Is this the punishment we get because we kept to our political opinions for socialism? Is this our reward? I wonder if this uncertainty, waiting and waiting, no answer, sabotage from the opposition? Why don't we get an answer, why? We are still sitting in this old damp place and the walls are falling down onto our heads! A few days ago the worker's newspaper announced that West Germans are returning to East Germany."

Following letter Gretel wrote to her brother clearly confirms the problems of a split nation, divided by different political views and the 'cold war' atmosphere;

"I have no luck selling my artwork here, especially in Maidenhead. In order to be able to sell the major's head I have modelled I needed to have been born here in Maidenhead with British qualifications. The talk about war, is taking away the taste to return, but a holiday must be possible."

Brother Hans advises Gretel and Peter to go over to West Germany first, but Gretel is not prepared to do that and would rather stay in England. Gretel's answer to this advice is; "Why can't we go straight to Dresden. We would have to be real idiots if we went to the American colony West Germany. Here it is not so bad, although prises are on the increase.
Hans is there really voices over war atmosphere? Isn't the cry coming from the other side of the ocean? What do you mean when you write that your good opinion is broken!"

That year, 1953, because my little sister was always seriously ill as a result of the bad damp housing we had lived in, we were to receive a council house and move to the Larchfield Estate by Maidenhead. We would now have a lovely house, plenty of room, no more cramped conditions and a garden.

July finds Gretel working hard in a garden centre but the situation was not ideal. The long awaited answer concerning Gretel and Peter's application to return to Dresden came just as we were preparing to move to the new council house; a refusal! This denial to Gretel's right to return home was devastating. No reason was given and no idea why the return was refused. Peter was extremely bitter and Gretel very upset. This was a most unsuitable position to be in for a future life together. Gone were the days when our 'two blues' were happy. The Russian authorities that were in control of East Germany refused to give permission to return. Gretel was so homesick for Dresden, for the beautiful countryside, the deep dark woods, and Saxonian Switzerland, the wonderful countryside at the border between Germany Saxony and Bohemia.

30th May 1953; in this letter Peter informs Gretel's brother Hans of the devastating bad news about the refusal from GDR authorities to allow them to return. Peter writes that they do not believe it is possible in their opinion to allow us to get the visa for return to the GDR. They gave no reason, just these few words which made no sense. My parents just could not understand this.

Gretel writes back to her brother Hans;

"Everyone knew that we were going back. Everyone else thinks the UK is the best country, in spite of conservatives, increased living standards and costs. Now Peter is forced to accept lies and to stay here. In a few weeks we are going to move and extra costs of moving are put on him. As we are now forced to stay here, no one can make us further accusations. He wants to protest about this refusal to give him permission to return, and to keep costs down to a minimum."

I was now starting secondary school, but what a difference to the happy times at the primary school. There was a lot of prejudice and racial harassment because of my German parents. The head teacher made nasty racist anti German remarks in front of the school about me and always looked down on me. His hatred was so obvious. Especially the history teacher was particularly bad. She looked like a 'witch', had a very red face and a particularly crooked nose, so it seemed to me as a child. Her face is still vivid in my memory. The very first lesson with her was spent, each of us standing up and telling everyone our names so that she could write them down. When my turn came and I said my name, she cried out, "Ha, we have a German in our class," that was 1953 approx. That ruined many friendships from the start for me. At that time I could hardly even speak a word of that language. As young children we could not even think of speaking German outside our front door, then stones were thrown at us.

After my experience with this secondary school, my parents decided to send my little sister when her time came to change schools, to send her to a different school, that was more into religion; a religious school.

The art and music teachers were good. I continued taking part in the class violin lessons, was top of the class in music, and wrote my own music that was later lost by Stasi intervention. I also played violin solo regularly, sang in the choir in school and was selected to take part in a major event in London singing in the choir at the Albertinum Hall. I cannot remember the composer who wrote the piece we sang. It was called ' The High Adventure.' The composer was very well known. My mother proudly reports to her brother that from 500 children in my school I was one of nine children chosen to take part.

By now I also went regularly every Saturday morning to the Berkshire junior music school in Reading. My parents were very supportive and paid privately for my music lessons. The music school in Reading was brilliant. We had regular concerts, I took regular exams and now I was also learning to play the piano. My mother also took me on a music course that took place in a cloister.

My parents made it possible for me to take part on an organized school trip to Scotland. I wanted so much to climb up mountains like my uncle Hans. Mum even bought me new shoes, but then the teacher only allowed the boys to do this. Instead, the girls were taken on a bus trip to the coast. I was so disappointed and upset. On the way to the coast the bus stopped by a lake for a short break. I had climbed down a small slope to look at the lake. It was a very lonely place and beautiful scenery, but how scared I was, when I climbed up the slope and saw the bus driving of in the distance without me! Those teachers had not checked if everyone was in the coach. I ran after the bus, waving desperately. Luckily, someone on the bus noticed my desperate vigorous waving and eventually the bus stopped, but it was already quite a way of. I was so shocked, but the teachers were so ignorant and uncaring.

How glad I was when this school ended. There was too much racial harassment in that school.

One problem my parents had in those years was the fact that they were always regarded as unwanted foreigners. If we children had any problems, were harassed or experienced any kind of danger from certain individuals and my parents wanted to contact a person in authority, or the police to complain about something, they were just ignored and not taken seriously. However, my childhood was a very happy one. I had wonderful very supportive and protective parents. They did everything they could possible to make sure we both were happy, and kept their worries as much as possible away from us.

Gretel continued to exhibit in Cookham, every other year 1954, 56, 57,58, 59, and 60, also at the Slough Arts Festival, often together with the well-known artist Stanley Spencer. There were further exhibitions in London at the Hampstead Festival. She never stopped working and created many fine artworks. My father eventually bought most of them with over to Dresden, but many fine artworks are lost, were left behind in Maidenhead.

Now we were living in a proper house, had more room and a garden and because my little sister was so often ill, my parents decided to keep chicken, so as to give her fresh eggs. They were concerned to offer us good and healthy food. It was jolly having our own chicken, hearing them clucking away in their enclosure that dad had made. Often the neighbour's children came round with left over scraps of food for our chicken. They usually received an egg as a present. Once mum asked a little boy who had bought something round; "have you got the egg I gave you?" He slapped his pocket with his hands and the egg broke. It was so funny!

We had also other pets. One day we came home after a visit to the cinema only to find out our beloved tortoiseshell cat was gone. Dad told us it had died and he took it away. We were, as can be imagined in a distressed state and went to look for it. The next two evenings we went out looking for our cat. She had been such a great and truthful companion. Eventually we found her, but never found out why and how it had died so suddenly and unexpectedly.

My father did not like cats. This was not always the case. We believe that a cat running across his path may have caused the accident he had, also some boys had been making fun of him and teasing him.

There is the story about my pet tortoise Oswald. He was a sweet little fellow and my little white mice. They often had baby mice and we used to take the young mice down to the pet shop where I got some pocket money for them. One day, whilst on my way to the pet shop, I looked into the box I had them in and counted; one, two, three,...one is missing, one little mouse had somehow disappeared. I wondered why the man in the shop was laughing when I gave him my little young mice, telling him one had disappeared. On the bus on the way home a woman began staring at me, gasping and said breathless;
"Little girl, little girl you have a mouse by your neck!"
That's what had happened! That little mouse had hopped out of the box without me realizing, crept up my sleeve and had made itself comfortable by my collar.
The time came when I did not want to keep mice any longer. I had one little old lady mouse left. She was, for a mouse very old. As she was now on her own she became depressed and hung hours upside down on her feet from the little platform where her nest box was.
Mum insisted; "Go get her a companion," and I got her a nice young male friend. She livened up instantly and had baby mice again.

One day out walking with mum and my little sister we noticed a little bird on the street flapping around. I picked him up and he sat on my finger, beak open begging for food. It was a little baby starling obviously lost. No other birds were around and we were anxious that no cat would get him. He was from the start quite tame. We took him home, all the time he sat on my finger looking at us, beak open chirping and begging for food. We called him Henry and he was a wonderful pet.
At first, he could not feed himself, only flying to us with opened beak expecting the food to somehow fly into his beak by itself. This was a problem. How can we show him how to feed himself? We had a canary and so thought that if we placed his cage next to the canary's cage he might be able to learn. It took some time. Henry would look at his food with opened beak expecting it to fly into his beak by itself.
He often sat by the kitchen hatch when we had supper always begging for food, beak open. Regrettably he became too tame and stayed with us. We gave him as much freedom as possible allowing him to fly around the house as he pleased. Mum was anxious that we treated him correctly and thought it a good idea to enter him in a competition in town for the best-kept pet bird. We took him there in his cage and he sat happily chirping looking at the other birds around him. How surprise we were, when at the end of the show we went to fetch him and perhaps have a talk with someone about our Henry, when we discovered he had won the first prize as best kept bird.

Then there was Pixy, our little dog. One day on my way home whilst passing the pet shop I saw little tiny puppies in the window. One little dog waggled forward and glared at me as if asking; 'take me with please woof woof!' Next day mum went with us to the pet shop and we took her home. She was a very special little dog, a fox terrier.

'The Ice-cream Van.'

'When the music of the ice-cream van
Makes the children to their mothers run,
My dog, running along the garden path,
Standing at the door,
Trying hard to say,
"It's ice-cream I adore,
Dear mistress, as the season is ever so hot,
I like the ice-cream better than the stew in your pot".

(Written appox.1958)

I had a lovely time at that council house with friends, roller-skating around the estate, my music, painting pictures with mum. Although I knew she longed to return home to Dresden it was a happy time. I loved playing with my puppet theatre. I loved telling stories and the children often came round to listen to the tales I told them. One morning during school holiday time, I woke up to find a group of neighbours children sitting in the garden peacefully waiting for something!

When mum asked what they wanted, they said; "We are waiting for the puppet theatre. There is always puppet theatre here!"

2. Unexpected arrival of uncle Hans.

At last we had a proper house, but this luck was over shadowed. A short time after we had moved to our new home 1954, my father had a serious road accident. It happened on his bicycle on his way home from work. It seems that some boys were teasing him, cycling round and round my father and causing a car to collide into him. He was ill for a long time and had to suffer under the effects for the rest of his life. The police were either unwilling or unable to find the culprits of this accident. Peter was in hospital for four weeks, seriously ill with a head injury, concussion, lame in one leg, and the nerves of one of his eyes paralysed causing loss of sight in the one eye.

Gretel's letter to her brother Hans, reports of the seriousness, even though Peter was now back home, how very ill and helpless he still was. Luckily Gretel had work, picking apples in an orchard. She still hoped for a return as soon as possible.

My father never fully recovered from his accident, and life became difficult living with him. This accident, and the disappointment of the refusal to return without any reason given, made him very vulnerable. My poor father, he suffered so much, and now submitted to giving up hope ever to return. He was so ill, had no strength and no energy left. He now often became very angry.

A return was now not possible because of my father's ill health and his accident. Gretel's desire to see her brother again and her longing to return to Dresden increased daily. All work and worries were now on Gretel's shoulders alone. She had some work during the school holidays. Although some sick money was coming in, the authorities took of more money, and they wanted to take more. Gretel felt as if Peter had forgotten her.

Short while later, Peter was sent to a convalescent home. Workers from his work place organized this convalescents home and Peter had paid into the scheme for many years. Gretel complains to her brother that it took a long time for him to write to her from the convalescent home.

Gretel writes to Hans; "My home country is so far away like the moon from the earth. I wish so much to see you, dear Hans at least for a few days, perhaps somewhere at the border between East and West."

To add to the worries Lindy was seriously ill again with asthma and bronchial catarrh. Gretel also had stomach complaints and could not eat certain things, Her next letter to Hans tells of her new job, working in a garden nursery, and now has the possibility to earn a little more money. Again asking;

"Where can we meet? My stomach is a little better now. Peter is much better but I think he will never really recover from the accident. He does not want to leave the new house but I still want to return. I am concerned that a return will not be a financial improvement but hopefully I will eventually receive recognition for my artwork. Here, alone the name Klopfleisch is enough to refuse me recognition. I receive loads of invitations to take part in exhibitions, but work is taking my time away. Peter can stay here. I want to return. Peter is now working overtime again and too tired to do anything else."

There is talk about getting the English nationality and that would mean easier travel. There is constantly the wish and hope to see her brother Hans again. Gretel is aware that financial things will not be better in Germany, and that we would not get such a nice good house but she wants to return for completely other reasons;

"I feel like crying when I hear old German folk songs in the radio and see pictures of Saxonian Switzerland. I wish my children would be able to speak my mother language. Life is passing and we still live as foreigners here. As much as I fight against it, my love for my home country is always present. The relatives from Düsseldorf have never invited us over ever. Otherwise I would have gone there long ago. Peter's six sisters have never come to visit us. Also here, my artwork is regarded as foreign. They say, they do not have the English feeling and the English spirit. A short while ago, a friend from the Burnham orchestra came to visit us. She expressed that my work was not British enough! Most of my artwork is far to free thinking, there is too much of this in my work."

Years pass by and still Gretel has the urge and desire to return.

A letter sent to Hans about 1956 asks; "I wonder if it would be better for permission to enter the GDR with an English pass or a stateless emigrants pass. Which is better? Peter now has no longing to see his home country, he is only curious. The question is not if I can live from my art, I can't live on it here either. It seems that I am condemned to live in banishment, in exile, while others travel to and fro. For me there is no possibility. In the mean time my strength is disintegrating and disappearing."

"The English wet and damp foggy climate is a disaster for my health. One has to be prepared to accept Peter's 'April weather' moods. Any time a thunderstorm could break out. This makes it difficult for us to live here. It made me quite nervous that I was unable to take care of him properly because I had to go to work. When the children were small I could leave them with Peter. Now I was trying to go with a group of English tourists to West Germany, but because I was ill could not. It will not harm the children to learn some German. My children talk so much about uncle Hans that the children on the street played uncle Hans, (he seemed to be a sort of fairy tale figure)."

Gretel is so very sad.

Peter and Gretel made an application to claim for compensation as Victims of Nazism, (odf)[1] through the West German authorities. Now they were expecting an answer. This claim for compensation would have given them some financial security. It was later turned down. A denial was not something they expected. They were told that there was not enough evidence. According to West Germany laws Gretel and Peter did not need to flee from the Nazis. There were no witnesses that the SS wanted them. In order be eligible to receive compensation my parents should have been Jews, not anti-fascists.

One day, 1956 something unexpected happened. Mum was working at the garden nursery, it was summer holiday time and I had just made something for lunch for my little sister and myself. We were just about to have lunch when there was a knock at the door. On opening it we were greeted by a little man, dressed in an unusual way. He had knickerbockers[2] trousers on, a huge rucksack on his back and wore a hat with a feather in it. I did not understand what he said and only understood; "…Uncle Hans, uncle Hans.. …."

There was no doubt in my mind who he was. At last, there he was, suddenly standing in front of the door before us, our fairy tale uncle Hans. He had come to visit us at last. He just appeared one day that summer holiday at our door. We had no idea that he was going to come. His visit was so unexpected, a complete surprise. We shared our lunch and then set out to my mother's work place.

I will never forget my mother's face on entering the garden nursery with uncle Hans. She was sitting there with her workmates also just finishing lunch. The surprise to see her brother again so unexpectedly after so many years was nearly too much for her. She knew nothing of this unexpected visit. The shock was great, but how glad and happy she was to see him again after such a long time. Somehow, my mother then managed to get free of work.

Uncle Hans had managed to come over to Britain illegally. As a pensioner he was able to obtain a permit to visit West Germany and with help from friends he came over to Maidenhead, but he got into trouble later on for that with the East German police who somehow had found out about his illegal visit. He was not happy that Gretel wanted to return to Dresden. He already saw what was going to happen later on.

Uncle Hans came again to visit us the next year but on his return journey was confronted at the border by the Stasi and had to undergo a scrupulous interrogation. This interrogation resulted in a court case1957. Uncle Hans was fined 250 DM[3] for unlawfully taking out and bringing back East German money. He was also fined a further 200 DM for doing something that was against the law.

I found the documents concerning this court case. They report that; before 1933 he had belonged to the workers organizations, the red sports organisation and the socialist workers youth organisation. Because of this activity he was punished with illegal activity and preparation to high treason. He was punished with imprisonment for one year ten months. Because of this he was declared unreliable for military service. He was not taken for service in the fascist army in Nazi Germany. Instead, 1943 he was put into the 999-probation battalion and sent to Greece.

January 1945 he sent to a hospital in Germany because of illness and from there, into a prison camp. Through the frontier clearance he was dismissed out of the English prison camp and sent into the Soviet prison camp, which was not realized. Instead he was sent back to Dresden. He then helped rebuild his father's cabinetmakers workshop, which had been

---

[1] (odf) ; Claim for compensation from West German authorities.
[2] Knickerbockers; short baggy men's trousers clasped below the knee. Also know as 'plus fours'.
[3] DM; East German money.

destroyed during the bombing of Dresden. 1950 he took his master exam. Because of illness and accident he received a disability pension, was recognized as VDN, was member of the KPD. By a party inspection 1951 in East Germany, through his own comments and because of his opinion of the ideological weakness of the East German party was thrown out.

Apart from the fascistic punishment during the Nazi time he was not previously convicted and he was not on remand. The documents state further that he wanted to visit us in England, but was only offered two English pounds. He was of the opinion that this was insufficient, that he would have to be too much reliant on our pockets, that it would cost us too much to keep him.

An uncle of one of his friends who lived in the West was prepared to help him and offered uncle Hans to leave him 200 West DM in Hannover at a post office. Uncle Hans could fetch it on his way through. The permission for this trip took too long, was delayed. Because of this uncle Hans feared that this money would no longer be available for him and so he decided to take 400 DM East German money with, hidden in his bag. His fear was not necessary. The money was still at the post office in Hannover for him on his way through. East German money was of no use any way and not accepted in the West. He stayed six weeks in England with us, went back over Holland. During his absence there was a change in Money currency. But he did not know about the circumstances.

He had about 600 old East German DM money that was not valid anymore. He then said at the East German border on his way home that he had 1000 DM left. Obviously he was forced to say how much he had at home and would have been able only to exchange that amount. Because of this, he said he had 1000 east DM left. He was then taken to a room and given a thorough interrogation, an examination and threatened with a body search. Because of this he admitted that he had this 400 East German money with him. Because of this he was punished and fined. He now had a criminal record!

During his stay with us in Maidenhead there were currency exchanges and the old East German money was no longer valid. It was forbidden, against the law to take out of the Soviet zone any money into the other occupied zone of the country. Also, he had brought back with him 105 West DM. To bring back West money into the soviet occupied zone was also forbidden.

According to the document of the court case 13th October 1957 an exchange rate happened that was necessary because a large amount of money was put into circulation in uncontrolled channels that lead to damaging conditions for the GDR. They wrote that it was to be recognized that this exchange was made necessary because of criminal activity against GDR currency laws. Any one found guilty of this crime was given sever punishment. My uncle Hans was very lucky to have avoided a prison sentence. He was even forbidden to bring in the 105 West DM. This money was probably confiscated. The last paragraph of court case states that; after considerable consideration the court came to the opinion that the accused did not belong to those that needed a prison sentence to come to their senses and that a fine would be sufficient.

My parents were not fully aware what was happening. Perhaps my mother would have thought differently if she had known the full facts of this case. But things were not good in Maidenhead, my mother's constant wish to return home to Dresden and the fact that although I as a child was happy, and mostly unaware of my parent's problems, we were still regarded as foreigners, as Germans.

Modelling uncle Hans

In the meantime life in England continued. My time at the secondary school ended and I was very glad that it was over. I was hoping to study at the art school, but I was not accepted. I wanted to take after my mum. Instead she made it possible for me to attend Elmsly School for girls, a private school in order to get the necessary GCE exams needed to study. I went there from 1958 to 1960. My mother went extra weekends working at a hotel and put the money aside to pay for my studies.

Here also certain teachers were prejudice against me. An English teacher spoke in class about 'how life would be in heaven' and that in future certain children from poorer working class parents would be influenced from earliest childhood to do simple work in factories etc by putting some kind of recording devise under their pillow when sleeping so that they would not want anything else.

The French teacher was also very racist. Her racial hatred against black people was incredible. Once in a class lesson she said that coloured people were only half human. She gave me a leaflet about her religion, telling me how important this was. I felt so angry, and at first wanted to stand up and tell her to stop, but I did not want to spoil my opportunity to get my GCE exams. A little while later, I was able to payback. My chance came to tell her what I thought of her.

I had elocution lessons, and loved acting. The elocution teacher was a fine lady. As part of my elocution lessons I took part in a play at the end of term at Christmas time. I was given the part of Ritter Blue beard. The poor elocution teacher gave up trying to get me to act cruel and vicious, especially one part where I had to go to the front of the stage, stare into audience, laugh viciously whilst rubbing my hands together because of what I had done to my wives. I just could not be cruel enough. But on day of the performance, I saw this racist French teacher in the audience and I stared and glared at her and I did it. She got so red in her face. For the second performance I purposely searched the audience to find her and did it again. My acting was good and the audience laughed, but that teacher knew why I looked at her so.

This teacher was not popular and everyone knew why I stared at her. Once the pupils decided to play a joke and tied all sorts of things, old tins and bits of coloured paper on the back of her car.

But the other teachers were very good, more progressive and better. The maths teacher was very good. She belonged to the CND. Christmas time we went carol singing to collect money for the CND. The German teacher was a very nice and friendly lady. The art teacher was excellent and very supportive. She knew my mother as she also exhibited in Cookham and was also a member of the art club. The science teacher taught us how nature developed. She spoke of how life on earth progressed, the various stages of development, the science of evolution, the different periods in time, from dinosaurs to early humans and today. This was a particular difficult task in such a religious environment.

In this school there was such a mixture of teachers of different social opinions, that racist teacher as mentioned earlier and teachers of more positive social opinions. The head teacher was also a very fine friendly lady. This school was good for me and I am so grateful to my parents for making it possible for me to complete my studies for the GCE exams.

I took part in concerts at the Saturday morning music school, continued with serious studies with my violin, composing melodies and wrote poems. To this day I do not understand why these compositions I wrote as a child should have been stolen! The poems prove that I was a very creative child. Why should the Stasi have taken these away?
How best to write about my happy childhood other than to describe it in my own way by the poems I wrote that time;

'The Fiddler' (aged 13)

'I hear their sweet melody,
All the summer long.
Of crickets and grasshoppers, do I see,
And of birds singing their song.

All summer long,
Are grasshoppers, in bright green waistcoats,
As I listen to their merry throng,
I hear a fiddler's merry tune,
Happy that winter is over so soon.

That merry fiddler, I went to find,
And I wondered, if he was as kind,
As I imagined him to be.
I looked, my fiddler I could not see.

Then a voice seemed to say,
'Looking for me?'
I looked, and there, starring at me,
Just tiny enough for me, to see,
Dressed in a waistcoat of green,
Was my fiddler so keen.

It was a grasshopper,
Yes, a tiny grasshopper.
The fiddle was it's back,
The bow was it's tiny back legs.

With legs and back, to me he played,
The violin, all day.
Then with a skip and a hop,
Before I could say pop,
He hopped and flew away,
Saying, 'I'll come back another day.'

And as I went on my way,
All through the long day,
I heard my fiddler, fiddling so keen,
Dressed in a waistcoat of bright green'.

150

'My dog.' (written 1957)
Concerning our little dog Pixy.

'She welcomed me,
With a woof and a bark,
And a wag of her tail,
I saw in the dark,
A pair of large eyes,
A small tiny face,
With a look rather wise,
She's young and frisk,
And full of play,
I'm just glad
She came my way,
She came to me
At Christmas tide,
Into the world
That's big and wide,
Christmas joys to us
Did she bring,
And carol with us
She did sing.
I hope that in future days,
A lot of fun she'll bring our ways.'

Graphic; 'Music'.

3. The Easter March.

My mother had told us many tales about the early demonstrations in Germany against the Nazis and the Keglerheim protest and demonstrations for peace. So when the Easter peace march began 1958, it was certain we also would be part of this event. Now we would experience what it was like and what it meant to take part on a demonstration like this. Those next three years 1958/59/60, this experience will forever be in my mind and when I returned to school that first year after I had been on the Easter peace march and proudly reported where I had been over Easter, it was with dismay that I received as a reply from a lady at school; "We are bound to blow ourselves up." I just could not understand someone saying this. Contact with people on the CND march helped my mother to return to Dresden.

My own words about the Easter March written 1960;
"I lived in a country, where although the trees had leaves and the sky was blue, a black cloud hung over the land. It was like a claw, like a horrible shadow, it was a thing, not wanted. The river continued to go its way, through fields, woods and towns, the grass continued to grow, the flowers to bloom and the sun to shine, sometimes. But there was often rain, and fog, and the people slept. The people were friendly enough and quite helpful to strangers, too much. There were of course some good eyes, they knew the truth but had not yet let themselves be seen. At last it got too much to bear, ' We want peace, we want a world without that black cloud, we want to live' was the cry. And then it happened, the next three years that I will never forget."

It was an incredible experience spending Easter this way. The first year, on the way through Chiswick, London we were exhausted, as again we had been marching in rainy weather, there came a lady towards us and offered to take us to her home. She wanted to do something, to be part of this event and so she let us stay that night in her house. This was her contribution to the march. She was a widower and her only son had died in the war in Japan. We said we are also marching so that never again a mother would lose her only son in a war.

The next year she stood there waiting for us. She had clapped her hands sore. This time she stood there with a rattle in her hand. Again we stayed the night at her home. The third year1960 it was certain that we would see her again.

I found following report my mother wrote about the Easter March. I believe she spoke about this experience at a peace meeting in Dresden 1964.

"1958, about 50 young London workers and students decided to demonstrate against the Atom bomb, to march to Aldermaston where a large hydrogen bomb factory was. Parts of London were still in ruins, and already again there was preparation for another new even worse war; the Atom war. These courageous 50 Londoners marched through storm and rain. It was a four daylong march. Their cry; ' Ban the Bomb, we want to live in peace', caused great excitement. The march started with only 50 people, but at the end of the march it grew to over 500 people and they were greeted heartily everywhere they went.

1959 an already excellent organized march met at Aldermaston for this year's anti-war demonstration and marched to London. This time it started with 600 and grew rapidly to thousands. Many countries sent delegations to join and demonstrate with us. The unity and discipline between the different delegations from the different countries was exemplary and became for everyone taking part an unforgettable experience.

We slept on bare floors in schools and town halls. It was a great strain, but in spite of this, many took part from all walks of life, from all stages of society, all ages and religious groups and many with political differences. They all came together in one mighty united front, ' for peace, equality, and for a humane life'.

1960; at the end of this year's march there were over 100 000 people demonstrating. It was the biggest demonstration in England since 100 years, not seen since. This cry for freedom against the atom bomb was heard all over the world and found many enthusiastic followers. In the year 1963 Aldermaston was closed.

It was a great experience for my daughter and myself, to be part of this event and to be among the hundred thousand people that demonstrated in London, to raise our voice united for peace.

Class-conscious workers and political indifferent citizens of all classes and professions marched together in unity for peace and against the atom bomb. Many well-known people were on the march; Cannon Collins from the English church march at the front of the demonstration in his priest robes as well as many other well-known religious clergymen, for example pastor Niemöller from Germany. There were delegations from all over the world.

Hundred thousand people got together at the end of the march and from that, about forty thousand had been marching all the way, about fifty-five miles, that is about hundred kilometres on that long four day march. Our night quarters were on the floor of some schools and church halls; our meals were taken often during the long walk or at the edge of the road and we continued to march in wind and rain.

The idea was to inspire the population as we past by to come and join in, to convince and explain and clarify the dangers of an atomic war. We called out again and again, 'join the march, ban the bomb.' And we met many sympathetic people.

Many of us had sore feet from walking, but we continued on our march and we grew and grew. We sang many peace songs and our peace call rolled from one end of the mighty crowd to the other. A group of Scots in their national costume played the bagpipes and one Scotsman played on his drum to help tired feet to continue walking. You could hear many different languages being spoken. The dancing and singing of a group of Africans contributed to an even more colourful picture. There were delegations from America, from Japan and India, also from Sweden, Holland and Franz. There was a special delegation from Hiroshima.

Youth was strongly represented and there was a large group of socialist youth and a large group of Jewish youth. United the communist party, the socialist party and trade unions marched together. Also there were many nuns, monks and priests in their religious robes on the march. There were wanderers with rucksacks and some had dressed themselves in fancy dress in carnival costume.

Children were pushed in prams and carried on their father's shoulders. Even war veterans with war injuries came along with us some of the way. I played on my mouth organ worker songs and peace songs. I marched together with a delegation from West Germany. My heart laughed as I discovered an English lady carrying a peace banner from Dresden; A white dove on a blue background; Coventry – Dresden. I managed to convince her to allow me to carry this banner part of the way, then Dresden is my hometown. Of course there was also opposition. A car with a loud speaker on it appeared often, and spoke out for the rearmament. A group of unschooled young boys cried out propaganda; 'bigger and better bombs'.

During the second year a group of Catholics lead by their priest in his robe and followed by the choir and their parents walked in protest on the other side of the road. It was a very small and ridiculous looking protest. This last Easter, two young girls and a boy made the 'marvellous' effort at the entrance of a large villa to burn our CND symbol over a fire they had made!

In television only a few tired wanderers were shown, although the newspapers were more truthful about their report of the march. Sometimes you could feel an ice-cold opposition towards us. A film was made and disappeared into the archives of the police. I heard that at first, the banners of the communist and socialist party was asked not to be carried openly with the remark that the demonstration was only for marching against the atom bomb, but last Easter both banners were carried proudly the whole way. This peace movement had now a three-year tradition. In the first year two hundred demonstrators marched through Maidenhead, a small town about half way between London and Aldermaston. Originally it was only fifty people marching. It grew to six, seven hundred.

In the second year, at the end of the march we had grown to nine to ten thousand, but this last year we grew to hundred thousand.

Back home we displayed our banner ' Ban the bomb' in the window of our house. It was well known that my daughter and I had taken part on the march the whole way, for many months afterwards the children on the road called after us, 'ban the bomb' and they played 'Aldermaston march' on the road.

I must not forget to mention the lady we met in Chiswick, London, how we met her on the roadside clapping, so enthusiastic about the march. That first year we went a little ahead, we were so tired and she met us talked to us and offered us accommodation and said it was her part for the march. She was a very lovely friendly lady. She had lost her only son in the war".

It was a great experience and Gretel was so happy, especially as she now had contact with this lady from Coventry who had contact with someone from Dresden. This lady help gain contact with certain officials over there so that a visit to Dresden was made possible.

4. Desperate to Return.

The report from letters from my parents to uncle Hans show a completely different picture, a picture of constant struggles and desperate attempts to return without success and the feelings of alienation and nowhere wanted anywhere. Where do they belong? My uncle Hans during his visit to us, tried hard unsuccessfully to convince his sister Gretel to stay in Maidenhead. But Gretel's longing to see her hometown Dresden again was too great. Meanwhile my mother worked hard to afford to pay for my music studies, violin lessons, and later my visit to Elmsly School for Girls in Maidenhead in order to allow me to take up my exams. My mother never gave up hope to be able to return to Dresden sometime in the near future but my father became increasingly bitter and very disappointed that the occupying Russian authority in East Germany had refused a return when they had applied earlier, in the late fifties. They refused to allow my parents back. They knew how active my parents had been and the Russian authorities refused to give any reasons for this refusal. My father could not forget this. Meanwhile life went on. My mother continued to attend sculpture classes at the Reading University. She was then able to exhibit her work in London, Maidenhead, Eton, Glasgow, Windsor, Reading and Cookham. In many of these exhibitions my mother's artworks were shown together with other well-known artists such as Stanley Spencer.

Open-air exhibition in London

154

'**An artist's nature** does not need to say anything at all,
An artist's work can have a very strong call,
To the world, or to yourselves,
Like children dreaming of fairies and elves,
Perhaps you never thought of that,
What fun to have modelled your children's head,
What fun to see yourself, from all sides and round about,
What fun to have a statuette,
From the animal that is your pet,
In the garden, the fountain figure between the flowers,
Will give you company and talk to you for many hours,
Stone, wood, terracotta, big or small,
With pleasure, I will do it all.'

Gretel wrote this poem as an advertisement for commissions for her artwork and placed it on the table where her sculptures were exhibited.

I always thought 'aliens' was a term for extra-terrestrials from outer space, but at that time this term was used for anyone not from the UK. 1955, my parents were still regarded as outsiders, as 'aliens'. They obviously still had to go to the police station regularly for interviews!

A letter my father wrote 25th November 1956 to uncle Hans, reports of Gretel's membership with the Burham orchestra where she played, an amateur orchestra, something like this was not available in GDR. He writes about her increasing desire to return and that it would be best to do everything to make a visit to Dresden possible. About this time we went for a wonderful holiday on the Isle of Wight and Gretel praise the English youth hostels, how good they are, but dad did not want to come with us.

1958 my cousin Hannelore moves over from Düsseldorf to live in London. She came to visit us several times while we lived at Hareshoots, but I never saw her again when we came back 1984.

13th August 1957 finds Gretel still hoping to return to Dresden in spite of the refusal. My parents reapplied again for compensation from West Germany for what they had gone through, fleeing from Nazi Germany but their application was again turned down. The West German solicitor dealing with their application asks in his letters for many documents and letters from witnesses, but wittiness cannot be found, as they are all most probably dead. A letter dated July 8th 1958 from the Reading and district international advice bureau and refugee committee confirms that my parents were refugees from Nazi oppression. But this letter is obviously not sufficient.

Gretel applies for a post as illustrator. The company are extremely pleased about her work and at first it looks as if Gretel might be successful, but then she is told that they could not employ foreigners. One day Gretel discovered an announcement in the newspaper that 'Mr and Mrs Klopfleisch' had applied for English citizenship but Gretel did not know about this. Obviously Peter had applied for it without informing Gretel. She is anxious that this application could harm her and prevent an eventual return to Dresden. Peter did not want to wait until it could be found out if it would be better to stay stateless or have the English nationality. It could be wrong by law to apply for English nationality without consent and without willingness to become British? There were so many questions still open. Gretel wanted to have the British nationality ten years ago, but now she was not sure what was best.

This restless feeling, rootless and not knowing where they belonged cause frustration and unhappiness, their marriage now coming to an end and the yearning to see Dresden increasing. We lived for many years only for that day when we could return. Peter was now like a volcano that could blow up any time. His illness caused by the accident was now the reason for many upsets.

Gretel writes to her brother that; "Lots of things upset him; the cat sitting on the chair, speaking when Sonja eats. If Peter would be a little more comfortable to live with I could settle down in England. It was better when you were here. We are living in an unhappy house"

She writes that she is not happy here in England and that her art was never really understood here, that in the Czech republic it was different. During uncle Hans's visit Peter was friendlier and happier.

19th October 1958 finds Gretel and Peter still waiting for news about the compensation claim they made, but the solicitor has no news and keeps asking for witnesses.

Gretel writes to her brother that; "Sonja makes serious efforts and progress in school, went to Reading to take part in a competition, one for violin and one for acting. Her school sent her there."

It was agreed to go over to Dresden next year for a few weeks. Gretel wants to keep her German nationality, although at the moment she only had an emigrant pass.

She writes to her brother; "It would be better when we stay together and that it would be good for the children to think more socialist ideas. I cannot stand the British climate. In Prague we had to starve, but there I was happy and could work contentedly with my artwork. The permission to enter the GDR has been put of for years and years. Next year I will get the permission myself. It will be possible even without your help."

The solicitor from Berlin writes that it should be possible to get this compensation but at the same time Peter wants the English nationality without Gretel's agreement. Gretel wants to return desperately. She wants to return now while she can still work and not just as an old woman to die. Uncle Hans obviously tried to become a sort of marriage counsellor but as he himself was a bachelor had no idea about marriage. The situation was not good.

I found a letter from the lady we met on the Aldermaston Easter March. We were together for two days during the march. She writes she had the impression that Gretel was homesick. Because of this, she writes to uncle Hans, and asks him if there is a possibility for Gretel to visit Dresden, if only for a few days. She writes that Gretel admits her homesickness only with hesitation. My mother had no passport and it was unclear how she was to pay for the journey through West Germany, but this friendly lady was prepared to help financially. She writes and asks uncle Hans to contact the authorities in Dresden.

"Please do contact your sister, as Gretel is worried not to have heard from you for sometime."

20th Jan 1960; the plan to go ahead for a holiday to Dresden was now making progress. Gretel found out that it was possible to get a holiday permit. Preparations were now being made.

"Sonja will finish school and her exams in summer. I will bring only Lindy with. She needs me. Sonja as the older one can quite easily be without me for a few weeks" she wrote to uncle Hans.

About the same time Peter received the final message that his application for compensation was not accepted. The West German authorities refused to accept that Peter was wanted by the Nazis before he fled to the Czech republic. They wrote that Peter could not prove that he was wanted by the Nazis because he was working against the Nazis. They wrote he did not belong to any political party. They refused to accept that he would have been arrested. Again no witnesses could be found.

My parents had requested compensation for;

Damage for loss of freedom.

Damage for loss of personal asset and property.

Damage for loss of earnings.

Damage for loss of career, job and professional progress.

The West German authorities refused to accept that my father had been an active member of the antifascist organisation.

On the 15th May 1933 Nazis came into Peter's apartment to arrest him. He was not arrested while luckily he was not at home that day. Next day he fled over the border to the Czech republic. Again they refused to accept his repeated application. If my father had been arrested and imprisoned, then they would have accepted his application.

Feb 1960, my parents received a further letter from the solicitor dealing with their claim for compensation entitlement. This letter confirms again that compensation was refused. They, the West German authorities just did not want to accept that my parents had the right to have compensation. If their claim had been because of racial reasons, there would have been no problems, but because of political reasons this was refused.

The West German authorities wrote that there were no more witnesses around to confirm that the applicant was at all a member of an antifascist organisation. They wrote that if the applicant would have been an antifascist working against the Nazis, and by a supposed house search they would have been taken prisoner, but as such, nothing could be proven. It is to be noted that in East Germany after 1960 – 65 both, Gretel and Peter were recognized as VDN.

My parents were optimistic believers - idealists. They never gave up their ideals and hope. When my parents applied to return in the 1950's, the GDR authorities did not want them back. Perhaps my father already realized something was not right. He was bitter and very disappointed that they had refused a return without any reason. He had done so much before1933 working in the underground against Hitler and the East German authorities did not want him. His application to return 1950 to the GDR was refused and no reason was given why. This was something he could not forgive. He had been a red front fighter.

My parents still counted officially as foreigners, as aliens living in Britain! It was different for my little sister and myself, we both were British born with all recognition and rights as all British born citizens. But although we had British nationality by law, we were still regarded, unofficially, by certain authorities, neighbours, and schools as foreigners although we never had been in Germany.

I went on a school exchange trip over to West Germany 1959. This trip proved to be very useful for the journey the next year over to Dresden. As I passed through Düsseldorf my aunts were there at the railway station to greet me, but I did not stay there. We never knew our relatives from Düsseldorf. The next and only time I saw my aunts was the following year on our way over to Dresden. We knew Hannelore a cousin and once, another cousin, Arthur, who came over once some years later, to Dresden to visit my father.

There were still some problems with obtaining travel and permit papers. A letter Gretel wrote to her brother 1960 informs her brother that his letter had arrived open! Her brother had obviously suggested that Gretel should say she has a Jewish connection. But Gretel wanted to keep to the truth. The travel papers had not arrived yet and Gretel was worried that the contents of letter would harm her.

There were obviously problems with getting into Dresden. Officials in Dresden did not realizing that Gretel still lived as an emigrant and under emigrant conditions in England. Gretel informs her brother that Peter would be recognized as a West German citizen without problems from West Germany and that the children have their own English passports. It is clear from this letter that only a holiday was planned. I was to stay behind because of my future plans to continue my music studies. Gretel had only an extremely old German passport from May 1933, no III 500/33 and then one from Czechoslovakia, passport no 714 on the name of Grossner. The birth certificate, copy that her brother Hans brought over with is the only proper certificate she had. Eventually she received permission for a two-month stay. She had been busy working extra hours to save money for the journey. She was fed up with living abroad, living in England as an 'alien', a foreigner

My mother should have stayed in the Czech republic where she had the most recognition as an artist. My father was so unhappy and extremely upset that the return to the GDR in the 1950's was refused without any reasons given from the Russian occupying authorities in the GDR.

If the British authorities had treated parents better, and given them certain rights as British citizens this might have been a different story.

If the British authorities had treated my parents differently when they arrived in Britain fleeing from Nazi terror and not interned them, putting them both behind barbed wire, something they had fled from, if they had not been treated like Nazis criminals and not mistreated, my mother given the right treatment in time on the IOM after her miscarriage, later if they had been given all rights and equality, respect, not treated as aliens, but as human beings, not treated as outcasts and kept as stateless persons they might have stayed. If they had been given compensation for their suffering from Nazi oppression, they might have been happier living in Maidenhead and my mother might not have gone on this holiday of no return.

The constant fleeing, rushing from country to country, internment camp, my father sent to Australia, my mother to the Isle of Man, her miscarriage and lack of treatment for 6 months before her life saving operation contributed to sadness and longing to return. The failure to return earlier with the other émigrés when my little sister was born, and Gretel's illness 1946 did not help the situation. This illness, later 1972-1973 was used as an excuse to put all blame on my mother for the theft and destruction of her artworks. It was used to cover up and protect the real culprits, the thieves and to try to hide Stasi intervention in our lives. My father could never really forgive my mother that he did not return to Dresden earlier. His accident and illness 1954, shortly after we moved to the new council house and fact they both were always regarded as 'aliens' as unwanted foreigners whilst living in Maidenhead did nothing to convince my mother that it would be best not to go over to Dresden, not even for a visit. Anyone reading this will hopefully understand the reasons for Gretel's urge and desire to see the place of her birth again once more.

A visit to Dresden was now becoming reality for Gretel. At first I thought I would need to prepare myself to study in London, and so stay behind while my mother and sister went over to Dresden for a visit. But then after the interview I was told to come back the next year after some more lessons, so instead I went with for this ' holiday of no return' to Dresden. I had a very happy childhood, in spite of the difficulties my parents faced. They made sure that we both, my sister and I were happy. I still, even today often long to go back to Maidenhead, but I never got back. My childhood was a happier and healthier one than my mother's with her experience of that bad stepmother.

3.

A Vision

"When I was still a child, things looked different. Today, happiness and prosperity travels laughing from house to house". (Translation from a poem Gretel wrote, approx 1965- 1968).

'Das Lachen in unserer Stadt.'

'Das Lachen ist wie eine Blume so fein,
Es blüht nur im warmen Sonnenschein.
Fast wäre das Lachen erstorben in unserer Stadt,
Es lag da nieder sterbensmatt.
Man hörte nur Stöhnen und Schreien,
Im Bomben krachen und Flammenschein.

Nun durch vereint Arbeit und fleißiges Mühen,
Konnte das Lachen von neuen Erblühen.
In unserer neu erbauten Stadt,
Wo jeder Recht, Ruhe und Arbeit hat.
O pflegt es, das Lachen, es ist so schön,
Das niemals mehr es möchte vergehen.
Behütet es sorgsam, es ist jeder beschieden,
Die schönste Blume, das Lachen, Sonnenschein und Frieden.'

Translation

' Happy Laughter in our Town'

Laughing is like a flower so fine,
It blossoms only in warm sunshine.
That happy laugh nearly died in our city,
It laid there deadly tired.
One heard only groans and cries,
During the bombing and burning fire.

Only through united strength and active labour,
Can happy laughter again bloom.
In our newly built city,
Where all have rights, peace and work.
O take heed, that happy laugh, it is so beautiful,
That it may never again disappear.
Guard it carefully, it is for everyone,
The most beautiful flower, that happy laughter, sunshine and peace.

CHAPTER 9.

A Dream World 1960.

Aquarelle; 'Still Life'

1. Just a Visit?

1960 was a turning point in my life. Until then I had lived in England in Maidenhead, and had just finished general school education. Important contacts had been made over the CND Easter march through the lady from Coventry whom we had met whilst on the march. The contact she had with someone in East Germany and the letter she wrote to my uncle Hans helped and enabled Gretel to obtain a visit permit. It was with great delight that Gretel saw this poster; 'Coventry - Dresden' that this lady was carrying on the CND march, and of course they made friends. As Coventry is twinned with Dresden, and both cities were heavily bombed it made sense for Gretel to ask to carry it part of the way on the Easter March demonstration.

As a result of the contact this lady had with the GDR, Gretel received permission at last for a visit to Dresden. We received a visitor's visa and started our journey to Dresden, to Germany, 'for a holiday of no return.' I was seventeen and my sister was thirteen. I did not know what to think at the time. I had no idea what a socialist country would be like. I had always been very close to my mother, and I knew she was longing to return home, to her place of birth and childhood and to wander again through the beautiful countryside surrounding Dresden. Dresden is a beautiful place, a beautiful city. Gretel was homesick for the place where she was born, grew up, where her ancestors had lived and longed to be part of a socialist society.

Gretel had saved up years to buy the tickets to Dresden. At the travel agency her request for tickets to Dresden, a place behind the iron curtain was greeted with surprise and astonishment. It was not so easy to sort out travel tickets, and timetable. The travel agency had no idea where Dresden was. Dresden was a white spot on the map, no-mans land. She did not even get a proper timetable for the journey. Instead, she was told to meet a stranger in London at Victoria station at night time and he would give us details, timetable and tickets for the midnight train to Dover, passenger seats for the ferry and seat reservations for the train from Ostende through Belgian to Düsseldorf in West Germany. This man was supposed to be from the travel agency.

It was all very peculiar, and bizarre. Gretel was most critical about this. We had to cross the East German border at a certain place and at a special time. That was a condition of the visa permit. None of this had been considered by the travel agency and Gretel could not help thinking about horror stories of missing persons and she was most unhappy and concerned that she was expected to meet a stranger at the railway station at mid-night. So from the start there were some strange things happening.

Because of this she decided to leave a day earlier and to travel without a timetable. The travel agency had not given her one!

Luckily, my knowledge collected a year earlier on a school exchange visit to Stuttgart was most useful and together with my mother we made our plans ourselves.

The day of departure arrived. It was not the day decided by the travel agency who expected us to meet some stranger at night time at the station for timetable and passenger seats for the ferry and train but the day and time Gretel decided upon. We had no tickets for the afternoon ferry over the channel to Ostende.

2. A holiday of no return.

The last days of school were filled with preparation for the journey to Dresden. At long last my mother would be able to satisfy her desire to see her hometown Dresden again. I still had several exams in school, but I was actually too excited about that approaching adventure to concentrate properly on those last exams. Well, I thought, when I am back after the holidays there will be enough time for homework.

I nearly stayed back behind in Maidenhead. My visa came late. Actually, I wanted to study in London to become a violinist, but I was told at the audition to come back a year later, after more private lessons. My mother then applied at the last possible date for my visa.

We were going to visit my uncle Hans, and my father was not coming with us. We thought we would be back in a few weeks. None of us knew, or even could imagine, what the next months had in store for us. I knew, and felt that we were on the verge of an adventure, a new life, a journey to a different planet, another completely different world. My mother's yearning and desire, to be able to step along the road of socialism to see her ideals become reality, and most important of all to be part of it was overwhelming. I remember well those last days in July 1960 in Maidenhead. It was strange that I had to draw and paint a poster of refugees for my last art lesson at school. It seemed this was a sign, a finger pointing into an uncertain future. Our future rested in the hands of destiny.

As we were going to travel into 'uncertain territory' we decided to sort out various important items as well as some favourite things and to pack them into bundles. I remember well writing notes on them: 'important', 'not so important'. It was good we did this; our 'holiday' was to last over two decades! We spent hours in my mother's room packing her pictures together, just in case!

Gretel was unhappy living in England and her marriage had become a daily torture for her. She was dreadfully homesick and Peter could not understand this. Having lived in Dresden I understand her homesickness. Dresden is a wonderful city. Peter was so ignorant of all that was going on around him. He lived in his own personal world, still bitter and very angry that the government from East Germany had refused to accept him as a GDR citizen and had refused to allow him to return. The reason why was left unclear and vague. Before 1930, Peter had stood in front of crowds, speaking against Hitler and warning of the fascist danger ahead. He had to live illegally in hiding, he had written illegal leaflets against fascism, he had to flee from Nazi Germany because he wanted a peaceful world and he was not wanted, not accepted in a socialist Germany? It had been his dream, to live to experience a better peaceful socialist country. My father could never forget or forgive this fact, and I want everyone reading this to understand his feelings at this moment and not misjudge anything.

My parents were two great contrasts. My mother was a great idealist, an optimist and always greeting the beauty and good sides of life. But she was completely dissatisfied with life in Capitalist England.

Dad's health had suffered since his accident; he was clumsier and more interested in comfort. The ten years difference in age and contrast in character were now making life difficult.

That last day is still as clear before me as it were only yesterday. We had as many cases as we could possibly carry and our violins, the most necessary clothing for a holiday and our little dog Pixy. She was such a faithful companion. We knew that on our return she would have to be in quarantine for six months, but we took her with us, - again, all in case of what might happen. Our other pets were taken to their temporary homes Strangely enough, many neighbours looked out to see us off, no one expecting that it would be the last time. I believe many were curious, because they knew we were going off on holiday, behind the iron curtain!!!! I felt no remorse or sadness leaving Hareshoots, just a curious passing sensation of the future adventure before us. I was happy for my mother; at last she could see her beloved Dresden again. She would be able to visit the places of her childhood and the beautiful Sandstone Mountains in Saxon Switzerland. This was for me important. I wanted to see my mother happy. After twenty-seven years of absence she was now about to return to the place of her childhood. She could visit her mother's grave and she would see her brother Hans again. Is there anything unusual in this wish? Anyone reading this should admire the courage of this woman – to set out in the world with her two children, leaving everything else behind her and going of into an uncertain future, then in 1960 there was very little or no official information about life in East Germany. She had only her strong belief in Socialism and that life in this other part of Germany could perhaps be what she was hoping for; a better peaceful world? But how would they welcome her? Would they understand? In 1953 we were refused permission to return to the GDR. It seemed they regarded us as spies. Who was right? My father who could not forgive their mistrust, or my mother's great idealistic optimism?

We had now permission to enter East Germany for a six-week holiday. In order to leave again and return to the UK we had to reapply for permission, how bureaucratic could that be?

We gave our home; 22 Hareshoots a last fleeting look. We had been happy here, in spite of the 'dark clouds' of a marriage gone wrong.

Dad came with us to the station. I cannot remember if we went by taxi or by bus. But I remember the loads of luggage we had and the neighbours staring at us. Just that last glance is still so vivid; it dominates all else. The house looked as if we were going to return. Gretel's sculptures were still standing on the windowsill and the modelled goat's head still over the front door, the flowers in the front garden bright and the morning sun beckoning us a farewell. The mini rose bush had grown well that last year.

We arrived at the station and for some reason dad decided not to come up to the platform to see us off. The farewell was quite cold and he seemed pleased to be rid of us for a few weeks. He was still living in his known private world, sometimes ignorant of all else around him. Gretel was sad and heavy hearted. She would have liked him to come up to the platform to see us off. I remember clearly the vision of my father leaving us at the bottom of the stairway. He did not even turn back to wave us goodbye. None of us realized that four years would pass before we would see him again and five years before he would join us.

I remember the next scene clearly; standing at the platform at the railway station in London waiting for the train to Dover and whom should we see but our Aunty Dinah. How glad we were to see her, little realizing that only I would see her again much later after twenty-four years.

At Dover, our tickets had to be sorted out. The captain was good-hearted; looking at our dog he said, 'well a dog is also a living creature' and allowed us on board the ferry. The boat glided out of the harbour, England disappearing in the distance, the last sight of Britain the white cliffs of Dover, little realizing the situation I would be in when I would see these white cliffs again! We stayed on deck, enjoying the fresh sea air and our little dog Pixy was quite curious about her surrounding. She was already tired, but glad to be with us.

3. The Journey to Dresden.

I cannot remember the time we arrived at Ostende, but it must have been early evening. The voyage had been a pleasant one, the sea quite calm, only Pixy our little dog was restless. The journey was too long for her. In Belgian she pulled us hurriedly aside to the first few green grass shoots on shore. Her joy at being on land again was overwhelming. My little sister Lindy looked tired. She was not really healthy, often ill with asthma. The doctors hoped she would grow out of it and my mother hoped that the continental climate might do her good. How right they were. My sister never had another attack of asthma as long as we still knew her. But I have no idea about her health from the year 1972 onwards. Those next twelve years proved be so fateful. In fact, it is as if she stayed behind, then the sister I had in Dresden was a completely different person, with a different personality and even different character. She changed completely.

None of us could imagine a tenth of what was to happen. We had no fixed timetable and no reserved seats for the train. The further journey proved tiresome and difficult. The journey through Belgian was anything but relaxing. Continuously we had to move to the next compartment, the seats were also reserved and we had so much luggage. Some how, due to the constant moving and carrying our luggage from compartment to compartment I must have injured my thumb. It became infected and started swelling. We were to meet my dad's six sisters in Düsseldorf on our way to Dresden and had arranged to stay two nights there. This was to be the last time I ever saw them. By now my thumb was causing me great problems and I was in considerable pain. The aunty we stayed with said I should not worry; she put some ointment on it and a bandage. Nothing helped. Luckily, the next day a visit had been arranged to see a sick relative in hospital. My mother was very worried and used this visit to ask for help. We had no insurance arranged for medical care and at first because of this, the nurses said they could not help. But when my mother took the bandage of my hand and showed them my by now very swollen thumb they just gasped and ran for help. Within minuets I was on the operating table and had my thumbnail taken off. I had nearly lost my thumb! No one at the hospital questioned how, what, why; they helped me immediately. Still it was quite nice to see my aunties and we had a little get together. My aunty gave my mother a sausage to take with for our journey but said that it would be taken away from us at the border.

My mum just said; "Well then I'll eat it" and took a bite out of it.

The next day our journey to Dresden continued. I was still a bit shaky and my arm in a sling, so I could not help much with carrying the luggage. We arrived at Marienborn, at the border control. It seemed that the officials were more concerned how much money we had with than anything else. We had 75 West Marks and 25 English pounds with us. Here we had to change trains.

My first impressions of the GDR on the night train over the border to East Germany to Dresden were mixed, then the train was full of drunken Russian soviet soldiers and the wooden seats were uncomfortable. The journey was so tiring, sitting on those extremely hard wooden seats, my poor arm in a sling and my head ached. I had been given tablets because of my injury. It was a journey I will never forget. Those soldiers were so noisy; drinking and singing, the train was crammed full of them. What first impression these were! The journey seemed endless.

At last we arrived in Dresden. It was midnight when we arrived and we had an extra long wait at the empty railway station. After that noisy train full of drunken soldier the eerie quietness of the lonely railway station seemed unreal. Nothing was anything to what we were used to, and I hardly understood much of the German spoken. My uncle Hans was there at the railway station to meet us, and took us into a small room from the Red Cross. We were given a hot herbal drink that tasted extremely bitter. I had never tasted anything so awful like that drink before. This strange tasting herbal tea we were given was something we were not used to. I do not know what sort of tea it was then back home in England we never drank that kind of tea.

We had to wait until early morning, and then came the typical slow tram journey through Dresden to my uncle's home. He lived outside Dresden in Klein Schachwitz.
My home was so far away and our adventures only just beginning! That early morning tram was no better than the train, also hard wooden seats, and little Pixy snuggling up to us for comfort then who of us was more confused?

Some years later someone complained that we already arrived with spots on our cloths. Our cloths were not tidy enough, they were not ironed. We had just completed a very long tiring train journey. Was the Stasi already observing us, and why? These first petty impressions of the GDR were so typical.

My uncle lived in a basement flat in an old villa. There was a large hallway with gallant stairs. My uncle's living accommodation was quite basic, but his flat was part of an old large villa and must have belonged to some rich person before the GDR time.

That year, 1960 in July, my mother took us, my sister and myself to the GDR, to Dresden for this holiday of no return. Our allowed time for the visit eventually became overdrawn. 'Nice words and promises' from the GDR authorities, also the fact that Gretel was not aware, did not know that we would have had to apply again for a permit to leave. We could not, would not have been allowed to leave without! This did not make things easy.

Gretel had suffered all sorts of experiences, life as an alien, (that's what foreigners were called in Britain that time), as the wife of a known German communist. She had suffered internment camp during the war; illness and she had become an artist. We arrived with just a couple of cases and our violins. Gretel was now back home, after so many years, now she could see her hometown again.

Those first weeks at my uncle's place were quite confusing then there were many things that were different to what we had been used to. We were 'a little spoilt' by the life we had back in Maidenhead, my sister and I too young to really understand what was happening and the confusing talks and discussions between Gretel and Hans, and the GDR authorities only contributed further to the baffling situation of now living behind this so-called 'iron curtain'. I knew how homesick my mother had been and was happy for her that she was now back home, at least for a visit? It took some time before I could understand sufficient of the German language and get accustomed to the different way of life. The food was different, the accommodation; my uncle's flat was quite basic, upstairs in a small room lived that stepmother, Trudy. She never left that room.

My uncle took us up to the mountain hut property and Gretel could at last see this wonderful place and enjoy the view over Dresden reaching far into the distance. Gretel was already making enquiries about possible work as an artist. One day, my mother came back from an appointment she had with someone from the VBK; (Artist organisation of the GDR). It was the first time she was to realize that they were not willing to accept her straight away. We were up on the mountain hut property waiting for her. When she came back, her distress and disappointment was enormous. My uncle was concerned that our stay was slowly becoming overdrawn and we had no idea what the future had to offer us.

Meanwhile Gretel continued to enjoy her stay in Dresden in spite of the advancing disillusion. Another time my uncle took us on a trip to Saxon Switzerland. We were to climb up one of the sand stone rocks. Brilliant, now I was to see for myself how my uncle and his friends climbed up those sand stone rocks, and we were to join them. By now, my poor thumb was much better. During the first week back my uncle took me to the hospital in Dresden to get my injury checked and here also was no problem concerning any health insurance.

That climb up the Mönchstein was magnificent. At last I had now experienced this sort of climb myself, and with rope. Each of us were partnered with one of Uncle Hans's friends to climb up that rock. On the top of that rock was a silhouette in metal of a monk that my uncle had created. Every year on a specific day this group of climbers that my uncle belonged to climbed up there. It was quite an experience. The weather was fine and there on top of that rock was a mountain book where we could write our names in.

Gretel had endless visits to the authorities. It was a most confusing time and finally we stayed in Dresden. I obtained a student place at the music school 'Carl Maria von Weber'. Our British passports were taken away in spite of my mother's request for us to keep them. At the same time they were persuading us how good and wonderful everything was in the GDR. I was given the opportunity to study music, to become a professional violinist, my dream.

4. The first months.

After the dramatic experience of Nazi Germany, the GDR, the first German Republic governed by the working class and farmers themselves, was for many a sign of hope.
In spite of everything, many German anti-fascists and socialists like my parents wanted to be proud of this. It was something they had wanted badly, something they had dreamed about, worked for and many had lost their lives for this new Germany.

It was certainly difficult for any previous GDR resident who had left the republic under similar conditions like myself to stay a socialist, and to think straight. I came back very confused and I am still searching for answers. But certainly only someone who has lived in the GDR can report of how life was there.

My mother saw that things were not as they should be already during our first months on arrival for this supposed holiday trip in 1960. But once we had arrived in Dresden there was no 'going back'. My mother always saw the good side of things, and this loyalty to her socialist ideas is evident in her artwork. Our stay in Dresden in the summer of 1960 was supposed to be a holiday, but the GDR authorities did everything to keep us there. My father was still in Maidenhead. We had come over from a capitalist country and because of that we were regarded either as stupid or with suspicion.

The fact that my mother was regarded only as 'alien' in Britain with little or no rights made things easier for the GDR authorities. Also the behaviour of the GDR authorities made things 'easier' for our stay. I had at this time the British nationality, given to me through my birth in Britain. We were then given GDR documents and GDR personal ID documents.

At this time, 1960, the GDR authorities ignored, or forgot for whatever reason to comply with their laws from 28th November 1957 that all foreigners and stateless persons must apply and sign some sort of documents if they were to become GDR citizens. They did not ask me to write or make an application for GDR citizenship and because of this they could not give me a document confirming my supposedly GDR citizenship. Because of this neglect, I had been a British citizen all the time I had lived in the GDR. I found this out only 1983.

Gretel met again old friends. There was a lot to talk about. After all Gretel had not seen Dresden and old friends for so long and many things had happened since their last meeting. After some weeks we move to friends living in Weißer Hirsch, another part of Dresden. Gretel's friend with whom she went to art school back in those early days in Dresden before she had to flee from Nazi Germany had invited Gretel to stay with her so that Gretel could sort things out. This lady and her husband whom we called the red priest because of his religious belief were very good friends and wanted to help Gretel. They were good people and so different to my later experience 1984 on my return to the UK, having to experience a fanatic religious group that insisted on dominating my life. We have a lot to thank this family for. At that time, they also obviously believed in life in the GDR for peace and freedom. We still have contact with the children of this couple to this day. This lady's husband accompanied Gretel on her endless journeys to town to the authorities. He helped with writing letters and filling in countless forms. He also helped with gaining contact with the music school in Dresden for me.

The GDR authorities had been extremely 'busy' talking to Gretel. I found following statement on a letter she wrote to them;

"As I fled from the Hitler fascists and had to leave Germany I swore that I would return one day. My heart and thoughts were always in my home country. It is the fulfilment of a great life to come back here and to stand up and fight for world peace."

How did the GDR treat my mother? How did they reward her?

Further letters to the Dresden authorities confirm Gretel's longing to return, her forced compulsory stopover in foreign countries and how she lived in England as a foreigner.

She wrote; "Although my children are born and according to laws have British nationality, they are also regarded as foreigners from authorities, schools and neighbours." How very true these words are still today, how sad.

Here in Britain we are German, but over in Germany we are English!
The GDR authorities, Stasi and neighbours never really regarded us, even my daughter as German. My daughter was taunted in school in Dresden the year before we left as 'dirty English girl' although she could not speak one word English. We were never trusted or given the same treatment as others born in the GDR.

What about here in England? During my childhood as my mother wrote we were taunted as German and racist remarks made about us. Still today, the same situation, nothing has changed, certain neighbours still call after us; "German, Nazi, Hitler".

Uncle Hans

Photo of one of the huts on mountain property

Gretel somehow finds contact with her first love, Kurt. He never forgot Gretel and wished he had stayed with her. He told Gretel about the fate of his sister, that she had died during

Nazi time and that the circumstances surrounding her death were unclear. He came to visit Gretel regularly and the two had many a long chat.

How happy Gretel was to find a post at the theatre in Dresden as stage designer and sculptor. She worked there for nine months, but working with certain materials there did not agree with her health, damaging her already bad stomach. The paint she had to use for her work was poisonous.

About this time the Polish Peace Committee from Warsaw bought her terracotta sculpture; 'Hand with Dove of Peace.'

 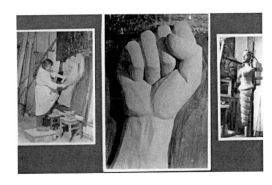

Gretel Worked as a stage artist, 'Bühnen Bildner' at the Dresden Staats Theater[1] 1960-61.

5. A New Life.

From the start, we were 'not normal' people for the GDR government or the public. We were regarded with suspicion and even as some sort of 'criminals because we came from England and I, as well as my sister had a British passport. Although the GDR authorities did everything possible 1960 to convince us to stay, spreading 'honey around our mouths' with all sorts of talk, it was clear that they only did this to stop us returning to the UK after our holiday in Dresden. They did the same with my father 1965 with all sorts of bogus promises which they had no intention of keeping. In fact I am convinced that both of my parents, as well as my uncle Hans were purposely disposed of, murdered. But I have no proof to give for this accusation. They were uncomfortable for the GDR government and as I stuck to my principals and my beliefs I also was an uncomfortable citizen. All those years we lived in the GDR we had to balance as if on a tight rope between two political sides, the GDR government and also from normal GDR citizens who also regarded us critically; 'what are they doing here? They must be spies for the government.'

These were extremely difficult years for my mother and my sister Lindy suffered greatly under this stressful situation. She was so young and easily influenced. She did not want to appear different, but was very concerned to be and look like any one else. She could not cope with this 'tight rope'-balancing act we were forced to undertake. The Stasi although invisible, were always around us, watching us, and creating difficulties in our lives. It was an easy breeding place, for fear, hate and suspicion and most probable the birth situation for future events.

Eventually we move to our first flat on the Ermel Street in Dresden. It was only a small place, a two-bed apartment with no bathroom but there was a small garden going with it. It took some getting used to, as back in Maidenhead we had a three-bed council house. My sister Lindy and I started to continue our studies; I was now at the music school, 'Carl Maria von Weber'. My dream, to become a musician, a violinist and composer became reality, my sister went to the local state school and later became an apprentice as a technical drafts

---

[1] 'Bühnen Bildner' at the Dresden Staats Theater; stage artist at the state theatre in Dresden.

designer. For both of us, this change was a challenge, a new life, a different culture and language. My first impressions of the GDR were of a young state, still coming to terms with the legacy left by the Nazi reign, a city still with many ruins but with optimistic views and some very good laws for equal rights, a country where everyone had work, no unemployment, no homeless people. It seemed Gretel's wish had come true.

Not everything was perfect, the neighbours looked upon us queerly, not understanding why we had come over from Britain and now lived in 'run down wrecked East Germany' as stated in the letter I received years later, sent to me supposedly from my sister.

Today my sister is missing. I do not know where she is. I think she may be still in Dresden and this situation is thanks to the GDR policies of that time. Years of sabotage and distrust did their utmost to increase our difficulties.

It took my mother many years to regain the recognition for her artwork she had as an artist during the emigration years. Only one year before she died did she regain the recognition that was due to her, after a wonderful and very successful exhibition of her sculptures in Dresden. But at this moment we were very vulnerable and most of all, my sister. We had come from the 'Western world' and both sides treated us with disbelief, making this forced upon us 'tight rope' balancing act, unbearable.

Before my mother received her VDN[2] pension, enabling her at last to have a financially easier life, she worked firstly in a garden nursery and then as a post woman in order to earn sufficient to live on. It was not much and financially things were a struggle. She did not receive work in her profession.

Gretel's longing to see Dresden again was fulfilled, but her artistic abilities were never accepted until 1981. The return to Dresden, my mother's longing to see and visit the place of her birth and childhood came at a price. But at that moment she was still optimistic and positive and I had been offered a place of study, my dream come true.

> **'Da steht eine ruine** auf den Berg, am rauschenden Waldesrande,
> Schon funfzig Jahre steht und schaut sie verwundert ins Lande.
> Das hät in ihrer Zeit nun garnicht gedacht,
> Was man hat da alles gemacht.
>
> Sie sah noch den Pflug und den Knecht mit der Peitsche,
> Sie sah noch den gepeitschten Knecht.
> Heut rattert der Pflug durch den goldenen Weizen,
> Heut hat der Knecht das Recht.
>
> Sie sah noch grausam barbarische Zeit,
> Sie sah noch den Hunger, die Mühsal der Leut.
> Und was sie sieht Heut ist wie Glocken klingen,
> Die Menschen in friedlicher Arbeit neues erringen.
>
> Da wachsen die Häuser säuberlich fein,
> Und die stählernen Vögel fliegen in den Himmel hinein,
>
> Da flüstert die alte Ruine, nur wenn Ihr erhaltet den Frieden,
> Ist Euch Menschen Wohlstand und Fortschritt beschieden'.

---

[2] VDN; An organization in the GDR for help for victims of Nazism.

There stands a ruin on the mountain, on the edge of the rustling woods,
Already now for fifty years it stands there and looks wondering into the land.
In its time it had not thought at all,
What now man has made so much.

It saw the plough and the labourer with the whip,
It still saw the wounded labourer,
Today the plough moves through the golden wheat,
Today the labourer has the reigns.

It saw once cruel barbaric times,
It saw hunger and troubled people.
And what it sees today is like ringing bells,
The folk in peaceful work creating new.

There the houses are growing clean and fine,
And the iron birds fly up in the sky.
Then the old ruin whispers, only then when you keep the peace,
Is wealth and success possible for all folk.

(Written approx 1964 – 1965?)

Why did we leave Britain to go for a holiday behind the 'iron curtain'? The answer is simple. Dresden is my mother's birthplace. She loved Dresden with her childhood memories of good and hard times. Our ancestors 'Birken von Tuba' lived in Saxony and Bohemia. They belonged to the knights of the Bohemian aristocracy and when impoverished in the 15th century became robber knights. On warm summer evenings we gathered together, relaxing on our beloved 'Mountain' property listening to the tales my eccentric uncle Hans told us. He just could not resist speaking about the stories and past history of our destined ancestors. He also told us about his many adventures in the resistance against the Nazis. So, with our regular stays, our 'Mountain' property became something special and personal. Another reason for my mother's longing to see her hometown Dresden again after many years living abroad was the fact that my parents in 1960 were not recognized British citizens, but still living as foreigners, as aliens. My sister and I are British by birth and we have had a British upbringing and Germany always was a foreign country to me. I never felt at home living in the GDR, but the wonderful countryside, the deep-rooted connections and my mother's grave keeps sending me back to Dresden for visits.

We went for a holiday to Dresden Summer 1960, after gaining contact with Dresden through connections made during the Easter CND peace march. It turned out to be a holiday of no return.

Twenty-two years later I returned to the UK with my daughter.

It took a long time for the GDR artists to recognize her abilities and talents. My mother had some very good friends who recognized her talents such as Dr Gerd Gruber and Dr Diether Schmidt also Gallery Kühl who exhibited her artworks later on a regular basis.
Dr Gerd Gruber, at that time was a young man who began to collect artworks and was very keen to promote antifascist artists and their work.

With their help Gretel slowly began to be known again in the artist world. She was able to exhibit some of her artworks at Gallery Kühl in Dresden regularly during the years 1967 to 1970. One of the most important exhibitions was 'Kunst gegen Fascism' 1969.

The Legend, part 7.

<u>Another Legend of Jutta von Duba</u>

There is another tale about a knight in disguise, incognito as an artist. He was Bernhard von Kamenz who had known Jutta from earliest childhood and now in this disguise wanted to be near her. Because both fathers were in disagreement and constantly quarrelling he was unable to be near his loved one. His plan did not work and the two lovers were not united.

Jutta took the veil. She never forgot her beloved. Bernhard went into battle against the unbelievers and found fame in death.

The legend reports of a figure of a lady that can often be seen in the Amselgrund, at full moon at the hour of midnight; the ghost of Jutta von Duba. Her cloak is white as fresh fallen snow and her face full of deep sorrow. Jutta von Duba is the maiden from the castle, the daughter of the knight from Rathenstein. Her ghost wanders silently through the forest until she comes to the cave.

The tale reports of this young knight from Saxony, and how the two lovers met one last time by the Amsel waterfalls at night by moonshine before he went to the holy wars. The knight said his last farewell to the maiden from the castle. They swore to be faithful to each other, forever over their graves. With tears in her eyes she gave him a farewell kiss. He never returned. He met his death at enemy hands in the holy lands.

Now by full moon, at the hour of midnight, the ghost of the castle maid wanders through the Amselgrund to the Amsel cave, longing and waiting poor soul for her beloved knight to return.

The birds hear her lamenting about her heartache. They sing to comfort her, poor maid, and bring greetings from afar, from her dearest, from his grave in foreign lands.

Saxon Switzerland; 'Mönchstein' [3]

---

[3] <u>Mönchstein;</u> Rock formation in Saxon Switzerland.

170

'Schlangen in unserer Stadt.'

'Schlangen in Osten, oh welches grauen,
Im roten Osten ist da zu erschauen,
Schlangen von Menschen, jung und alt,
Sie stehen in der Kälte, werden Kälter und Kalt,
Und so berichtet man im Westen,
Die Menschen seien hier nicht die Besten.

Recht haben sie, man kann sehen,
Die Menschen Schlange stehen,
Und schaut mal, Ach wie schön,
Ins Theater und Kino wollen sie gehen.

Du meine Stadt, in der Zeit vergangen,
Was hattest du doch für schreckliche Schlangen?
Von Elend und Hunger und Arbeitslosigkeit,
Hat der Sozialismus nur, dich Befreit'.

Translation

'Queues is our town.'

Queues in the East, Oh what a cruel sight,
Is there to find and see in the red East,
Queues of people, young and old,
They stand in the cold, become colder and cold,
So are the reports in the West,
The people here are not the best.

How right they are, you can see,
Queues of people standing,
And look, how nice,
In the theatre and to the cinema they want to go.

You my town, in past times,
What did you have for dreadful queues?
From poverty and hunger and unemployment,
Only socialism could free you.

Woodcarving; 'French Revolution' 1953

CHAPTER 10.

Woodcarving; 'Leaping Panther'

Behind the iron curtain, 1961 – 1968.

It seems that the British authorities did not wait long to take away the council house we had. Dad wanted to send my sister Lindy also to Elmsly School, the private school I had attended when we return to Britain after our holiday, but we were unable to return. Dad had sorted out everything. We left the UK in summer 1960 and obviously dad was forced to move soon after. The Maidenhead authorities were not willing to wait for our possible return. But dad hoped to see us soon sometime in the New Year.

Once we had crossed the border into East Germany we were on a completely different planet, another world. It could have been somewhere else up there in space; life was so different. If the permission to return to the GDR 1951 had been granted, our lives most probably would have taken a different path. Instead, after the long two-year wait on packed cases a refusal came without any reason given why.

By now we were living a year in the GDR[1]. It was a year of mixed feelings, and it was not easy to cope with a different culture. Our small flat was very insufficient; there was no bathroom and the neighbours watching us with curious eyes made us feel often out of place. Perhaps here was the seed sown for my little sister's later strange behaviour and her Stasi involvement. She had to cope with a different kind of school in a 'socialist' country and an education so different to that back in England. Back home, we had been used to a large three bed council house, but here in Dresden, her health improved and she had no more asthma attacks. The change of climate had been good for her.

Life was not easy. Money was short, but my mother was optimistic and very positive in her views. We were living now in a 'socialist' country, looking into a bright and peaceful future, into that 'socialist' future that my parents had so hard fought for and believed in. By now, our heads were high in the clouds and due to newspaper reports we now could not see clearly how actually things really were.

I was studying at the music school ' Carl Maria von Weber', and so happy to have this opportunity to fulfil my dream. Music was my life, is my life and my destiny. My mother now back in her beloved hometown Dresden, and although many political situations and events were unclear, living conditions still primitive and many shops often empty, we were not

---

[1] GDR; German Democratic republic.

unhappy. Dresden is a beautiful city, surrounded by the most gorgeous landscape, especially the Saxonian Elb Sandstone Mountains. For me, life was an adventure, and main thing, my mother now no longer suffering from severe homesickness. I received a regular monthly student grant and so, was able to help my mother financially.

Gretel was home at last, but her artistic qualities and artwork were not accepted. She received a letter 21st September 1961 from the Verband Bildender Kunstler (VBK),[2] informing her that her application for recognition was refused. She was told to wait until she was able to get her artwork sent over from England. The work she had with was not accepted.

Woodcarving; 'Dreaming', approx 1969

1. First Impressions.

'Wir, die Soldaten des Sozialismus,
Zum Schutz des Friedens sind wir stets bereit,
Wir Arbeiterschaft, mit Optimismus
Marschieren wir immer froh und bereit,

Jeden einen Freundschafts gruß wir bieten,
Rings um die Welt, und übers Meer,
Arbeiter, kämpft immer für Frieden,
Und für Einigkeit mit der DDR.
Die junge Saat fängt an zu sprießen,
Das sonnigen Himmelsblau uns lacht,
In der frischen Morgenröte Pracht
Unter unser roten Fahne Macht,
Marschieren wir kühn des Sieges bewußt,
Wir, die Soldaten des Sozialismus'.

Translation

'We the soldiers of socialism,
To protect peace, we are always prepared,
We, the workers with optimism
We march always joyful and ready,
We offer everyone a greeting in friendship,
All over the world, and over the sea,
Workers, always fight for peace,
And for unity with the GDR.
The young state begins to sprout,
The sunny blue sky smiles to us,
In the fresh morning sunrise delight,
Under the influence of our red flag,
We march keen, conscious of victory,
We, the soldiers of socialism.'

(Written approx 1964)

---

[2] VBK; Verband Bildender Kunstler, - Professional artists
organisation from the GDR.

It is so obvious how positive, optimistic and happy my mother was.

There were at first many good intensions and positive plans for the new GDR, but certain authoritarian and dictatorial laws made life as time past, increasingly difficult and stressful.

This Republic governed by the working class and farmers themselves, after the dramatic experience of Nazi Germany was, in spite of everything, the name of hope and joy, something German socialists and communists, like my parents, wanted to be proud of. This was something they had wanted badly, something they had dreamed about, worked for and many socialist and communists had lost their lives for this new Germany.

It is certainly difficult for any previous GDR resident who had left the republic under similar conditions like myself to think straight. I came back very confused and I am still searching for answers. But certainly only someone who has lived in the GDR can give a full report of how life was there.

East Germans couldn't get out into the west world. They became very narrow-minded, imprisoned within this society. The people in the GDR were very clothes conscious. It was most important what you wore, and how you wore it, your appearance. Living in a community in flats, the house duty, sweeping and cleaning the stairs and similar things were of great importance. Decisions were made, what sort of person you were, firstly under these aspects, your home, the wallpaper, the curtains, and the colour scheme. If there was something different to others, like my mother's artwork, this was a disadvantage. This gave the impression that socialism was being built up on such small petty things, small unimportant things counted. Everything had to fit into a certain dictated norm. But I was impressed with the quality of the school system, of the equal rights and equal opportunities to learn all subjects. The high standards were very impressive. Education was free. I became a professional orchestra violinist, but a 'big brother' situation was everywhere and this worsened as years went by.

There was a very eventful and busy cultural life in the GDR. Prices were affordable and accessible for all. In every town there were theatres, professional orchestras, art galleries and cinemas.

There seemed to be far less violence and crime on the streets. In fact you had the impression that the streets were a safer place.

There was work for everyone, no unemployment, but not necessarily the work you wanted. If you were under Stasi surveillance for a certain reason, this could cost you your job, as I experienced myself later. Colleagues could be extremely unwilling and reluctant to accept such a person in their midst, if the Stasi were always making enquiries about them, or they were not the right person politically for a certain post, or the Stasi wanted them somewhere, so as to keep them under observation.

There were no homeless people. Everyone had somewhere to live, not necessarily the place they would like, and the amount of space per person per family was restricted. If a single person, or a couple bought a large house, they were not allowed to live in it on their own. It did not count if it belonged to them, if it was their own private property. A certain space was given to each person, something like one room for each, or two in certain cases. But there were ways around this depending on the sanitary arrangements, if for example a house had only one flushing toilet and bathroom, then it was possible to have more space.

There was a lot of jealously and envy around, then certain people were given priority for housing accommodation, e.g. victims of Nazism (VDN).
Travelling to West Germany and abroad to other capitalist countries was made nearly impossible then West currency was practically unattainable and had no value in the West.

There were many elements of socialism in the GDR, and I have experienced what it could have been to live in such a society but it was a caged society, cut of from the outside world.

Gretel applied for continued membership with the SED[3] from 1931 onwards, but this was refused because she had no connection with any political émigrés from 1946 – 1949 due to the birth of her second child 1946 and illness. Membership was given to her at first only from 1962 onwards. Some years later, the authorities offered her continued membership. We lived in a very bureaucratic society.

2. The First Years.

Our first years living in East Germany were not easy. We lived in that very small insufficient flat and financially things were not easy. Although Gretel was not accepted in the VBK she was positive and hopeful that the near future would bring better times. 1963 found my father still living in Maidenhead. He was fed up with life in England and now no longer lived at our house in Hareshoots. He complained about the rough racist neighbours there and was glad to have had to move away. He was seriously considering coming over to visit us and asked if we still have the return tickets from three years ago. He had hoped to send his letters registered but was told, "they don't register letter over to the GDR, only to the West." Gretel wrote back asking him to "send us things, clothing and food parcels, to help out." He was not allowed to send tins. It was a demanding time, lack of contact and a divided world between us.

A letter he wrote on the 17th November 1963 reported how he was now used to living on his own, likes to live on his own and does not want to be burdened but still discussing a possible visit to Dresden. He is concerned about the paper work to apply for a visit and reports; "Tricky question of the exit visa without which one cannot return from you, I never thought of that, but it says quite clearly on the instructions that before starting the return journey one must have the exit visa which one has to apply for while there."

December 1963; my father's intended journey to us is now reality and he completed the necessary forms. He still has our belongings from 1960 when we left.

January 1964 found my father fed up and concentrating on the pending journey to us. He was still working and had a weekly wage of £14. He hopes that one of us at least can come over to England to help him pack and sort out things out. But this wish was not possible, we were not allowed to go over and help. He sends us greetings from a friend, 'Jolly' but she does not want direct correspondence with East Germany as it could have 'adverse' influence on her business.

Whilst looking through old papers, I find the date 3.10.64 on a document. This confirms that Gretel again tries to get recognition as an artist, and applies for admission to the VBK. But yet again she was not accepted. Reason given; not enough work available to prove her ability although she had worked at the theatre in Dresden 1960 – 61 as a stage artist for stage decoration, and now had contacts with other artists who knew her from the emigration time. It is recommended that she should continue her studies at evening classes at the art school. This stubborn refusal to accept her does not put her off. In February1965 she repeats her application and yet again is refused. This time Gretel is told that her work is not good enough. This disappointing message only creates a very busy time for Gretel continuing to create more artwork. It is already clear that her work does not 'fit in' with the standard style on show. She had tried so hard 1960 – 1965 to get work as an artist, but was not taken seriously anywhere. All efforts to get work as an artist and to become a member of the Verband Bildender

---

[3] <u>SED</u>; 'Sozialist united party of East Germany.

Künstler have negative results. At this time, due to the bombing of Dresden during the war there was a large amount of work available in the museums and Dresden Zwinger. As my mother had experience with stone carving and qualifications it would have been no problem to employ her to work with the other artist who were at that time already working to rebuild and repair sculptures that were destroyed during the war.

1965 at last she receives a VDN pension, although at first only a small one, but this pension enables her to have at least some financial security. Gretel can now concentrate completely on her artwork in spite of all difficulties put on her. The result of starvation in the emigration and daily struggles has a bad effect on her health and she suffers from stomach ulcers, heart complain and glaucoma but she never gave up, had great courage and optimism believing in a better socialist future. 1964 Gretel is given the possibility to have a relaxing time in Karnow a VDN convalescent home. She has a wonderful time, swimming, boating, walking and watching the wild animals in the forest. Until 1945 this castle belonged to an old Count lord who lived there. For fear of the Russian army he obviously committed suicide, throwing himself into the lake. Now the castle belonged to everyone.

Now Gretel had VDN recognition and was a respected member of the SED, helping and campaigning for certain issues. Also at the same time Gretel was a voluntary helper for other VDN comrades. She used to go round regularly to see if all was ok and if they needed any help. She was also on the committee for the local area. One story comes particularly in my mind about this time. A friend, a lady, Mrs Gothardt, whose husband had died as a result of bad treatment from the Nazis, had a disabled son, Rainer. He was born during the bombing of Dresden and his disability was a result of this. Gretel went regularly round to her, and she came visiting us many times. She was concerned about his welfare and had made arrangements that after her death Rainer should be cared for by friends in the countryside. But the bureaucratic GDR authorities ignored her will and refused to accept her wishes. When she died Rainer locked himself in the flat not letting anyone in or even near him. When at last the authorities got him out they simply put him in a home instead of taking him to his friends. There he hanged himself, committed suicide. When Gretel asked why her friends wishes had been ignored the authorities simply said they thought he would be better of in the home.

I found a copy of a letter my mother wrote to the violin teacher I had when I lived back in Maidenhead. In this letter my mother informs her that I am doing well at the music school, composing for various instruments, have a good violin teacher who was a member of States Opera theatre in Dresden, that I receive a grant of 160 marks monthly, and that she receives an extra 100 marks for me from the state.

Just compare that with the help students now get to help finance their studies, students now end in debt. She also informs her that I will be an orchestral player and will get work as soon as I finish studying. This was true, but then, later things went wrong due to Stasi involvement. Proudly she also writes about my sister Lindy, that she is on the way to a good profession as an engineering draftswoman for the building industry; that Lindy has one-week practical work and one-week school, working on the drawing board and lots of mathematics, cheap lunch and sport to keep healthy.

At this time Gretel was employed at the post office, working for half a day, and receiving a pension of 153 marks because of her ill health. She hopes to be accepted as a member of the artist organisation and feels quite positive that things will work out. Again the artworks left behind in England are missing to make her wishes reality for acceptance in the artist organization. Our dog Pixy had to learn German as well, but she was so pleased to hear English spoken and expressed her pleasure by wagging her tail.

This letter was clearly written before 1965. My mother was very optimistic and it is important to note the positive socialist points of how life was in the GDR.

About this time, 1964, Peter was preparing himself to come over for a visit. Gretel is quite excited about this and pleased that the visit permit had been granted. She was looking forward very much to seeing him again. It seems that the GDR authorities were concerned with our West contact and once he came over for a visit did everything to persuade him to come over permanently. In fact, Peter was practically persuaded by other people to come over. It was of great importance for the GDR authority that we would then have little or no contact with the western world, and they hoped that later contact to the west would stop completely. Many promises were made, one of them that they would give us a better and bigger place to live. This promise was never realized, not kept and obviously not meant.

As a result of his visit, the promises made and the persuading talks from the authorities with both my parents, my dad returned to Britain with the plan to return the next year permanently. January 1965 finds both making preparations, Gretel in Dresden and Peter over in Maidenhead. In one letter, Gretel reports of the promise made that we were to get better accommodation, even before dad arrives. There is also the promise of a full pension for both, but before anything else, before dad would be allowed to enter the GDR for permanent he would have to stay at the 'Aufnahme Heim,' (reception home) first for two weeks! It is so clear how positive and optimistic my parents were, their positive views of the Stalinist state, their heads in the clouds. Gretel was still working at the post office and very impatient to get things sorted, to be back together with Peter again.

She wrote; "We have friends in the party and we cannot disappoint them. We will get good accommodation and you will get a good pension and we will make ourselves useful for the party. It is best; I believe not to tell too many people about your plans to move over to GDR. Be careful with Hans. He has an impossible scandalous opinion about the GDR, but I think the state does not take him seriously He is a very ill person, has progressing blindness. I am so glad that I am on a friendly foot with him."

She tells dad to be patient with the reception home and that it's no convalescent place. He can then go to VDN convalescent home when he is in Dresden. He would get his GDR papers, will meet old friends and old comrades.

"We are a young socialist state and things are not easy when so many capitalist countries are like hyenas out to hurt and ruin us" she wrote.

"In February the VDN will get us new accommodation. Hopefully, by then, we will have a new flat." She writes that she had to be without proper GDR papers for a quarter year and that was very unpleasant. All this talk were only words, we never got what they promised us. It is also clear how my uncle thought, and tried to warn us of the Stalinist state.

My uncle Hans looking out of the window of the mountain hut

3. My father arrives

And so, after we had already lived in Dresden for four years, the East German authorities during my father's visit to us persuaded him to come over to Dresden permanently. I wanted to go back to England, and help him pack, but the GDR authorities would not let me go. I was not allowed to go over to help him. He then joined us permanently the following year. All those many attractive promises the GDR government made - 'Oh, you'll have a house, you'll have this, you'll have that!' now my father eventually came over, that was it. We were all together again, but living in this very small old flat. The promises were just lies; then the GDR government wanted us to stay for some strange reason, and they did everything they could to persuade us, that it was right to keep us there, although people were fleeing at that time.

There were high-profile defections going on during the Cold War, people would go to scientific conventions in the West and never go back. I suppose they wanted the propaganda value of people going the other way.

My father arrives at last summer 1965 to live permanently with us in the GDR. I had not been allowed to go over to help him pack. He left many fine sculptures behind and to this day I do not know where they are. When my father wrote that he had placed all artworks with certain friends we immediately wrote back that they were needed because of Gretel's pending recognition as an artist with the VBK. Regrettably, he did not manage to get everything returned. Uncle Hans had given him bad advice. One small sculpture is found. It is one sculpture Gretel modelled in Prague and managed to bring over to Britain with her. The family who has this particular sculpture insisted that it was a present, but this is not true.
My father was persuaded by certain persons in authority, that on his return to Dresden we would get a better place, he was persuaded that it was the right thing to do to return. Of course we were delighted to see him again after those long four years. But it did not take long for my parents to decide that separation was best. There are many reasons why this was inevitable, but certainly, if all the promises had been kept, the story would a different one.

Due to circumstances my parents' marriage since years was no longer; it existed only on paper. They married 19th June 1939 in London Hampstead England, and divorced in Dresden end of that year 1965. At least my father also received a good VDN pension and very soon his own apartment, in a block of newly built flats. There are many reasons why a future life together was no longer possible.

We were still living at that very small flat, an apartment far too small for a family of four, with no bathroom. My parents had now been living apart for five years and their marriage was already ruined at the time we left England 1960. Due to his accident it was not easy to get on my father. Also, he had to be persuaded to bring my mother's artworks back with. He gave them away as advised badly by uncle Hans and only after several letters could he be persuaded to fetch them back. Not all were returned and many valuable works remained back in Maidenhead. This may have also contributed to the divorce.

The disastrous refusal from the Russian zone to allow my parents to return earlier, the constant struggles, Gretel's home sickness and desire to return, my father's anger at the refusal and his feeling of hopelessness of a return, all these points were not in a favour of a positive life together. Yet they were both determined to want to try to have a family relationship once more. Nothing happened. Although both at first were looking forward to be together again it did not work, there were no tenderness and affectionate behaviour between them any more. My father unconsciously never really forgave my mother that they could not return already 1946 with the other émigrés. The birth of my sister prevented this. Both parents hoped it would work, but it was not possible. They tried so hard to make things work those few months in Dresden 1965 without success. Such a large gap had grown between them; it could not be put together again, especially now that they both had lived apart for five years, this fact did not help. These problems may have been the reasons for my sister's later strange behaviour. In spite of these problems, both parents were very good friends and cared for each other. They were both good parents.

The break-up of the marriage of my parents was inevitable.

- They were practically 'thrown' together in their youth through political circumstances and their work in the anti-fascist underground movement and life together in the emigration.
- Constant stress-internment camp imprisonment, IOM and Australia. Then unable to return to their homeland with the other emigrants.
- Refusal of Stasi to allow them to return in the 1950's
- Constant longing to belong somewhere, both living as 'Aliens' in Britain.
- My mother's return, ' Our holiday of no return.'
- Dad's lack of enthusiasm to help save her artwork when he joined us in Dresden 1965. I had to write to beg him to get the artworks back he had 'given away'.
- All this contributed to the break-up.

'Old Trees after the storm' Charcoal graphic.

'Wenn all die Roten Fahnen wehen.'

'Am ersten Mai, wenn all die rotten Fahnen wehen,
Ist unser Dresden besonders schön.
Dann denk ich, all ihr Leut, welch ein Glück,
Und Heimlich denk ich dann zurück,
Zurück zum Kampf und welches grauen
So viele Menschen hatten zu Erschauen.
So viele, die nun nicht mehr unter uns sind,
Doch Ihre Fahnen wehen im Wind
Und Ihrer zu Gedenken,
Wir unsere Schritte lenken.
Auf den Fabriken und im Schacht
Überall bauen wir den Sozialismus auf, mit Macht.
Für Völkerfrieden und Einigkeit
Sind wir jeder Zeit bereit'.

Translation.

'When all the red flags fly'.
'On the first of May, when all the red flag fly,
Our Dresden is particularly magnificent.
Then I think, all you people, what luck,
And secretly I think back,
Back to the struggles and fears,
So many people had to experience.
So many, who are not with us any more,
Still their flag wave in the winds.
And for them, in memory,
We direct our steps.
In the factories and shafts
Everywhere we build up socialism with manipulation.
Peace for all and unity
We are ready at all times.'

(Written approx. 1964 – 1965?)

4. My sister Lindy.

Our lives at our first home in the GDR, living in that very small flat on the Ermel Street was of mixed experiences. My mother was extremely busy working in order to earn the most necessary income for us. On the one side we were very happy, unaware of the already vicious observations from Stasi officials, happy to be together, my music studies, thinking we were living in a positive peaceful ' socialist' society, and on the other side my sister's increasing strange behaviour and the often unexplainable findings of missing money. Although my mother was financially very careful, then we did not have much in those days, she made sure that there should be enough for every day needs. But often, for no apparent reason when she wanted to go out shopping money went missing. Her purse was empty! What can we do? It made no sense and we wondered why. For some reason money was disappearing, at first only small amounts. At this time she was friends with Frau H., the wife of the son of previous friends who also had to emigrant from Nazi Germany. She thought she could trust this lady. My mother decided to go round to Frau H. and asked to borrow money sufficient to buy some food. This alone was strange, how come, why were certain things missing, particularly money for no apparent reason. We did not understand really what was going on and unaware of many things happening around us, but my sister knew and told us nothing.

Later we discovered the theft and carefully constructed destruction of mother's artworks But Gretel 'fought back', created many more artworks and managed to repair her wonderful sculptures. It is clear that during those first years in the GDR, someone from the Stasi made contact with my sister. We do not know exactly what happened, but her behavior changed. We all wanted a normal life. It is now 30 years since I last saw my sister, her last spoken words informing me that she could not keep contact with us because it would bring us all in danger! We both have been victims of that previous East German government.

Lindy at this time had started her apprenticeship and I still went to the music school. Only years later could we fully understand why particularly money went missing regularly out of mum's pocket, at first only very small amounts. Later my mother believed Lindy took the money, larger amounts in a desperate attempt to get out of the 'spider web' she was caught in. She did not want to appear different to others around and did everything to be like others, not to want to fall out and tried at all costs to keep on a good foot with her bosses and work colleagues. Fact; she had always money and bonuses. She was never short. Later on pictures started to go missing. At first we noticed nothing as things were done very carefully so as not to be too obvious. Once, whilst living at this flat my sister did not come back after an evening out with her friends. My mother became increasingly worried as time went on. I cannot exactly remember the full details, but eventually somehow the police became involved bringing her back early morning. What had happened I do not know but she received a telling off not to do this again. We never received any explanation why she had disappeared.

Lindy was often in great despair, often crying but she never spoke out and kept things to herself. She used to sit in the kitchen in the old flat we lived in, before we moved to the new built apartment, her head in her hands. She had quite a temper, throwing things around and seemed often distraught about something. Often she became extremely cross and angry. She would start to stare at the wall at an empty space. We had so many pictures so that if one went missing we did not always notice. Her increasingly strange behaviour, becoming upset about something, she started fiddling about with her hair, pulling bits out and banging her head on the table. She began to have fits of anger. But she kept silent and never talked about what was troubling her.

My sister's silence has harmed her greatly. She changed so much. Here in England, we would call that what happened with her, brainwashing. Nothing was left of the sister I had when we left England. The Stasi ruined her and they are responsible for her desperate change.
About this time, certain people, Stasi and most probably Neo-Nazis, perhaps in disguise as Party members made themselves onto Lindy, manipulating her and perhaps interrogating her to work for them. This would explain her desperate attacks of despair. She never spoke out.

It is now quite clear that my sister could not cope with the change, life in England and then life in the GDR; the change was too much for her. I have lost contact with her since 1972.
When she started work, she always had some sort of bonus, never short of money. In contrast, my mother at that time seemed always to be missing something and often found it

necessary to borrow something from friends. She did not like doing this and it was a hard time.

My music course was nearing completion and I took my sister with to a dance evening event at the music school. There was a lively band playing, I was happy and content, we were dancing and talking with friends but my sister just took of with a complete stranger.

One weekend we decided to go rambling of to the Sandstone Mountains in Saxon Switzerland. It was only half an hour's journey by train from Dresden and we wanted to head towards Hohnstein. Perhaps we could stay there at the youth hostel. My mother had to work and it was good to be with my sister, to go out with her. It was to be the very last time we went wandering together. The weather was fine, Pixy our little dog was delighted to be with us, and we enjoyed the unique Elbe Sandstone Mountain scenery. On arrival at the youth hostel I sorted out our stay for one night, sorted out our night accommodation, even Pixy was allowed to stay. The kind hostel warden found a comfy place for her in a shed. Pixy was a special dog, very well behaved and if we told her to stay put she would do so until we came to collect her. We left a rucksack with her to give a sense of 'duty' to look after it. I went back to our night accommodation to make the beds and then wanted to sort out our evening meal. I was hungry after our tiring long but lovely ramble. On my return to where we had left Pixy, then we wanted to take her for a short walk before we settled down ourselves; no one was there, no sister, no dog, both gone. I was so worried and spent the evening searching for her looking and asking. I felt responsible for her safety. Where was she? I was frantic. She and Pixy were nowhere to be seen, disappeared. Midnight arrived, still no Lindy. Then suddenly I saw her. She came towards me smiling, arm in arm with a stranger, never seen before and never seen again. I was so worried. I felt responsible for my sister's safety.

5. Student Years.

My student years were happy times. Now I was studying for the job I had since childhood dreamt about. After my first violin teacher died I had to change teachers. I was sent to an excellent teacher who was also a member of the 'Staats Kapelle' Dresden [4]
I remember well my first lesson with him. I arrived at my lesson early and had time to listen to the previous pupil. It was fascinating to hear the virtuous playing of this student. Then it was my turn. Instead of being distressed about it I was positively happy and content. This teacher made me relearn everything correcting many mistakes and I made good progress. How upset I was, when on my return to the music school after the summer holidays I was told that it was decided that I should go to another teacher. The difference between these two teachers was like day and night. I just could not get on with her. Her methods were strange and for me unacceptable. One idea she had was to tie a pincushion under your arm in order to hold your violin up! She was a really bad teacher. Luckily I managed to return to the good teacher who supported me throughout my studies.

It was also custom to start the term with helping out, bringing in the harvest, especially when there was an urgent need due to weather circumstances. Part of our monthly grant was sent to us. One year we were sent to a place near Berlin. I kept 10 marks and sent the rest to mum, as she needed it more. One supper we had was particularly upsetting. Can anyone imagine, coming back early evening after helping with the harvest hungry and tired only to be served with a 'maggot sandwich'! The food was that bad. Many of the students were upset

---

[4] Staats Kapelle Dresden; State Orchestra Dresden.

about these bad conditions and decided to protest. Next day many refused to go onto the fields to help with the harvest. For my sister Lindy I bought some seamless stockings, the shops were full of them. In Dresden they were hard to get.

I can never forget the first year at the music school. At first I could only speak limited German, just about GCE level. It was not easy studying in a different country, a completely different society and having to learn also a new language. As well as my music lessons all students had to take part in certain other lessons. Of course we all had language tuition in Russian. This was a particularly difficult subject as the writing is so different, but I found it interesting. I was not particularly forced to do it, as I had no previous lessons. Other students came to the class with a limited knowledge from school, but I wanted to take part. Often, at first, I had to translate back into English and then into German! I was learning two languages at the same time. There were other subjects we had to take part in. Everyone had to study Marxist theories. Our teacher was excellent. He said; humanity needs to go back to our native origins, but on a much higher level; then a socialist society, a friendlier and peaceful world would be possible. In one session he talked how the value of money would no longer be necessary, how certain supplies would be available without money. The world he described was 'paradise on earth' a world without war, without poverty, a world of plenitude and peace; a socialist world! One session will forever be in my mind; we were discussing the possibilities of this future world without the need for money. Our teacher described how at first many, especially young people would travel on the trams just for fun not having to pay and being able to travel anywhere for nothing and that in time one would get so used to it and only travel when needed. I often wonder what happened to this fine teacher with his optimistic views and the fall of the Berlin wall! One difficulty I had with this session was, having to read those political books in German. That was very difficult. Luckily my father managed to send me some copies of those books in English, so I could read them first in my native tongue. We also had sport sessions. It was an interesting and happy time, but not all students believed or accepted what was told. Many looked over to the West, having relatives in the other part of Germany and saw only the full shops and plenty on offer there.

I was the only female student at the music school having composition lessons and I also took part in conducting classes. There were many fine laws for equal rights for women, but regrettably often not acknowledged and existed only on paper. I was very keen and very happy to be able to have composition and conducting lessons. At first my composition work was written in a more traditional classical style. One day my composition tutor looked at me and said my music is not personal enough. So I went home and put dissonances and discords in the harmony and distorted the melody. I still have these particular pieces. These pieces changed my tutor's attitude to my work overnight. He never said again my work was not personal enough. Contrary, he encouraged my work.

The head of this music school was completely different. He laughed at my work and made ironic remarks during a concert when one of my compositions was performed, but this did not put me of. It did not deter me.

On the one side art form in GDR was pressed into one certain form, one certain style and individuality was not wanted as well any critical views. My mother had this problem with her artwork as well as myself. On the other side I was given a very good foundation for the future of my composition work. My tutor made me study Hindemith's harmony theory and this has proved valuable for my future as a composer.

Of course we all had to take part on the May demonstrations, but these demonstrations were just for show.

Woodcarving; 'Lady with dog' in memory of Pixy.

' Liebe Herrschaften.'

'Liebe Herrschaften, Tischkasten und Kommodenschieber,
Heute könnt Ihr machen was Euch beliebt,
Heute könnt Ihr zeigen wies bei Euch piept,

Heute könnt Ihr lachen und fressen,
Heute könnt Ihr toben wie besessen,
Denn liebe Freunde es ist gar fein,
Einmal recht lustig zu sein.

Wir möchten Euch alle recht herzlich begrüßen,
Und legen Euch unser willkommen zu Füssen.

Nun haben wir Heute,
Verschiedene berühmte Leute.
Da ist mit der Geige die Bini,
So klein und ohne Bikini,
Und da ist die Anke,
Sie war bei der Inge lange nicht da,
Und da ist die Zeichnerin Lindy,
Manchmal ein bischen ein launiges Kindy,
So ist da auch Sonja sonnenschein,
Doch manchmal fängt sie laut an zu schreien.
Das wirs nicht vergessen zu bringen,
Herzlichen Glückwunsch der Inge,
Auch fur Ihren Mann und Kind,
Damit es Gittarre spielen lernt geschwind.

Dann ist noch zu begrüßen Martin Zimmermann,
Der auch Gittarre spielen kann,
Er ist auch Segelflieger und Schornsteinfeger,
Und ein berühmter Mädchen jäger.

Manchmal gelingts beim scherzen und Necken,
Ein bischen Warheit dahinter zu stecken,
Doch schmeißt mich raus in großen Bogen,
Wenn Ihr beliebt wenn ich gelogen.
Wohl auf nun zum Essen und Trinken Ihr Leute,
Ich sag Euch dann noch was wir feiern Heute,

Die Nacht ist lang, Frohsinn ist unsere Devise,
Wir schlafen dann aus, auf unseren Berg auf der Wiese.

Nun wer nicht genannt,
Ist trotzdem bekannt,
Denn jeder, selbst wenn scheu und zahm,
Kennt ja seinen eigenen Nahm.

Zum schluß möcht selbst ich mich vorstellen,
Mit meinen Hund der so schön kann bellen.

184

Jetzt denkt Ihr gewiß,
Schluss, nun zum Teufel zur Höll,
Schon gut ich bin fertig und verschwind auf der Stell'.

Translation.

'Dear ladies and gentlemen,'

'Dear everyone, table boxes and cupboard pushers,
Today you all can do anything you like,
Today you can show how 'barmy' we all are,
Today you can laugh and eat,
Today you can be rant with obsession,
Then dear friends it is quite fine,
Once to be right jolly this time.

We would like to greet you all heartily,
And lay our welcome greetings to feet.

Now we today,
Have several famous people.
There is with the violin Bini,
So small and without bikini,
And there is Anke,

Woodcarving 'Mother with children' approx 1963

She stayed away so long from Inge,
And there is the designer Lindy,
Sometimes a little moody child,
So there is also Sonja sunshine,
But sometimes she begins loud to scream.

That we don't forget to bring,
All our hearty wishes to Inge,
Also for her husband and child,
That it may learn guitar really quick.
Then is also to greet Martin Zimmermann,
Who can also play the guitar,
He is also a glider pilot and chimneysweeper,
And also, a famous woman hunter.

Sometimes it is possible by joking and teasing,
To attach little truth behind it,
Then throw me out with a big swing,
When you believe I have lied.

Now off to eat and drink you people,
I'll tell you then what we are today celebrating,
The night is long, happiness is our motto,
We'll sleep it out, on our mountain on the lawn.

Now who is not called,
Is still well known,
Then each, self when shy and tame,
Knows their own name.

Finally I would like to introduce myself,
With my doggy who can so nicely bark.
Now you must surely think,
Stop, now to the devil to hell,
Alright I'll stop and disappear on the spot'.

(Written approx 1968).

Goodness! How happy and content we were those days. How ignorant of future stress. What happened to all our good friends, to Inge, her husband, Martin and my sister and the others? I miss so much the socialising and friendship we had that time, and my dear sister! Why did the Stasi destroy it all? This poem was written for a party we had with our friends.

My course was now nearing completion. I had taken my final exam, my dream to become a professional violin now reality. I even had a job waiting for me, violinist at the theatre in Freiberg, a small town about thirty minutes train drive outside Dresden. All students who had successfully completed their study course were given jobs. We did not need to go out searching, as is custom today.

We were sent to auditions during our last term. So now I had my degree, a job in my dream profession and the future world looked bright and good. I still needed my teacher's degree and I wanted to continue my composition work, but now I could begin to earn something, help my mum and I was independent. My application to continue studying part-time, one day a week was also granted, and I could continue taking some private lessons if I wanted.

I was so happy. This event needed celebrating, and I said to my friends; lets get together, be happy celebrate and have fun. First I wanted to express my thanks to my violin teacher, how best than to propose a party up on our mountain hut property in Wachwitz outside Dresden. My uncle Hans agreed and even allowed us to use the main good hut. It was a beautiful place, up there on that mountain property that once was a vineyard. The view was stunning, the weather great, the sun shining brightly. It was July 1968. We were a group of about five student friends, my uncle and my mother. We had afternoon coffee and cakes, enjoyed the view over the whole of Dresden out of the window of the mountain hut, the river Elbe like a silver band winding, past Pilnitz, and stretching far into distant Saxon Switzerland where the Elbe Sandstone Mountains stood.

My uncle Hans always said that this stunning view was his television. When evening time drew near, the sun spread its magnificent sunrays, and the changing colours in the sky were superb, everything seemed to turn into a golden blanket. The sun sinking in the distant horizon beyond Dresden and when the darkness of the night sky came gradually approaching, on clear nights the stars appeared twinkling in space above.
After our afternoon coffee and cakes we all went up in woods above for a short walk until we came to clearing from where we could see the Television tower reaching into the sky above the trees.
The world was good, my future looked bright although we still lived in that small flat.

View over Dresden from the mountain hut

We still had contact with friends back in England and we wrote many letters particularly to my aunty Dinah although many letters, 'got lost' on the way, but we never lost contact. On my return to England we met again and she was the same aunty for me as she had been in my childhood and also an aunty for my daughter.

One friend I had during my student time is worth mentioning. He was a student from Burma and was studying in Dresden. We had many interesting talks together. He eventually settled over to West Germany and came one last time to visit me about 1970. At this time we were already living in the new flat. It was strange and disturbing that he was constantly 'looking over his shoulders' and seemed very anxious not to be seen. Interestingly, he became a dedicated and enthusiastic socialist whilst living in West Germany. Living as a student in the GDR had done nothing to make him a socialist!

Why was he so restless during his visit back in Dresden, why was he constantly so alert? Did he already know what was happening and was he aware of Stasi intervention?
At that time we were still not aware what was already happening. I liked him a lot, he was a fine and honest young man.

Summer time was holiday time and we often went camping in the Erzgebirge[5], a smaller mountainous area outside Dresden. We had a very small tent and we slept only on straw sacks. Often we met a horn player from the Staats Capella Dresden. Each summer he camped there with his family. He had an extremely large oversized tent, nearly the size of a circus tent. He was a very friendly chap and helpful in rainy weather. Of course we often went wandering in the Sächsische Schweiz[6], up to Hohnstein, the place of our ancestors and over to the Bastei. Train journeys and steamer trips on the Elbe were cheap and affordable.

We discovered one freedom GDR citizens enjoyed during our holidays on the Baltic coast. One day, during our first visit, whilst walking along the beach we suddenly noticed that everyone was walking around and bathing naked. Can you image our surprise and astonishment? Everyone was extremely friendly and very well behaved, just enjoying the fresh air and sunshine. It was like going back in time, clothing was not needed, and it was so warm. This FKK[7] culture was custom all along the Baltic coast outside towns and built up areas. You could wander along the beach naked, clothing in rucksack on your back and then

---

[5] Erzgebirge; 'Ore mountains,' mountainous area outside Dresden.
[6] Sächsische Schweiz; Saxon Switzerland , Elb Sand stone mountains.
[7] FKK; Freie Körper Kultur, Free body culture.

when you arrived at a town or built up area you simply put your cloths back on, only to take them of again when you past the town! We discovered that it was very pleasant to bathe this way and indeed it was colder to bath with something on than without. We had many pleasant holidays on the Baltic coast. My sister Lindy was with us. Gretel's friend Ina from the Czech Republic was often there as well as many friends from Dresden. It was happy and jolly times.

Graphic; Darßer Landscape, (Baltic coast)

My mother wrote the following poem about her friend Ina during one of these happy holidays;

'Die Seejungfrau.'

'Ina Zuckermannova, die Seejungfrau,
Im Schwimmen ist sie eine große Schau,
Mit Angst und wunder
Haben wir immer vernommen,
Wie Sie immer ist in die See hinnaus geschwommen.
Auch wenn das Wasser noch so kalt,
Wieder kehrt Sie niemals bald.
Heute nun habe ich entdeckt,
Wo immer Sie hat so lang gesteckt.
Ich ging in schönen Darßer lande
Einsam lang am sonnigen Strande.
Da stand er vor mir mit all seiner Macht,
Der Meerkönig der unsere Meerjungfrau immer so Glücklich gemacht.
Versteinert ein Baumstumpf in einer Majestic pose,
Noch hielt er in den Händen ein Stückchen von ihre Hose'.

Translation.

'The Sea Nymph'

'Ina Zuckermannova, the sea nymph,
In swimming she is great show,
With fear and admiration
We have always noticed,
How she at all times swam out to sea.
Also if the water is so cold,
She never returns so soon.

Now today I have discovered,
Where she had always stayed so long.
I went along the beautiful Darßer land
Alone on the sunny beach.
There he stood in front of me complete in his splendour,
The sea king who forever made our sea nymph happy.
Turned to stone in majestic pose a tree trunk,
In his hands he still held a piece of her shorts'.

(Written approx 1968).

Although Gretel's recognition as an artist was still not acknowledged she had several successful exhibitions of her work and 1965 her sculpture; a woodcarving; 'Mother with child' carved approx 1943– 1948 was bought by the gallery in Halle Moritzburg.
She also exhibited artwork at the gallery Kühl in Dresden 1967 as well as an exhibition together with the Dresden artist Otto Schubert. 1967, some works were also exhibited in the Leonbaad museum in Dresden.

Saxon Switzerland

The Legend, part 8.

The legend from Schandau

There came a king from Bohemia, with his army, who fought a fierce battle in the Kirnitzsch valley. The fighters fought wildly with their swords and some brave knights fell into a deathly sleep. The duke 'von Duba' was also hit, he was knocked down by a friend's hand in a fatal assault. This friend, who stood by the duke's side, had only treachery in his heart, this betrayal and disloyalty, unforgivable. Seriously wounded, struck down by the murderous weapon, he laid there covered in blood and dust.

And as the night descended, with cold wet dew, he called out in his death cry, 'Ha shame on this place, and disgrace.'

His loyal faithful followers heard his cry. They were his last words and since then, that place has been called 'place of shame'. But as the legend reports, a mountain spirit had a word to say. He came down to the valley, and said, 'no curse, but blessings for this place'. So spoke the gnome king. The waters, the springs and fountains, the forests and forest fragrance are its greatest treasures, and the views of the mountains and the pure fresh air. Where the duke fell, where scornful breach of faith and disloyalty took place, there, mankind will find convalescence and recreation year after year. And so was as the spirit promised, far and wide over all the land, the name Schandau is well known as a spa and health resort.

Perhaps, sometimes, on summer evenings in the glowing twilight, you might see the gnome spirit sitting on the top of the high rocky mountains. There, the evening sunrays shine on the mountains and the dwarfs line up in wonderful dance like pearls sparkling on the damp green moss. The water nymphs from the fountains and springs appear from beneath their castle.

And as the sun sinks in fiery glaze, the gnome spirit gives his Schandau blessings and keeps it in faithful and devoted trust.

It certainly is a wonderful place, these rocky mountains of Saxon Switzerland. Once you have lived there the longing to return is inevitable. Gretel was now back home, her desire to see her beautiful Dresden at last reality. Life was good and her wish to be part of a socialist society had come true. No matter what 'small and insignificant ' difficulties we had such as living in this insufficient small flat and lacking financially, also still no full artistic recognition for Gretel, we were happy.

Hardly anyone had a telephone. The world that time was a far more social and caring place than today. It was no problem to just go visiting friends unannounced to have coffee, cake and a chat. This was custom, especially at Christmas time. It seemed that Christmas was far better celebrated over there in a socialist, non-religious country than here in England. Anyone could come up to our mountain hut and visit us, and uncle Hans. We had many wonderful happy moments up there enjoying the fine scenery and fresh air.

This was supposed to be the life behind the iron curtain, a dull and boring life without any positive future! What went wrong? This question is still open and unsolved. I often wonder what happened with my friends, especially my sister. It is so clear how positive we all were that time in spite of any 'short comings' we may have had. They, the Stasi tried to ruin my mother's growing recognition as an artist and also ruin my possibility to continue working in my chosen profession as a professional violinist in an orchestra. Of course everyone worked hard and often there were limited goods in the shops, but we learned that money was not the most important thing in life, but happiness and contentment, the belief that we all were working towards a peaceful and happier world.

Woodcarving; 'Mother carrying her child on her back'

CHAPER 11.

Happy Years 1968 – 1970.

These happy years will forever be in my memory, especially because of the disastrous events that followed. We were, that time very happy, confident and believing in a positive bright future in spite of some 'dark clouds', my sister's increasing strange behaviour that we put down to 'teenage' years, and my mother's still lack of artist recognition. But it seemed as if things were improving.

The years 1968 to 1970 were pleasing, happy and content. We were in good spirit. The world was looking good. We believed we lived in a socialist society. We experienced the good side of socialism, life was here in the GDR at that time, better than in England, and we believed we were all equal.

'Um die Welt geht ein Lied.
Das schönste was uns erblüht,
Das Lied für den Frieden
Das Lied für den Frieden.

Die schönste Blühte der Menschlichkeit,
Zu streben fur Recht und Freiheit.
Für den Frieden das Lied,
Für den Frieden das Lied.

Und wenn es von allen Menschen gesungen,
Dann haben einen großen Sieg wir errungen.
Für Freiheit und Frieden,
Für Freiheit und Frieden.'

Translation

'Around the World travels a song.
The best that for us can blossom,
That song for peace,
That song for peace.

The finest blossom of humanity,
To aim for justice and peace.
For peace this song,
For peace this song.

And when it is sung from everyone,
Then a great victory we have won.
For freedom and peace,
For freedom and peace.'

(Written approx 1968).

1. My first Job.

My course at the music school was now completed and I was about to start my first job. Wonderful, now I could earn something, had a job at the theatre in Freiberg as a violinist in the orchestra, had even my own little place to stay, although it was a very primitive accommodation in a very old house. Freiberg was not far from Dresden and I could travel home anytime. This needed celebrating with my friends.

We decided to have a party at my friend Inge's place where we had a little more room than at our old flat. Inge had also just completed her music degree. We were a jolly party; my mother and sister came along, as well as Bini and a couple of other friends.

Each of us played something on our instruments; I even composed something special for this occasion so we had our own little concert. Mum played something on her mouth organ and some of her favourite gypsy tunes on her violin. It was the same violin she had in Dresden, used for hiding illegal leaflets for the underground movement, the same violin she took with over into the emigration. If this violin could talk, it would be a story in itself. We still have this instrument today and my daughter is it's proud owner.

It is highly likely that my sister already had some problems with Stasi officials then she seemed very keen to want to talk about something with my friend. Later this friend and her future husband made some strange remarks informing us that we should have a good look around our flat. But at this moment in time my mother had no idea of the disastrous events already beginning to evolve. We were happy and celebrating our graduation, our new jobs in our chosen profession, also my friend was about to get married, so there were several reasons to make merry and have fun.

'Heut zu Euren Hochzeits Feste,
Wünschen wir Euch das aller Beste,
Viel Lust und freud auf allen Wegen,
Und einen reichen Kindersegen.

Glücklich müßt Ihr sein, Ihr beide,
Wie Adam als er seine Eva freite,
Doch werdet ihr nie vom Paradies vertrieben,
Denn Inge tut lieber Hans stat Äpfel lieben.
Was schwatz ich viel von Glück und Segen,
Es gibt den Sonnenschein und auch den Regen,
Und eines ist so nützlich wie das Andere,
Für Zweie die gemeinsam durch das Leben wandern.

Nun laß die Glässer hell erklingen,
So hell wie Glockengeleut,
Was sollten für Wünsche wir Euch noch bringen,
Ihr beide wünscht es Euch selbst noch Heut.

Es mischt sich Lachen und die Gläsern klingen,
Es mischt sich Blumenduft und kuss,
Alle die wir Wünsche bringen,
Verschwinden dann mit stillen Gruß'.

<u>Translation</u>

'Today, for your wedding feast,
We wish you all the best,
Lots of fun and happiness on your way,
And a blessing of many children.

Happy you must both be,
Like Adam as he freed his Eva,
Never to be banished from paradise,
Then Inge loves Hans instead of apples.
Pardon my chatter of luck and blessings,
There is sunshine and also rain,
And one is as useful as the other,
For two who travel through life together.

Now let the glasses ring,
As bright as bells sounding,
What else could we wish you both?
You both wish it for yourself.

After a mixture of laughter and glasses ringing,
And flowery scent and kiss,
All of us our best wishes bringing,
Disappear with silent greetings'.

(Written approx 1968).

About this time, a friend in Dresden, knowing my mother's love for music and my beginning career as a professional violinist presented us with a gypsy violin. She said she wanted to give it into good hands, to a good home. The story behind this instrument, how this lady came into possession of this violin is indeed extremely tragic. During the Second World War, a gypsy sold this violin for a piece of dry bread. He was so hungry, starving and obviously threatened with deportation to a concentration camp. Can anyone imagine the pain and suffering behind this heartbreaking tale? We still have this instrument today. It is a beautiful piece, with a carved dragon's head as the scroll.

Now I had a good job. I was a professional violinist, playing in a professional orchestra at the theatre in Freiberg and I enjoyed it so much, my dream had come true. Also I continued my studies part-time for a teacher's degree, just in case I should need it in the future. I also continued my composition work and had further lessons.

It was only a small theatre, but we played everything possible, from orchestra concerts, to operas and musicals. It was a good start, I thought for my future. I had only a very primitive flat in a very old building, and it did not even a flush toilet, but the accommodation was meant to be only for those nights when I had rehearsal the next day after an evening performance. The train fares were not expensive and it was only approximately half an hours train journey back to Dresden, hopefully I would get a slightly better job nearer home in the near future. At first I started as a second violinist, but soon was promoted over to the first violin section. If there were no rehearsals the next morning I joined the others, travelling together as a group back to Dresden. We were a jolly group, always joking, chatting and up to mischief.

Especially the singers were always plotting something. One evening, after the summer holidays, one of the singers seemed extremely restless. He kept biting and chewing on his train ticket. We looked at him puzzled but he continued chewing and said, he's just nervous and in need of a break, had too much work! Then the conductor came, asking to see our tickets. All was well, we all had valid tickets. So we thought! After the conductor left the train compartment, this singer stopped fidgeting and with a big grin on his face confessed his actions; "I was only chewing the date of the ticket as it was an old one!"

We all had a good laugh.

Another time, two of the singers kept discussing, ' how are we going to portrait the kissing scene, how are we going to kiss each other?' They talked about this in a jolly way, laughing all the time. She was an excellent singer with a wonderful voice, and he was quite a comedian. These types of discussions happened in particular when we performed musicals and light operetta. Once, during performing an operetta from Offenbach, this singer presented his 'darling' on stage with a bunch of parsley instead of flowers. It was very difficult for them to keep their laughter under control in front of the audience, but once of stage and in the train on the way back home there was no holding back, and we all could not hold back our tears of laughter! One more event is still particularly in my mind. We called the front of the stage where the orchestra sat, 'the bath tub'. It was quite stuffy there. Often there was time between music bits when playing musicals and operetta. It becomes quite tiring performing the same piece many times, again and again. During the performance of one operetta, the actors and singers had to walk onto the stage from the audience seating area. For this, boards were placed over 'the bath tub' on each side, where the singers were to be seated once they had walked onto stage. I wondered why the violinists over there were whispering and looking up! One of the boards had a small hole where you could look through. The singers had large crinoline dresses on and a tiny bit of the singer's dress could be seen. Those two violinists kept giggling and poking with their fingers up that tiny hole until they managed to get hold of a bit that dress, tugging at it, they got a bit more through, enough to tie a knot in it. That poor singer had great difficulty to keep her laughter at bay, tugging at her dress to free herself, as she was then to stand up! Never once was there ever a bad word said to any colleagues, we were all just happy and everything taken in good spirits.

Back in Dresden after the train journey, I had to wait a while for the tram, but they travelled regularly throughout the night. I usually arrived home 2 o'clock in the morning and it was quite safe in those days in the GDR[1] to travel home so late. Crime rate increased, only after the wall came down. Sometimes, if the theatre employed another musician temporarily for an evening's performance, and he, she was from Dresden, I usually could get a lift back home.

Theatre visit prices were very cheap and affordable for all. The prices for tickets at the theatre in Freiberg were; 1.50 to 4.50 DM.

It was a most enjoyable job, playing my violin at that theatre, in the orchestra, and often each night, a different piece. We also performed symphony concerts and went travelling to the neighbouring towns and villages. Sometimes it was tiring when we performed the same piece too many times. But in those days, in the GDR, culture was high on the agenda and theatres were hardly ever empty.

---

[1] GDR; German Democratic Republic.

2. We move to a new flat 1968.

We still lived in that old flat we had moved into when we came over to Dresden 1960, but now at last we were offered a new place, much better with bath and a modern built in kitchen and balcony. Although it was a bit small we were very happy to get it. My sister was not enthusiastic about the move and her strange behaviour continued. It was as if she wanted to hide something.

On the night before we moved to our new flat on the Ender Street my sister refused to help pack. She insisted on going to bed early. She was not really sleeping, just keeping her eyes tightly closed. As can be expected when moving there were many last minute things to do and pack. Later we found empty boxes where paintings should have been; perhaps she was hiding something under her blankets?

We moved to this new-built luxury flat in Dresden 1968, away from that small apartment that had no bath. The new flat was very small but we were happy to get it.

Now we no longer lived in that small old flat, our new apartment was much better and we had our little hut up on that wonderful mountain property outside Dresden with that superb view, far reaching into the distant. My mother now had a good pension, full VDN recognition, and time to continue with her artwork, and my sister was working, also in a good job as a technical draughts woman. Gretel was for the first time in her life without financial worries and she had succeeded to build up a regular exhibition possibility by Gallery Kühl in Dresden. She also was active in the SED, (East German Socialist Party, but this party was Stalinist dictated as we found out a little later).

All was well for the moment, we thought, until those catastrophic events of the coming years.

We did not realize that the Stasi, and most probably my sister under pressure were already making their disastrous preparation for the events of 1972 and 1973. It is now well known that the Stasi, with threats and promises, manipulated many GDR citizens. This resulted in family members spying on each other, the end effect causing families to break up, and as in my case lose contact. Anything could prompt the Stasi into blackmailing a person to work for them. This could be contact with the western world, ability to speak another language, appearance, anything and everything possible was used.

It is more than likely that the Stasi already as early as 1967 began their evil activities and my sister was by now also a victim of Stasi blackmail and subject to constant intimidation to work for them. Perhaps Stasi activity might have began even earlier, about 1963?

My mother always stood up for her beliefs and positive socialist views. But our lives in the GDR became a balancing act between different worlds, tight rope walking. Some people told us how silly we were to leave Britain and others, SED party members, regarding us with suspicion and mistrust, as spies.

As long as I lived with my mother in the previous GDR we could not talk freely about what was happening. We were always under strict observation from Stasi.

Lindy could not stand this pressure much longer and married as soon as she could. We always said, 'she married a car' because the waiting list for a car was so long and her husband had one. It was difficult to get a car in East Germany with a ten-year waiting list. His attitude towards us was from the start weird and uncomfortable. Then her son Frank was born. So with the poor boy was born into very unhappy circumstances although Lindy would say she was happy.

My sister married about 1970. I was not even allowed to attend the official wedding reception, and only allowed to attend the diner party afterwards at the pub. I think it was the only time I ever saw my sister's husband's relatives. She requested that I undergo all sorts of special treatment, had to have a special hair do, and buy extra special clothing. In the end I was not even permitted to attend the ceremony and only allowed to go to the pub afterwards. I was not good enough for her.

When dad came over to join us from England he was promised all sorts of things from the GDR authorities. 'Honey' spread round his mouth and promises were made that were not kept. That time we were regrettably still ' blind'. Don't forget I was studying at the music school, my dream coming true and my mother still hoping for artist recognition. She was back in her beloved Dresden, home again at last. We just did not understand what was going on. When we did discover the facts and the disastrous events increased to full extent the physiological pain was unbearable.
Lindy despaired, disappeared, stayed silent, and is still silent to this day. I was deeply occupied with my music and loving every minute of it. I did not understand what was happening with my sister.

When we then moved to our new flat on the Ender Street the situation with my sister was no better. My mother now had a good pension and financially we were better of. We were at first unaware of individuals meddling in our lives and the constant strict observation from Stasi officials until things escalated to the disastrous events of 1972. We were too happy and blinded by the so-called socialist world and did not see the changes that gradually took place around us. It was not too late to save Lindy, but it was clear that the Stasi entered our flat on a regular basis and not only Lindy but also my dad knew about these regular 'visits' in our absence without our knowledge.

I never stayed long away from home whilst working at the theatre in Freiberg and always came back as soon as possible. My accommodation on Freiberg was after all extremely primitive!

After my sister got married and had moved away to her own home with her husband she was obviously sent into our flat from the Stasi for whatever reason, and most probably forced to do certain things. But at this time, 1968 – 1969 we still believed that my sister just wanted to be with her fiancée, have her own life and have her own family, something quite natural and understandable!

3. Our holiday 1969 on the Isle of Rügen at the Baltic coast, (Ost See).

We had many wonderful holidays together, not always did we write a diary but here is one holiday we wrote about.

1969 was a happy year. I had spent my first year as a professional orchestra violinist at the theatre in Freiberg. My wish and desire to take up this profession had now become reality. Lindy, my little sister was now independent, and going her own way. She had her job as a technical engineer and had her own wishes and desires. She was already together with her future husband.
The summer holidays were about to begin. It was a wonderful holiday we had, my mother and I, my friend Halline, a friend from the Czech republic and my friend Sabine nicknamed 'Bini'

who joined us later. We were a jolly group of five by the end of that memorable holiday. Bini and Halline were sisters. I met Bini at the music school in Dresden. We had studied together.

We both, my mother and I, kept a diary of that memorable holiday. My mother's diary starts on the 2nd of July. The journey began in the train with my friend Halline as 'replacement daughter' and Pixy our little dog went with. My mother and Halline took the night train to the coast. The journey was tiring, and I was to come two days later, then I still had two performances at the theatre.

My mother's diary starts on the 3rd of July. She reports;
"We had a two-hour wait in Bergen before we could continue our journey.
Outside the railway station is a small very well laid out cemetery for fallen soviet soldiers. It is very well kept and impressive. Now we have built our miniature palace on the small campsite here. We had to fetch our luggage from the post office. Luckily, the post office was not far from the campsite. This camping place could be better, but it is not too far from the wild rough stormy coast.
Our GDR does not care much for holidaymakers. The footpath to the coast is rather overgrown and wild."

My mother continues to report about the events of the next day, 4th July;
"Today was an exciting day. Halline is now feeling better. The journey was tiring. Fetching our camping equipment from the post office and building up our 'holiday home' was obviously a bit too much for her. Today we went wandering around the island, from Stutzen Kammer and then to Königstuhl enjoying the wonderful landscape and view over the sea."

We were disappointed that we could not find a beach where we could bathe in the same way as we used to during our previous holidays at the Darßer coast. It was custom there to bathe free and naked. (FKK coast – free body culture).
As reported before, this was one freedom the majority of GDR citizens had and took at the coast and nothing would stop or take away this one freedom. No one could travel free to the West but here we could be free in a 'different way'.

My diary notes start on Thursday 3rd July that year;
"It's evening and at last, the final show of this summer season's performances.
On my way to work to the theatre I met that very nice young friendly cellist and we chatted about this and that and all sort of things. I wonder if I will hear from him again? He has my address. Today we played the comical opera 'Oben und Unten', (Above and Below) by Robert Hanell. As we arrived it began to rain quite heavily. It was a right thunderstorm and I got quite wet. I wonder how the two lucky ones are getting on at Rügen?[2] Yesterday, mum and my friend Halline set of with Pixy, our little dog. As the train departed from the station, disappearing in the distance, I ran along the platform trying to keep up with the train as far as possible waving to them.

After the performance, I had luck, then the tuba player from the Dresden Staats Kapelle, (Dresden state orchestra) who was helping out took me back to Dresden. He is a very nice jolly chap."

Friday 4th July I went early into town and went to dad's place. He had just woken up, so I made him a cup of tea. He was lazy and not dressed properly. I gave him a daughterly kiss that embarrassed him. Dad was not one for that kind of affection.

I took an earlier tram and arrived much too early at the railway station then I did not want to carry my luggage all the way.

---

[2] Rügen; an Island of the Baltic coast.

I had a friend whom I nicknamed ' Boxer' and wondered if he would see me of at the station but he did not come, might have missed me then I fell asleep sitting on the bank at the station whilst waiting for the train. If he did come, then he must have walked past me without seeing me. I had laid my head on my folded arms then I was quite sleepy. ,

For the first part of my journey to Berlin I shared the train compartment with an older couple from Hungary. They had already travelled twenty-four hours and would arrive Saturday morning at last in Norway where their son lived. They were a very friendly couple and we chatted a lot.

In Stralsund I had some time before my journey continued so I went for a walk and fed the ducks with some biscuits I had.

The sun was shinning brightly when I arrived in Saßnitz but there was no bus connection to continue my journey to Nipmerow until late afternoon so I went looking for a taxi and arrived 1pm at last at the campsite. I found our tent but how disappointed I was, no one was there, so I quickly changed my cloths and went searching for two ladies with a little black and white dog.

The beach was disappointing, everywhere stones. It was quite impossible to bathe here. Five o'clock arrived and still no one there at the tent, so I went again for a walk over the fields to the other beach. This time I found the bathing place. The weather was fine, the sea dazzling in the sunlight.

At last, on my return to the campsite there they were, and what a luxury I can settle into a finished built nest, they get top marks for a perfectly built tent. After an evening feast I slept like a log, but before we went to bed we went for an evening walk around the small lake and listened to the croaking frogs and the rustling noises in the bushes.

The next day; 5th July we rambled through the forest hoping to find a shorter way to the stony beach. The scorching sun shone down onto the earth but in the forest in the shade it was cool. The path was endless, became narrower and smaller as we trekked down it finally ending as a rough stony pathway only possible to scramble and climb down leading to an area belonging to the NVA[3]. We had to turn round, go back and at length landed at the Stubbenkammer.[4]

Not many people were at the beach, so we could bathe in Darßer fashion[5], then we climbed onto a large rock and sunned ourselves also in Darßer fashion. This one freedom we experienced on the Baltic coast was custom nearly everywhere and especially on the Darßer coast. It was as if the lack of freedom to travel to the west was compensated in this fashion to bathe at the coast naked in free body culture way.

We played a jolly game, if we thought someone was coming, quickly put something on, then we were not sure if this lonely cove we found was an official free body culture place, although the majority of the Baltic coast was. Pixy was angry and annoyed about the stones making it difficult for her to walk over them and we had to carry her over them.

Three sea nymphs seated on the rocks in the sun by the sea, singing and watching the boats and ships sailing by on the horizon. Ah, we are not the nymphs from the Lorelei, from that story of those nymphs locking sailors to their destruction. Can people from the Stubben Kammer see us through their telescopes? Well if this is the case, they have something interesting to see.

Before we made our way back to the campsite we went up to the viewpoint. The scenery was stunning, the sea spread out endless before us. No one was there anymore to cash in the fee, so we saved the fifty pence.

---

[3] NVA; National folks army
[4] Stubbenkammer; cove by the beach.
[5] Darßer fashion; here is meant bathing in 'free body culture' way.

At last we found a shorter way back to the campsite, three quarters of an hour later we arrived at our tent.

We woke up 6th of July, Sunday, the weather undecided how it was to treat us, cold, warm or windy! Again we sat at the stony beach by the Stubben Kammer. I had to carry Pixy over the beach in the rucksack, as it was too difficult for her to walk over the stones. My unusual luggage amused people and photographs were taken.

We stopped at the 'soldiers cove'; a cove we renamed while often soldiers visited this part. Today we were not alone on the beach and so could not bathe in Darßer fashion then some sailors had arrived. Before they came, we had hollowed out a place in the stones, built a wall as refuge from the winds, and went to fetch some wooden boards for us to lie on.

The sun was warm and the sky blue, the scenery so beautiful. It's such a shame that there is no sunset here, only until about four pm in the afternoon, then everything is in shadow.

The chalky rocks ascend steep. Above by the 'Königs Stuhl'(rock formation) people are leisurely strolling along, or having lunch at the café at Stubben Kammer. But we are sitting on our wooden boards in our 'stone castle' having a wonderful picnic.

As the sailors arrived we ran, actually scrambled over the stones into the water to get to our place on our 'Lorelei' rock. Quite right we were to do so, then the sailors also scrambled over the stones into the water and onto our rock. It was quite a squeeze, eight folk on our rock, there was just enough room for all of us. Continually we, and the sailors sprang from the rocks into the water. There were two other smaller rocks sticking out of the water and sailors sat on them also.

It was a jolly picture; the green sea, the three rocks in the water, on the one larger rock a whole herd of folk sitting there, on the other two rocks the bathers sitting on their on, single or in twos and allowing the salty waves of the sea to splash over them.

That evening we went for an evening walk in direction Saßnitz. It was supposed to be a two-kilometre climb, so we scrambled over the stony coast, carrying Pixy in the rucksack. At various places little streams came flowing over the rocky cliffs into the sea. We called these streams 'doggy restaurants' then here, Pixy could drink as much water as she wanted. At the Darßer coast on our previous holidays poor Pixy often went thirsty if we did not take sufficient drinking water with, but here there were so many little streams flowing over the rocks into the sea.

Everywhere stones and chalky cliffs, but at last we found an ascent by the Keiler stream. Up above on the cliff top we were greeted with a wonderful panoramic view over the sea, the white chalky steep cliffs and above in the sky many seagulls flying and calling. Obviously they had their nests here and had made themselves quite at home.

A small insignificant track led further up through the bushes and we arrived at the viewpoint. Here we found a notice from the military informing any visitors that it was forbidden to take any photographs. Why, was a bit of a puzzle! The track improved with wooden steps to climb up followed by a steep ascending wide path. The wood here is beautiful, quiet and peaceful, birds singing and we are alone with ourselves meeting no one on our way. Pixy is so delighted not to have to walk over those stony rocks. We arrived back at the campsite far too early; the sun was still shining so bright and warm.

The next day Monday 7th July found us travelling over to Glowe, and at last a sandy beach. We swam from buoy to buoy like fish. The campsite here by Glowe, is situated right by the seacoast; the sandy beach stretching far, Pixy was especially pleased about the sand. An approaching thunderstorm surprised us; luckily some campers offered us shelter in their large tent.

Tuesday 8th July arrived. Today we wanted to continue our wandering from Sunday. This time we wandered direct through the woods to the 'Fisher Bay'. The sun shone so bright and hot. Actually we wanted to bathe in Darßer style, but the presence of a fisher boat changed our plans. Everywhere were fishing nets thrown out to catch eels, so we could not bathe here after all, also the water was chalk white and laid out with many rocks showing out of the water, the waves splashing over them. We searched for a shorter way back; our walk became an evening stroll. Well we had stayed at the 'Fisher Bay' all day instead of the planned coast walk.

On our trail back to the campsite we stumbled upon interesting wild life; a herd of wild boars disappearing into the forest grunting, then a stag appeared majestically in front of us on our path, his head held proudly his antlers high. As we wandered over the field two hares, scared by our presence ran away from us. Pixy would have loved to catch and play with them. And then, to complete our wild life encounter, a bull snorting and threatening tried to prevent us from walking further over the field.

Wednesday the 9th July arrived. Just as we were having our breakfast it began to thunder. Well its mum's fault, she wanted to have a day's rest, so now I'm sitting in the tent, the rain drumming on the tent roof, Pixy laying comfortably behind me wrapped up in a blanket. Mum is busy eating and Halline is writing a letter. I want to go shopping to buy some food, then rain day is a day for feasting.

Late that afternoon the sun decided to appear through the clouds so we went for a stroll around the 'Herta Lake'. Somewhere here was once a castle, standing pompously in the scenery. According to a rumour from a legend a Goddess of fertility lived here bathing in the dark black waters of the 'Herta Lake'. All her attendants, servants and slaves were murdered, sacrificed to the Gods at the sacrifice stone nearby. The lake laid hidden here in the forest, calm and still, surrounded by trees and bushes. Wild boars dwelled here also and we were only too glad to see them in the distance. We stumbled across an old ancient burial site on our way back.

Halline received a telegram from Usti, her friend Jitka is coming tomorrow and Sabine also to follow shortly. Ha, then we will be a right jolly crowd.

Today, 10th July dazzlingly shining sun shone down on us. Halline's friend Jitka from Usti had already arrived. Mum had found out that if one walked back from Juliusruhe in the direction of Glowe that there is a free body culture beach. Now I am sitting on a rock by Lohme and mum is painting. We waited in vain for Halline and Jitka. We then decided to continue our walk along the coast. Here were no steep cliffs; the forest edge came right up to the water where large stones and boulders emerged out of the sea. Folk here bathing behaved a little suspicious, hiding themselves behind the rocks, surely they had been bathing in free body culture way. Here the evening sun shone down onto the beach and at last we could sun bathe at leisure till late.

The journey back took us along a dried up slippery streambed and then across some wind still fields. Here we decided to sunbathe again, it was so warm. The rest of the journey continued across cornfields, blue cornflowers and red poppies smiling at us, an invitation to pick and take them back to the tent. This was so tempting that we could not resist taking a bunch for our camping table. Someone had already trampled a path across the cornfield. The evening sun in the clear blue sky was smiling down upon us, the sea shimmering in the distant. We past a fenced of area where horses and a cow roamed freely resting and grazing peacefully in the evening sun. Finally we arrived at a farmhouse, greeted by ducks and chicken quacking and clucking. The friendly farmer showed us the way back. It had been a lovely peaceful day.

Friday the 11th July arrived. It was a really mad day. The weather was not specially and Halline and Jitka had to go to the police station in Sassnitz to report her arrival. The officials here in Nipmerow are simply dreadfully bureaucratic. Today we decided to leave our dog Pixy back at the tent so before we set off we went for a ramble with her around the pond near the campsite. Halline was going to take care of her. Tiny little frogs were hopping around our feet making it difficult to walk in case they got squashed. So we had to step really carefully. Anglers had made a primitive raft to use for fishing. Poor Pixy was so cross with us when we left her back at the tent, but it was difficult for her small paws to scramble over the rocks. Our ramble led us over to Stubben Kammer where we had an excellent lunch.

There is a legend about the black woman at Stubben Kammer. She sat all alone in a cave guarding a golden goblet. A white dove sat before the cave. A man condemned to death was given the option, either to die or to fetch the golden goblet. He of course decided to acquire the goblet and made his way to the cave. As he stood before the cave the black woman changed into a beautiful virgin maiden. She talked to him trying to persuade him to take her instead of the golden goblet. The condemned man took the goblet because this would save his life. The young virgin changed back into the black woman and sighed; ' Alas, can no one help me? Can no one release me from my curse?

After our lunch we went bathing at the 'Soldier cove'. It was bitterly cold, the water icy and freezing.

We continued walking along the coast up steep chalky cliffs. At last we arrived at the 'Fisher Bay'. Today the water was so wonderful clear, the view, breath taking. Now began the best part of our walk, continuing over even steeper and frail cliffs, the sky on the horizon became darker as if a thunderstorm was approaching. From the 'Fisher Bay' you could see in the far distant the top of a high chalky white cliff. That's where we intended to head for. Can we find another way to climb up? The trees hung a half to one meter over the rocks so that it looked as if they would tumble over and down the cliffs. We had to climb over fallen trees. At some places the water was quite high, the stones round and smooth. Streams were flowing, tumbling down the rocks. If Pixy were with us, she would be pleased to drink the fresh clear stream water. At one point a stream plummeted over the rocky precipice and here we found a path going further up.

Now was time for a well earned break and mum just had to paint a picture, even it was just a small one. Of course I painted as well but obviously I need a bit more time to practice and get back into painting.

We had hardly continued our wandering when we noticed a strange peculiar movement or reflection in the water less than fifty meters away from the shore. We gazed and wondered what it could be; perhaps seals? It could not be stones or rocks, they do not change form from something pointing out of the water, something long like a snake form, moving around. Then we saw quite clearly seals, two of them playing with each other undisturbed and ignorant of our presence. They turned and rolled showing their white bellies, their noses and flippers then disappearing as a dark shadow in the water. This game repeated many times over and over again. We could have watched for hours how the seals played and rolled and bounced back into the sea but we had to continue our long wandering. We still had a long way to go and it was already five o'clock. Now we arrived as planned at the top point and looking back once more we could watch the seals at play. Here the cliffs were steeper; the tide coming high up the stony shore and the waves spraying over the rocks at this stormy corner. We had to climb over a fallen tree.

It was a comforting feeling after that lonely wonderful and eventful time to meet people coming towards us as soon as we past the viewpoint. It's still three kilometres walk until

Saßnitz. As it was now quite late we went up the next ascent. Here the beach was even a little sandy and a couple of men were fishing. Now the way led up a steep ladder to the ' Waldhalle' café. Here we had supper. It was already 6pm and we still had to wander through the woods to Wipmerw then at this time there was no bus. At first it was wonderful in the woods until we noticed that something was not quite right with the path. The map showed so many paths crossing through the woods. But today these paths are now not in use and overgrown. Obviously only the path by the shore was useable, a few disappearing overgrown paths into the woods and the main road.

Until we found this out we had another unique experience. With the map in our hands, we continued bravely happily and boldly. We had to keep left towards the main road but the path gradually disappeared. Everything was fine until we came to the stream. Here the path was completely overgrown with trees across over the path. There were grunting noises on all sides around us. We were surrounded by wild boars and their fresh tracks could be seen on the ground.

Mum did not lose her confidence. She did not want to go back the way we had just come. That would have meant going back along the whole of the shore, also it was now beginning to get dark and we already could hear noises coming from the main road.

Our search and investigation for the disappearing hidden track was unsuccessful. In the end, disappointed we had to admit defeat. Are we going to have to spend the night in the woods? How is Pixy back at the tent? And Halline and Jitka? Hope they are not too worried.

The trail that once existed disappeared subsiding into grass. Are we going to find our way back to the stream? Yes, we did find it after we went astray in the woods. Now began a long ramble always along the cliff. Here were no grunting noises. Obviously no wild boars came here. The darkness of night ascending, sea and sky melting into one, the horizon was no more; the view was ghostly and eerie in the dusk.

At last we arrived at Stubben Kammer. In the café one lonely light was still burning, the chairs were placed on the tables, the place was deserted and empty. We decided to go back along the road so as not to get lost again. The journey down the country road was endless, and now it was quite dark. The ghostly effect of the darkness of the night around the 'Herta Lake' made this area look even more creepy and unnatural, the fallen rotting tree trunks shone ghostly in the darkness. Occasional we heard a wild boar grunting again. Perhaps we disturbed a deer as we continued our walk into the dark night. The road was endless; mum complained about the stony paths, her sandals were not made for walking on them.

We were so glad when we arrived at last at the campsite. Halline and Jitka were both fast asleep. We were beginning to think we would have to find some sort of night quarters in the woods amongst the wild boars without Pixy. Pixy was fine and delighted to see us when we arrived at last, wagging her tail so fast it nearly fell of. We drank some milk and soon slept soundly.

Saturday 12th July; familiar voices woke me up. Bini had arrived, great now it's going to be really jolly. Halline was convinced we had gone to the cinema in Lohme last evening because we came back so late. I thought she would say that.
Today we went the 'soldiers cove'; bathing and sunning ourselves in 'Darßer' fashion with lots of fun and laughter.100 metres away, a man was also bathing in 'Darßer' fashion. We hid ourselves behind the rocks. Yesterday we found a hidden notice; 'FKK'[6] that we had not seen before. I went into the water at first with my bikini on. The man came towards us and said 'don't catch cold with something on'. Fact; bathing with a wet swimsuit on is colder than bathing in 'Darßer' fashion. Also important to note that anyone bathing on these 'FKK' beaches were all very friendly, polite and decent people. How it is today I do not know, but in

---

[6] FKK; 'Freie korper kultur' meaning 'free body culture.'

those days in the GDR no one needed to be afraid or fear of any indecent behaviour. We all just enjoyed the fresh air, beautiful countryside, the warmth of the sun and the freedom to bathe this way in the sea. Surely, this man must also have visited the 'Darßer' beach. It was our custom to bind our bikinis onto our heads and so we could keep them dry until we swam back onto the rocks.

Sunday 13ᵗʰ July; this morning howling winds greeted us, and no sunshine, so we had a lay in. It had been quite noisy at the campsite during the night. That afternoon we went to Stubben Kammer where mum sold two small paintings for 15 DM each. She could have sold some pictures earlier to the man who had a small shop selling souvenirs.
Earlier that morning we were awaken by Bini and Halline singing a duet that sounded wonderful. That evening we celebrated then next day we were going home to pack and prepare for our Tatra holiday. We drank and eat and sang, merry making until late. Pixy received a gigantic large ribbon to celebrate this parting feast.

Monday 14ᵗʰ July arrived, departure day. We packed early and sent off our luggage at the post office. The weather was fine, and the sun shone brightly. That afternoon we sunned and bathed at the beach in Lohme. We said our goodbyes to Halline, Jitka and Bini and now we are sitting in the night train on our way home to Dresden. Hopefully we will have good weather for our Tatra holiday."

4 Our holiday in the Polish Tatra.

I wanted to celebrate my first year in my profession in a special way, and so we decided to pre- book a holiday abroad, somewhere we would be able to travel. This had to be in one of the other east block countries and it was not so easy. Such particular holidays could only be pre- booked at one specific time early in January and often booking such a vacation was accompanied by endless waiting in extremely long queues. You had to watch out for special announcements in the local newspaper for that particular day when these special holidays were on sale. Many GDR citizens started queuing up all night for the priority to buy one of these. We were extremely lucky, then often, before your turn arrived after queuing so long, the place you wanted might be sold out. And so we pre-booked a holiday to the Polish Tatra.

I had a whole month free before returning to start my second year in my profession. Our camping holiday on the Isle of Rügen was over. Now we wanted something more comfortable and different. My sister did not want to come with; she was by now already with her future husband, engaged, but still living at home. She wanted to go her own way and had a holiday booked with her fiancée. We had a most wonderful time, my mother and I, the memories still vivid in my mind. Dad took care of little Pixy. She was such a well-behaved dog and no trouble to take care off.

Our diary notes begin on the 19ᵗʰ July 1969
"It is now twenty-four hours since we left Dresden at about 21.30 pm. But I'll report about everything one at a time.

We arrived back in Dresden very tired from our camping trip. As soon as I collected the papers for our Tatra journey we went up to our mountain property in Wachwitz outside Dresden. We wanted to rest before the night journey to the Tatra. This was disappointing then we had not expected to have to travel through the night.

Our Budgie, 'Jimmy' was so pleased to see us again. He was quite a chatterbox constantly calling after us, ' Bist du da', 'Gib küsschen Rindvieh!' Translated meaning 'Are you there?' 'Give a kiss, you cow!' From whom our budgie picked this up, I don't know, but he was very quick to mimic any sounds and words he liked. Pixy was also glad, at last, no stony beaches to scramble over any more.

Wednesday we went up to the mountain property in Wachwitz. There was still no message from 'Boxer'. The weather was wonderful, and extremely hot, so that we could sunbathe a little. In the night things became a little spooky, there was a constant cluttering noise, animals were creeping around our hut.

Back home Thursday evening I found two postcards from 'Boxer' waiting for me with a time to meet him. Well, at the Görlitzer railway station I wrote him an apologetic letter hoping to meet him after our holiday. Our journey began Friday night. Pixy was so well behaved still hoping that she could come with us. As the train departed out of the station she stood there with my sister Lindy looking sadly after us. Hope she will be all right. Dad and Lindy had agreed to take care of her.

The journey was long and tiring. First, we took the express train to Görlitz and arrived there at midnight. Here at the border we were supposed to meet the others of our group at 3 o'clock in the morning. The three hour long wait in Görlitz past by uneventful. We drank very strong coffee mum had made which kept us awake and cheerful. The waiting room that was also a café was horrible, noisy and dirty, so we went onto the platform, sat on a bench to have a rest. We could not find our group. Three o'clock arrived and still there was no tour guide to be seen, but instead we finally met some others from our group also waiting. The train from Berlin arrived early at 3.17 am and we had to get onto the train quickly without having met the rest of the group. The train was absolutely filthy. The customs officer on duty said we should wait, then our tour guide was already there. The train was crammed full and still this uncertainty, where was she? Finally we all had to walk through the entire jam-packed moving train with our luggage before we found the rest of our group and our tour guide. By then it was 4 o'clock in the morning. At last we had found her, what a relief that was and we also had a sleeping-carriage, now we could have some sleep. We were so tired; it was now 4.30 early in the morning.

The rest of the journey until Krakow past peacefully and we chatted with the other friendly fellow holidaymakers in our compartment. They told us that in Poland hardly any state owned land existed as in the GDR, perhaps only about twenty-five per cent, most of the land was privately owned as in earlier days. Indeed only smaller parts of the fields were in use and often worked on in the old fashion way with scythe.

In Krakow at lunchtime we were given a feast fit for royalty, a four-course meal; as starter a cooked egg with mayonnaise followed by dill soup, pork fillet and finally a pancake, far too much. Now the journey continued by bus another three hours travel through boring dirty industry countryside, then further into the mountains. It was harvest time. At first the countryside looked similar to the Chiltern Hills back home in England, hilly with small fields in stripes and patches. The hills became larger as we continued through woods and valleys further into the mountains. Then we saw those wonderful mountains towering high into the sky, at last the Tatra. The bus took other people with who happened to want to travel the same way. Also in Zakopane the bus stopped extra to let someone in, now that would not have happened in the GDR. Everyone is so friendly here. In Krakow we met the tour guide from Poland. Except for the tiring first part, the rest of our journey was good organized.

We arrived in Zakopan, the only main town in the Tatra with those towering high mountains in view in the near distance. The town was swarming with people; folk dressed in their traditional costume, everywhere were signs with the number twenty-two on it. Obviously their twenty-two-anniversary year was approaching. Outside Zakopane the houses became smaller and smaller, less and less. Our tiredness disappearing with every second our journey continued, admiring the splendid landscape, the magnificent mountains reaching high into the sky. The bus stopped in Huciska where horse drawn carriages awaited to take us on our last part of the journey, a pleasant drive through the valley between the mountains. The horses trotted happily along, on each carriage sat a local man in the driver seat in traditional costume; coloured embroidered trousers and a little round hat on his head. It was a very special joyful drive through the Chocholovska valley. The horse from our carriage was so sweet. At one point he just went to the side and drank water from a little stream. We gave him some sugar as a farewell gift.

Soon we arrived at our destination in a valley with several wooden huts and a wooden church on the hilltop. We wondered if people were living in them. No, that could not be possible that people lived in these primitive huts, surely they are for animals only. But there were people living in these poor wooden huts situated on the mountainside without light, no electricity and they were very friendly, looked happy and healthy.

We were given a one two-bed room in a mountain hotel situated on the edge of wonderful woods, before us superb flowering fields with old primitive huts, cows and sheep and a mountain stream flowing over the rocky stones. The view was magnificent. The valley with fields and primitive huts surrounded by mountains and forests. These huts had no or only one window and were built from wooden planks, any gaps stuffed with grass and paper; people really lived in these huts.

Seven o'clock evenings we had a superb supper, again a feast and then went for an evening walk in the valley over to the huts where we were greeted by two friendly little dogs and children playing. They showed us two small puppies, their eyes hardly open, so sweet. The mother dog sprang up barking angrily, but after we gave her something to eat she became friendlier.

Sunday 20th July; we slept so well after that long day yesterday and had a hearty breakfast at 7 o'clock. If this continues we'll arrive home really stuffed. Mum can eat all the food on offer. She was especially pleased that milk soup was available, something light for her sensitive stomach. That morning we went for a walk to 'Grytze' at the Czech border enjoying the panoramic view, such a shame we had to be back for lunch otherwise we would have continued. But we still painted a picture only it began to rain smearing the paint. Again a feast for lunch and an afternoon spent in the valley; mum complaining about the bad weather, but it did not prevent her from painting another watercolour picture that afternoon. We met a little man in the woods in traditional dress with a dog, happily singing and playing the mouth organ. We tried to talk to the friendly locals, tried a mixture of a little English, Czech and German. In spite of their very primitive living conditions they are very happy and content.

A crowd of people stood in front of one of the huts where cheese was sold. Many tourists and polish youth visit this valley, as part of the mountain hotel is also a youth hostel. This mountain hotel was situated at 1128 meter above sea level, at the top end of the valley. In front of another hut sat an old woman in a cart chewing something out of a sack and a man played the mouth organ for her. Perhaps it was her birthday?

These people live so primitive, no electric, not even a cooking stove, only a simple open fire in the middle of the room. On one side of the single room the domestic animals were kept, on the other side the locals were living, sleeping on the bare floor on straw sacks. We saw a woman boiling some potatoes on an open fire in front of one of the huts. Inside another hut a woman was cooking on an open fire, the smoke floating out of the door. Most of the huts have no windows.

We continued our walk to the tiny church constructed completely out of wood, well kept and in good condition, situated on the hilltop between these wonderful mountains. Today, Sunday the locals were dressed in their best clothing, the women with bright coloured headscarves and the men wearing woollen white trousers, tight fitting with coloured embroidery on the side.

Children were looking after the cows and the sheep grazing by the edge of the woods were taken care of by a shepherd. To each hut belonged a few cattle, some sheep and poultry. We saw how sheep were milked.

We were amazed that people were living in such primitive conditions in a socialist country. Our polish tour guide told us that the locals living in these primitive huts do not live here in winter that would be a little too cold!

That night it rained heavily, again a superb breakfast, milk soup for mum and we all received our pocket money. (We were only allowed a certain amount of money, even on a holiday trip to another socialist country like this one. This is something unheard of today; now you can take any amount of spending money with you like).

We were told that the Americans had landed on the moon and now were on their way back home, so they got there first before the soviets. Our walk to the Raken, a viewpoint led us through a valley, the path filled with bright shining stones inviting us to collect them. Bears live in this mountainous area and there are hidden caves in the forest. Whilst walking we were startled by a strange noise coming from behind us, looking around we were greeted by a group of happy wanderers, laughing. It was rather foggy the mist had not ascended. Our journey up the mountain took us past a lonesome hut in ruins, the view over the endless mountains spread before us. Tomorrow we'll come here again, then we need a whole day for this venture. That afternoon we painted two pictures from the Chocholowska valley. Many painters must have sat here painting, the view was well known.

After supper we spent the evening singing in our hotel room with the friendly couple with whom we shared our table. Our room looks now quite artistic, six pictures on the shelf, a collection of large pretty stones and pieces of wood.

Tuesday 22nd July was a dull day; we hoped that eventually the sun would shine. First, our path took us along the rippling brook in the valley. For one minute the mist lifted and we could see the summit, our goal.

It was very cold, the clouds on the mountain became thicker, and the view between the trees had disappeared between deep hanging clouds and mist. Usually you could see the rocks in the distance on the mountain shining white. In one direction you saw the Kominiarski Wierch and Kominy Tylkowe, in the other direction the Kamz Rakon and Wolowiec, (2063 meters high). There are numerous streams flowing through the forest in all directions, gurgling and rippling over the stones. It's the last sound you hear at night before you sleep and the first sound in bed in the morning to awaken you.

We past two-deserted derelict huts and wondered if the shepherds sometimes sleep here, then the sheep, like mountain goats climb incredibly high up the mountain. We continued our ramble, climbing higher and higher.

The paths here are extremely good marked making it impossible to get lost. In spite of the cold we were quite hot and sweating after our climb. Here the air was noticeably thinner than below, the trees smaller, tiny fir trees, bushes and undergrowth insignificant. The higher we climbed, the more mountain flowers grew in abundance. Our pockets were heavy, full of those lovely glittering stones we had collected down below in the valley.

Finally the bushes and undergrowth stopped growing, only grass and these wonderful mountain flowers everywhere. Now we were climbing up into the clouds, seeing less and less. Today is a holiday in Poland celebrating their twenty-second anniversary year. Many other people were around as well. The Polish locals were very friendly.

At last we arrived at the top only now the view was missing. It felt like being in space on an asteroid covered in white, the world looked so lonely deserted and small. Now we continued further up the Wolowiec. Our joy arriving at the peak was immense then we found a booklet where we could write our names in it. So the whole climb had been well worthwhile, the wintry weather, misty, cold and damp air did not spoil our pleasure. We had made the whole walk along the ridge in mist and fog; it was such a shame that the mist did not lift for us to see the magnificent view now hidden from us. In spite of that it was a great day walking in the clouds high up the mountain.

Our climb down the mountain was a little insecure, so we asked a young Czech couple the way. Below the mountain, under the Gryeses we continued our ramble further along the border. We found a steep descending trail that looked similar to the trail in the Gries Grund valley in the Saxon Swiss mountains back home. Suddenly someone called after us, as we were about to descend. A young man came running down the mountain, he had taken of his shirt. It was the same young man we had talked to previously. He wanted to tell us that the path we were about to use was dangerous and he then showed us the correct way. We had a good rest before continuing, enjoyed the view as the mist, now late afternoon lifted.

When we came back to our hotel we found that our dinner portions had been saved for us so we had a double portion. So that evening we had dinner and supper at the same time; very nice, and plenty.

The next day was supposed to be a rest day, but instead it became an adventurous risky day climbing up the rocks behind the youth hostel. We fed the two dogs we had made friends with previously regularly with some tasty morsels. One dog reminded me of little Pixy, she was of the same colour and had two puppies. She was quite shy and not always around. The other dog, perhaps her doggy husband was bolder and daring, his tail wagging took most of the scraps given to him by the tourists. He was a very happy dog and the tourists smiled and laughed as if these tasty scraps were for themselves.

We wanted to paint the grandiose view over the whole of the valley so we climbed up the path the shepherds use. Half way up we heard bells tinkling. The sheep were on their way down the mountain. They wore bells around their necks. There they were, all kinds and all sizes, with and without horns jumping over the rocks down the mountain, amazing how they could climb such steep rocks. Passing, they looked at us astounded, 'what are you both doing here, you're in our way, bahh....' Then before continuing their journey jumping and climbing over stones and rocks down the mountain they stopped and stared at us. The shepherd, a middle-aged man, brown from the sun came whistling down the path surrounded by his sheep.

Not all have a bell and there were many young lambs amongst the herd. He looked at us surprised not expecting to meet anyone up that part of the mountain.

We continued our ramble, higher up a steep stony path, over undergrowth, through woodland and finally we came to the alpine pasture high above below the rocks, we still heard the sheep below. Early mornings you hear the sheep passing on their way up the mountain and the whistling shepherd calling them. Sometimes the shepherd is out at night, his whistling, singing and yodelling sounding over the valley.

Whilst sunning ourselves on this pleasant pasture, the shepherd's music and this picture of his sheep around him was never far from my mind.

We wanted to continue further up, it looked so easy and the view up there must be magnificent. First we searched for a path to ascend through the woods. The silence was eerie. Everywhere were footprints from the sheep. Eventually we lost our way and had to return back to the alpine pasture. Woodcutters had been here; all over the woods were fallen trees. How surprised we were when we noticed that the path was becoming steeper and gradually more difficult to climb down than to climb up. It was so hot now in the sun and we had to continue further up, often scrambling on all fours over the stones. The rocks seemed to be moving further away instead of coming nearer, but soon we arrived at the crest. We were more anxious for each other's safety than for ourselves. In front of the rock was about a whole meter or more of lose stones and one could slip easily walking over it. Luckily it was not far to the other side. My mum and I, we are quite tough and do not give up easily. At last at the top we realized that it was now impossible to make our way down, so we had to continue further up. First we had a good rest and admired the hard, well earned glorious view, the mountains towering high between the two rocks, the sky clear blue. It was such a wonderful view, such a shame we did not have the nerves or peace of mind to paint. How are we going to get down? To begin with, it looked as if we might have to call out for help to get down again. Is there an echo here? It's a shame I did not try it out. Down on the alpine pasture, were wonderful echoes from all sides. Our path downwards was hard and difficult to find, going over and under bushes, small deep growing fir trees and larches, around one rock and then around another rock. Perhaps we'll end up the Czech republic? But luckily things went smoothly and after our predicament we came at last to a little woodland area, then over a lawn, the view becoming even more impressive and magnificent. Here at last we found time to sketch the splendid view before us. Finally we found a way down a stony path with no rocks blocking our path.

That night in bed I thought of the sheep and chamois, a type of mountain goat that live here in the Tatra, climbing everywhere. We had seen them up there in the mountains as well.

The next day, Thursday 24th July, greeted us with glorious sunshine and our first official outing awaiting us, but it turned out to be quite a disappointing day. The bus took us to Moskei Oko, (the eye of the sea).

On the way to Moskei Oko we stopped at Zakopane and some of the tourists in our group wanted to go coffee drinking. This took valuable time away for our stay at 'Moskei Oko'. When we got there, mum had only just enough time for a quick sketch, and for us to walk half way round the lake up to the climb to the other lake 'Czerny Staw'. The view is supposed to be even better up there. Our time was far too short. Other tourists from our group ran up the slope as fast as possible. That was something we did not want to do. We did not want to hasten up and down the mountain, but to take time and enjoy the wonderful mountainous view and to be back well in time for the return journey. In the end we also would have had time to go up the mountain, then we had to wait a whole hour for the others to return. Our Chocholowska valley is the best with the magnificent mountainous view surrounding it. On the way back we stopped and went round the extremely attractive and interesting market in

Zakopane. There were two rows of women knitting exceptionally coloured jackets. Over there, on the stall a farmer's wife was sleeping, children were begging and one very friendly farmer's wife, who obviously could not write, spoke Polish and a little German, demonstrating with her fingers in the air gave me a jacket to try on. The visit to that market was the best of the day.

Friday 25th July dawned, greeting us again with radiant sunshine. Early every morning, we heard the bells of the sheep and the shepherd, whistling merrily like a bird tenderly for his flock of sheep. Each morning I had to jump out of bed quickly to go to the window to watch him, a strong sturdy man, brown from the fresh air and sun with his special little ' korallen'[7] hat on, a typical style worn by the local folk living here in these self-styled so-called 'korallen villages'. In winter, they do not live here in the Chocholovska valley, only one stays behind to take care of the huts and goods until the next summer.

Today, we had planned to be back by lunchtime. We set of in the direction of the Rakon Mountain. It was hot and there was no problem to wander around in bikini, this was quite fashionable here; cloths in the rucksack and bikini on, brown from the sun, that's how the proficient youth here wander up into the mountains. On the way up we collected stones glittering like gold and silver, our anoraks tied round our waists, bikini on, so in this fashion we continued. The view today was splendid and mum wanted to paint again, she was anxious that she would not paint enough watercolours, but for this, a wonderful view was necessary. Shortly before the deserted derelict huts we rested, but the view today was not grand enough for mum. At first she wanted to paint here, now today it's not good enough. As we rested, enjoying the view and contemplating our next steps the young teacher Mrs Baum from our group came up. We asked her to cancel our lunch in order to have more time up here, then we continued our ramble further up to the second rest place where we spent time painting. Wild blue berries grew here in abundance but they were not yet ripe. Here you can drink the clear cold water direct from the mountain stream. A group of rock climbers passing by also drank the clear fresh water. It was now getting late and although evening shadows covered our rest place our skin was still warm from the hot sun. Now we had to hurry to climb up the Rakon, the path becoming steeper the further we ascended. The higher we went the steeper our path, the stunning view becoming magnificent and grander, the mountains towering higher and higher above each other. We saw the rocks peering above our valley where we had been climbing the other day. Someone said they are called, 'Die Mönche' (The monks). Its great how the paths here are so clearly marked, made safe and secure, large slabs have been laid to make it easier to walk on. We were already quite high up when a young polish man spoke to us if we wanted to climb up to the top so late. It gets quickly dark here in the Tatra and there is still an hour's walk until Wolowiec. The polish people here are very polite and always greet other fellow wanderers.

At last we arrived at the top amazed at the superb view before us. Today no mist and fog like last time, the scenery spreading before us in all directions. Over there, the Czech mountains are even higher and grander than the polish ones. We were amazed and astonished at the grand panorama before us breathing in the fresh thin mountain air with delight and contentment. We could not stay too long up here so we soon had to dance hurriedly down the mountain leaping and hoping from stone to stone like gazelles. 'You are becoming a perfect dancer' mum said.

---

[7] 'korallen'; Ethnic minority living in this area.

That evening after supper we stayed up late talking to the other friendly tourists we had met up on our journey up. Mrs Lange was once fashion designer and through the encouragement from mum wanted to start drawing landscapes again.

That evening we went to sleep with the sound of the yodelling of the shepherd in the distance as he stayed the night with his only companions the mountain sheep.

Saturday 26th July arrived. Today, a group tour was organized to the neighbouring valley and caves. The weather was getting warmer and better as the day progressed. I had put my bikini on under my cloths for later. It is good to wander like this. You don't sweat and it is so airy. Many wander around like this. We passed the wooden hut where outside milk jugs stood and a cut down fir tree, the branches left as they had fallen. On the branches hung cloths, nappies, shoes and other things to dry. We passed by the hut where Muschka and Chapka live, that dear little doggy pair, obviously a very happy and contented doggy couple, father and mother, with their two sweet little doggy children. The mother dog is always so hungry.

We did not get far before we started peeling of our cloths, except for the bikinis of course. We wandered further down until quite near the other mountain cabin in the Chocholowska valley. This building is private and part of it belongs to the mountain rescue service. Now we turned away from our path in the direction of the Dolina Koscieliska always travelling up the mountain. The path continued to improve and as usual was very good presented and partly laid out with slabs. We were a happy and joyful group of different people, all of us in very good mood and content. Amusingly, those of the group who usually walked less were walking the fastest. The two sturdy chatty women, in fact ran up the mountain and Luzie, our Polish tour group leader never gave us enough time. The path led us through a forest. We came to a clearing where we could see the rocky mountains in front of us coming nearer, and our beautiful valley disappearing further in the distance. We came to an alpine pasture, again with some huts. This area was quite isolated and even lonelier than our valley. In the distance a part of the rocky Kominarski Wirch Mountains could be seen. If you looked inside one of the huts, obviously believing it was meant for cattle only, you saw how rough and primitive it was built; simple wooden boards, the gaps filled with straw and stuffed with earth. In some of the huts the holes were left unfilled and still they were lived in. The wind must be blowing through into the room. A dog was barking at the other end of the valley guarding a hut, cattle and sheep grazing peacefully next to it. The ringing of the bells could be heard throughout the whole valley. In front of one of the huts sat an elderly woman and a child was racing up the mountain. You could hear the gurgling of a stream nearby then of course water is needed to live. This was the only water supply they had.

We wandered further together up the mountain along the stream, through a forest and over a small wooden bridge. It was so hot, we all were sweating and we took a five-minute rest to cool ourselves down. Some of our group had a cigarette break. The water was very clear and icy cold. Our wandering took us further up the mountain, through another forest.

At last we reached the saddle before the climb up to the Kominarski Wierch, (1829 m high). Here we sunned ourselves before we descended into the neighbouring valley 'Dolina Koscieliska, where there are caves, everyone in our group sitting around us, all in shorts and sun costumes, it's so hot.

We all were thrilled about the wonderful view down to the valley and the glorious weather. The Kominy Tylkope, the mountain before the Kominarski Wierch reaching high on the right hand side, the valley Koscieliska with its secret caves stretching along in front of us. The mountains here were rockier. We looked at this glorious panorama admiring the view and mum took out her mouth organ and began to, play a wander song, softly all sang with. Now the steep descend into the valley began, always climbing from stone to stone. Another young girl borrowed the mouth organ and also played some songs, so we sang the whole way down. Wild strawberries and blue berries grew on the wayside. We had our lunch in the mountain cabin from Dolina Koscieliska. Our mountain cabin in the Chochlovska valley was better, elegant airier and lighter, not as dark but it still was a very interesting building like everything else here. Here were deer and stags grazing peacefully without any fear of humans. Many of our group were by now fed up with walking and wanted to get to a bus, have coffee and cake.

Here in the valley we parted from our group. No one else wanted to climb or walk anymore. We came with on this trip because we wanted to see the caves. It seems that the others got 'cold feet' as they saw we would have to climb further up the mountain. So we said our goodbyes and set of alone to continue our ramble. Luzie told us that the caves marked with red signs are the dangerous ones. There, 1962 a man went into the cave and lost his way, he could not get out. This cave had many tunnels. Two years later his bones were found. We thought that this cave was still unexplored. Now mum remembered a tale about a cave in the Harz in Germany, the 'Bauman and Herman' caves. Both of these men were explorers and wanted to investigate these unexplored caves. They both lost their way. Deep inside the caves they found stalagmites. One of them found his way out through an air vent, the other through a bat. The stalagmites are built only deep under the earth where there is no daylight. Both these men wandered days around in the caves before they found their way out ill and utterly exhausted. Both men died a short while later as a result of their stressful experience. In honour of these two men the caves were named after them. With this story in our minds we climbed up to the caves. We were also told that bones from dinosaurs were found in those caves. These caves were situated high up in the rocks, not deep down in the earth as one would think.

A stream was gushing and gurgling along the valley, flowing over the stones, and at some parts the stream came from above the mountain rocks or disappeared inside the rocks. That must be a true sign that down there are caves.

We climbed further up to the red-signed cave, the dangerous one with many entrances. We saw two entrances; the first one was not signed so we continued for another five minutes and there they were, those caves we were going to look at; a dark gapping black hole. Inside something was rustling, are people inside? It sounds like it. We put our cardigans on; it was cold inside the cave. We had torches with us. We went inside. At first there were no side tunnels, only such where you had to crawl on your stomachs in order to continue to make any progress forwards. So with it was safe to continue. At first we had to stoop, but then further on, the cave ceiling was very high, we saw a light in front of us, and an opening.

Then we saw them, the other tunnels, black gaping holes, as we thought, unexplored sections of the caves. Most probably there are stalagmites also down there, but no one knows about them. These tunnels were clearly marked with red signs.

The main tunnel made a sharp curve and led further deeper into the cave. Stones came rattling down, but we heard and saw no one else. The ground was muddy and our torches were insufficient so we could not continue. Later we found out that if we had followed the clearly marked path further on, we would not have been able to continue as the other exit had collapsed. We went back to the other unmarked cave. Suddenly three young men came equipped with lamps and everything necessary for exploring these caves. They soon disappeared down one of the side tunnels and only the rattling of falling stones told the tale that they were there. We investigated these also. At the end of the tunnel were two holes just sufficient for a person to squeeze and creep through with difficulty. The other hole led back to the rocks outside. It was so incredible eerie, but that's where those young men had disappeared and above us we heard sounds and the echoes of their voices slowly diminishing the further they descended into the depths of the cave.

Our investigation continued exploring the black marked cave that to our astonishment was situated higher as the red marked one. The path was very slippery and stony, but where was this cave? A path led round the rocks. We were about to continue when suddenly the sound of falling stones made us look up. There on the rocks was the black sign and chains were fastened onto the rocks for climbing up. A young couple came climbing carefully down, step by step, holding onto the chains. This unexpected change of direction, to climb up to a cave did not put us of. Without our experience and wanderings in Saxon Switzerland and the climb up the Mönch Stein[8] we would not have be able to climb up to the cave entrance.

We climbed up slowly foot by foot holding onto the chains not too fast in cause it might have got lose. No end was in sight. Of course mum wanted to go first. Suddenly she called out astonished and disappeared. How surprised we were, when we thought at last to have found the entrance, but instead only a gapping deep hole and a stepladder leading deep into the cave. At the bottom looking around we found ourselves in a very high grotto, perhaps about 10 meters in height, pitch dark, above us the daylight beamed into the cavern, a thunderstorm approaching and dark clouds spreading over the sky. A couple came down as well and joined us, as we were the only ones with some light. This cave definitely looked dangerous, although clearer marked. Large blocks of rocks and stones blocked the entrance to further tunnels leading deeper into the cave. Here you could easily slip and fall without proper climbing equipment and a rope. It was difficult to climb up and down.
Mum said, 'at last a proper climb; she is first- rate, wonderful and a genuine good experienced wanderer. There is only one mum like my mum to be found in the whole of the world.

Outside the cave once more, we met some German tourists. They asked us about the cave and told us that yesterday they had climbed up the 'Riesi' Mountain and that it is far more difficult to climb up from the Polish side as from the Czech side. Above were supposed to be chains and footholds for climbing up to the yellow marked cave that we also wanted to look at. We had little time left, as we had to be back by 7 pm for supper.

The thunderstorm was now approaching fast. We hurried over the wooden bridge following the yellow marking. In the front of us was a group of small school children with their teacher. Our path led us through a sort of valley, high towering rocks on both sides reminding us of the Saxon Swiss Elb Sandstone Mountains back home. We had to climb up to the yellow marked cave as well. By now mum was quite exhausted and tired. Later we found out that there were three different ways back, but we returned the way we came until the main path by the bridge and stream. High above, round the rocks was a path to climb up, with secure and safe chains and footholds, and then leading finally to the cave. On our arrival at the top we saw the other entrance where we would have come out. The path continued comfortable further a little down the mountain and then through the woods. Soon we arrived at Husiska place. Actually our group wanted to wait for us here but they would have had to wait too long. Our cave expedition took two hours and with that, we were only able to look at them briefly. It was now raining and thundering. I have never seen such large raindrops before. Now how to continue? Time was progressing and it was questionable if we would get back in time. I suggested that we go back the same way we came, over the saddle below the Kominarski Wiersch but mum said she could not climb any mountains anymore. No wonder it was all quite tough. We did not have enough money with to continue our return journey by cart and then bus. Also, now we were too late for the bus, so we continued as Luzie had suggested hoping to continue through the valley although I was sceptic that this would be the case.

---

[8] 'Mönch Stein'; Translated meaning; Monk's stone, a well-known rock formation in the Elbe Sandstone Mountains in Saxon Switzerland.

At Husiska we made enquiries about the price for the cart; 80 zloty, far too much and we did not have that much money with. Our legs are more reliable and so we continued walking, along the valley, over the bridge next to the gurgling stream flowing gentle on its way. Soon we found the path we had to follow, but it went uphill, becoming steeper and difficult and mum was by now so tired, but we had to continue. The path should split here, but it didn't. We searched and searched in vain, we continued over the stream in the most likely direction along the most probable trail. The path became steeper and even more difficult, soon no path could be seen and time passed by so quickly. Up on the hillside sheep were grazing and the shepherd looked at us astonished and the bells seemed to laugh at us. Although the map showed us otherwise, the path did not continue. So we had to go back and walk the longer way losing three quarter of an hour. Crucifixes and Madonna statutes were placed everywhere in Poland, by roadsides, next to the paths through the forests and also on alpine pastures, as here also. We passed a small wooden church, similar in style as elsewhere. The Madonna statute outside the church was decorated with flowers and paper. Now began the long journey back and mum complaining, we had thought the path would lead through the valley, then Luzie had said that there are only small hills that way. Halfway, we met two German wanderers that were going in the opposite direction also hurrying to get back before darkness descended. We still had quite a way to go and darkness was descending now rapidly. The others will have had their supper by now, what are they going to think? O well, main thing we get back by 9 /10 evenings.

At last the path continued descending. We passed an alpine field with one lonely hut on it surrounded by cattle and sheep, their bells could be heard from a distance. We heard sounds in the forest, like the ripping of grass. Could that be deer and stags grazing, so tame that they did not let themselves be disturbed? As we came nearer we saw it was cattle without bells so lonely far from any civilization alone in the woods. A little later we arrived at the alpine pasture, the shepherd playing on his accordion in the twilight before his hut surrounded only by his herd.

Finally we arrived at the Chocholowska valley. We were so tired and arrived point 9 o'clock back. Many of our group were still waiting up for us anxious that we might have got lost in the caves and thinking they might have to alarm the mountain rescue service. Theresa the waitress had even saved us our supper but the tour guide was very cross.

Sunday 27th at breakfast time we were given a lecture, and told how bad and naughty we were to come back so late yesterday. That was completely wrong, then firstly the tour had been planned with visits to the caves for all, and secondly, Luzie had completely wrongly calculated the time needed for the trip and the return journey. Mum told the tour guide off and in end, all was well again.

Today was a rest day, the weather was good and sunny, and we wanted to sun ourselves. The elderly teacher looked at mum's pictures and said she would like to buy one, but in oil a great opportunity for mum. Today, Sunday and we wanted to watch the locals going to church. Mum made many sketches and paintings from the valley. I was very lazy, sunning myself and watched a very old woman, or was she very old? She was so bent, walked so slowly with a stick. I jumped up to help her; she obviously wanted to go to church. The way to the church went straight over the fields, uphill all the way. She was very happy and thankful that I helped her and smiled at me. She suffered on gout, arthritis; it's no wonder by this way of life. Soon the other locals came on their way to church. The whole valley met there. The church bells rang, calling. Before the locals arrived for church service we had a look inside. The church was built of wood and the altar was decorated. The locals here are very religious. Mum made many sketches of the locals, their costume, and their huts. After we helped the old woman she sat down on a bench in front of the church praying. A little later others came up, women in fine costumes, children, young boys with their feather hats on, the milk woman with her family. Her baby had one of those typical pointed hats on. Everyone was extremely friendly and greeted us. Then came the more well off and richer locals from the village, a group of young women with the priest. These women were beautifully dressed in dazzling costumes. But these women could not greet, were quite snobbish, their behaviour high and mighty. The priest, modern civilised dressed walked along the field path as if it were the main road, in his eyes, it was quite obvious that anyone sunbathing in sun costume or bikini was a sinner. The shepherd was not there; you could hear his yodelling over the mountains in the distance and the sound of the bells round the sheep's necks. Later the sheep with their shepherd came down from the alpine pastures to be milked. The cheese from these sheep's milk tastes excellent. In one of the huts cheese was made, 30 zlotys a cheese. They are cone formed and covered in wax. The tourist guide leader was very glad that all were present today for lunch. Did he think it was a result of his morning predict? Today was going to be a rest day anyway. That afternoon, mum made more sketches and paintings then the elderly teacher wanted a painting in oil.

Outside the milk woman's hut we saw, tied onto three sticks a cloth hanging. At first, when we saw this at the beginning of our holiday, we thought quark was being made. Then one day we saw how the woman lovingly rocked the supposedly quark to and fro. It was a cradle for a baby. As we looked inside the 'cradle' a blue-eyed baby smiled at us.

Monday 28th July; Today Luzie organized a tour for all of us, a ramble over the crest of the mountains that we had already done in the mist and fog, but again planning far to little time for the trip. We set of for Wolowiec and the weather was glorious, better than yesterday. On the way up we stopped many times to admire the splendid view. At last, on reaching the top of the Rakon we caught up with the others. They had hurried up. We were very lazy today. Of course we continued up the Wolowiec, 2063 meters high. Deep snow still covered the mountains on the Czech side and mountain lakes glimmering in the sunshine. At the top of the mountain mum painted again another picture, I was lazy and just enjoyed the wonderful scenery. Each day better than the previous one, the clear fresh air, the mountains, everything was so wonderful. That evening we fed the two dogs Schapka and Muschka. They were replacement for our Pixy. How is she at home back in Dresden?

Today 29th again a tour organized for all of us; with the bus to Zakopane sightseeing, with the cable car to Kasprowy Wierch and evenings was to be a lecture about the Tatra.
Early morning the bells from the sheep awoke me together with the shepherds whistling and yodelling. It sounded every time as if he was whistling a love song to his sheep. I sprang joyfully out of bed and went to the window to look. Some of the sheep were quite lame from all that climbing. It is really surprising how they climb. Also the cows graze on quite steep slopes. Again glowing sunshine. In the bus, apart from the heat all were in good spirits, happy and joyful looking forward to this tour. Hopefully it will be better than the bus tour to Moskei Oko. Life in Zakopane was very busy again, the interesting market full of all sorts of people, quite a mixture of folk, farmers, shepherds and tourists. We looked at the ski-jump stadium in Zakopane; here ski jumping took place sometimes in summer. Our tour continued by bus, and then a cable car journey to Kasprowy Wierch. Everywhere on all corners, the locals and farmers were selling their goods; carved figures, Madonna statues, beautiful carved wooden boxes, mirrors and many more, also self-made shoes from leather. A man walked around in a bears costume making fun, but he must have been extremely hot under his bear costume.

The air in the cable car was boiling hot, so many people squashed together and the cable car swaying from side to side, sailing over Zakopane spread out below us, passing mountains, mountaintops, and jagged rocks, forests and fir tree tops full of clusters of fir cones glittering in the sun so near we could nearly pick them with our hands. On the right side was an alpine pastureland where a monk and also a nuns' cloister was supposed to be. The tourists made jokes about how near these two buildings were to each other. Also a tourist hotel was there. Today this is going to be a right comfortable mountain climb, something only for tourists who never go by foot.

Arriving at the top a wonderful panoramic view of the mountains and mountain lakes spread before us, and Zakopane laid before our feet, the houses so tiny like toys greeted us.
At the café we bought a light snack and a liqueur, a special sort of brandy that tasted great and we had never tasted before.   But it was expensive, about 60 zloty!
Many tourists, mostly speaking German were up here on the Kasprowy Wierch; it was a mass tourist attraction. Although it was really nice up here, we found it better on the Rakon. There were far too many people up here for our liking, but it was really good.
On our way back we stopped at Zakopane, and again the market place drew our attention. It was a pitiful sight to see farmer's wives with chicken tucked under their arms for sale. We felt so sorry for those poor chicken, completely exhausted from the heat, their beaks open in the effort to breath, panting for air, and their feet tide together. They laid there in bags and baskets squashed together. The women sat and stood at long tables making self-made quark and cheese, talking and chatting contributing to the general confusion, one woman offered us quark to taste, it was really good. Self picked blue berries in buckets and baskets were also on offer. We looked at the other side of the market, where the same women were sitting there like last time, knitting jackets and jumpers in a wide range of colours, patterns and sizes. A beggar sat at the side of the road, obviously with a walking disability, singing and playing the mouth organ.

After supper, back at the mountain hotel a lecture was planned. Actually we were all very tired and would have liked to go to bed, but the lecture was very interesting. A mountain climber, from mountain rescue service talked to us in broken German about the first settlers that came to live in the Tatra. The Tatra was a very isolated lonely uninhabited area. At first only criminals came and other people, who, for some reason were fleeing from society. They built their wooden huts and lived merely from what they could find on the surrounding land and their cattle. Also, other emigrants came, most probably from the neighbouring countries. The Tatra, had such an impact on these emigrants, they fell in love with the beautiful mountains and forests, they did not want to leave, and so, the foundation for the 'Korallen' villages were laid, quite a mixture of colourful folk of all nations.
He also told us about the founder of the mountain rescue service and the many tragic tales that happened, mostly during the winter months. One tale especially drew our attention, a tale of foresters and the dangers from glaciers. One night, whilst sitting in their huts, unexpected tragic events took place. One forester stood by the window, and that saved him. Snow and ice, a glacier, came tumbling down from the mountaintop. It must have been an exceptionally high uncanny wind. The man standing at the window, without shoes and only light clothing on, was thrown out by the force of the stormy wind, the others were smothered, buried by the snow and falling trees.
This forester, under great strain in the freezing cold made his way to the mountain rescue service to report what had happened.
We were shown various knots, ties, tools and kit used by the mountain rescue service. The mountain climber would have loved to climb up the wall of the room in the hotel to give us a

clearer demonstration of mountain climbing. I already knew many of these things; I had climbed up the 'Mönch Stein' with uncle Hans, with rope and climbing kit.

Wednesday the 30th July; and today was the best tour we made as a group. Today we went on a boat trip. Early morning we travelled with the bus to Dunnajeh, 60 kilometres distance away from Chocholowska valley. Here, there are also mountains, but smaller ones, just 900 meters high. The bus driver was a very jolly man and spoke continuously with Luzie and he laughed a lot. He had also bought young pigeons with. They were to be let loose for the first time to fly a longer distance back home. We were looking forward to this, but we all shared the bus driver's concern that all the pigeons would find their way home. Again the sun was shining as usual, the Tatra Mountains disappearing gradually in the distance and soon only a blue violet coloured outline could be seen against the clear blue sky. The bus stopped to let the pigeons fly. They fluttered excitedly in their box. The driver carefully took one out at a time in his hands and threw the pigeon high into the air. He opened another box and all the pigeons at the same time flattering flew high up, at first in circles. The pigeons divided themselves into two groups. One group flew in circles still searching for their way, the other group striving already homewards towards the mountains. The driver gazing after them as they flew away concerned, it was clear he was very fond of his pigeons and only then, when the second group stopped flying in circles and also flew homewards was he content and our journey could continue. As I so viewed the mountains in the distance I realized that soon we would leave this wonderful place and go back to Dresden. These gloomy thoughts that we would soon leave these mountains made me feel so sad, but we'll come again soon!

The bus travelled through Nowy Targ, past fields and houses, past Madonna statues and crucifixes by the wayside then through flat land with many houses and fields. Many people lived here. Luzie told us that it was planned to put this part of the countryside under water, everything here was to disappear and instead a large lake was to be created. The Dunnajeh appeared to be a shallow river flowing swiftly, rippling over stones and rocks. At last we arrived at the boat port and fresh air, it was so hot and stuffy in the bus, we felt like suffocating. Again we were greeted by a mixture of various folk, like in Zakopane at the market; farmer wives trying to sell us their goods, a small boy came towards us with some small wooden carved figures, quite simple made; boats, birds and eagles. Mum said the eagle will get broken, but the boy said, 'no, no, not break,' and waving his hands in the air bending the eagle's wings around showed how stable it was. It was amazing how much German he understood. By the harbour a gypsy band played; double bass, violin and guitar. They had pitch-black hair, dark eyes and a real gypsy temperament, the gypsy violinist leaping from boat to boat, playing gypsy songs. Many boats and many people were there. On each boat were two men dressed in their local traditional costume, one at the front and one at the back of the boat to make sure to ferry the boat safely through the waves. Each boat took about 10 to 12 people. Mr and Mrs Lange, Mr Mans and also the two teachers were on our boat. We were all very jolly, in good mood, sang songs and made jokes. A gypsy stood in the middle of the shallow river playing his violin, we would have loved to give him some money, but he was too far away. Suddenly, we noticed that photos were taken of us at various places, and I waved merrily to them. Models of a pair of storks were placed on a tree by the riverbank. At first we thought they were real storks. It was hard for the work two steersmen to keep the boat steady, as the river was not always deep enough at certain places and often too shallow. They were obviously very experienced in their work; the boat did not go on ground. Our two steersmen were very happy and slightly malicious when the other steersmen on the other boats were unlucky enough to go on ground. On the bank we past farm houses, fields, forests and castles. On the one side was the Czech republic on the other side Poland.

We continued joyfully, floating along in the middle of the river Dunnajeh, followed by more boats behind us and in front of us. The shining sun, a light-fluttering breeze and the water rippling over the stone, it was dreamlike beautiful. Mum took her mouth organ out of her bag and began playing and I sunned myself. It was a long trip on the raft, three and a half hours, and still far too short, not enough. Everywhere people on the bank waved to us as we past them. At one place a crippled girl was bathing and waved also to us and we waved back. We past a place where some huts stood, same sort of huts as built in the Chocholowska valley. The raft now continued its journey slowly into uninhabited areas, the mountains became higher, the forests deeper and thicker, less and less people were there to greet and wave to us from the bank. I stuck my big toe into the cold clear water wishing I could jump in and bathe. Luzie called something to us, we should guess on which side the mountain in front of us was; on the polish or Czech side, so began a jolly puzzle game. Wonderful that the 'weather god' was in such good mood, no wind, the clear cold rippling Dunnajeh river, scorching sun shine and fresh air. Time stood still for us, only we were here, a happy, laughing, singing group of people floating along on this raft. The steersman in front was an older man, and after a cigarette break he took some water and sprinkled some jokingly over my feet. Mr Mans sprinkled some teasingly over my back, so now I could not complain not to be wet because I could not bathe. I had now received an unexpectedly but not unpleasant shower bath. Ha, that journey could have been twice as long, soon we were called back into the real world, the mountains were becoming less, the forests thinner, now only parks on the river bank and then houses appeared, we had now arrived at our destination.

As we got out of the boat, people came towards us and pressed photos in our hands. How surprised we were to see ourselves, and of course we bought them, a permanent remembrance of this wonderful boat trip.

In a very smart modern café we ate blue berries with cream, coffee and cake. On our way back the bus stopped to pick up the steersmen. That was so nice and collegial. They were standing by the wayside waiting for a bus. Some of the other steersmen had already made their way back by pony carriage. Our rafts were already taken apart and loaded onto the carriages. For the horses, and the men who drove these horse carts, their work was only beginning, a long and boring trip down the country road. The steersmen were happy to get into our bus to get back home soon. A girl from our group was obviously not pleased that an older steersman sat near her. In fact they did smell after cow dung, but how can it be different? You can't expect anything else; after all they all live like we have seen in the Chocholowska valley. The bus driver chatted merrily with the steersmen and although he did not want it, we paid him something extra, we all collected money and simple stuck it into his pockets. The faces of the bus driver and steersmen reflected contentment and good mood. They were looking forward to their homes and families. For them a day's hard work came to an end, for us an unforgettable experience.

Thursday 31st July arrived and we had only two more days left for our holiday. Mum was very early awake. The sun shone brightly again, as if there had never any other kind of weather. 'Get up quickly, we must under all circumstances go up the Kominarski Wierch,' said mum, and I had thought, that today we were going to have a rest day! After that bus journey it was only right for me that today we would do something again. You can see the Kominarski Wierch from the mountain hotel. Every time we were in the dinning hall we could see this mountain, towering over everything else, high above the Chocholowska valley. Whatever the weather, the mountain was always there; dark and cloudy as on our first days here and clear radiant in sunshine like today, whether in evening or dawn or daytime, always seen as if it wants to safe guard and watch over the valley and people living in it. It seems such a shame not to climb up this magnificent mountain. We must climb up it, absolutely under all circumstances.

After the usual ample breakfast we set of, past the milk woman's hut, past the 'cradle' with the baby, past the hut where the doggy couple, Schapka and Muschka live. Children were playing outside and looked at us, we past the hut where cheese was being made, smoke rising above it, then past the hut where the old woman suffering from gout lived. She sat outside her hut and smiling greeted us.

Our path led us the same way as we had wandered on the 26th July, on the day of our cave tour, always upwards through the forest over streams and the alpine pasture until we came to the saddle under the Kominarski Wierch. Here we had a rest. Now the main part of our wandering began. Here we had sat together with the others some days ago happily singing. Beneath us stretched the neighbouring valley, in the distance mountains and mountains, rocks and rocks and a wonderful clear sky.

On our way we met some young people also from Germany who wanted to climb up the mountain. We met so many Germans here on holiday. We began climbing, at first, a steep grass slope, then our path led us through shrubs and many small dwarf pine. The view became grander and splendid as we progressed. Up there, on the mountain, edelweiss is supposed to grow; great we'll take some with back home!

In fact this mountain is actually two mountains; at first one has to climb up the Tylkope, the smaller mountain before climbing up the Kominarski Wierch. Soon we saw the top of the mountain. The path became steeper and steeper and we had to climb around the dwarf pine trees, steep rocks rose high into the sky on our right and left side. Over there, something gleaming white in the sunshine, edelweiss growing, it looked like a wonderful dreamlike rock garden, everywhere on the pasture, clinging with their roots fast onto the rocks using the small tiny bit of earth available, everywhere wonderful flowers in all colours. We had to watch not to get lost, the path was not as good marked as below. Where was the path? We climbed up the slope, is the path over there? No, not here, perhaps over there, by the rocks? Yes at last we found the sign. What a wonderful view, so many mountains, clear blue sky, and in the distance the bells of the sheep could be heard. Now began the proper climb. The dwarf pine trees here were especially small and wide. Between them grew wonderful flowers. To begin with, we climbed over steep large rock boulders, dwarf pine hanging onto it. The path was getting steeper and as we progressed less and less dwarf pines grew. We continued our climb up the mountain; everywhere grew all sorts of wonderful flowers and loads of edelweiss. We found out later that this year was a special good year for edelweiss.

At one place a large boulder blocked our way. In the rocks were dents made from many footholds from previous rock climbers, on some places quite slippery and smooth from rain and weather. After this obstacle was overcome we came upon a cavernous stony area of about 2 to 3 meters wide reaching from above to deep down below. If one stone falls, then at the same time many stones will fall creating an avalanche into the valley below. From the mountaintop people came towards us; ha we know them; they are our acquaintances from our cave tour. The path continued winding like a snake up the mountain and at last we reached the top.

There was a plateau at the mountaintop, and to our great surprise we discovered that the sheep were here also. The shepherd sat contentedly on a grass mound looking proudly at his sheep. There on the slope they were grazing, their bells sounding clear and distinct.
We looked around us, admiring the wonderful and breathtaking views, we saw Zakopane stretched out below us, the houses placed like toys, we saw our mountain hotel and Chocholowska valley laid out before our feet.

On our return journey we collected edelweiss, so as to have a permanent souvenir in remembrance to take home with us.

After supper, we presented a little exhibition of our paintings and sketches, mum's work, also mines as well as Mrs Lange's sketches. My mother received through this, another commission from Mr Mans. He was very interested in the photos of mum's sculptures. Finally we all celebrated, a wonderful final goodbye party from our beautiful holiday. Outside in the distance the Kominarski Wierch towering over the valley, the sun disappearing behind it, sending a last greeting with its sun rays over the valley. This time we could be satisfied and pleased with ourselves when we looked up to the mountain, we had now been up there, seen that wonderful flower garden and those magnificent views. It had been a wonderful day.

Happily we went to bed but still a little sad. Tomorrow was to be our last day. The shepherd yodelled in the distance, a dog barked and the bells from the sheep sang us a lullaby.

Friday 1st August arrived, and the sun shone brightly like yesterday, a farewell gift for our last day. Today, I wanted to go to Zakopane after breakfast, as tomorrow is mum's birthday. So I set of alone. In the bus I met the milk woman. She had her baby on her lap. The market was as usual full of life and activities, everywhere brightly coloured farmers' wives, this time small little dogs were offered for sale. I did some shopping and bought a present for mum. Latter that afternoon I was back in the valley. Mum had a good rest, made some sketches and went for a walk in the valley. Together we said our farewells from the locals, their primitive huts and the mountains. After the last supper at the mountain hotel we stayed up late, talked and exchanged addresses and we all were of the same opinion, 'we will come again' farewell but not forever. Goodbye Chocholowska valley.

Saturday 2nd August, departure day, the last things were packed into our cases, goodbyes said to the kitchen staff with a handshake, a last thank you, a last breakfast, now our journey starts back to normal life.

Horse drawn carriages came again to collect us. Of course we said our goodbyes to Muschka and Schapka, that adorable doggy couple. I would have loved to take one of the little puppies with, but our dear little Pixy was waiting for us back home. The warm shining sun and the mountains smiling a farewell greeting calling us to come back soon, of course we'll come again, it was so good here. The Chocholowska valley disappeared gradually in the distance, the ringing of the sheep's bells, and the shepherd's yodelling a farewell in the mountains. We waved to the local folk, and the mountain hotel disappeared around the bend as the horse drawn carriage took us away from this wonderful valley. Seldom, anywhere else have we found such friendly people. The horses panting and neighing, the driver, brown from the sun, smiling took us further away.

Our journey continued by bus, again the same driver with his pigeons that he let loose on the way and they flew all of in direction Chocholowska valley and Zakopane. We saw in the distance the outlines of the Tatra Mountains like a cloud on the horizon vanishing disappearing in the distance until nothing more of the Tatra could be seen.

Arrival in Krakow where we had lunch and we just did not like town life at all, it was so stifling hot and we were too warmly dressed. There is not much to report of the sightseeing tour we all made after lunch; the beautiful Chocholowska valley with its stunning mountains and fresh air completely occupied our thoughts. City life did not agree with us at all. We visited the castle and gallery, had to slide on slippery slippers through the rooms.

We were so glad evenings at last to be in the train and of course a compartment together with Mr and Mrs Lange and both teachers.

How happy we were to arrive in Gorlitz at last at midnight, quickly out of the train, quickly through customs without any problems and onto the platform for the earlier train to Dresden that departed a little late. We were so glad about this, then otherwise it would have been a very long wait for the next train. Later, we were told by Lange's, that our tour guide was unhappy that we did not take the later train and had 'disappeared' so quickly. Well, main thing we got back home safely, happy and content with an everlasting memory of a wonderful holiday. Goodbye Chocholowska Valley until next time."

Aquarelle painting of Chocholowska valley.

Sketches from our trip on the raft.

5. Prosperity.

After that memorable wonderful holiday, life was now back to normal. I continued to work at the theatre in Freiberg and continued my studies to obtain a proper teacher's qualification, just in case. Also I continued my composition work. It was a very busy time. By now, mum was also busy sculpting and painting, preparing work for further exhibitions. She no longer needed to work as she now received a good pension. Although my parents lived apart; dad had his own modern little flat, they were in constant contact with each other, on good term, good friends visiting each other regularly. My sister went her own way, had her job and kept much to herself.

One day, I found a letter in the letterbox of my primitive old flat in Freiberg. It was from my mum;

'Der Briefkasten.'

'Es war einmal ein Briefkasten
Um den wars traurig sehr bestellt.
Er fühlte sich so nutzlos
Und überflußig in der Welt.
Rings um ihn war ein hasten,
Und traurig dachte er,
Mein Bauch fühlt sich so leer,
Es fehlt was irgendwo.
Da kam ein liebes Kärtchen
Und es war wieder froh.
Nun rate mal wer Dir dies schrieb?
Es ist jemand der Dich hat sehr lieb'.

Translation.

'The Letter Box.'

There was once a letter box
His state of affairs were so sad.
He felt so useless
And redundant in the world.
Around him was such a hustle.
And sadly he thought,
My stomach is so empty
Something somehow is missing.
Then, there came a precious card,
And again he was happy.
Now have a guess who wrote this?
It's someone who loves you dearly.

(Written approx 1968).

My parents came regularly to Freiberg to enjoy a theatre visit and to see me play, also my sister came occasionally. Her last visit together with me to Freiberg ended somewhat odd, and still today I do not understand how she managed somehow to get hold of two strangers after the performance. Her behaviour was strange. A similar thing happened like previously when we went the last time wandering together to Höhnstein, flirting with strangers, never seen before and never seen again, but this time trying hard to get me involved.

Because of the approaching tragic events and Stasi involvement causing the loss of my profession it is only logic that I report of the variety of pieces and performances I played. Amongst them were; 'Madame Butterfly', by Giacomo Puccini, 'Nut Cracker' and 'Eugen Onegin' by Peter Tschaikowski, and 'Die Entfuhrung aus dem Serail', (The Abduction from the Serail), by Wolfgang Amadeus Mozart as well as ' Hansel and Gretel', by Engelbert Humperdinck.

It was particularly fun to play light-hearted and comical works. The variety was styles performed ranged from operettas to musicals, classic works as well as contemporary pieces. We also performed 'Calamity Jane', a musical after Warner Bros Film, music by James O'Hanlon, 'Die Fledermaus' by Johann Strauss and 'My Fair Lady', after Bernard Shaw's Pygmalien, music by Leonard Bernstain.

Of course we also performed symphony concerts that included works by Mendelssohn, Mozart, Brahms, Shostakowich, and Beethoven. We gave special performances of 'Peter and the Wolf' from Prokofjew for children as part of their music lessons in school. Culture during the GDR time was high on the agenda, and organized school visits to the theatre was part of the music program.

We gave special concerts for various special occasions performing many overtures and scenes from Richard Wagner's, operas, as well as many works from Johann Sebastian Bach, also works by contemporary composers. The program was a wide varied selection of many styles of compositions.

My life should have been spent continuing to play in professional orchestras, but Stasi involvement ruined all this. I was so lucky and incredibly happy.

Things were beginning to pick up for my mother with some exhibitions and sale of her work. Life was not bad at all and we were happy despite the lack of contact with the western world. We lived in a 'socialist' society where there was no unemployment, no homeless people and no one was starving. No, that 'socialist' society was not perfect by all means, and there were many things one found unexplainable and incorrect.

Before the stepmother died she gave us the very small hut up on that mountain hut, perhaps some bad guilty feelings made her do this. So now we had our own place up there and mum could use it as a place for her sculpture work. One very sad event happened during these happy years; we lost our little Pixy. That holiday on the coast was the last time we had her. She died later that year 1969. We had bought her over from England, something still from my childhood, and now gone. In remembrance mum carved a special sculpture, which I still have. How could we live without her, that thought was so depressing and so we decided to get Bella, she was also a fox terrier and turned out to be just as great as Pixy.

About this time, a young man contacted mum asking for the possibility to exhibit some of her paintings. He had started to collect artworks from antifascist émigré artists. He was concerned to help promote, exhibit and save works from artists that had been persecuted by the Nazis, especially where perhaps only a few were left and saved. Today he has a valuable collection that is exhibited regularly. My mother gave him something for his collection.

During the years 1970 –71, 72, 73 the gallery Kühl exhibited some of mum's works regularly. 1970 she exhibited together with Prof Dr Erich Drechsler and the Museum for German History in Berlin 1971 bought two sculptures; 'Prisoner' and 'Man from Concentration Camp', two very dramatic works in memory of those who died in concentration camp.

We also had a small allotment nearby, where we grew some fresh vegetables. It also had an apple tree and fruit bushes. The little shed was used as a work shed for mum. These were prosperous, happy and creative years.

landscape 1975

'Als ich noch ein Kind war.'

Woodcarving; Shepherd with flute and goat'; (Approx 1971)

'Als ich noch ein Kind war, da sah es anders aus,
Da gingen oftmals Bettler hungernd von Haus zu Haus.
Wo ist er den geblieben,
Der Bettler in unserer Stadt?
Er ist jetz in den Betrieben,
Er steht am Steuerrad.

Als ich noch ein Kind war, saß Hungersnot oft am Tisch,
Die Mutter maß das trockene Brot, es fehlten Fleisch und Fisch,
Wo ist sie denn geblieben,
Die Hungersnot die wir gekannt?
Wir haben sie fort getrieben,
Samt den Fabrikherren, fort von unseren Land.

Als ich noch ein Kind war, saß Hungersnot oft am Tisch,
Die Mutter maß das trockene Brot, es fehlten Fleisch und Fisch,
Wo ist sie denn geblieben,
Die Hungersnot die wir gekannt?
Wir haben sie fort getrieben,
Samt den Fabrikherren, fort von unseren Land.

Als ich noch ein Kind war, viel wollte ich Lernen und Wissen,
Am besten doch lernte ich das Arbeiter vereint Kämpfen müssen.
Im vereinten Kampf für Frieden,
Für unsere Arbeiter macht,
Sind viele dahin geschieden,
Haben viele Opfer gebracht

Als ich noch ein Kind war, da sah es anders aus,
Doch Heut geht Freud und Wohlstand lachend von Haus zu Haus.
Reicht Euch vertrauensvoll die Hände,
Freunde, Ihr in Sorg und Mühen,
Das keiner müßig abseits stände,
Vereint sind wir Macht und Frieden.

Als ich noch ein Kind war, konnt keine Ruine ich nirgends sehen,
Doch Heute, trotz großen fleiß Ruinen in unserer Stadt noch stehen,
Viele Wunden Heut sind noch zu frisch,
Doch keiner sitzt am leeren Tisch,
Vereint sind wir eine Kraft,
Die Neues baut und Frieden schaft.'

223

<u>Translation.</u>

'When I was still a child.'

'When I was still a child, things looked different,
Often beggars went hungry from house to house.
Where is he then now,
The beggar in our city?
He is now working,
Standing at the steering wheel.

. When I was still a child, hunger sat often at the table,
Mother measured the dry bread, missing was meat and fish.
Where is it now then,
The hunger we used to know?
We have thrown it out,
Together with the factory bosses, out of our land.

When I was still a child, loads I wanted to learn and know,
The best I learnt that workers united must fight.
United fight for peace,
For our working force,
Have many past away,
And many sacrifices made.

When I was still a child, things looked different,
Today, happiness and prosperity travels laughing from house to house.
Come reach each other trustingly your hands,
Friends in worries and troubles,
That no one stands idle aside,

United we stand in control and peace.
When I was still a child, could see no where any ruins,
Still today, in spite of immense activity ruins can still be seen.
Many wounds are still so fresh,
Yet no one sits at empty tables,
United we are one strength,
That builds up new and creates peace.'

(Written approx 1965- 1968).

Tatra landscape

224

How clear it is when reading this poem to realise the positive and happy atmosphere we were living in at that time, as well as our positive views on a socialist future!

Another happy holiday we had is worth mentioning, the summer of 1970. We went back to the Baltic coast. It was July and my holiday from my job at the theatre had just started. The last things were packed and our 'huge' rucksacks sorted out. Bella, our little puppy sat in the bag we had bought for her.

We went extra for walks with Bella to get her accustomed to the bag. Once whilst walking in the Heide, a woodland surrounding Dresden, it started to rain and little Bella happily crept into the bag. She did not like getting wet and so we covered her up with a bath towel. Another time we went for a walk with her in 'Grosser Garten', a park in the midst of the city, and took her with boating. She was still so small. Camping without a dog? This thought was terrible, impossible. Our sweet little Pixy had died and now we had Bella in her place. We were concerned how Bella would behave in the train but our fears were not needed.

Bella sat bravely in her bag and in the train she was very quiet and slept soundly. A young couple in the train compartment were also animal lovers and were pleased to see Bella admiring how well behaved she was for such a young dog. We had bockwurst for supper and there showed a little nose stretching in the air out of the bag sniffing. Bella liked to eat bockwurst, it was her favourite food and she got her portion. We admired how brave she was and how quiet. We had expected her to be restless.

The campsite had changed since our last visit two years ago, shrubs cleared away, tidied up and the place was not so wet, muddy and swampy as before. We went straight to our usual place under the fur trees with the memories of happy times here in past years still vivid. We had a good time, excellent weather, bathed in Darßer fashion and meeting old friends again a very happy holiday. Little did we realize that these happy years were about to come to an end. We still believed in a socialist equal society.

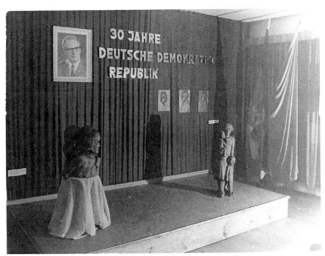

Exhibition; 30 years GDR; Two sculptures on show on stage

CHAPTER 12.

The Revenge. 1971 – 1976

Until now our lives in the GDR were happy and content. Yes, there was no unemployment; I now had my job as a professional violinist, my sister also had her secure post, and both my parents, although they were now living apart, both had a very good pension, enhanced through extra financial funding, as they both had full recognition as VVN[1]; victims of Nazism. We now lived in better accommodation, in modern newly built flats, and my parents were sent regularly to special wonderful holiday places, organized for recognized VVN members to convalescence and recuperate. We felt and thought we were living in an equal, more cohesive society, and we had our small part of the mountain property and a hut where we could stay up there and enjoy the wonderful view and landscape. It seemed as if our future would be embedded in this positive optimistic ideal world. But it was not to be. We held our heads high up in the clouds of mist that surrounded the reality. The Stasi had long been observing us, and we had been unable to see the psychological damage already taking place around us. There were many positive aspects of life in the GDR, and this 'socialist paradise' could have worked, but hell was already approaching in form of Stasi interference.

The Legend, part 9.

<u>Concerning the fiery hound of Schandau</u>

Perhaps, it is suitable at this stage of my story to continue to tell the tale of our ancestors, of the legend of the fiery hound, of the rich and powerful baron wanting more and dissatisfied with his wealth, of his cruelty and his banishment;

There are many different versions of these tales and the most gripping one is undoubtedly the tale of the fiery hound. A grandmother reports how she encountered several times in the darkest night this fiery hound, how it frightened her and her limbs still shake to and fro when she remembers her dramatic experience, something she will never forget as long as she lives. The hound was as black as you would think the devil would be, matted, shapeless and large in size, two eyes shining brightly under his bushy fur, like burning coals.

This frightful hound appeared from under the Zauken valley, from the old castle, dashing through the whole town, until the Kirnitzsch valley by the riverbank. Then he turns round and went the same way back, until he vanishes in the castle grounds. The locals living here often wondered what happened with this fiery hound?

The grandmother, as she span at the spinning wheel told her grandchildren sitting by her, listening to her, to keep quiet so she could tell the story, and so she started to tell the tale;

"Once a baron lived here, in that old castle. He was daring, bold and gallant on foot and in the saddle. All in the land knew Birk von Duba as a knight. He was rich and powerful, and possessed everything to make him happy. He lived like a prince, then everything your eyes could see, all the forests, meadows, mountains and valleys belonged to baron Birk von Duba. Although God gave him so much, his heart was corrupt. In spite of his possessions he could not find his inner peace. And although in vain the innocent begged and cried, he was a friend of burden and trouble.

---

[1] <u>VVN</u>; an organization to give certain help, support and extra financial funding to those who had suffered through the Nazis, had been in concentration camp or forced emigration like my parents.

He was driven only from a burning desire for robbery, looting and murder lust, and filling the golden goblet many times with his bleeding hands, there was no end to his cravings for wealth, fatal against humane feelings, the deadly final suffocating breath was his triumph, his victory.

Once complaining about their fears and needs, many of the poor begged for a little piece of bread, for mercy, sympathy and compassion. Ruthlessly he chased them away, hunting them with his hounds out of the castle grounds.
The heavens above were exhausted with forgiving and their patience gone, but still, the baron as long as he lived continued on his sinful path. He is now the one who appears as a black hound on his rounds every night. So appeared the old frightful hound for many hundreds of years, horrific payment for his wickedness, until compassion, mercy and forgiveness brought him the peace and deliverance he never gave."

Returning now to the present day, the sad truth how history repeats itself and how humanity is vulnerable to lust and needless desire for certain assets is heartbreaking. Until now, we still believed we lived in a socialist society.

1. Pre-warning of events.

1971 Easter; Thursday was my only day free from my job at the theatre where I worked as a violinist. We decided to go wandering into the beautiful Saxon Swiss mountains, only a short train journey outside Dresden. The weather was fine, the sun shining bright. We had the whole day ahead of us. After the train journey we crossed the river Elbe with the ferry, the picturesque sand stone mountains beckoning us.
We had hardly gone far, just behind the youth hostel and up the forest path leading into the rocky mountains when we found a man lying at the foot of the first rock, dead obviously fatally fallen. We hurried back to the hostel to alert the mountain rescue service.
Other wanderers had seen him also lying there, but had hurried on without doing anything, then on our way up the forest path we met some wanderers passing us hurriedly on their way down. This was a kind of pre-warning for the events that followed.

My annual holiday began in July. We usually enjoyed our vacation. The weather was fine, hardly any rain and plenty of sunshine. My mother had told me plenty about her life in the emigration in Czechoslovakia and we wanted to visit some of the places she had mentioned; the Tatra, the Mazurka caves, Prague, Zylina. But somehow, Gretel was not her usual self. It was as if she sensed the enormous tragedy that was already happening. We left the flat securely locked and safe, 'we thought'. My sister had a key. Although she now lived in a flat together with her husband at the other end of Dresden my mother had said to her, she was always welcome and could pop in anytime. It was still her home if she needed it. We trusted her and never thought, or realized what was going on in her mind, or the pressure she was under. Dad also had a key as he had agreed to come and water the plants during the week.

I found some diary notes about our holiday summer 1971. It describes the wonderful friendliness of the Czech people, so different to what we were to expect on our return home.

The diary notes start on the seventh of July that year.
Our journey began; everything was packed, rucksack, tent, painting material and Bella our little dog. The bell rang to inform us the taxi had arrived, but there were two taxis waiting

outside and we panicked, hoping they were not both meant for us! Our fears were unnecessary; there was one taxi for us, and one for a neighbour.

It was as if something was telling us not to go, as Gretel was not feeling at all well that morning. Bella our little dog was excited and did not leave her eyes from us.
It was holiday time, and the hustle and bustle at the railway station full of excited lively people, with packed cases and bags ready to set off on their journey became greater as time passed. The train arrived late. A very friendly young lady helped us into our compartment with our luggage. She seemed to be a botanist and chatted cheerfully with us about all sorts of things. Gretel felt sick again, but soon recovered.

Our first stop was Usti Nad Labem, a small town on the border of East Germany.
We had arranged to visit Ina, Gretel's good friend from past years. We had difficulty finding her place, as it was some time since we had been there last.
We climbed up the stairs to her flat, rang the bell, no answer. Just as we were beginning to wonder what to do we heard Ina's voice from her neighbours flat. She was taking care of a neighbour's child, and she had not expected us yet.
She was the same nervous person as she was when she had come to visit us. Lunchtime we went out to a restaurant. Gretel was not feeling well again and I was worried.
On the way back we went to visit Schrecken Stein, ruins of an ancient castle outside that small town, a beautiful place with sand stone rocks and woods, but the ruins were closed and so we left disappointed.

Ina was a strong, sturdily built and exhilarating woman, now of a slightly nervous nature due to her past, difficult and dangerous partisan life. The strength, the united fight against Hitler had given her, was still present. Her personality filled me with awe and her partisan stories with pride. She had been a partisan in France during the war. Her husband had died in one of the concentration camps. My mother and Ina had many mutual memories about their fight against fascism, the emigration years, and their everlasting chat continued till early morning
Some years previously, the VDN organisation, (Victims of Nazism), organized an excursion to Theresen Stadt, now a place of remembrance in memory of the many victims who had died in the concentration camp the nazis had erected there during the war. Both my parents had received VDN recognition and Gretel was with the VDN delegation to attend a meeting.
It had been at this meeting where the two friends met again. They fell into each other's arms, so delighted to see each other after so many years not knowing what fate each had to overcome. It must have been a very moving scene, and when Ina came to visit us in Dresden, the two friends talked through the night till dawn.

During our stay in Usti, Gretel felt ill. I asked her if we should go back home, 'no we'll continue, I'm sure I'll feel better soon' was her reply. She did not want to spoil my holiday. Unconsciously Gretel felt each blow that was done to her. At home, in our flat something was happening. Gretel's artworks; her sculptures and paintings were as much part of her as life itself. This life force taken away and destroyed left Gretel vulnerable, she felt wounded and helpless. She sensed something was happening, but at this time we did not know what, only that my mother felt ill, and strangely she had no will or strength to paint.
Gretel painted only one watercolour picture during this holiday. This was extremely unusual. Something heavy and evil filled the air. A series of traumatic events and victimization against us from the Stasi secret police began to take hold of us, and to change our lives.

The next evening we continued our journey, had good connections. In Prague we were able to get a taxi to the other station and had a whole compartment for ourselves. We spread out and slept soundly.

The morning sunrays awoke us and we enjoyed the presentation the sunrise gave of the beautiful countryside passing by. Peering out of the window of the train, the fleeting views of the dazzling panorama, the forests and mountains of Czechoslovakia made me understand completely the music of Smetana's 'My Father Land', his musical journey through the Czech countryside and the river Moldau. Sitting in the train and looking out of the window, was like listening to his music. Gretel had recovered and there was no sign of the evil forces at work back in Dresden.

We continued our journey to the Tatra. A jolly gipsy came into the train with his violin playing gypsy tunes. We enjoyed the wonderful landscape of Poprad Lomnica and found a campsite midst the wonderful mountainous scenery spreading around us. The weather was good and we had a wonderful time, although Gretel was still not really well, but she was not going to be put off.

We strolled through the forests and explored the caves. We met a gypsy selling wild strawberries that tasted so delicious. We took a cable car up into the mountains. But after a while Gretel became so ill she had to stay in hospital. Everyone was so friendly and helpful. I went back on my own to the campsite, but next day Mr Oswald Kerzmarok a friendly porter took me in with our dog and I could stay the night at his apartment. My mother stayed about four days in that hospital.

The diary notes continue on the twenty- second of July. That morning found us waking up in a hotel. The sun shining through the window and Bella was with us. We had a hearty breakfast; rolls, butter, good tasting jam, a boiled egg each, tea and coffee. We only paid twenty kronunas[2] for that lot. The price of the hotel accommodation was also not so bad, 51 kronunas for accomodation.

The Czech people were all very friendly and willing to help strangers. The waitress gave us a box so that we were able to pack up all unnecessary camping equipment to send back to Dresden.

We continued our journey to Dobra. We hoped to see the Beskydy Mountains. Gretel seemed to have recovered and her mood improved with every minute. The little chuckling train had wooden benches and stopped everywhere. Bella our little dog stuck her nose out of the train window sniffing the fresh air. We arrived at Dobra, a small country station with only a few houses. We were rather at loss how to continue but soon some friendly people came and showed us the way to the bus stop.

We headed for the campsite Jermanice that seemed to be situated by a large lake. As we struggled along the road an old woman came to us and chattered away in Czech. We were puzzled and could not help wondering. What a chatterbox she was. What does she want?

But soon we could understand enough to recognize that she wanted to help us. She insisted on helping me to carry our large bag of provisions and chattered merrily all the while. We wondered how far do we still have to go. At last there was the bus stop. The old woman chattering stayed with us, keeping us company. We had an hour to wait. In the meantime more people came to the bus stop, some talking about a place called Moravka. We must try to get there once, sounds a good place to visit.

The friendly old woman was still not satisfied with her help. She wanted to help us even more. After a while she disappeared to fetch a taxi. She came back with a young girl from the

---

[2] kronunas- Czech money.

milk shop who helped us carry our things back into the shop. The taxi would fetch us here, she said.

After a hearty goodbye the dear old friendly woman left us. She reminded us a lot in her behaviour of Mrs Glatho. The milk we drank here in this milk shop in Dobra was so good, 'fresh good milk at last,' was my mother's comment. We also ate some ham sandwiches and strawberries with cream.

At last the taxi man came, he turned out to be the local butcher and did not want any money. The sun was shining brightly and the lake shone like a mirror as we arrived at the campsite in Jermanice. The price of the campsite was much cheaper here than in the Tatra.

Soon our little tent was put up and Bella was skipping and jumping around with pleasure

The sun was shining brightly the next morning and we were up early. We had a good breakfast and intended to hire a boat for the whole day, but this was possible for the afternoon only. The campsite was very clean, with electric cooking possibilities in the building, everything much better than in the GDR.

That afternoon we hired a boat to paddle round the lake. People were camping everywhere by the waterside, especially round a half island, and we called merrily to them. Someone seemed to have brought a hen with them – for eggs? It was clucking merrily and did not seem at all distressed to be with at the campsite. Further on we passed a children's holiday camp. They were merrymaking getting ready for a carnival festival.

Many were camping wildly on the half island making bonfires to cook their food. Soon we found a quiet spot where we had a good dip in the cool waters, wonderful. In the distance some hills, mountains and a little village church came into view. The lake was large and it took us a long time to paddle round it. On shore a dog glimpsing Bella started to have a good 'doggy' conversation with her, barking. Bella would have loved to leap into the water to swim over to him. Everywhere, where people had put up their tents, their food was being cooked on open fires and the smoke and smell of food tickled our nostrils. On the lake, speedboats with water skiers passed creating waves and our boat began to rock.

At last, fed up with paddling round the edge of the lake we decided to row straight across, leaving the half island behind us. Willow trees and branches were growing in the water and we had to watch out not to get tangled up within the roots. On the other side some anglers seemed angry that we were disturbing their peace and chasing the fish away by rowing past them.

Suddenly it looked as if as the weather was turning and we made our way back to the shore towards our tent. It had been a lovely trip, in the bathtub as mum called it, because the boats were made from metal.

The landscape was beautiful; we passed little wooden weekend huts, weeping willows, geese and ducks waddling around and a kingfisher.

In the evening we made a campfire and I fried sausages over it and cooked tea. Gretel played her mouth organ and the stars shone brightly.

During the night Gretel woke up again in pain. Her back was full of boils. The day was again wonderful hot, but today, the lake was overcrowded. Bella made friends with a cocker spaniel enjoyed playing with him, but soon got fed up. It was a pleasure to see the two dogs playing about, racing in and out of the water. Really, Bella liked it here; there were so many holes in the ground so she could dig to her heart's content. Midday found us still lazing around enjoying the hot sun.

Towards evening we decided to continue our journey. It was so much better to travel when the heat of the day had passed. We decided to stay the night in Frydek Mistek.

The waiter at the station restaurant was very friendly and told us where we could stay. As we walked along the road to the hotel, after a good supper, a man came towards us and wanted to accompany us. We were very suspicious. What does he want? But he turned out to be just as friendly and helpful as the old woman in Dobra. He took us to the hotel in Frydek.

This friendly man came with, translated and spoke for us with the hotel personal. At the door of our room he shook hands with us, and with a friendly smile said goodbye. We had a lovely view from the balcony; the main room had two sleeping couches, a table, two chairs and also an extra room with shower, bath and toilet, all wonderfully modern. Bella was pleased to have a balcony again, just like home, but she was afraid of the great height, she then looked about the room, saw the open cupboard, crept in and curled up to sleep.

The Last entry in my diary is on Sunday twenty-fifth of July.

We had travelled on to Friedland, but first we had to go to the hospital. Gretel needed a doctor again; her back was so painful, full of boils. It turned out to be an after effect from the hospital treatment from Poprad.

Afterwards we passed a little park zoo and we decided to have a look at it. The garden was very neglected but the woman who sold the tickets was very friendly and kept Bella in her ticket box until we had completed our visit.

We saw only few animals in this zoo, birds, peacocks, two donkeys, a friendly looking bear, two little monkeys and then some little kittens strolling about. They seemed rather neglected and bitten.

In a hut was a small sleepy dog eyeing us warily as we passed it, then we passed a friendly red dingo. At first he was quite wild, jumping up and down in his cage, staring at the little kitten we had seen, and giving the impression that he was rather hungry. Later on when we passed his cage again he was quite peaceful sitting there blinking in the sun, waging his tail, a rather unusual behaviour for a wild dog. Glancing us, he got up pressing himself on the bars of the cage, it seemed, he was just asking to be stroked, and he seemed quite tame. He then begged for a piece of ham we had in our bag.

Time passed and we had to move on to continue our journey. We said our goodbyes to the friendly lady, the friendly dingo and continued to the station.

Our aim was to travel on to Frydland. We wanted to wander around in the nearby wonderful mountains.

We arrived at Frydland and Bella was so pleased to be out of that stuffy train. 'When are we going to build up our house?' she seemed to say as she sniffed around the camping bags.

We managed to get a taxi and found a campsite. We had hoped to get one of those little wooden huts to sleep in but they were all full. The campsite was full of young people, and more expensive than those in the Tatra. We wanted to be alone, but a group of young people came, putting up their tents and then sitting around playing guitar and singing.

Our concern was unnecessary, they were very friendly and the night passed quietly. They played around with Bella who had decided to 'sing' with them. That pleased everyone.

Bella decided to catch her own supper. . young mice. We could do nothing to stop her. We could not save the mice. The mother mouse was already dead and the baby mice laid there defenceless, like little tiny pink sausage balls. That reminded me so much of the time when I had mice myself as pets as a child back in England in Maidenhead.

The young people could speak English and one of them said he was Scottish, which we found hard to believe.

That evening we all sat around the campfire. The young people singing. Bella was particularly tired. She had such a busy time and slept soundly her tail sometimes wagging in her sleep. That mouse super had made her particularly tired since she had swallowed the mice down alive.

It was a lovely holiday, but we had no idea what was awaiting us at home.

2. Discovery of theft and destruction.

On entering our flat on our return home from this holiday trip we felt uneasy and troubled. Something in our flat seemed to have changed. We couldn't quite put our fingers on it.

I was now back at work at the theatre in Freiberg, playing my violin in a professional orchestra, doing a job I loved and had worked so hard for.

At the same time we tried to locate reasons why we didn't feel at home? The changes in our apartment were made so that at first glance it was difficult to realize the shocking truth. That picture on the wall there, staring at us. It didn't seem right. That sculpture, why had it such fresh marks, can't be, not possible. Then we couldn't find certain things; some things were missing. In my room looking around, I was sure I had put that folder over there. Why wasn't it in order? There were many telltale signs of disturbances, and I hurried home as soon as I possibly could after performances, not staying in Freiberg in my tiny little old flat I had there. I rather preferred to make the longer journey home to Dresden daily.

My father came to visit us and seemed to try to want to tell us something, but could not quite get it out of himself. He just said he had told Lindy not to do something. He seemed restless. A friend I thought I could trust, suddenly wrote to me and informed us to look around the place! It was all very weird. The neighbours began behaving oddly towards us, mentioning certain loud noises that came from our flat. It made no sense at first. Then there was this constant uncanny feeling we had when looking around us. My sister came to visit us together with her husband. He was a strange person and we did not feel comfortable in his presence. He told many ironic tales and behaved oddly, often with a sarcastic smile on his face. My sister and her husband left then hand in hand and once it seemed as if they had picked up something from our flat, then they left with a folder and a bag. We were sure they had arrived without these things.

A little later, on one memorable evening that I will never forget, Lorna's father had come to visit us; we discovered the theft and destruction of my mother's artworks. We discovered that many pictures, sketches and also some sculptures were ruined. Later we found out that some had even been stolen, sold or exhibited under another name. This was a great shock for my mother.

Lorna is my daughter. Like any one of my age at that time, I was looking forward to a positive future and to having my own family.

I wanted to show Lorna's father my mother's paintings, scenes from my childhood, from Maidenhead, the Thames, the Berkshire countryside and the English seaside. These paintings meant a lot to me. They were memories of childhood scenes. On opening the trunk we discovered that many of the paintings were missing. We looked at each other in dismay and disbelief. Next day we reported the theft.

The following day, a young policeman came round to take up the case. He stared at a painting on the wall and said we should look around the flat for other unexpected changes.

We never saw this policeman again as he was sent to another department, he had lost his job. In our absence someone or some people had entered our flat and messed around with things. Pictures had been taken out of their frames, small changes made to them; a spot of paint here, a mark there, changes that were not visible to our immediate attention. These pictures were then put back in their frames and hung back on the wall. These cruel changes created an eerie feeling of restlessness and uncertainty.

The majority of my mother's life drawings had also been attacked, certain parts strongly outlined and viciously changed and distorted to give the impression that they were made by someone of perverted character. They were desperately trying to declare my mother unstable and insecure because she stood up for her beliefs and positive socialist views. A sketch of a man was changed to resemble a portrait of Hitler and her wonderful woodcarvings were attacked.

The Stasi had been in our flat, planting bugs. When we were out, they were in. No locked door was safe. The damage, the distortion of my mother's artworks may have started as an extremely bad joke that got way out of hand, but to mutilate these artworks like this, that person had in mind to eliminate my mother in a way that would discredit her.

Why was this young policeman, the first to deal with our case, reemployed into another department, and was demoted to a lesser post? He had made us aware of certain things that he obviously was not supposed to do!

Christmas time arrived. I still worked at the theatre, still had my boyfriend and positive thoughts for a good future, but more dark clouds were gathering on the horizon.

That memorable Christmas 1971 was the last time spent together as a family. But what a distressing time it was. We set off to visit my sister on Christmas Eve. When we arrived we were quite in happy spirits and sang a Christmas carol. But it did not seem as if we were really welcome, then we were greeted with frowning faces. The atmosphere was cool and hard. My father was there also. The room at my sister's flat was full of smoke from supposedly cigarettes that they had been smoking. These cigarettes had a strange unusual smell. It was unusual, then my dad was a fanatic anti smoker. Suddenly, after a short while my mother felt extremely sick. Something had upset her stomach. Was it the smoke, the cigarettes, the food? Today I believe that drugs were used that evening. My mother was very sick. My sister fetched a bowl thrusting it under my mother's face. We had to order a taxi and return home as quickly as possible. My mother was seriously ill for the next couple of weeks.

My time was spent between working, further studies, then I wanted to improve my qualifications, trying to help my mother sort out the theft and destruction of her artworks, visiting my dad and getting to know my boyfriend's family better. It was a busy time and I wanted so much to be happy and positive. We hoped so much that the police would help us. I liked my boy friend's mother very much. She was a very friendly lady, with a big family and I could talk to her about anything. I always felt so welcome at her home. The police were still messing around and we heard nothing for many weeks. In the meantime we still felt restless and ill at ease in our own home.

One afternoon, 1972 my uncle and my father came to visit us. They tried to stop the police investigations that were already underway. At that time we still believed in justice. That my sister and her husband could have been involved was something we found extremely hard to accept. The tragedy of the actual reality sank in only after further events and my sister's husband's strange behaviour.

My sister's husband was particularly fond of making extremely bad so-called jokes. One day, shortly after that memorable Christmas, a letter arrived from my sister and her husband. The date on the letter is, 28/1/72. On the envelope my mother's name and the street name was written purposely incorrectly; Greta Klopfleich, Endte straße; **66**

The number 66 was made to look like eyes, and my mother's name should have been Gretel Klopfleisch. Actually my mother now usually used Margarete as her Christian name, and it was strange to receive a letter calling her Greta. Also Dresden was changed to Treßden. Obviously this was meant to be funny, a bad joke. My sister Lindy still had a key to the flat the whole time. This letter was full of deliberate written mistakes, words purposely spelt wrongly, making fun of my mother all the while. It was full of purposely wrongly written words, and deliberate wrong spelling. For example; 'sisch' should be sich, 'filleicht' should be vielleicht, 'Dier' should be Dir, 'Mudder' should be Mutter, 'dehm' should be dem, 'Paum' should be Baum. Even my sister's name was incorrect. He wrote 'Llindy' instead of Lindy. Then my sister's husband wrote that his little boy was looking so distressed, sitting on mum's lap and wondering why a tree is growing out of her head. He had sent a strange photo with that letter.

We were not happy with this letter and the so-called jokes in it. But a little later, after further investigations because of the picture theft and destruction of my mother's artworks, it began to become clearer what had happened.

This man was especially keen on making bad jokes. Once whilst on holiday with Lindy, he made fun of an old couple that also were staying at the same hotel. He put something up the exhaust of their car and then watched in delight and enjoyment how the poor couple kept trying to start their car without success and could not find out what was wrong with it. There was no such thing as AA roadside recovery in East Germany.

Another time during a short visit to us they talked about putting pins and needles etc in my piano to make it sound differently.

Something was happening all the while in our apartment and these continued events seemed to say; "Ha Ha, - don't you see what is happening!"

Peter, my sister's husband was obviously a member of the Stasi although I have no real evidence other than these tragic events.

Did my sister's husband, and any one else, as well as other members of the Stasi actually think they were having a wonderful time in our flat, amusing themselves with the ridiculous absurd playing around with my mother's artworks, and then, afterwards, wondering how to conceal their malicious deeds by putting the pictures back on the wall? Also, obviously other so-called friends had been involved. Mrs I. R. and her husband used to be, I thought, good friends? Were they also influenced to spy for the Stasi? The last time I had contact with Mrs I. R. she said I should have a good look around!

It seems that someone wanted badly to damage my mother's reputation and bring her artwork into disrepute, - her pictures had been stolen and some of them sold. We discovered her watercolours in a shop in town. There was a different name under it. We wondered why they looked so familiar, and it took some time before it sank in, that they were my mother's paintings. Gretel had been so busy the first years back in Dresden, working hard as a post woman and in a garden nursery, it took some years before she was able to get her pension. Often there was little time to put her signature under her work and regrettably some of her paintings were not signed. She painted in her free time, on holidays and then put her work in folders in a case, thinking it was safe there.

My mother's possessions in our flat were messed around with. Spies sent into our flat, remarks made on pictures, and certain changes. On one document a picture was drawn of a woman with something coming out of her head and smoke out of her mouth, a bad joke?

It seemed that orgies and parties were held in our flat in our absence, then the neighbours even mentioned that there was something going on and made remarks about the noise, but we were not aware who had entered our home without our permission.

Her newspaper critics and exhibition catalogues had disappeared. There were empty envelopes, the contents missing, and a photo album with photos of her sculptures, exhibition catalogues, as well as certain newspaper cuttings of articles where her name was mentioned, gone. Luckily mum had duplicates.
We discovered that sketches, watercolour and life drawings have been ruined, distorted and scribbled on.

A portrait of a man was so distorted, so as to look like a portrait of Hitler! This was something absolutely unbelievable and unthinkable that my mother would draw a portrait of that evil being!
On one picture; mother with child, the mother's short hair was changed to long hair. The hand holding the child was deformed. On the top right-hand corner, lightly drawn in the shaded area were nazi crosses.
Gretel drew this picture again as it once was, and repainted many of those missing and ruined pictures. According to how these vicious changes were made, a person with some experience and knowledge must have completed them.

Small extra drawings of little birds and rabbits were put on some of the sketches. Was this supposed to be a joke?
A photo album was torn apart and not put together again. Most of the missing photos were from those artworks that were either ruined or changed in some way.

On an article about the Keglerheim event [3] was an amateur drawing scrawled on it and there were scribbles over the writing on the pages.
Loads of watercolour paintings were missing, far more than the hundred reported, especially those paintings from England.

The thieves made a mistake about certain documents concerning the Oska Kokoshka league[4] my mother still had from her time spent in the Czech republic. They changed a photo of a sculpture that had been presented to the president Dr Benesch before she left for England. The thieves changed it with something created in England. Only family members could know about this,
My mother said that if she had been murdered it would have been more merciful.
She said; "An artist lives and dies for his, her artwork."
Her sculptures were also affected, a certain smile changed, little chips carved to destroy the original carving. Luckily my mother was able to correct these. I can still point out the changes made on them. The destructive forces could not destroy the beauty of her sculpture work. In spite of the changes they are still of great value.
Even my paintings, sketches, notes and early compositions were affected. Someone had scribbled on my poems I wrote as a child. My GCE certificate in music was torn and some documents of a music course had disappeared. Later on my very early compositions that I had written as a child and teenager disappeared completely.

---

[3] On 25th January 1933 a powerful demonstration against growing fascism was held in Dresden at
Keglerheim - (house for skittle players). Hitler came to power on 30.1 33.
[4] Oska Kokoshka league – was a group of emigrant anti-fascist artists lead by the well known artist Oska Kokoshka.

It was unbearable to see how my mother suffered. The contact to my sister broke off completely and our request to the police in the GDR to find out what had happened, to investigate why and who was behind all this was refused. Instead we had to live isolated, withdrawn as much as possible from society, step back from all activities and live completely for ourselves in order to have peace from certain SED members who were '1933 – 1939' on the other side, members of the Nazi party!

After searching through our cupboards, cases and drawers we reported a large amount of missing watercolours; 25 sea landscapes from our holiday at the Baltic coast, all missing between 1971 – 1972, 18 paintings from England from the English countryside, seaside, still-life and flowers, all presenting typical English landscape and English seascape pictures, some went missing as early as approximately 1963.

At first, single pictures went missing, and then as time went on over the years, larger quantities of her pictures disappeared. We reported approximately 100 missing pictures. Recently, after looking through papers and reading my diary notes about our wonderful holiday in the Polish Tatra 1969, it is quite obvious that even more pictures have been stolen than we originally reported missing to the police. During that holiday that year, my mother was especially busy sketching, painting and sculpting many new works, yet, when I look through what is left after reading about the large amount of sketches and paintings my mother made, there are only a few to be found.

Years later, after my return to the UK, a friend after hearing what had happened 1971-1973, tried to help find some answers why my parents had been so victimised and observed by the Stasi.

This friend believed that my parents, like all socialists and anti- fascists that immigrated to England had either direct or indirect contact with a comrade Heinz Schmidt and perhaps also the American Noel H Field. In the eyes of the Stasi, they were highly suspicious individuals, and if they returned to the GDR late, or even later like my mother and father, this made them even more suspects. This comrade Schmidt had an official position within the GDR government until 1976.

The Stasi were always very persistent and investigations carried on for many years. It is highly likely that my sister Lindy was at first blackmailed by the Stasi and then forced to become an informant against her own family as a so-called collaborator employed by the mfs.

It is certain that Stasi intervention caused and influenced her to spy on us, her own family members. This was common practice of the Stasi. It is more than likely that someone from her group of friends was a member of the Stasi.

Her behaviour certainly pointed out that this was a possibility. This person helped out by the destruction of the sculptures and paintings. We were told by a third person that her husband had been a Stasi member. This friend suggested that I should write to her and make her aware of the possibility to apply to look at copies of the Stasi files, and that she should tell the truth so that the last feelings of guilt could be taken from her. It would be wonderful if we could reach our hands in reconcilement by the grave of our mother.

I have tried to contact her many times without success. I am still scared to get in touch with her, but I have written letters, suggested ways to meet and also tried contact over Red Cross family search service.

This Mr Schmidt, after his three-year imprisonment 1934 - 36 fled to the Czech republic. He was a member of the Hallenser KP newspaper, ' Klassen-kampf'. 1933 he took part and helped build up illegal work by Halle. He managed to flee before a second arrest could be made.

He represented the 1939 group of anti-fascist German refugee emigrants as a member of the Czech refugee trust fund. He helped Austrians as well as Germans to flee to Britain in exile. He made the necessary talks and attended the necessary meetings with London representatives and the American Noel – H Field. In Britain he was Chief editor from the newspaper ' Freie Tribune'. He was concerned about social contacts with other comrades.

In autumn 1949, because of Schmidt's many contacts to the west and his civilised way of talking to others of same thinking, he was ridiculed by the ZPKK[5]. The mfs[6] made ludicrous and absurd accusations against him. This friend meant that this was probably the reason for the refusal to allow my parents to return 1950 – 1953.

This may have been one of the reasons why we were so victimised by the Stasi, but it is no excuse and nothing can justify what happened to us during those years.

Early 1972, Gretel became so seriously ill that she had to be taken to hospital, but the doctors did not treated her correctly. Something did not make sense. She had stomach ulcers and serious heart problems and her complaints were completely ignored. The doctors refused to give her the diet she needed, instead they gave her food that was too heavy and which she could not eat. They wanted to treat her for something completely different.

Because my mother could not stand the food they gave her, the doctor then said;
"Ah there might be something wrong with her heart and stomach after all."
It was devastating to visit her at that hospital and frightening, the doctors were so ignorant of her ailment.
My next visit to that hospital was so devastating that we decided together that the best thing would be for me to take her home and ignore the wrong treatment that was given to her. She would be safer at home and I would take care of her.

So there we were, Gretel was now at home seriously ill without any medical help whatsoever and under constant threat from the Stasi. I was still working full time at the theatre, studying part time as well, I had one day each week free, and I tried to live a normal life at the same time.

April 1972, my mother received a letter from a Mr. Gelinek. He was the police official, (Stasi member) dealing with the theft. This letter contained false disfigurement and misrepresentation of the truth. It was a mockery. She was not well enough to go to his office as ordered and wrote a letter of apology asking for postponement. Instead the following happened;

She had informed him that certain people from galleries and artists, who knew her, would be able to support her artwork. These included the museum for German history in Berlin, Gustave Schmidt, a painter and sculptor, Hans Peter Schulze, author, and her friend Ina from Usti.

A little later I was ordered to go to the police. I believe it was also Mr. Gelinek. I will never forget that meeting, it was one of the worse experiences I have ever had in my whole life. Instead of trying to investigate what had happened, I became subject to an incredible interrogation. I was taken into a small room and this man with a sarcastic smile on his face ordered me to sit opposite him. Mr. Gelinek began questioning me endlessly. He would not stop but began ordering me to confirm his lies. He wanted me to agree to his tale that my mother waited each time for me to disappear of to work to the theatre and then she would start destroying her own artwork. As soon as I came home she would return to her normal self. I

---

[5] ZPKK– top committee, part of East German authority, the Stasi.

[6] mfs – top committee, part of East German authority, the Stasi.

think I must have been in that room for at least two hours. It was well past midday and he ordered himself something to eat and drink. I felt treated as a criminal; in fact I was treated as a criminal. I sat there throughout and had to watch him eat his lunch.

He kept on questioning me about my mother, saying she was not normal and did certain things herself to her own work. He continued, endlessly and would not stop. I did not know how long I would be able to hold out. How long could I take this cross-examination? I tried to stay calm. It was an absolutely awful experience. After about two hours I began to lose my patience and thumped with my fists on the table so that his cup nearly slipped, and said;

"My mother is not mad, she did not do it herself, that is rubbish!"

He laughed. It seemed this is what he had been waiting for, and at last I was allowed to go.

By now we both were very suspicious and careful of anyone. I found it difficult to concentrate on my job and part time studies. It was a relief when we went visiting friends and I still had my boy friend. We still believed in some kind of solution and peace at the end of it all.

I had continued my music studies part-time, as I wanted to improve my composition work and my teaching qualifications. One day as I came home from my lessons, a man, obviously a doctor of some sort, dressed in a thin white coat accompanied by two nurses was coming down the stairs and greeted me as I went up the stairs to our flat. He told me that I was to make an appointment to see him concerning my mother as soon as possible and he gave me the address and the phone number of his office.

I had left my mother that morning very ill in bed. Due to the worries and stress, she was again seriously ill with stomach ulcers and serious heart problems. Don't forget that earlier on I had to take her home from hospital due to the wrong treatment. We could not trust anyone, especially a doctor. In my absence, this man, so-called doctor with his two so-called nurses had forced their way into our flat under false pretence, and unsuspecting mum had let them in.

My mother told me that a short while earlier there was a knock at the door and on opening it she saw this strange man in this thin white coat accompanied by these two nurses. They told her that there would be no further investigations and requested that she signs a document. She was forced to put her signature under it. My mother was very distraught about these strangers she had never seen before, knocking at our door and asking her questions and the fact that a 'nerve' doctor had forced his way into our flat. This man even wrote to my sister – not to have contact with us ever again.

As I opened the door she called out that I should stop them and question them who they were, who had sent them and what was going on. I rushed down the stairs but they had already gone. It was obvious that the Stasi had sent these three individuals round, waiting for a suitable moment when I was out. Our flat was obviously under constant observation.

I had tried to get some help for her, but the doctors were ignorant of her stomach and heart complaints, they wanted to treat her for something completely different.

That afternoon Mrs. Glatho came to visit us. She was a good friend. We told her what had happened and she suggested phoning up and to try to find out what was going on. We then found out that this man was a psychiatrist. She had put herself under great risk to do this, as any sort of help and involvement from another outsider could have put her also under threat from Stasi observation.

Mrs. Glatho began to argue with this man on the phone as he tried to convince her that my mother was unstable.

After my father died, we found a letter my sister had written to him, dated 25th April 1972. She wrote; "A week ago I got a letter from mummy's doctor that he wanted to talk with me. So I went there. He said, the whole thing is not my fault, the police have obviously, I am not quite sure, stopped the investigation. Nothing can be proved. He advised me to stop all communications with mummy and Sonja to stop further excitement. He told me not to write or go there, so I think it is better to follow his advise."

This letter, containing these Stasi orders has been followed up to this day. I saw my sister a last time, 1976 shortly after the funeral of my father. The doctor mentioned earlier was not my mother's doctor, but a psychiatrist ordered by the Stasi.

My mother disowned Lindy. She found it now necessary to write her testament to secure her artwork for the future, and in spite of damaged parts, they still had material value. Since then, she restored and recreated many of her lost and damaged artworks.

Lindy's yearlong heartless, strange and loveless behaviour to her mother, in spite of continuous efforts to regain her daughter's love, and the fact that her daughter's behaviour got worse as time went on proved fatal. The truth was based on the fact that things were damaged and taken away from a family member who knew where they were. My mother's, heart was imbedded in those artworks.

My mother was dying. We could not trust any doctor. I was helpless and saw how she suffered. One evening she was so ill and ailing. Her stomach ulcers broke and she was bleeding, a bucket of blood pouring out of her mouth, she was so sick.

I looked at my mother and prayed; I was desperate. How could I help her?

"Please help my mother. Give her ten years of my life if necessary. Don't let her die."

She lived exactly nearly to the day another ten years!

I had to fetch the emergency ambulance. Now there was no time to look into certain files. She had a life saving operation and recovered.

About this time my mother wrote a letter to the director of the Freiberg theatre where I worked as a violinist in the orchestra, asking for permission for me to be freed from work for a few weeks in order to help her sort out the theft and destruction of her work. I think this was in February that year. At that time we still believed in help.

This letter informed the director that something dreadful had happened, that I was helping her to sort it out and that I was finding it difficult to find time to do my job and at the same time to assist her. She also wrote that I loved my job and would then return with fresh strength.

It was obviously a mistake to inform the director of the theatre about the incident and to ask for permission for me to be freed from work for a short time. This letter informed him that a Mr. criminal inspector Jenz was dealing with the case. It also informed him that the Stasi were observing us as obviously suspicious persons.

This was the beginning of the end, and the reason why all future efforts to get back to work after the birth of my daughter as a professional orchestra musician was made impossible, sabotaged and refused.

In April that year I made an application asking to regain my British nationality. My mother wrote a letter to support my wish. She wrote that she was sorry that she had brought both children over to the GDR.

She wrote, that as the official authorities were obviously unable to remove the treacherous persons or even unable to find them, she regrets there was no other alternative than to support my wish that she found correct. How was it possible that political sabotage could take place in her own flat, her work ruined and that her artwork, that was a weapon in the anti-fascist fight for peace and a better world was not accepted.

She also wrote that it was obvious that her younger daughter Rosalinde in the GDR had come under bad influence, and was put under pressure. (We called my sister Lindy for short). In her own words she wrote; 'in the capitalist world abroad you stand in the open opposite the enemy. Here, he is undercover, hidden, and often in a safe position. Because of this many innocent people become the victims'.

My mother had a recurring dream. She dreamt of an endless long snake, it was so long she could not see where the head was. Was this a dream version of the Stalinist state we were living in?

In spite of all efforts by the police and some still today unknown forces to ruin my mother's growing reputation and recognition as an artist they did not succeed. She carried on working, creating more and more sculptures and paintings. My main concern at this time was to help and save my mother and so we lived isolated and withdrawn. It was obvious that the Stasi wanted me to move away from Dresden, I would have then been absent from home and the Stasi would have had an easier opportunity to do their damage.

We wrote a letter to Mr. Gelinek dated 27th April 1972 requesting the return of certain contents. We were sent this letter back. In this letter we wrote;

"Dear Mr. Gelinek, as you have discontinued our case, why have you kept following things?

1) A letter from Mrs. R with remarks; (wrote we should look around).

2) A letter from Mr. Boehme with envelope.

3) Several documents; one of them, a document that was corrected with a red marker.

4) The picture list is not required any more. Why have you decided to keep it?

We want to know why?"

We never received an answer.

About this time my mother received a letter from Theo Balden. He advises my mother to contact the Verband Bildender Künstler[7] and wrote that he was also a victim of burglars, but his artworks were not touched.

Thinking the SED[8] might help, as we still believed in justice, we wrote to them, asking for assistance to solve the theft case and destruction of the artworks. The police had written informing us that they had stopped the investigation. We disagreed and appealed against their decision. The answer was devastating; the police had written to the SED and we now received a joint answer informing us that in their opinion no crime had been committed, the case did not confirm that a crime had happened. It remained unsolved.

The destruction, intrusion and meddling in our lives was immense. Even today I find it hard to deal with the results these devastating events had on our lives. Not only were my mother's artworks affected, but also my own creative work violated. I began to write my own small compositions already as an eight year old, from the moment I started to learn to play the violin. At first, during these devastating months, I noticed some strange marks written on my early composition pieces. The handwriting on these music manuscripts looked like my sister's handwriting. Short while later, these early music manuscripts disappeared altogether.

Although I kept them in a safe place, someone had also thought it a joke to steal them as well. Today, the earliest compositions I can find that I wrote exist from my time as a student at the Dresden music school; my early work before 1960 has 'disappeared'. For what reason these early compositions have been stolen is still today unsolved; why?

---

[7] Verband Bildender Künstler; Association of artists in the GDR.

[8] SED, - Socialist united party of East Germany.

Woodcarving; determined

Sketch; despair

'Es war einmal ein Röslein,
Ein Kindlein hübsch und fein,
Es war so froh und munter,
Ihm schienen Sonn und Sternelein.

Nun ist sein Herz erkaltet,
Das Röslein ward zu Stein,
Und Dornen wurden Schwerter,
Zu bereiten Qual und Pein.

O sag warum ist das geschehen ,
Das schlimmste das Mutter Augen mußten sehen,
Wie sich verwandelte das liebe kleine,
In ein Monster mit einen Herzen von Stein.

Ein Künstler arbeitet mit seinen Herzens Blut,
Und diese seine Arbeiten zu verschandeln,
Tut dem Tater nimmer gut,
Es ist ein Qualvoll Streich,
Einen Morde gleich.

O Götter, Ihr warum ist das geschehen,
Ein Gewitter wird hernieder gehen,
Auf den Täter mit Gewalt,
Die zerstörten Kunstwerke werden neu Erstehen,
Denn wahre Kunst und Künstler,
Bleiben immer jung und werden nimmer alt.
Das Röschen war ein Bild von einen Menschlein,
Klug hübsch und fein,
Ihr Götter, o, wie, warum und wer hat es zerstört?
Ein blütend Herz stellt diese Frage,
Denn sie ist noch ungeklärt'.

<u>Translation.</u>

'There was once a little rose,
A child, sweet and bright,
She was so happy and alert,
Sun and stars shining for her.

Now her heart has turned cold,
The little rose has turned to stone,
And thorns became swords,
To prepare pain and sorrow

Oh tell me why has this happened,
The worst that mother's eyes could see,
How changed the dear little one,
In a monster with a heart of stone.

An artist works with his heart's blood,
And to shame his work,
For the offender this is never good,
It is a painful stroke,
Equal as a murder.

Oh Gods, tell me why has this happened,
Thunder will descend,
With force upon the offender,
The destroyed artworks will arise again new,
Then genuine artworks and artists,
Stay young and never grow old.

The little rose was a picture of a little person,
Clever, beautiful and bright,
You, Gods, Oh why, how, and who has destroyed it?
A bleeding heart asks this question,
Then it is still unsolved.'

(Written approx 1973 - 1974).

This poem is proof how my mother suffered under the disastrous intrusion and destruction from Stasi interference in our lives.

Woodcarving; crying

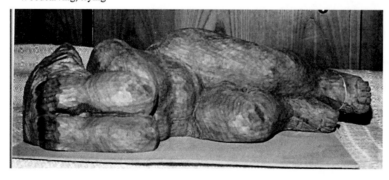

The Legend, part 10.

<u>The salvation and deliverance of the fiery hound.</u>

Returning to my tale of the legend of the fiery hound, the banishment was to be lifted, at last after many years, and so in my report of devastating events of the years 1971-1972, the birth of my daughter brought peace and new life into our broken world.

Many years had passed by since the old grandmother told her tale about the fiery hound and everything was still as before. Each night the hound with the fiery eyes came as always, at the twelfth stroke of the bell at midnight, by storm, by clear starry night when everyone was asleep, restlessly roaming through the town to the Zauken valley.

Then, in a time of peace it came to pass, that a master's faithful servant, a good, godly, simple and righteous man, passed away. His daughter, in loving memory, crying with passionate tears, her heart nearly broke for longing for her dear father. Nearby in the Zauken valley, in the silent graveyard, in a painful and distressing hour, her father's body was laid to rest.

Once in the stillness of a cool evening, the daughter went to the grave crying tears in painful abundance over her sleeping father. Quietly she sat by the precious mound, alone with her grief and sorrow. She did not notice how the night, like on dark wings came descending gradually.

As the bells rang at the twelfth hour, the last tones sounding and trembling, there appeared on his rounds the dreadful apparition of the hound.

He approached the peaceful grave, where on a green twig a flowering white rose grew, there the maid was kneeling and crying. He sat down sadly opposite on the moss of the neighbouring grave, and silently looked at the maid's flowing tears. Painfully smiling through her flowing tears she stepped over to the edge of the grave to her silent fellow sufferer, her companion in misfortune and stroked him gently with her soft hands.

"Oh," she said, speaking mildly;

"You also are pursued by pain. Poor animal your heart is nearer to suffering and full of sorrow and grief."

And the maid's flowing tears fell onto his matted fur, and brought him at last the longing for peace, for pity and compassion.

The result was amazing, then look, the hound sprang up barking around the maiden, caressing, fondling, licking her soft hands, he was wild no more. His sparks of wildness did not show the usual fierceness and his eyes were glowing in a delighted milder light. Now he had found compassion and pity at last. He could go home now in peace, and since that night he has disappeared and has never been seen again.

Back to the twentieth century, after the devastating events and the now absences of my sister our lives were brightened by the arrival of my daughter.

3. 1973 Arrival of my daughter.

I cannot exactly remember when I met my daughter's father. Naturally I was planning a normal life, family, friends, socialising, but Stasi intervention and my sister's obvious involvement took that all away from me, as well as a permanent post in my chosen profession as an orchestral musician.

I continued my studies in order to obtain a teacher's degree and composing was something I was particularly interested in. I was the only female student at the music school 'Carl Maria von Weber' who studied composition as well.

When the Stasi started to bug our home, to put us under continued observation, I had a choice; to do what my sister did, move away, ignore and leave my mother, and her artwork to an uncertain destiny, or, to help protect her and to keep her artwork for the future but also to stand up and tell the world the truth, then both my parents were heroic idealist believing in a better peaceful world. It is certain that if I had gone away, something would have happened to my mother earlier. She would have been taken away and I would not have even been told, or informed where they had taken her.

My daughter's father's family was large. It was jolly to meet his mother, sister and brother. We spent many happy hours together.

One holiday is particularly in my memory. We went to the Czech republic together with his cousin and fiancé camping by a lakeside. Although I was used to more extensive walks, wanderings and adventure it still was pleasant and normally I would have stayed and returned with the others. It was summer 1972, I think. Because of what had happened I felt restless. We had arranged to make it possible for me to contact my mother somehow on a regular basis while I was away. I cannot remember how we arranged this; I think it was per telegram.

Under normal circumstances I most probably would have stayed with Lorna's father, but as things were, I left for home earlier than the others. The Stasi were at work observing us, I felt restless then my mother had just recovered from her serious dangerous operation.

I returned home and we spent some time together up in the mountain hut. My uncle was still alive at that time and we still had only the very small wooden hut at the top. Life seemed now to return more or less to 'normal' as far as that was now possible under the 'new' circumstances. I returned to work, enjoyed my position playing my violin in the orchestra, and continued my part-time studies. But the Stasi were not going to leave us alone for long. Contact with my sister had now broken completely, and my mother was devastated about this. She now spent much of her time repairing damaged sculptures and reconstructing, repainting scenes of missing paintings.

The New Year arrived, 1973. Hopefully it would be a better year. The month of March arrived and Stasi interference began again.

We were not informed about any illness that my uncle was supposed to have. Yes, he was not a healthy person, but there was nothing to point out that he was about to die. It came unexpectedly swiftly. His vision was now impaired but it did not stop him doing things, He spent much of his time up in the mountain hut, continued his marquetry work and spent time together with his many friends.

My uncle Hans died under strange circumstances, 24th march 1973. I believe the Stasi have been messing around, not only in our flat, but also among my uncle's belongings and his apartment. There were loads, far too many syringes around in his place. Who gave him these? It certainly was not the doctor. Why did he die so shortly after the discovery of the theft? Although my uncle suffered under progressing blindness, he still could read and write, he still saw sufficient to write letters. It seems certain that 1972 the Stasi talked to uncle Hans as well as to my father in the effort to try to discredit my mother.

My uncle died Autumn1973 and left many unsolved problems. Uncle Hans was never without money in his apartment, but there was nothing there when we were finally able to clear his apartment. His place was in a right mess. Many things from uncle Hans's apartment and mountain hut were missing and stolen already before we got the keys.

My uncle had also criticized the Stalinist state and problems with the East German police already as early as about 1953. My mother was so homesick and her marriage to my father breaking down. He wanted to convince my mother to stay in England at all costs. He had used the possibility given to him to visit the West to come over to England to visit us in Maidenhead. The GDR authorities found out and he was taken before a court. It was a criminal offence to criticize the state and even worse to travel over to a capitalist country without the GDR authorities' permission. He now had a criminal record!

If he knew or suspected what was going on in our flat in our absence and thought of trying to warn us in some way through that visit together with my father, this might have put him in danger. His death left us with the problem of solving his assets. My uncle's girl friend told us that she came that day to see him as she usually did only to find him laying there already dead. Instead of alarming the doctors she went crying to a friend. She must have had a key to his apartment, or the door was open.

Uncle Hans left us with a heritage problem of dissolving a joiner's workshop and many other things. We had problems with his so- called friends. We did not know them. Everyone seemed to be after his assets and especially the mountain property that belonged to him. The testament he left behind was extremely confusing. He gave each of these so-called friends a hut. There were five huts up there, each in various stages of condition. We had the smallest which was nothing more than a small wooden shed. There was nothing mentioned in the testament about the land on which the huts were built. At one time it had been a vineyard.

Many of uncle Hans's 'friends' turned out to be old Nazis. We did not want anything to do with them. He had now come to a phase were he could not determine the difference between true friends and so-called friends using him. My uncle Hans, like my parents, had criticized the Stalinist state, and this put him also at risk.

He had many visitors up on the mountain hut, known also as the apple mountain because there used to be apple trees up there. My uncle was eccentric. Often something was going on up there, merry making, telling tales of our ancestors, tales of his journeys as a youth, how he, with a group of friends in Italy stopped in front of a tall building, started to look and stare up at it until a small group of people had gathered around also looking up to see what was going on. They left and after two hours returned only to find an even larger group of people still looking up, and wondering at what. He told us of his adventures in the underground during the nazi time. He told us how he managed to deceive the Nazi officers many times when he was deported to the punishment regiment in Greece because they had found the weapons he had hidden in his father's workshop for the resistance. He had, as my parents, the full recognition as a victim of Nazism. He was a good and jolly man.

His so–called friends started quarrelling about his assets. Who gets what! We did not want to sit on a table together with family ' A' or family 'von H'. These people were old Nazis. It was difficult for my mother to get it sorted out, but eventually things were settled and we now had the whole of the mountain property.

My uncle and grandfather, as well as my parents my daughter and myself have spent many happy and peaceful times up there, on this land with the wonderful view over the river Elbe and Dresden, reaching far into the Erzgebirge (Ore Mountains) and the Saxonian Swiss mountains in the distance. During the bombing of Dresden it was a refuge, a safe haven for my grandfather, his second wife and my uncle.

'The mountain' as we called this weekend home because of the exceptional beautiful view, had a special place in my heart with many wonderful cherished memories and this was the 'unmovable assets' I intended to keep for my daughter.

I still believed in a positive future with my daughter's father and we had loads to sort out. My mother went with him on his motorbike to my uncle's place to sort things out. She now had the authorisation to enter his apartment as his sole heir. His apartment looked as if someone had been messing around with things. We never found out why his place was full of syringes. Why? We reported it to the police, but they refused to take it seriously and after our own continued experience with the Stasi we were unable to do anything. Other personal possessions went missing as well. We found many personal letters but strangely enough no letters sent to him from England from my mum and dad.

The first time Gretel went to her brother's place with my daughter's father she found these later missing documents about our ancestry. Regrettably mum did not bring it back with her thinking it was safe then she had the key.
When we went there a couple of weeks later to collect some of his assets, among the missing items was this document concerning our ancestors 'von Duba'. Why?

A short while later I decided to stop further contact with my daughter's father. We did not know whom to trust, - who was involved. By now we had no contact with my sister.
Before I stopped contact with Lorna's dad after my uncle died we decided to use the money inherited to buy ourselves a house and I wanted to find a nice place, where we all could live peacefully together, myself, my child and her father, but also enough room for my mother. I could not even think of leaving her alone under those circumstances. But Stasi intervention, disturbances and bugging in our home continued. We withdrew further and further living only for ourselves. I remember writing a letter to Lorna's dad informing him of my decision to stop contact. He never tried to answer it or to try to find out exactly why I had made that decision.

Shortly after I stopped contact with my fiancé I found out later that my dad went to visit him. I do not know what they talked about but perhaps his family became afraid to have contact with someone whom the Stasi was observing?
Now, with no contact with the father of my child, this would have discredited him, his parents, sister and brother, then the Stasi had now taken that possibility away from us to become a family, we were alone.

Why was it not possible for Lorna's dad 1973 to come back just to talk things over with me? He just stayed away. Why? After the Berlin wall came down Lorna's dad came over to England on a trip to London. He came over with his son and wife. The first thing he did was to contact me and arrange for us to meet up.
Shortly before the Berlin wall came down I managed to go over back to Dresden for a holiday and we met up again. I managed to arrange to stay at a friend's place, our first visit since we had returned to the UK. We had studied together at the music school in Dresden. During this short holiday we saw each other again, and my daughter saw her father for the first time, I was now over there, as a visitor from the West. We had much to talk about.

Today we have regular contact with each other. We found each other again although certain circumstances had changed and he is married with a son, but that does not spoil our renewed friendship, we are all good friends and we visit each other regularly.

Why could this not have been possible for my sister? Has she a bad conscious? Feeling guilty? Where is she? Is she still alive? I do not know.

At home, on the Ender Street we had problems with the comrade V and his grandmother living on the ground floor. The grandmother was especially bad and vicious with us, complaining about all sorts of things that we never locked the front door, always left it open, we did not sweep the stairs properly. She complained about many trivial things.

We could never speak with this woman, She always spoke to us in the most awful manner, quarrelling and shouting to us, treating and talking to me as if I were a small child.

I was already expecting my daughter Lorna. But because of all the problems and our own wariness and the previous theft, we lived already isolated, not trusting anyone.

Obviously neighbours were aware of Stasi observation. This victimisation from these people began in approximately late 1972.

On the tenth of March that year, this woman as always greeted us with swear words, shouting and bad language. We tried to ignore her and wanted to go quietly into our flat. This lady lived on the ground floor by Mr R, who was Mr V's son in law. We were always treated with aggravation and swear words etc from this family. This time Mr V and his wife came towards us threatening shouting unintelligent talk, refused to talk quietly and bashed into the door of our flat, breaking the frame. At this time I was already pregnant.

My fiancé was not present; in fact I had to stop contact with nearly everyone I knew, because we could not trust anyone.

After the theft we changed the locks on a regular basis. Because of this incident and the broken door, the Stasi would have been able to gain easier access again into our flat.

It was very difficult to get such newly built apartments like the one we had, and they were quite small. We had a small two-bed apartment and it was highly possible that this family were after our flat. Perhaps the Stasi had made promises to them in return for continued observation?

Except for the harassment from that horrible neighbour and constant Stasi observation, the second half of that year past comparably peaceful. I enjoyed my last days in my profession and prepared myself for the birth of my child. I was going to make my mother a grandmother and I wanted her to enjoy her grandchild, something that my sister had taken away from her. I remember well the last performance in Freiberg before the birth of my daughter. It was a sunny day and we gave a concert performance in the open air at the market place in the middle of the town. I believe it was to celebrate some sort of anniversary. Little did I realize it would be the last time I played in Freiberg.

It was not planned to be without a father but I felt happy and at last somehow positive.

My mother would have bought us a house and we could have lived happily together. We now had the mountain hut for ourselves and we spent many happy hours up there. I must not forget to mention how our little dog Bella took particularly care of me.

During the time I was pregnant with my daughter, she was always by my side. It was as if she knew that I was expecting. One day I went down to the village for shopping. Our little dog was very concerned and as I strolled down the hill she suddenly appeared by my side insisting on following me. She continued this habit after Lorna was born, always sitting next to the pram and if anyone wanted to look at Lorna she would growl and bark.

My daughter was born in October 1973. She was a beautiful baby and nothing could take my newly gained motherly happiness away. She brought much pleasure to my mother. She was just as good and loving to her granddaughter as she had been to me. It seemed as if for at least a while the Stasi were leaving us alone. Enough harm had been done. I was now without my fiancé. The destruction from Stasi interference in our lives was overwhelming; we had no idea whom we could trust, but I was of the opinion that living in a socialist country there should not be any prejudice to live on my own with my child, she was wanted, a gift from the heavens. I still believed we lived in a 'socialist world' where all should be equal. But 1972 – 73 our world broke down, our belief in socialism destroyed and in pieces.

Gretel with her granddaughter Lorna 1973   Woodcarving, 'Two Generations,' (approx.1976).

Although I had now a teacher's degree I could not find work as a violin music teacher. The experiences of the theft and destruction had an extremely negative effect on my search for work, and Stasi intervention was everywhere notable.

Naturally I believed I could get work again nearer home but this proved negative. I received negative messages from the music schools, Bautzen, Dresden land and Paul Büttner music school in Dresden. I was told that there were no vacancies although at the same time vacancies were supposed to be available, but for me there was nothing; there was no work in my profession in Dresden or surroundings. There was work for musicians from other socialist countries that came over to stay. This ironic inconsistency to the so-called GDR laws that there was work for everyone, no unemployment proved to be fatal for me. At least I managed to build up a private practise and was quite successful with it.

Not all neighbours were horrible, one neighbour, the lady from upstairs came down regularly, was friendly, but checked regularly on Lorna, especially when mum was in convalescent and in hospital. I had started to teach privately and she sent her son down for violin lessons.

I did not want to stay too long away from home because of Stasi interference, so this new possibility to teach privately suited me. They were still after my mother. We had to keep together and be vigilant.

'Es greift mit kalten Fingern.
Nach meinen Herz so wild,
O grausam qualvoll des Totes Krallen sind.
Mein Leben lag noch ruhig, so wie ein Bergsee,
Gebettet zwischen Bergen von Freud und Weh.

Doch da ein Sproß von mir erzürnte,
Ward wild, ja ward Gaunerin,
Das trübte so mein Leben,
Nun geh ich darüber ein.

Ich leb wie in der Wüste,
Im Menschengewühl ringsum.
Die Menschen sind wie Steine,
Sind kalt und taub und stumm.

Ein Stück des Lebens leuchtet,
Noch in heller Glut
Das ist mein erster Sproß,
Er ist so ehrlich lieb und gut,
O gütiger Götter gebet
Das diese Glut nicht vergeht,
Sonst wers um mich geschehen,
Mein Leben wer verweht'.

Translation.

'It grips with cold fingers,
At my heart so wild,
O how cruel and painful is deaths claws,
My life laid still quiet as a mountain lake,
Bedded between mountains of happiness and pain,

Then there, a sprout from me became aggravated,
Became wild, yes untamed,
That overshadowed so my life,
Now because of this, I fade away.

I live like in a wasteland,
Midst crowds of people around,
The people are like stones,
Are cold and deaf and mute.

A bit of life is shining,
Still in glowing light,
It is my first born,
So honest, dear and good.

Oh, dear Gods please give,
That this light never fades,
Else it was for nothing,
My life would fade away.

(Written approx; 1973 - 1974).

4. My father's last years.

About 1974 my father was sent into an old peoples home against our will. He was forced to go. He complained that there were Nazis in that place. He was given a very small room with an impossible long walk, approx fifty meters to the bathroom and toilet; no consideration was given that he had difficulties walking, a problem that related back to his accident about 1954.

He used to sit on a bench by the tram stop and regularly complain that there were Nazis in that old people's home. It was a great mistake to talk like this openly in public. We wanted to help him, to get him out of there. At first, he used to come round regularly telling us about certain people living in that place and complaining. We also were not happy, as Stasi observation had increased making our lives difficult.

He kept saying that he had told Lindy, my sister, not to do something; "No she can't do that," but what exactly, he never got round to say.

The plan we had was to buy a house outside Dresden and to move as soon as possible and then hopefully get dad out of that old peoples home. We never got round to informing him of our idea as he also had contact with Lindy my sister and her husband. We could not trust them and had to be careful because of Stasi contact.

A short while later after my dad had made these comments about Nazis he was put in another room at the top of the building, I think on the fourth floor! He had fallen down several times on his way to the bathroom. The home officials then shoved him up to the top of the building to share a room together with someone else saying, "you don't need this, and you don't need that" his belongings now disperse to the utmost minimum. My dad never got out again. We were left in the dark what was happening. It was always painful to visit him and see him in such an appalling condition.

Why was my dad shortly later forced into this old peoples home, against his will?
What about the remarks he had made before he was pushed even further into an even worse situation and smaller room up on the fourth floor where he would find it even more difficult to get out, and his remarks that; "there are Nazis in this place?"

He was trying to tell us something, and what did he mean telling Lindy;
"No, you must not do that." What exactly was he trying to tell us?

We tried so hard to persuade dad not to go into that old peoples home. We warned him again and again. We told him, he would lose his freedom.

I went to visit that place as it was still being built and as a result warned him;
"Do not go, no green lawn, still a big building place, not completed yet."
I could not see the room where my dad was to be put in, and there were no balconies. I told him that you could hear what was going on in next room, as the walls were so thin. There were very small rooms with a small sink only. He was told that he could take some furniture with, but not his typewriter. There was a long passage to walk down to visit the bathroom. There were no toilet facilities in the rooms. The porter said, you would be asked to come first for an interview. You can cancel the application at any time, but once you are in the home that is it. There would be no going back.

One peculiar fact; old people were not allowed to take their savings with them. Any savings had to be given up to someone else in that home for safekeeping. No sun shone into the rooms. I advised him again and again; "No way don't give up that flat. I guess someone else is after it."

I promised to visit him each week to go shopping for him. I also wrote a letter to him with an idea;

"Dad you have two children. I take care of mum. Can't Lindy take care of you? Tell Lindy to move to a larger apartment with enough room for you all. But please, stay where you are. Don't move."

Lindy never bothered about anything. He could have got a larger place from the VDN services. He should wait until he could get a better place.

Meanwhile at home we were constantly under control, the family living in the flat opposite and the flat below always watching us, insulting us and making life impossible. The Stasi were in and out of our flat continuously. Often when we came home we noticed that someone or some people had been in our flat again. Sometimes we saw a strange face looking down out of the window of our flat when we came down the road on our way home. But we met no one on our way up. Who ever had been in our apartment must have disappeared in one of the neighbour's flats. Lorna was just a small baby.

Why were we continuously victimised from bad neighbours and that Nazi SED secretary? He was an extremely unpleasant person, arguing and disagreeing with my mother, making our lives difficult. We disagreed with too many things and we were not traditional enough.

On 29th January 1976 my mother received a letter from this SED local party secretary. It stated; "As you have during the year 1975 insufficiently taken part in duties and because of your unsatisfactory attendance at party meetings and given no excuse or apologies for not attending meetings and you even did not attend the most important meetings for the reports about voting, (something like AGM), and also because of inadequate duties to your party contributions, you are ordered to attend a meeting. If you do not attend this meeting, a party disciplinary action will still be given to you."

This ridiculous message was a hand written note. My mother was again seriously ill. This time due to her glaucoma and she had just come back from hospital after an eye operation.

This man who was the local party secretary from the SED had been a Nazi during the war. So at the time when there was a warrant out for my parents arrest, when my mother had to hide in an empty factory building, and my father was working the political press and had to escape over the border into the Czech Republic, in fact as we found out, this man had not only been a Nazi, but also an active member of the SS - and here he was, a secretary of the SED, the East German communist party in a position of authority.

During the time my parents were starving and fleeing, living in Czechoslovakia in the emigration in poor accommodation, this man, as a member of the SS most probably was searching and hunting down anti-fascist. On the outside he appeared to be a socialist, but he had just changed his colour. Inside he was the same Nazi as before. It was a cat and mouse game he played with my mother.

The last few months had been gloomy and we spent most of our time up on the mountain hut, in all weather. The peace up there compensated us for the continuous harassment we were subject to from Stasi and the local SED secretary.

My father had now been in the old peoples home for about two years. He was not happy there. Although we had told him not to go, he went. He said the SED had told him he must go and that he had been told from other comrades that it was a party commission to go. This old peoples home was supposed to be a special good one for old comrades. It was an order from the SED party. He was forced to go into that home.

It was April and we had lived most of these last months up on the mountain hut in all kinds of weather, snow, ice, cold winds, and rain. My daughter was just two and a half years old. We had no running water at that time. We had to fetch water in a bucket from the people living at the bottom of the hill. We went home regularly just to have a proper bath, and to wash our clothes. The situation was becoming unbearable. We had plans to buy a house and to move away as soon as possible. We planned to get my father out of that old people's home to live with us at last. The house on the Bahnhof Street was big enough, but he died before we could do this.

One day in May, as we came home, a lady whom we only knew by sight greeted us. She informed us that my father was ill. Next day I went to visit him. An official person met me, as I was about to enter his room, I was then told that my dad had just died, five minutes earlier. I was not allowed to see him and given no further explanation. We had received no message or information, either from officials from that home or from my sister. He had been shoved again into another room and left to die and they looked in at certain intervals to see if he was dead. He was no longer in the room I had seen him in last. My immediate reaction at first was anger; no one had informed us about what had happened and the unbelievable cruel cold attitude and ignorance of those working in that home was unbelievable. I was not allowed to see him but sent away without being given any explanation.

My father received a medal for recognition as fighter against fascism for his work in the underground and his anti-fascist activities on the 15th April 1976. It was a very high award. He died one month later, 13th May.

My sister phoned up the old people's home, she knew he was ill, —just to find out if he was still alive. She did not inform us.
The Stasi did not want him to talk to us. Perhaps that is why they prevented us seeing him when he was still alive! He might have told us something!

Shortly before the memorial service, my sister came round once to see our mother, mainly to talk about certain arrangements.
One of the things we had to do was to sort out the few things my dad left behind.
The next day we went together to dad's room to collect his belongings. My sister was very concerned to prevent me taking and looking at a certain package and bundle of papers. I was too stunned and shocked, as my dad had just died.
She rummaged and poked around in his cupboard took up this bundle and said;
"I'll take this. You don't need these things, you're not getting this."
She took it away so hastily and quickly without showing me what it was. But she but did not care or want anything of dad's other papers, letters and his diary notes. Could it have been something to do with the Stasi, with the picture theft, and the desperate attempt to discredit my mother with a report about her illness 1946 to the police in an attempt to save Lindy and her husband from being made suspects? The police were so keen to try to make me believe that my mother had psychological problems that occurred as soon as I was out of the house, during which she damaged her own work. Then when I returned she was again normal. They forgot that during our holiday together to the Czech Tatra and our visit to Ina in Usti the main damage had already been done!
Another possibility could be that this package, perhaps because of my father's physical disability, was deposited in his room for safekeeping. Dad had said to us during one of his last visits before he was unable to come round that he had told Lindy;
"No she must not do that."

What exactly he meant, he never explained.

Our father was to be laid to rest at the Heide cemetery outside Dresden. Here was a permanent memorial erected to commemorate all victims of the Nazi regime. We had not seen my sister since 1972. This was the only time my mother had the chance to see her daughter again, and the only time my sister saw her niece, my daughter now two and a half years old. My mother saw Lindy a last time at the memorial service at the cemetery, but what a final meeting it was! We met my sister and her husband outside the memorial hall. Apart from us, there were only about two or three other people there, mainly old comrades. We did not know them. Mrs Glatho came with us to take care of Lorna and to take her for a walk during the ceremony. I did not want to stay behind, and I did not want to take Lorna with to the cemetery. She was still so small to really understand what was going on.

At my father's funeral we were not even allowed to grieve privately. We had hardly walked together a few yards after he was laid to rest when my sister suddenly stopped. I will never forget the expression on her face, it was cold and rigid; in fact her whole body froze.

She refused to walk further with us, and said; " This is as far as I go with you."

A moment earlier, we had noticed a movement, a rustling in the bushes by the side of the path. Someone was hiding behind the bushes, following, spying and watching us, and we saw someone peering through the branches.

We could not be left alone, even at this moment of great sadness, and my sister could not even go the full way with us together out of the cemetery. It was the last time my mother saw her younger daughter Lindy. Was it the Stasi, and why? The pain, the loss of her younger daughter in this way was so great, my mother never recovered from it. It was a nail to her coffin. She never talked about my sister ever again; she only said once, 'at least she is alive and well'.

Shortly after the funeral, my sister and I had to go to the bank, as he had left each of us some money. I asked her, please don't forget mum. Come and visit her, talk to her, get things sorted out.
She answered: " If I contact you, if I come to see you, mum and your daughter, I would put you all in danger"!!
These were her last words spoken to me. The next sign I had from her was a letter concerning the tragic accident of her son Frank 1992.

Now, looking through old papers and old letters, although I brought everything back with me, because I had no time to sort things out when I left Dresden in 1984, I found that there is nothing available around the time of my mother's illness 1946 – 47. Only a single remark could be found on one letter, that she was fed artificially during her first days in hospital. She was obviously seriously ill.

Why couldn't I find any letters from this time? I have found many letters and documents from my parents, from their time spent in Prague, - diary notes about my dad's departure from Prague, how he fled to safety, his letters, and the diary he wrote when he was sent to Australia in the internment camp, my mother's letters to uncle Hans, dad's letters to uncle Hans, but nothing about 1946, - 47. Why did uncle Hans die in 1973? The Stasi were also in his flat.

Did someone choose to steal certain things relating to my parents time 1946- 47 and to give them to the police?

My mother's serious stomach operation 1973 and the blood transfusion, although it saved her life, but there certainly was something wrong with the blood given to her, perhaps contaminated, HIV. Taking into account certain remarks made by friends, officials, and doctors, this could have been a possibility.

It is a most unbelievable story what happened from 1971 – 1974, hardly believable. Why and to what sense. Many things still do not add up. But it happened and is true.

Later that year we managed to find a house that we bought with the money my uncle had left, and we moved to Bahnhof Str closing our doors to everyone, even to Lorna's father, lived isolated and cancelled our SED membership. We couldn't trust anyone.

By now, Gretel was very sad and regretful that she had brought her two children over to the GDR. She was so sorry, but I understood why it happened. She was a great idealist, and Dresden was her home. Dresden a beautiful city surrounded by stunning landscape of mountains, the sandstone rocks of Saxon Switzerland and the deep forests creates an everlasting call to return. It was her birthplace and the home of our ancestors. The dream of a better world, of equality and peace, of freedom and happiness was so strong in her that she risked to return in 1960, although it was supposed to have been only for a holiday. That holiday lasted over twenty years. Although she had some recognition in Britain she was not free from prejudice, because the after war years created a hatred and discrimination against Germans whatever their background. She was living in England as an alien and her marriage to Peter was in decline, breaking. How was she to know that a return would be to another society of a different kind of hatred, of suspicion and mistrust? Her belief in a positive socialist society was great and like many others, she and my father were bitterly disappointed and disillusioned. But I know, nothing like what happened over there in that Stalinist dictator regime would ever have happened here in the UK although she was interned on the Isle of Man and my father sent to Australia during the war as possible enemies!

By now, I had no more chance of ever returning to my dream job, playing my violin in a professional orchestra, the Stasi made sure of that and I wanted to leave the SED party. I had full support from my mother. I remember how we stuck our party membership cards together, and as one we resigned. Gretel wrote in her letter of resignation, that because it was impossible to find the political saboteur that came into our flat and ruined her work that was a weapon in the fight for peace, and the official authorities were obviously unable to find the persons responsible, and that she also feared that her younger daughter Lindy here in the GDR had come under bad influence she gave her full support and resigned also.

She wrote; "I spent many long years of homelessness and haunted life; I always kept the flag held high and never gave up. But because of the behaviour and lack of understanding from friends and comrades; for example, the behaviour from party secretary Boehme and Raack as well as the impossible performance of certain individuals when we gave up our flat, and above all, the fact that it has now been made impossible for my daughter to work in her profession, I will also resign my SED membership. I have never been given an explanation, how it was possible, and why party secretary Boehme from Schmiedeberg str Dresden 8021 was able to threaten me with a party disciplinary action, while he knew that at the time I was seriously ill in hospital. I could not go to meetings. Also the previous year, I was also prevented to come to meetings because of my stomach problems, illness and operation.

When I was on the committee we went to visit ill comrades informing them what was happening, gave them encouragement and help."

My mother had party recognition from 1931 onwards because of her anti-fascist work. She received her recognition as an artist only one year before she died. It was a privilege to have my parents, and to know them, for what they stood up for.

We continuously changed the locks to our apartment since the events of 1973. The Stasi were trying to regain entrance to our flat. 24th March 1976 we received a letter requesting us to allow workers into our flat to do repair work. What work? There was no repair work to be done. The people above and below were also VDN and were members of Stasi. They wanted our flat for their old mother. At this time we were practically living up on the mountain hut in all weather. Dad was in the old peoples home dying, and Lorna was just three years old. It was an awful hard time and contributed further to mother's ill health.

5. Reasons for Stasi observation.

We lived from 1973 – 84 isolated and withdrawn. Life in the previous GDR was becoming impossible for us. This resulted in my departure from Dresden 1984. I believe that the Stasi killed my mother. She did not die a natural death but died from an injection given to her. I have no real proof for this. The Stasi ruined any possibility of a family life.

Although I had worked for many years in my profession as an orchestral player and music teacher, I was not wanted as a musician.

The Stasi (after 1973) wanted me to leave my mother so that they could get at her without me around. They did this by trying to force me to work in a factory, or as a carer for older people. There should have been room for me in my profession in the GDR society. I did get some part-time work with the orchestra in Pirna and at the operetta theatre in Dresden.

I managed to get permission to teach privately. I had permission to teach piano as well as violin, and got hold of a viola and started to relearn so that I could also play this instrument.

Certain rules were placed by the mfs.
1) Generally anyone observed from the Stasi, for example anyone who had made an application to leave the GDR, or had contact with certain persons were forced to give up their profession. (Berufs verbot, or Berufs einschränkung, in English meaning; prohibition, or part exclusion to work in your profession).
   In my case I was allowed to give private music lessons. Private music lessons were given at a rate of 15 DM per lesson. In my case I was only allowed to ask for 8 DM per lesson.
2) The work I received as an orchestra musician after the birth of my daughter was only provisionally and part time work, not full time and not permanent.

The reason. The bosses of the orchestra ensembles where I worked part time after I left Freiberg theatre were responsible to give information etc to the mfs and to follow Stasi orders. This made a permanent post impossible.

Because of this, I never received a proper explanation why I never got a full time post again. The bosses of the orchestras were not in a position to report the real motive to me. My qualifications were ok, perfect, but in fact they were glad to lose a person that was constantly observed by the mfs.

In this connection a certain Prof Böhme from the TU (technical university) from department Marxism, Leninism played a certain vicious bad roll.

This man certainly was a member of the Stasi, a top person. Because of his profession and post he had a position in the mfs. He was behind everything because of his position.
3) My mother was ill for many years, especially after the theft and destruction. I looked after her and also wanted to keep her safe from mfs hands.

When we still lived at the old place before we bought our house on the Bahnhof

Street, the mfs sent this nerve doctor into our flat. This Mr. Gelinek wanted to send my mother away to an asylum.

We left the SED. We did not get any proper help to solve the theft and destruction of mother's artworks. We were regarded as dangerous enemies of the state. My mother continued to request an explanation and to ask to shed light on what happened, to find the thieves and the reason for destruction of her artworks. The letter from my sister Lindy later confirms this. Because of this I had problems with my job.

There was work for everyone, no unemployment, but not necessary the work you wanted. If you were under Stasi surveillance for a certain reason, this could cost you your post, as I experienced myself. The colleagues were either extremely unwilling and reluctant to accept such a person in their midst, then the Stasi were always making enquiries about you, or you were not the right person politically for a certain post, or the Stasi wanted you somewhere, so as to keep you under observation.

I have found out following facts;

Goose-stepping at demonstrations was an old Prussian tradition and people who associated it with Nazis were ignored. In the GDR, Nazis were working on top as Stasi.
Until 1950 Soviets re-opened Buchenwald again and filled it with Social Democrats and other opponents of the Soviet Regime.
Franz Erich Giese was deputy commander at Buchenwald. East Germans hid his identity so that he could run a luxury hotel on their behalf.

History was rewritten to confirm that Nazism was a form of capitalism and that Nazis were only still around in the West.
The purpose to rewrite history was to prove the innocence of all East Germans, and that no Nazis were in the East.

There were still hundreds of thousands of German ex soldiers and their relatives living in GDR. Lots of lies were told; According to GDR law they were not anymore, or never had been Nazi fighters, but had been working all along secretly to help liberation from fascism. Those who fled to West were Nazis.
Those who stayed behind had secretly been communists all the time.
It was a crime for anyone to criticize or question the official authorities.
My dad reporting that there were Nazis in that old peoples home and my mother's artwork criticizing the GDR state was not acceptable and highly dangerous.
From about 1980, anyone trying to study the past in a manner not approved by state was severely punished.

Honnecker's attempt to create a 'socialist state identity meant that debates like in the West were impossible; my mother's remarks confirm this. She even wrote it a letter; 'in the capitalist world abroad you stand in the open opposite the enemy. Here, he is undercover, hidden, and often in a safe position. Because of this many innocent people become the victims'.

My daughter was born October1973 and we were constantly watched by neighbours. The fact that we then started to live isolated saved her from being taken away from me.
I had to be careful so as not to be regarded as a 'politically unreliable parent', otherwise they would have taken my daughter away from me.

The totalitarian system meant parents easily lost control of their children as they were expected to go to nursery from babyhood.

The banning of certain styles; art had to be all in one style.
The squabble about who is to get my dads flat, and the same happened with our flat.

Inner emigration, to keep quiet and not talking in public, only open talk with reliable friends or those wanting to leave-open.

A privileged few lived by other rules. Those on top had long ago abandoned original socialist ideas of equality. They had special treats, special shops, special holidays and received special accommodation.

Open criticism brought swift and severe punishment.
Hidden cameras, informants and microphones where everywhere. I am convince that my parents' and uncle's death were not by natural causes.

The Stasi were working everywhere and controlling anyone applying for jobs; this resulted in the loss of my profession.

Successful Stasi could rise high in the system and the rewards were immense. They had access to all sorts of special things, to West products and to luxurious apartments.
It was a serious offence for GDR citizen to have 'unlawful contact with the West
Everything was observed, letters and contacts. Spies were everywhere in all walks of life.
Agents were kept alert to watch all foreigners and any contact they may have with the West.
You could be locked into the system of spies and working for Stasi by just doing one thing-being blackmailed.
Children could be forced to spy on parents, husband on wife and reverse.
Important medication was withheld if you did not co-operate. Many were forced to co-operate actively with the ministry for state security, and were forced into doing things.
Victims had no right whatsoever, and no right to appeal.

The Stasi controlled your post, and apartments were bugged, like ours.
The Stasi would make sure that people out of the building, then they would move in.
Polaroid's were taken of entire flats so that everything could be put back into place again.
The Stasi would look for foreign currency and suspicious letters.
Many were targeted again and again.

Virtually anybody could be targeted and found guilty.
Incarceration in an asylum was one punishment for some who disagreed with the system. Was this why my dad was forced into that old peoples home?

Production of artworks that seem critical of the workers and peasants state was unacceptable and any intellectual writers wanting to rise to significant importance in the GDR had to created works that were in guide lines with what was ordered by the SED.

Some who returned voluntarily, out of their own free will to the GDR genuinely believed that there was socialism over there, (like my parents). But many became disillusioned with the Stalinist state. Some left again to return to the West, like myself after death of my mother. Others who had campaigned against Stalinist system were sent to prison.

We lived, escaping from Stasi observation up onto our mountain hut.
Some artists and writers were forced out of the country if they refused to break contact with the West, (like myself).

This 'tight rope walking' situation never left us all those years we lived in the GDR. On the other hand, there was no unemployment; there was work for all. I was able to study and received a job as a violinist at a theatre until I was victimised because I stood by my mother's side. Education was free. But a 'big brother' situation was everywhere and this got worse as years went by. I had no choice and had to leave and often wonder what would it have been like if I had stayed. This would have meant giving up my British passport, my passport to my freedom!

The guilt of this Stalinist regime is great.
I lost my parents under 'strange' circumstances; my father was sent to this so-called old people's home and my mother threatened with being taken away as an unstable ill person. My uncle departed also under strange circumstances and my sister is missing to this day.
My parents have suffered greatly and to this day I am convinced that their passing was not of a natural nature.

My parents stood up in defiance against fascism and for their ideals of a better world. They should have been given more credit and honour for their heroism in a time in history when mankind was threatened with war. Instead they were   maltreated, victims of the Stalinist regime.

Woodcarvings; 'Man in concentration camp', and 'Prisoner'.
Both sculptures are now in Berlin; Museum for German History,

6. The Truth about this report.

There is no mystery surrounding this part of my story, although it may still seem to be shrouded in a mysterious cloud.
Today, many stories about Stasi involvement in the lives of ordinary East German citizen have come to light. This alone confirms the truth of my tale. Even the only letter I received years later that was supposedly from my sister confirmed and stated Stasi participation in our lives.

A quote from this letter; "Did it never come into your head that it possible was the Stasi, just sending some young careless fellows to control us."
At this time, the Stasi, so-called doctors, my sister and especially her husband were trying hard to manipulate and control my mother's reputation as an artist. These 'young careless fellows' mentioned in this letter were no other than particularly my sister's husband, some so-

called friends and my sister herself. She had a key to our apartment at the time of the destruction and theft of my mother's artworks. She alone knew where certain things were and what newspaper article belonged to what artwork. It is certain that she was blackmailed to spy for the Stasi and most probably the spying in our flat got out of hand. In order to hide certain tell tale signs they decided to 'have fun'. That would have been her husband. Then he had already made remarks about putting pins and needles inside my piano and told tales of so-called fun to an older couple whilst on holiday, putting something up the exhaust of their car, and watching how the poor couple reacted!

Nothing can excuse the treatment my mother received as a result of this.
Why were the Stasi so against us? Firstly, the Stasi would have been more interested in hiding their entry into our flat to a certain degree, and not making such changes on the artworks, as was the case. Yes, the Stasi were everywhere, spying on everyone and searching through belongings, but what happened in our flat was done purposely, with the intention to harm my mother's reputation. We were away on holiday when the destructive changes were made. Certain comments, and those so-called 'fun letters' we received point to one certain person. We tried to talk to my sister, but she refused. My father tried to tell us something, that he had told her, 'no you must not do that'. What it was, he never got round to tell us. Those last words my sister said to me, 'that if she would keep contact with us, it would harm us!' Why?

My mother was a very optimistic person, believing in a socialist future and in spite of lack of recognition as an artist, until her last year, very positive in her views about the future of the GDR as a country working towards a peaceful and free society. But after 1972 the destructive forces that were working against her devastated her socialist views.

I could have 'made my life easier' if I had agreed to work with those destructive forces and most probably I would have then been able to continue working in my profession and I might still be in Dresden now! But I stood up, spoke out the truth and helped my mother in this time of despair and rejection. I am so glad I could be there to help her and our last years in Dresden, in our wonderful house on the Bahnhof Street with my little daughter were peaceful and happy ones, in spite of the dark cloud that continued to accompany us until my return to England.

I have made many applications to look into the Stasi files that now are available to look at, but from my mother is nothing there, just lots of sentences blacked out. There are files about my return to the UK and something about my dad's past before he had to flee into the emigration, but nothing else. Those files that I am looking for have either been shredded or disposed of, then the Stasi kept files on everyone.

A last question is still open; why was I not allowed to see my mother when she died? Why was I only allowed to lay her to rest two weeks later after she died? Why was I not allowed to see my father when he died? I was told he had just died some minutes earlier when I went to visit him the last time?

My sister never forgave my mother for taking her over to Dresden, she never understood why. Perhaps what happened 1972 was unconsciously a kind of revenge act! I do not condemn my mother for taking me over, I understood and knew why, especially now after my own similar experiences. If my parents had been treated differently in England, not interned as dangerous enemies and later felt happier and at peace living in Maidenhead with the possibility of permission to visit Dresden, they might have stayed in England.

The story of my parents proofs how in dreadful ways events had an effect on certain people. The story of my parents would have been different. They could have helped built up a better world instead of fighting against fascism.

Working class thought they had control of factories and firms. State control was only a thing on paper. Stasi spying and lives made to hell contributed to the feeling of mistrust and envy for many people in the GDR.

Anyone could be an enemy of the state and those who did not co-operate letting Stasi in apartments, spying on others – they themselves were suspicious persons.

I have never received anything from Stasi files about my mother, from the time she lived in Dresden 1960 – 1984 and I am convinced her passing was not a natural death.

So many questions, still unanswered and my sister is still missing today. Why was my mother so victimised, why her artwork so ruined? And why, when told at the hospital that she had died, was I not allowed to see her?

I was not allowed to see my father when he died either. Why was I not informed that dad was dying?

Why was our life in the GDR made so impossible and finally I was forced to leave?

When we arrived in the GDR 1960, although it was as if we had entered a different planet, life was positive, so we thought and we believed we were living in a socialist society. There was no unemployment and I was studying at the music school.

Aquarelle; Darßer Landscape

Exhibition in GDR

Watercolour painting of view from our mountain property and painting of woodland

Woodcarving; 1966/67 'A Summer Day'

CHAPTER 13.

Peaceful Years at Last in Dresden. 1976 - 1981

Christmas in our new house at the Bahnhof Street

The Legend, part 11.

As regards to this legend, it goes unmistakably far back into cruellest history of no exact time, back into the middle ages. And when a Birke von Duba plays the leading part, so is this statement at least not untrue, because these rich well to do and powerful ancestry were well known and recognized for their thieving predatory intentions and dishonest frame of mind. This lineage occupied the largest part of Schandau.

As history reports Schandau itself was occupied by the heirs of the Birken von Duba until 1490. But it would be very difficult to research and find out exactly if the forbearer of our legend was really a Birken von Duba, and so, we accept the story as it is told here.
At that time, of course it was a shame to acknowledge and admit that they were robbers. That was too shameful. They called themselves; 'Schnappbahnen'. Translated this could mean; snap catchers, snap and grab, and their thieving activity; 'Reuterei'. Translated meaning that they did not acknowledge their robbers activity, but considered it something less shameful. So they became robber knights, impoverished knights, raiding and looting, plundering and ransacking strangers passing by, beneath their castle.

So the knights continued their mischief and disorder from the 12th to the 15th century. At the end of the 15th century a German author called the German aristocracy; 'eine große Räuberbande'; translated meaning; a 'vast band of robbers'. The Dubas' had become robber knights, impoverished knights, so the legend.

1. Closed Doors.

Our late return to the GDR 1960, my mother, myself and sister, and my father's late return 1965 made the Stasi suspicious of us. This most probably contributed to the Stasi believing that my parents were sent over as West agents with some sort of commission to fulfil. No one trusted anyone.

Although both parents were also members for the SED, they were not considered as trustworthy persons. Evidently, in order to get rid of them, sabotage and provocation was organized, especially against my mother, ruining her reputation, her artwork and sculptures. My sister still had the key to the flat when she moved out to live with her husband. My mother let her keep the key after she married saying to her that she was always welcome.

The suspense between my mother and my sister was most likely the result that certain 'helpers' were in direct contact with the Stasi and had influenced my sister, putting her under pressure. They completed this deed that hurt my mother so much.
Gretel received no help from leading members of the SED to clear the theft and destruction of her artwork. I also received no help to get back to work in my profession as a professional orchestra musician.

It was 1976 when we moved to our new home. Dad had died shortly before we had moved and we obviously cancelled our membership at the end of that year. We just sent our membership books back, stuck together without the official form that was supposed to be filled in when you resign your SED membership, and we did not go to the compulsory interview about our resignation. Since that time we were regarded as deserters, as dissidents, that meant that we were now enemies of the party!

We lived isolated and couldn't trust anyone. It is thanks to my mother's strong personality that she stayed true and faithful to socialist ideals throughout her life in spite of these disastrous experiences. Although Gretel gave up her SED membership, she never changed her views on life. She was till the last the same antifascist fighter as she always had been.

After my uncle died 1973 we inherited the mountain hut property, this beautiful place outside Dresden where we spent so many happy hours. It was clear that we could not live in peace at our flat and so we found this old house on the Bahnhof Street in Schachwitz. There at last we could live in peace. We managed to move and closed our doors to everyone. It was an old farmhouse, with plenty of room and a very large garden. There was a green house at the back and plenty of rose bushes. At the side was a building that Gretel used as a work shed for her sculpture work. At first two ladies lived downstairs when we moved in, as there were two single apartments, but there was no flush toilet only a primitive 'dry' toilet arrangement that we wanted to get rid of. We had a proper flush toilet upstairs in our apartment. Eventually the two ladies moved out and we then had the whole house for ourselves, now plenty of room for my mother's sculptures, and I had a special room for my private music teaching arrangements. As there was a certain law allowing only a certain amount of space pro person it was to our advantage that downstairs was only primitive facilities available. Because of this we were able to get permission to use downstairs for ourselves.

We were very happy there in spite of past events. How wonderful and peaceful it was in summer sitting in our garden, surrounded by fruit trees, flowering shrubs and rose trees and bushes and slowly my mother recovered her artist recognition again.

'Die Blumen Wiese.'

'Des Sommers goldener Sonnenschein,
Liegt auf den blumigen Wiesen fein.
Die Blumen strecken das Köpfchen
Wiegen sich und flustern.
Käfer stolpern zwischen den Blumen Geschwistern
Schmetterlinge taumeln in sonniger Luft,
Die durchweht von Blüten Duft.
Seelig hängen die Schmetterlinge
An den Blumen leicht beschwingt
Und mein Herz ein Liedel singt,
Bienen summen, Grillen geigen.
Die Blumen tanzen einen bunten reigen.
Wie könnte da mein Herz schweigen.'

Translation

'The flowering meadow'

'The summer's golden sunshine,
Shines on the flowering meadow fine.
The flowers stretch their little heads
Swaying and whispering.
Beetles stumble between the flowers sisters
Butterflies staggering in the sunny air,
Surrounded by flower fragrance.
Delighted the butterflies suspend
On the flowers lightly swinging
And my heart sings a little song,
Bees buzzing, grasshoppers chirping.
The flowers dance a colourful gig.
How could my heart keep still.'

'Woodland' 'pen ink and watercolour.

2. The year 1976.

This was the year we managed to move at last. I believe it was sometime in early summer after my father had died under those strange suspicious circumstances mentioned earlier. For the first year before we resigned our SED membership whilst already living at our new home I worked part-time as an orchestra musician in Dresden operetta theatre, but the theatre did not keep the contract. I also worked at the Pirna state orchestra for a short while. Then one day I received a letter that no more work was available. At this time we were still members of the SED. Conductor and orchestra members were against employing anyone who was a member. Every work place had an SED committee, but in my job it only contributed to lack of work. Most normal members of orchestra were not SED members.

The Stasi and SED members had tried hard to get me to move away from Dresden, to leave my mother alone. With this it would have been easy for them to, 'take her away'. It was made nearly impossible for me to get any kind of work in my profession as a musician in Dresden or surroundings. I was told that there was no work available for me. In contrast, many foreigners were employed from Poland, and Bulgarian. There was supposed to be no unemployment in the GDR. There is no doubt that I was terrorized and put under pressure from the Stasi and if I had complied and accepted Stasi orders 1973 then my tale would be different.

A short time later I was practically unemployed; there was no more work for me, no more work playing in the operetta theatre orchestra, no more work playing in the Pirna orchestra.

I received a letter from the party secretary from Pirna orchestra. His letter was brutal, condemning me and dismissing me. He himself was no musician but as he had a position of authority he was most probably a Stasi member. Every workplace whatsoever had to have some person from the Stasi in charge. This party secretary had condemned me in such a way, with the aim to ruin and destroy completely any further possibility for work in my hard earned profession. This was my loan for standing up to protect my mother, her artwork and her socialist ideals. This was my loan for not resigning to Stasi rules, for not deserting my mother, for not accepting the Stasi's ridiculous discrimination of my mother's artworks and for not 'helping' them in their endeavour to discredit her.

I cannot remember much of this time, but I found a letter, written in my name in answer to this, to the party secretary from the Pirna orchestra.

I was so upset with the loss of my work as a professional orchestra musician. The letter stated that the party should be helping me to represent my interests instead of trying to ruin me and to hit me in this hard way. This letter I had received concerning the loss of my profession was the final straw to resigning our SED membership. I believe my mother wrote this letter for me, informing him that his letter, with his signature under it made him responsible for our resignation. This letter stated that to discriminate their own 'comrade' in such a way, and to condemn a person in a profession from which he himself had no idea or knowledge after I had proven myself in my job for many years and often under difficult circumstances was a negligence of great concern. He had the 'wonderful idea' to present me with 1000 East German Marks compensation for the loss of my job. This alone was a great offence.

I had been given the position and had the contract, but as was custom, a foreign person from another East block country got the job instead. Obviously the orchestra members feared to have an SED member in their midst. This secretary obviously feared for his position, he feared the Stasi. I was brutally pushed out of my hard earned profession and now without a job!

Most of the orchestra members feared the Stasi and feared anyone who might be involved in anyway. They were concerned to keep their orchestra free from any 'suspicious' characters. Because of Stasi observation, we were constantly balancing between worlds. Because of the events of the past years I was now a suspicious person with a kind of 'criminal' record! After this, I concentrated completely on private music teaching at home.

Part of us still believed in socialism. Already at this time many people were restless and many were leaving the GDR continuously. If I had had a more reactionary and neo-nazi ideology, or even been a person with no political opinion and above all, nothing had happened1973 – 1974 it would have been a completely different case and I would have been able to continue in my profession.

3. 'Double-tongue speaking.

A typical feature of life in East Germany was 'double-tongue' speaking. When my daughter Lorna was born I started to teach privately. For this, you had to apply for permission, renewable every five years. I was grateful to be allowed to do this so that I had time to take care of my daughter and my mother. I had children coming to me for private music lessons. They were very openhearted. There was this little blond child who came for violin lessons. One day he came to his lesson complaining that he had to learn Russian in school. He stood up straight, thrust his shoulders back and said: "Hah! German nearly became a world language!" This was a typical example of the 'double-tongued' language spoken in the GDR; how you spoke in public, in school and what was spoken at home. Because I taught children privately, they generally did not speak their school 'tongue' to me!

One thing that distressed me greatly was the preparation of students and older schoolchildren for civil defence in case of a nuclear war. There were lessons given to students on how they should behave, and what to do in emergency cases.
One day a piano pupil said to me; "Well, through this lesson, we won't panic. We will know what to do."

In the last years of the existence of the GDR state, the government was especially concerned to point out to children, the bad West, the bad capitalists, the bad world outside. There was a certain amount of military education in schools and preparation for school children for military service. Girls and boys had to do a certain amount of military exercises. But nothing was taught of the results a nuclear war would have. This developed in the 1970's.

Another time two brothers who also came to me for music lessons were so frustrated and agitated that I was unable to give a lesson because an army official had visited the school that morning telling the children all about army life, what you had to do, what would happen if you refused to do what you were told.
These two children opened their hearts to me. We were all very distracted and distraught about what we had just heard, then this army official had told these children many unpleasant things. But this event ended up in laughter because the younger brother asked me if I had, 'shot my husband dead' and my mother who was present came back from the kitchen with a cup of tea for me and had absentmindedly used vegetable water to brew it up with. Of course I made quite a funny face when I tasted it. We all had a good laugh and these two children went home with an easier lighter heart.

Before my daughter started school I tried to see how it would be if I sent her to the 'kindergarten' as was custom. It did not take long for me to decide against it. There were too many practises that I thought queer, especially the daily midday nap. All children had to sleep facing one side only, every child facing the same way. Was this some sort of early military education? I do not know what the reason for this was. We were still too concerned about Stasi observation and so we decided to discontinue her kindergarten visits. She was much happier at home. Once, when I took my daughter for her usual regular visit to the children's doctor, also as required, then they wanted to know how she was getting on, the doctor asked Lorna again and again questions, wanting to find out how her speech was progressing, if she could talk! I will never forget the expression on Lorna's face. She obviously was finding this continues questioning bothersome. Her smile turned to a frown, the frown to a scowl.

The doctor by now had given up that my daughter would say anything;

"Well shake hands at least" she said.

The result was comical. Then suddenly my little daughter's hand shot forwards, at the same time she said very loud; "So"!

"At least that's something," the doctor said!

By 1980 certain basic foods and clothing became difficult to obtain. Although East Germans worked hard and generally earned enough, certain necessary products were becoming more and more difficult to obtain. Most of these necessary products were exported to the West in order to get foreign currency. Inter-shops were becoming a customary thing where one could get certain products.

4. A peaceful home.

Our home at Bahnhof Street.

The peaceful years at our house on the Bahnhof Street were busy years. I now had a private practice, giving private music lessons, teaching violin and piano. It was a successful time although I missed playing in the professional orchestra. Slowly we regained a little trust and confidence in our surrounding world. Any Stasi spying was not as noticeable at this moment. Gretel also gave drawing lessons to a couple of children who also came to me for music lessons. Their mother thought this a good idea as she felt something was missing from their normal school sessions. There was a large amount of gardening to be done and we were able to sell roses from our garden. We made many new friends during this time. It seemed that now we had resigned our SED membership we were free from certain interfering persons.

Once while gardening my little daughter came up to me, and looking me straight in my eyes said;

"So mamma is papa," then off she went to her gran in the work shed to 'help' with her gran's sculpture work.

Today my daughter is also an artist sculpting many fine sculptures. This was the only time she ever mentioned a father. I was both for her. Apparently she had watched the neighbours working in their garden and compared it with me also working in the garden!

Not all was peaceful, and one day we experienced something very sad. We still had our little dog Bella; replacement for Pixy. She was a very happy dog and very friendly, especially caring for my daughter Lorna, following her everywhere she went, at the same time very protective for our property. The garden had a secure fence all the way round it. There was no way our little dog could get out on her own. That memorable day she went out in garden as usual, the lady from downstairs was in her shed chopping wood. We still had this one lady living there. The other one had moved out. We wondered why our Bella was suddenly not to be seen, a short while before we had heard her barking. We went out and looked everywhere. The gate at the entrance was closed. This was strange. Just by chance we looked out on the road and there she was lying there, dead. This was distressing and when we discovered that there was a deep cut across her back, her backbone cut through, we knew what had happened. No way could this have happened by a car, the cut was on her back as if chopped and the gates were all closed, that lady from downstairs still in her shed and looking at us strangely.

Bella must have been barking at her and she chopped our dog and then threw her onto the road so as to look as if she had been run over!

We did not take long to make up our minds what to do next. The next day we went to a dog breeder and bought Lux. He was a pedigree dog and as such, more likely to have more protection if something would happen to him. This time we trained our dog to be particularly critical to anyone else, training him to bark at strangers, particularly to this lady. There was no way we could have involved the police and there was no such thing as animal protection. Lux also turned out great and now we had a watchdog! A short while later this lady moved out.

My daughter Lorna began her school years and at first all was well. It is custom on the first day of school to celebrate this event with special presents and a 'sugar bag'. The school was not far, practically just over the road and round the corner. The school day began very early, usually finished by late lunchtime but loads of homework expected at home. Whilst looking through old papers I noticed how cheap certain necessary services were; for the bin collection service we paid only 19 marks 36 pfennigs for the whole year!

As hardly anyone had a telephone, only certain privileged persons, you went round unannounced visiting friends, had tea with them, socialising in a far more friendlier atmosphere than today. This was especially noticeable in the winter months. There was a certain great Christmas atmosphere that was not influenced by profit making industries, as there was nothing special available in the shops This resulted in more visits and socialising. It was wonderful going round to friends at Christmas time chatting and the children could play peacefully with each other.

Another interesting event is how we got our car. Buying a car in East Germany was not easy and involved long years of waiting if you wanted a new one. A second hand car was usually quite expensive. We had not lived that long in our nice house when one day we received a letter informing us that we could come to collect our new car. At first we thought someone had played a joke on us, then we had not ordered one. That day we went to visit friends and told them about this 'joke';

"Don't you know, uncle Hans ordered a car ten years ago? You have inherited his order. Don't hesitate go get it. You can sell it for double the price if you want."

So that's how we got our car, and I couldn't even drive at that time. That was in the year 1976. This friend went round to fetch it for us, as I could not even drive it. So now we had a car and I started having driving lessons. There was a long drive at the back of our garden and I used to practice driving forward and backward along this back garden path. Wonderful, after I got my driving licence I could take my mother everywhere in the car and we had some fine holidays and outings with it.

' Die Eule'

' Diese Eule war einmal ein stückchen Apfelbaum,
Es saßen Eulen drauf im Mondschein und Blütentraum.
Sie wünschten sich, glücklich zur zweit,
Zu leben in alle Ewigkeit
Ein leben in frieden und freud.
Das wünscht sich wohl ein jeder heut,
Sie hatten wohl auch manch stürmische Nacht,
Doch immer haben sie wohlbedacht
Das sie mit allen Baumvolk eben
Immer müssen in Frieden leben,
Und so ihr Wunsch ward wirklichkeit,
Nun stehst du kleine Eule da für alle Zeit'.

Translation.

'The Owl'

This owl was once a piece of apple wood,
Owls sat on it in moonshine and trees in bloom.
They wished, in luck to be together
To live for ever
A life in peace and happiness.
This wish has everyone today,
They had some stormy nights,
Still always they thought well
That they with all tree folk
Must live for ever in peace,
And so their wish became reality,
Now there you are little owl for all times.

This poem was written after Gretel carved an owl from a piece of apple wood from an apple tree that once grew on our mountain hut property.

An old lady 'friend' who lived round the corner who made friends with us introduced me to a young man who was interested in me. After I went out with him a very short while he told me that he had been in prison for ten years! What exactly he was supposed to have done is still unclear to me to this day. He told me about the hard time he had, prevented from looking at a single flower that was growing in the prison yard. I believe he was sent by Stasi to spy on us in this way. He was not a bad person and I believe he was sent to prison for trying to leave the GDR.

The years in our new home were peaceful and quiet although the Stasi continued to watch and observe all our movements and we still could not trust anyone.

October 1981 arrived and at last Gretel was accepted in the VBK.[1] This was a result of the extremely successful exhibition in the Dresden Gallery Comenius, 19th Sept –1st Nov. 1981, Kulturbund der DDR[2]. The exhibition was such a success that the VBK came uninvited and took my mother at last up into their organisation. They could not refuse her any longer. At last the recognition she deserved and had worked endless for. Dr Diether Schmidt opened the exhibition.

Seascape, aquarelle 1982.

It seems that the Stasi again tried to find a way through me to get to my mother. At the exhibition I met a friend whom I had not seen for many years. The strange thing was that when I originally met this 'friend' he was particularly against the SED or any involvement with that party. In fact he was not political and did not want to know about any politics. Now when this 'friend' suddenly appeared again after so many years, his ' political views' had changed completely. He was a member of the so-called SED, but I was not a member anymore. It is quite clear today, that again the Stasi were involved.

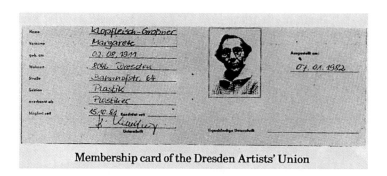

Membership card of the Dresden Artists' Union

---

[1] VBK; 'Verband Bildender Künstler der DDR. (GDR professional Artist organization).
[2] Kulturbund der DDR; Culture league of the GDR.

I am glad my mother lived to experience and see the recognition of her artwork through this wonderful exhibition. Since 1972 she had continually struggled with her health. The shock of the destruction of her artwork and the shock of losing her youngest daughter proved to be a nail on her coffin. If she had not experienced this traumatic event she might have lived longer. Also the doctors had refused to treat her ailments properly. They gave her the wrong diagnosis and repeatedly the wrong treatment. But the last six years of her life were fulfilled with peace, creating more artworks and she had at last financial security and a fine grand home.

Wandering with gran and Bella.

Watercolour; 'Tree forms'

Further exhibitions of my mother's artwork took place in Wittenberg 1983, 'Kunst Gegen Faschism'[3] in VEB[4] Chemische Werke Buna.

There were a variety of small exhibitions in clubs, one of them in the Pujatkin House in Schachwitz Dresden 1980. Also 1981 Kulturbund der DDR Stadtleitung Dresden opened by Dr Diether Schmidt.

1982, from Dr Gerd Gruber's collection; 'International Graphic since 1945.' Haus der Kultur und Bildung [5] Neubrandenburg Germany and 1983, 'Sie haben eine Welt zu gewinnen'[6] Exhibition of graphics, Lutherstadt Wittenberg.

---

[3] 'Kunst Gegen Faschism'; Art against fascism .

[4] VEB Chemische Werke Buna; Folks owned factory in Buna.

[5] Haus der Kultur und Bildung; House of culture and education.

[6] 'Sie haben eine Welt zu gewinnen' They have a world to win.

Woodcarving; 'Der Leidensweg', 'The path of suffering', approx 1976.

The Legend, part 12.

The Bastei and Felsenburg Neurathen are first mentioned in the year 1361. The castle belonged at that time to the bohemian masters of Michelsburg. 1406 Berka von Duba, a member of the bohemian aristocracy came into possession of this castle. After many quarrels and feuds the castle fell into the hands of the family 'von der Oelsnitz'.

The Bohemian aristocracy became robber knights in the 15th century and their fortresses were destroyed in the year 1469.

Whatever the reality of the legend, it seems that there were many feuds and quarrels about who should own these castles.

There are many legends and stories about this part of Saxony and the wonderful Elbe Sandstone Mountains. Once you have been there, you will understand why my mother had such an intense longing and craving to go back home to the far reaching roots of her family, her ancestry.

I also have this longing, although I grew up in Maidenhead Berkshire. I spent many long years in that part of the world, my mother's hometown, her place of birth and my second home. When I think what happened there, the Stasi, my lost sister, the destruction of family life, my heart is filled with sorrow and tears.

At least my mother was able to return to her hometown, her place of birth, Dresden, to see her brother again and experience a kind of future socialist society, how it could be, although this experience ended in disaster. Also she was for the first time in her life financially better of and finally she did receive her artistic recognition even if it was so late, one year before she died. In contrast I was not able to return to the place of my birth Maidenhead and I will never see my sister again. She is lost forever.

Gretel's last exhibition in Dresden 1981.

CHAPTER 14.

The Last Years in Dresden

'Auf den Wachwitz Höhen.'

'Der Nachtwind flüstert in dunklen Zweigen,
Müdes Herz jetzt darfst du ruhen und schweigen.
Da bricht die Stille
Der Eule geheimnissvolles schreien
Und da dort fällt ein Stern vom Himmel,
Und mischt sich mit dem Lichter gewimmel.
Mein Herz, hier darfst du froh sein,
Hier bist du frei,
Hier von den Wachwitz Höhen
Mein Dresden wie bist du schön zu sehen,
Viele Lichter groß und klein funkeln,
Und ringsum steht der Wald so dunkeln,
Einsam hier oben am Abend und in der Nacht,
Die funkelndes Lichter gewimmel da unter bist eine Pracht,
Und weiter weg dort in der ferne,
Da mischen sich Lichter und Sterne.'

Translation.

'Up on the Wachwitz[1] Hights'.

'The night wind whispers in the dark branches,
Tired heart now you may rest and be silent.
The silence breaks
The owl's secret call
And there falls a star from the skies,
And mixes with the other lights.
My heart, here you may be happy,
Here you are free,
Here up on the Wachwitz Hights
My Dresden how beautiful you are to see,
So many lights large and small sparkling,
And around us the woods stand so dark,
Those sparkling lights down there are so magnificent,
And further away in the distance,
Lights and stars mix.'

This poem describes the beauty of the mountain hut property we had, and wonderful scenery, and views surrounding it, up there we always we free and happy.

---

[1] Wachwitz; On the outskirts of Dresden. The mountain
   hut property was situated up there

The Legend, part 13.

There are many versions of the tales and legends. Hohenstein castle and its owners seemed to play an important role. Ernst and his brother Albrecht Duke of Saxony, Landgraf of Thuringia and Markgraf of Meißen give an edict 1467. George Birke sold and brought onto himself all rights, honours and independence etc, from the whole parish, their offspring and descendants of the above named village Rathmans dorf with its owned and assigned judges, for all times.

The people of Schandau were obliged to serve at the castle Hohenstein whenever there was a need for them. Schandau and Rathmans dorf were both under the care and control of Hohenstein.

So it seems the Dubas' were quite prosperous at certain times but obviously greed and envy played an important role and eventually they lost their wealth. But at this time George Birka was obviously a significant noble man with certain priorities and the whole community was committed to providing assistance if he should be in need of it.

Legends, tales and history merge together when searching back into the distant past. The tales of the 'von Duba' robber knights and their misdeeds as well as the tales of the bravery of the hunting master back in the year 1085 seem to be the start of these stories, and are part of the history of Saxony itself. The landscape around Hohnstein, with its sand stone rocky mountains and the ruins of castles are so impressive, they alone are sufficient to create legends of battles, love scenes and imbedded secrets of historic events. No one should have to be forced to leave the place of the roots of their family tree in such a way as my parents, and why was Stasi intrusion in our lives possible?

1. Gretel's Last Year

I did everything to protect my mother, and so we lived for ourselves, with a self-imposed isolation until she died. The Stasi is guilty of the destruction of our family, and our parents suffered greatly. 1989 many East Germans discovered the extent to which they had been controlled and manipulated by this GDR regime. The extent of spying was revealed, and thousands of the population had willingly co-operated to spy on friends, neighbours and colleagues. How could we survive in this situation? The GDR was a totalitarian state, highly centralized and every aspect of cultural life under strict control. This system meant that parents risked losing control of their children. There were informants and hidden cameras everywhere. People were blackmailed and bribed into working for them. Many victims locked into the system. My sister was desperate to be the same as everyone else, and so, she married and disappeared.

My story is not complete with the death of my mother. Her legacy, her artworks, many fine sculptures and pictures need to find a safe home. Fact; if I had left them behind, they would have been lost forever.

But one important fact I must not forget to mention; there were many aspects of socialism, life could have been wonderful if certain Stasi officials and neo-Nazis under cover, calling themselves communists had not been given the power to sabotage and ruin the dream of many anti-fascists and socialists, no unemployment, no homeless people, work for all, free education, freedom and peace as described in Gretel's poems and in her artwork. I often think back on the good things we had in East Germany, and I miss them dearly.

Woodcarving;
Mulatto on cross 1972

That last year summer 1982 Gretel became seriously ill again. It was not really clear what she had; most probable heart problems but it seems that something was wrong with her blood. Someone mentioned that something was not quite right with the blood transfusion she had years earlier. Once whilst walking in town a stranger passing made some odd remarks about her health. This was really weird then we did not know this person. My mother never received the correct treatment she needed for her ill health because we were unable to trust anyone under this Stalinist regime.

Gretel managed to recover and we had one last good holiday together but Gretel was not herself. She kept saying; "I was up there by Him. I am only back for a short time."

She had been a short time in hospital early summer before we had our last holiday and it seems she was far more seriously ill than the doctors wanted to accept.

1981, one year before Gretel died, she had this one last most successful exhibition in Dresden Orbis Pictus 27 Gallery Comenius[2]. She died 1982 on the 13th November one year later. Three weeks before she died we went to visit the British embassy in East Berlin. At this time, many GDR citizens were leaving the country for various reasons. The shops were becoming increasingly empty. It was getting considerably difficult to purchase many necessary things. Gretel's friend from her youth time, the wife of the 'red priest' was no longer living in Dresden. She went regularly over to the West for better medical treatment and overstayed her allowed visit as a pensioner, that last time she stayed and did not come back. It was a very unsettling time, defection to the West becoming daily news, life in the GDR becoming increasingly difficult, lonely and friendless. The Stasi were increasingly becoming overactive and no one trusted anyone. Gone were the times of happiness and positive ideals of a future socialist world. The GDR was dying although it was still only 1982 the signs were inevitable, West propaganda and Stasi interference in personal lives causing only more confusion. My mother and I were still living a withdrawn existence because of what happened 1972. Once we went to visit a friend living outside Dresden only to find the family sitting on packed cases prepared to receive the order to leave any minute.

Can anyone imagine the unrest and lack of confidence in a government that caused this? Because of this situation, my mother's ill health and her latest experience in the hospital she had just left, then the treatment, as before had been everything but satisfactory, the Stasi were still trying to manipulate her reputation, my mother insisted on taking me down to Berlin to visit the British embassy, at least to have my British nationality confirmed for an emergency case. My mother spoke out against what she thought was wrong. She kept saying that she had only come out of hospital to sort this problem out! She insisted, and so during the autumn school holiday we set off. Lorna stayed at a lady's place whose son came to me for music lessons. At this time, my daughter's schoolteachers were already making certain remarks that pointed to Stasi making enquiries about us. Their interference was never ending and lack of work in my profession was making decisions easier. What was there to lose?

The day came when we finally set off to Berlin to visit the British embassy. We did not have a fixed appointment. We just went. We had no problems finding the embassy and at this time it did not seem as if we were being watched. We were most welcomed at the embassy and on hearing that I once had a British passport that the East German authorities had taken away 1960 and that I also possessed a British birth certificate, it did not take long before we could see the British ambassador. We were offered a wonderful tasting cup of English tea and soon we were able to have a talk. He then told us that as we had come over for a holiday 1960 and soon after, 1961 the Berlin wall was put up, this was an important point in regaining my British passport. All my mother wanted was to secure my rights by birth, to keep my British

---

[2] Orbis Pictus 27 Gallery Comenius; Gretel's last exhibition in Dresden organized by the culture association of the GDR and opened by Dr Diether Schmidt.

nationality and if necessary regain it, as originally 1960, she was not happy that the GDR had insisted on keeping our passports. It would have been nearly impossible for us to return to Britain after the Berlin wall was erected 1961.

Originally we came over on a visit that had now lasted twenty-two years. This was an important fact and played an important part in the events that followed. The ambassador promised to help and would let us know as soon as possible of the outcome of his investigations. I hoped this would enable me to visit England, Maidenhead, the place of my birth and old friends and my aunty Dinah again. The intension was to go over for a visit, not for permanent. We stayed that night at a hostel and returned to Dresden the next day.

This event set the ball rolling for my forced departure from the GDR. If I had stayed I would have been in constant observation, no job, certainly not in my profession. I was, because of this visit, (and also because of the theft and destruction of my mother's artworks 1972 – 1973) now also a threat to the GDR in Stasi and GDR authorities eyes.

Three weeks after this visit, my mother fell ill again, and was admitted to hospital. She was only two days in that hospital. Again it took time before the doctors even accepted that she was ill. Perhaps she should have been admitted earlier? I saw my mother the day before she died and although she was very ill, there was no sign that she was dying. I remember that last visit and it seemed as if my mother was worried about something. She asked me to bring in the heart tablets she had at home. I thought this puzzling. Also the doctor wanted to talk to me and kept me waiting a very long time after the visit. I had to wait so long that in the end I went home without being able to see that doctor saying, 'I will come back tomorrow'. Lorna, my daughter was waiting for me at home. The doctor was very vague about the reason why she wanted to see me.

The next morning I woke up early. I had a strange feeling, a sensation that morning as if my mother was calling me. Short while later I received a telegram asking me to phone up the hospital as soon as possible. Not even on the phone would the doctors tell me what they wanted, only that I should come in immediately. I rushed to the hospital and was told to wait a while. I was not allowed to go into the ward to see her. Then this doctor came and told me that my mother had died. The tone was cold and heartless.

I asked what she wanted to tell me yesterday when I came to see my mother;

"Oh that does not matter now," she said.

After this, I was sent away and not even allowed to see her. The hospital refused to allow me to see her. It was the same heartless behaviour I had experienced when my dad had died just five minutes before I came. I also was not allowed to see him.

I noticed that other visitors who had relatives in that hospital were allowed to see their loved ones. But I was not allowed to see my mother. A couple of days before, someone, a visitor was allowed to see a friend, or relative who had just died. The talk between doctor and relative was completely different, friendlier.

Many questions are left open concerning the circumstances surrounding the death of my mother:

-Why could I not see my mother the day she died?

-Why was I only allowed to lay her to rest 14 days later?

-Was she really dead when I was told? Other people were allowed to see their loved ones. I was not!

-Also the authorities were too eager to settle her assets far to quickly.

I believe to this day that she did not die a natural death.

-When I at last saw her I could not see the scar she had on her face by her jaw because of the accident she had as a youth. Maybe I was too distraught, but things did not seem real.

-Why did she ask for her heart tablets that she had at home? My mother was ill yes, but it did not look as if she was at deaths door!

-She died at the same hospital where she had been years earlier and I had to take her home because they wanted to treat her for something else.

-Why that heartless cold behaviour informing me she had died?

I will never find an answer to my questions.

That day I was in a state of confusion and bewilderment. I went home, fetched Lorna and went round to my friend's mother, Mrs Glatho. She was a very passionate and friendly lady. She knew what the Stasi had been up to. She was the same lady who came round our flat that day back in 1972 short while after the Stasi had sent that psychiatric round and had phoned up to find out what they were up to. We stayed that first night with her after my mother's death. She was very comforting and helped me the next two weeks sorting things out and helped prepare my mother's funeral.

One last question I had to sort out? My sister? What should I do? Since 1972 we had no contact with her whatsoever, only 1976 when my father died and then, what about those strange words my sister said to me! " If I contact you, if I come to see you, mum and your daughter, I would put you all in danger"!! Also I did not know where she lived anymore.

There was so much to sort out. I certainly did not want any Stasi contacts. My mother had disowned her and now it was only myself, and Lorna left behind. In the end, I let the authorities sort it out. I wanted my mother's funeral to be rather a celebration of her life and her work. How thankful I was that Dr. Dieter Schmidt was there.

Christmas 1982 I received at last a letter from my Aunty Dinah. I had informed her of the death of my mother. I found out that for two years no letters got through to her. All post to her must have been confiscated, also letters she sent to us and a parcel she sent to Lorna never arrived. How many other letters have been mislaid?

2. The Year 1983

After my mother died many people came round telling me to sell my property and that I would not be able to keep it, even the previous owner of our house came round. Finally I was so fed up with these curious neighbours and other people knocking at our door telling me that I should move out because in their opinion I would not be able to keep the property that in the end I put a notice board out informing that I am staying, not selling. This was most distressing for me.

During recent years I managed to receive copies of Stasi files. The Stasi reported that I was born as a child from German anti-fascists who had immigrated to Britain as ordered by the party. This statement is incorrect. My parents fled to the Czech republic because of the pending warrant for their arrest from the Nazis. Then, as the Nazi fascists invaded the Czech republic, they had to flee again and this time managed to escape to Britain. True, my parents left Dresden because of the warrant for their arrest by the Nazis. What happened then had nothing to do with the party.

The obvious neglect 1960 to get us to apply and write for an application for GDR citizenship was now used to determine my uncertain future. The Stasi files forgot to mention that my sister was also present, and also did not make an application. At that time I was still only 17, my sister 13. My mother, I know for certain, was always concerned that we should keep our British citizenship. She told the GDR authorities this 1960 when they demanded to take our British passports away. The Stasi ignored this fact. My daughter Lorna was born 1973 and the Stasi had a copy of the certificate confirming that Lorna's father had accepted his fatherhood. They then wrote that because I was 'annoyed' with the refusal to let me go on a visit that I then made an application to return to the UK.

The truth is, that once I had made the application for visit I had no option. In fact, once we had visited the British embassy that was it. There was no return. If my mother had lived still after 1982, who knows what would have happened. The Stasi papers reported that then on the 10th July 1984, they began to work on the decision to decide if I would be allowed to take Lorna with. I had to be extremely careful all this time. The Stasi knew exactly when I phoned up the embassy and knew exactly the time and dates when I went there. The Stasi files were catalogued as ' strictly secret'. They reported further of discussions about my person and nationality. They knew all the dates when I visited the embassy. Thankfully, the British embassy was very helpful. I was now under their protection. If it were not for this protection, who knows what my fate would have been and I might have lost my child!

The British consulate contacted a member of the British foreign administration in London to help clarify my situation and obviously helped me with the problem to take Lorna with.
It was an extremely critical and dangerous situation throughout those two years. When I managed to get some copies of existing Stasi files, I found out that the files gave on the date 1st September 1960 as the date for us to have received permission to stay in the GDR. It is the date they gave us, the date they decided we were to stay. We had no real choice. When we arrived 1960, my mother was stateless and I was a British citizen, as was also my sister. At the start of our 'holiday of no return' we were given East German documents and our British passports were taken away from us. My father, when he came over 1965 had a West German passport.

It is important here to mention, that these Stasi file papers wrote, that according to the laws from 1957, a GDR citizenship can only be given to underage children, when a legal representative applied for a GDR citizenship by the appropriate authorities for home affairs and a citizenship certificate had been handed out to the citizens concerned.
We, my sister and I were both underage when we arrived in the GDR 1960. As my mother did not put our names on the application form for GDR citizenship we were never GDR citizens. This accounts for my sister as well. My mother put only her name, not ours on the form. Because of this we were always British. I suspect my mother did this purposely as she always wanted us to keep the British nationality. Does this mean, that according to this information that my sister is still living illegally in Germany as a British citizen? I will never know if she was aware of this fact, as I have never again seen her since 1976.
I was under constant pressure, no work in my profession, no opportunity whatsoever, also I was told that I would never ever get permission to visit Britain. I was homesick.

After our visit October 1982 to the British embassy, my citizenship was now being investigated. They helped me, stood up for me and sorted things out with the MfAA and one day in Spring five months later after our visit. I received my British passport.

Now that I had received my British passport again I decided to try to apply for permission to visit Britain again. Was this so unusual for someone who had spent their childhood in another country? Was it wrong to wish to see again the places of childhood, especially after the dramatic events of 1972-1973, and now my mother's death?

At this time I was still regarded as a citizen of the GDR. I had no relatives in Britain, and because of this, a visit to Britain was refused. I was informed that 'because of missing application rights' I had no reason and no rights to visit Britain.

Did my mother know something I did not know, or did not tell me? She was so adamant, persistent to go to the British embassy October 1982 to regain my British nationality. Right from the start, the contact with the British embassy gave me certain protection as I found out later when I was ordered to attend an interview at the police station. All along, my application was for a visit only.

Early 1983 I received letters from friends from England. One lady who had purchased two sculptures wrote that she understood my mother's longing to return to Dresden, just as much as my longing now to visit England again. It became clear, that if I had stayed behind in England 1960 as was originally planned because we thought I might continue my music studies in London, I might never have seen my mother again. My friends informed me that there was a high rate of unemployment, that the country not the same as it was when I left.

My old violin teacher wrote to me informing me of the bad state of affairs in England, the high rate of unemployment, 13 ½ million out of work and advised me to be careful and not come over for a holiday, that we should stay in Dresden. One teacher from the last school I attended before we left 1960 wrote that you cannot expect a country to be perfect just because it is a socialist country and everything is not quite what you expect. She wrote that people are better housed, fed, and educated in GDR, and concerning demonstrations, she was surprised I wrote that people joined in only because it's expected. No one understood what was going on and why I had to return. They informed me that Maidenhead had changed a lot.

After my mother died the Stasi concentrated on me alone. When they found out that I had now a British passport I was told I was not allowed to have own property. The constant pressure from Stasi made life difficult; no work, others were given priority. I was practically thrown out of the GDR. My life there was made impossible. I should have been given the status as a banished person. This has never been recognized or acknowledged from Germany to this day.

1983, after the GDR authorities found out about my British nationality, I was told that it was not possible to keep my British nationality if I stayed. My application was turned into an application for permanent leave without my doing anything for this.

3.Concerning my application to visit England again.

It was spring 1983. The obliging and very friendly British Embassy soon sent me my new British passport. Now I could apply for permission for a holiday trip back home to England, I thought! Now, as well as my East German document that every GDR citizen had to have, I also had my British passport again at last. We had been forced to give it up late Summer1960. We, my sister and I, had arrived in the GDR as British subjects with all constitutional rights and civil liberties that all British born had. Now hopefully I would be able to visit England again after an absence of twenty-two years.

All I wanted was to be allowed to go over for a visit. After all, Dresden was now my second home; my daughter was only ten years old and had friends. We now had a lovely home with a large garden that included a large greenhouse. We had that wonderful mountain property outside on the outskirts of Dresden with that stunning breathtaking view over all Dresden way into the far distance. It was with some reason my uncle had always said he did not need a television; he had a better one up there on the apple mountain as we also called the property. At one time there were apple trees up there. When the night descended and the sunset came the dazzling view was all the more mesmerizing and the stars up in the heavens in the sky on clear nights looked so near. When a storm was approaching you could see the dark clouds gathering in the far distance. It was a beautiful fascinating place. And there was also my mother's grave! Did I want to leave all this behind? But I had no job although there was supposed to be no unemployment in the GDR. I had my private pupils, I could have sold up and left Dresden to live in another part of East Germany! Or I could have given up my profession as a musician and gone to work in a factory or to work for Mrs. H as a carer with her team! Since my mother had died she was always talking to me to do this, she did her utmost to persuade me. I was determined and resolute not to do this. We were living in a so-called socialist state and I believed I should have the possibility to work in my profession.

The political and economical situation in East Germany was becoming increasingly difficult to handle. Many people had left, the shops were empty and the mistrust and envy from certain people seemed to grow daily. Although we had now lived only seven years in our house on the Bahnhof Street they were the best ever and most peaceful years we had in East Germany. Regrettably it was to be a very short-lived time my mother had left to enjoy it all. I wrote a letter to the authorities asking for permission to be allowed to visit England again. I wanted to see the places of my childhood once more. I wanted to see Maidenhead again. I wanted to walk along the river Thames as we used to. I wanted to wander along the paths of my childhood and to see the English countryside again. I wanted this so desperately. Now my mother had gone and so many friends had left, I felt alone with my child. There was no contact with her father and there was no contact with my sister. I was homesick. I needed to go back home for at least a short holiday.

My life was about to change, and I was at this stage not sure if I wanted a permanent return to the UK. Was this wish I had really impossible, isn't it normal for someone to have this desire and longing to go back to your place of birth and childhood, for a visit, especially after some traumatic event?

It did not take long for the East German authorities to respond to my letter. It came. The angry tone of the letter they sent me was alarming and disturbing. Was I now regarded as a criminal? I obviously had done something against the law. I had to be careful. I was ordered to attend an interview at the police station because I had applied for permission for a holiday trip back home to England.

I left my little Lorna alone at home. She was a good child and I could trust her, she was still at school when I went and I did not think the visit to the police station would take that long. But that visit turned out to be an interrogation; again I was reminded of that visit in 1973 when I had been ordered by the Stasi officials to go to their office and answer certain questions why I believed my mother's artwork had been ruined, and stolen! This latest situation had all the same signs of a possible similar repeat.

I had my British passport with me as well as my East German personal document that every GDR citizen was ordered to carry with at all times. I had to show it on entering the police station. My British passport was still hidden in my bag. Until that moment I had not shown it to anyone, except I think might have shown it to some friends who were also feeling the pinch of this extremist Stalinist state we were now in.

I am sure, in fact I am positive the East German officials knew about our previous trip to Berlin to the British Embassy that last week in October 1982, three weeks before my mother had died, and I am convinced they knew about any letters, phone calls and visits to Berlin. But they obviously did not know that I now had acquired my British passport again after twenty-two years.

I was shown into a room on the first floor. A youngish man, possibly in his early forties sat there. At first he did not show any signs of aggravation, just a slight annoying ridiculous grin on his face. He began by me informing me about the GDR laws, that it was not allowed for GDR citizens to visit the West. I was not of pensioner age and had no rights to apply for such a trip. Any kind of visits to West Germany or any other part of the Capitalist western world was prohibited. He ordered me to give up any such ideas and again repeated himself informing me that such ideas were forbidden and illegal.

Instead of leaving the room as the official had hoped, I took my newly regained British passport out of my bag and placed it on the table together with my East German personal document and said; "I would like to inform you, to make you aware, I am also a British citizen."

The reaction on showing him the two documents, my newly regained British passport and my East German document was incredible, unbelievable! He looked at me, mouth wide open. He stood up and then sat down again. He did not know how to responded at the sight of my newly gained British passport. He seemed to try to want to say something, opened his mouth again, closed it, and sat down then stood up yet again. He did this several times. If the situation had not been so serious it would have been a scene from a comedy play, it was a laughable situation, but I was not in the mood to find the situation amusing.

He then took my British passport, looked at it, and ordered me out of the room telling me to sit outside on the bench in that long corridor and wait. I waited and waited. I sat there waiting for about two hours. Lorna would be home now from school and I still sat there on that bench, in that long cold corridor waiting. I wanted my passport back. They had no right to keep it.

During those two long hours I sat in the corridor waiting there was a great deal of movement, officials rushing to and fro staring at me fiercely. Each time they passed by, they looked with stern eyes and a severe frown on their faces at me. Some of those officials could not help themselves and kept staring at me when they walked past me. It was an uncanny eerie situation. If looks could kill, I would not be alive today. My worry was for Lorna, now waiting for me at home alone.

Something else happened during those two long hours while I had to wait. The shops at this time were empty, no fresh fruit or vegetables were available at the greengrocers or any shop, only crumpled up old rotting apples, onions and stale looking cabbages. That was all that was available. There was little else you could get, and there were long queues at the shops. There were hardly any imported products in normal shops in order to save hard currency. I wondered what was going on at the other end of the corridor. I saw many officials going into a back room and coming out again loaded with some sort of goods in their arms. They hurried past me and I could not believe what I saw. It was like looking at paradise. Your mouth watered because nothing like this was seen in normal shops. It was bliss. Their arms were loaded with fresh fruit, bananas, oranges and vegetables. Was that a cucumber? That official had a bag of tomatoes! Where did they get that? After the long wait I was ordered into another room up onto the fourth floor of that building.

I was shown into a room on the fourth floor. An older police official sat behind the table with papers on it and looked at me sternly. He was an unsympathetic and scrupulous man. He sat there with my British passport in his hands. My heart was pounding and I was tired and frustrated after having had to wait so long. He looked at me and said that what I had done to get a second nationality, to go to Berlin to the British embassy and obtain another passport especially from a capitalist country was forbidden and against the law. He said I was a citizen of the GDR republic and always had been, that my parents never meant me to belong any other country than East Germany. He kept telling me how wonderful things were in the GDR, and my parents had done a wonderful thing bringing me back. Here was where I belonged and had to stay. He then said how good everything was in the GDR how wonderful life was there and how excellent that so-called socialist society cared for us. Finally he handed my British passport back to me, but hesitant and with tears in his eyes, so it seemed. He said he had to give it back to me but that it was illegal for me to have it. He would have so liked to keep it. He reluctantly gave me back my newly regained British passport. Whilst cautiously handing it over to me he ordered me never to go to the British embassy again, that it was forbidden and I was breaking the law if I did and to make no further contact with them. He forbade me to visit the British Embassy again, and told me that it was against the law to obtain dual nationality. I had committed a serious offence.

I hurried out of that building as fast as I could, shaking and trembling with anger and fear. At the corner of the next road was a telephone box and I did exactly what he said I should not do, I phoned up the British embassy and told them what had happened.

They were expecting my call;

"Come as quick as you possibly can" was the answer.

It was now urgent and vital that I went down to Berlin within the next days.

With that visit to the police station and my phone call to Berlin my future fate was sealed. Nothing could change my destiny anymore. I had now joined the crowd of many East German citizens waiting to leave. We all were waiting for the final order to leave. No one under such circumstances had any choice. The Stasi made the decisions and we had to comply. This order I received to go to the police station concerning my repeat application for permission to visit Britain resulted in the Stasi examining my nationality.

A letter I received from the British embassy in July 1983 confirmed that the GDR authorities still did not recognize my British nationality in spite of the note they wrote to the Mf AA.

On the 15th March 1983 I had received a letter from the British embassy informing me that my British passport was ready for me to collect. On the 9th July 1984 I had to write an application for recognition by GDR authorities as an English citizen.

The Stasi constantly observed me. We did not live a normal life 1973 - 1984 we lived isolated. We were practically thrown out of the GDR and I returned to Britain penniless.

Many decided to co-operate with Stasi rather than criticise. This situation could not go on for much longer and was condemned to fail. From the moment we gave up our SED books without any explanation, from that time we were regarded as dissidents, party enemies of the state.

I originally wanted to visit to England only, not a permanent leave. 1982 I made an application to visit England. 1960 the GDR authorities took away our British passports. Once the GDR authorities recognized my newly gained British passport, my application to visit England was turned into a permanent return without my permission. They just did it.

4. 'I had lived in the GDR illegally!'

My visit to Berlin to the British Embassy was made within the next couple of days. I was prepared, nervous and restless. The British Embassy made me aware of the seriousness of the situation, and warned me how far the Stasi could go. I was now at risk, on the danger list. The Stasi could come any time, take my daughter Lorna away - anything could happen. It was an extremely risky situation. I had now joined the many, the mass of people waiting for their so called 'run notice' to leave the GDR.

The GDR authority did not want to recognize my British nationality and they decided that I had lived in the GDR illegally for 22 years. The British embassy found out that I had always been British a long as I had lived in the GDR. According to investigations I had lived illegally for over twenty years in the GDR with illegal papers. My GDR documents had been invalid. Our British passports 1960 have never been returned. What had happened with them? What did the GDR authorities use them for?

I was ordered apply working backwards to stay in the GDR and to apply for permission to live there after I had already lived there for 24 years! I told the officials informing me of their orders that I was proud of my British nationality as I was born in the emigration and it was part of my parents past. They had to live in the emigration because of what they stood up for. If I gave up my now regained British passport I would be lying, denying the anti-fascist past of my parents.

According to copies of Stasi papers from Berlin November1983, they obviously knew everything I said to British Embassy. The Mf, Stasi were making constant enquiries about me. Now I could only wait and see what was going to happen. I was worried about paying for the luggage to Britain, and concerned to save my mother's artworks.

What would have happened if my application for permission to live in the GDR from 1960 onwards, that I had to make 1984 had refused? Confusing, but that's how the GDR authorities were. As I was now a 'foreigner' in Dresden and I was not allowed to have any property or assets! I was told I had to go. I had to leave! My application was until the last for a visit to England!

I was forced to sell my property. I could not afford to refuse as I was threatened with loss of my child, and I did not want to leave Lorna behind alone in the GDR. The house we had on the Bahnhof Street in Dresden was my home. It belonged to me and I had lived there together with my mother and my little daughter.

I found out that when the East German authorities had taken away our British passports 1960, that they were never returned to the British authorities. It was possible that our British passports might have been used for spies.

My daughter Lorna had to write her own letter with her own reasons why she wanted to leave the GDR with her mother! Lorna had to apply herself as a child to be allowed to come with me. She had to be made stateless first in order to be allowed to leave. Perhaps the reason why the GDR authorities wanted us to stay 1960 was that they were after our British passports from the start?

My sister and I were British citizens when we arrived in the GDR 1960. We were handed out GDR documents and our British passports were taken away from us. We were not allowed to keep them. If the GDR authorities forgot to, or did not want to bother with realizing certain laws that were in existence is not known today, but they were obviously too concerned with keeping us there in the GDR, and so with thought it unnecessary to comply with their own rules. Perhaps they already planed to misuse our British passports! This law stated 'that to comply with the decree about questions concerning the practice of nationalization from 28th November 1957, only those foreigners and stateless persons who had applied for an application and were handed a nationalization certificate would receive the GDR nationality'. Because of this I was then registered as a foreigner, as British.

5. Preparing to leave.

There was a whole group of us, each helping each other out. Because no one knew exactly what would happen, you had to be prepared. There were a whole group of us going for one reason or the other. It was difficult to find out what you had to do. What are you going to leave behind? What can you take with, and how? Each situation was different. Everything taken out of the GDR had to be valued and certified every bit of mail, every little hairpin, even our dog had to have his own certificate to prove that he was not valuable for pedigree breeding purposes. Some of those officials who had to hand out these certificates were very sympathetic and so I saved my mother's artworks and my instruments.

It was good that I brought back with what I could manage. Many of the things and any money I had to leave behind were either confiscated by the East German authorities or taken away from local people. I was able to pack everything myself, and brought back all my mother's sculptures, paintings and other necessary things I wanted.

I was forced to sell my property. There was no other way out. Although I was now 'recognized' as a foreigner from England I was still not allowed to go back to Britain. I had to wait. After living there 24 years I was not allowed to travel. First I had to prove that I did not possess any property or assets anymore. Only then, on the 3rd October1984 was I allowed to go. A visit was not allowed, not permitted and my daughter had to be made stateless first. The situation was incredibly stressful and anxiety was a daily hazard. We were all very vulnerable. All sorts of difficulties, sabotage and obstacles were put in your way; loss of a good job, even the consequences of a prison sentences could affect someone who perhaps did not comply with the orders of the Stasi.

No GDR money could be taken out of the country to capitalist states. So anyone leaving arrived on the other side penniless. All cases, all leavers were regarded as deserters and suffered from the pressures of waiting indefinite time sometimes for years. When the final notice came, a normal GDR citizen was given up to 24 hours to leave. I was extremely lucky. We were given one weeks' notice, because I had a British passport.

Two of my friends were given one day, 24 hours notice to leave. One family with three small children were only given only a few hours notice. After Gretel's school friend, the wife of the 'red priest' had left, her two sons with their families eventually also left. It was a mass exit out of Dresden. So many friends were leaving.

What had happened to my parent's dream of a socialist world? This restless life, not knowing what the next day would bring. How come we were now all treated as bad and corrupt?

That last year, I used to sit outside my lovely house and drink champagne for breakfast. My GDR money would be useless. I would only be allowed to take out per day a very small amount when and if I came back for a holiday. The GDR authorities would confiscate anything left behind, so I used most of it up. I bought clothing and cuddly toys for Lorna that I used for packing up my mother's artworks. - I knew, when I came back here, I would have nothing. I knew I would not be able to take any money with me, from the sale of my house in Dresden. What was I to do with money that I could not take with? East German money was of no use in the western world. It seems, many were relying on this fact and trying to gain for themselves from assets and money I had to leave behind.

As I now had double state recognition, the GDR authorities did not like this and did not want to accept it. I was expected to give up my newly regained British passport. This situation was used by certain people who were after my property, after the mountain hut and after my house on the Bahnhof Street.

Mrs H was once a friend of my mother's. Her husband who had died shortly before my mother was the son of friends who also had to emigrate from Nazi Germany. I thought I could trust this woman, and at first wanted to give her the mountain hut in care only, and not sell it. She did not accept this, but also the authorities forced me. Finally I decided to 'pretend' sell it to her on the grounds that she said she would keep it safe for the future for Lorna. We then agreed to this 'pretend' sale. Concerning my house on the Bahnhof Street, I had no choice. It was a forced sale. In August that year before we left Dresden, she said; 'we have spoken and talked about all measures necessary to safe guard yours and Lorna's mountain property. We have dealt with the GDR authorities and the sale contract to save guard the property.' She always spoke with me alone. There were never any witnesses around when she talked to me. She agreed to keep things safely for Lorna for later. The daughter of Mrs H remarked shortly before I left Dresden, that when we come over for a visit we could stay at the expensive Dresden hotel. This was supposed to be a joke!

I did not trust Mrs H, but I had no choice. My thoughts were first for my daughter and my mother's artworks. There was no room for any other thoughts. My mother had died nearly two years earlier, before I was able to leave and I had no idea what the future would hold for us. The pressure I was under was enormous.

I now have the suspicion that Mrs. H, particularly her daughter were Stasi members. Mrs. H's daughter, Dr S, was working at the university in Dresden. I did not know whom I could trust. Certain People were very keen for their own gain that my application should be changed into a permanent leave. Were they after my house on the Bahnhof Street and the mountain hut property? What was I to expect on my return to England? I had been away too long and many things would be strange to me. I had lived in a different world. It was not possible to just pack away things to take with. For everything a permit was needed.

Many people used this situation, if there was something to get for nothing! I was powerless. I saved as much as I could. I wanted to be careful, then any friends still in Dresden could get in trouble with being in contact with me. My best friends were gone. I had to accept everything that happened. Our departure was more of a flight, an escape; we fled out of Dresden into an unknown future, uncertain. I had to keep quiet and hope and see how certain people misused the situation. No letters or files have been found about my loss of work or anything about my mother.

I had to think of the most important things, my daughter, clothing, instruments, music notes, books, even my own compositions had to be certificated that they were not valuable and that I could take them with.

I had to get a special permit to bring back all my mother's artworks and any antic items. I was lucky. The man who came round was more interested in antic items and antic furniture than in the artworks.

Most probably, because my mother received her recognition as an artist from the East German artist organisation only one year before she died, she was not so well known. That man had no idea about the antifascist organisation; the Oska Kokoschka artist league my mother had belonged to in Prague. This most probably saved her artwork. At this time it was in my favour that the East German authorities had tried to damage her reputation as an artist.

I had to leave two items behind I wanted to bring with; an antic small sewing table in Biedermeyer style[3] and an old hand printed trunk with the date 1813 on it. I did not sell these things and so I gave them to my friend Bini. Her husband gave me 75 Swiss franks for them in very last minute, something he had left over from his trip abroad with the Dresden philharmonic orchestra. As he had a job as a professional viola player in this world famous orchestra he had certain privileges. His job often took him over to the West.

I was anxious not to lose my mother's artworks. It was very important to bring them back myself. I did not trust anyone else with this. I was concerned for there safety. When I got the 'run note' I wanted to be prepared. I took all sculptures with, about 80 pieces, of various sizes, and boxes full of pictures. It was a most exhausting stressful time.

All certificates needed to take out personal assets were of a limited time only. It was an endless running around from office to office and all extremely bureaucratic. Everything had to be written down. Even the luggage we took with us on our departure had to be noted. We took as much as possible with, all we could carry.

If I would have had to wait a few more weeks longer, the certificates I had; valuation certificates I had to have in order to bring out my goods would have had to be reorganized and revaluated. All my certificates would have been invalid as there was a time restriction on them. If I did not get the so-called 'run note' the permission to depart from East Germany by 14th October I would have had to pay again for all those certificates. I would have had to reapply for permission to bring my mother's artworks with.

There was more old antic furniture up on my mountain hut. Most of it too big to bring with, also I would not have been allowed to bring it with, too valuable as antic. Mrs. H was supposed to take care of these items.

My uncle was a cabinetmaker, his apartment and workplace was full of good furniture, and also some of these valuable pieces had been in family possession for some time. I organized the transport of the artworks all by myself, all on my own, my two pianos and our little dog, Lux. I was hoping to take him with. Even he had to have a special certificate for permission to take him with. The breeder had to certificate that Lux was not a valuable breeding dog. His tail was bent; he did not hold it straight enough!

Everything was now ready. I just had to wait for my final notice. My heart was heavy and sad. What did the future hold for us?

If I had known that I never would have got back home to Maidenhead I would have insisted on staying in Dresden, or going over only to the West. Now I still feel uprooted. Where do I belong?

The date in my UK passport, stamped by the embassy is 16th March 1983. The stamp from the GDR police is 2nd October 1984. My daughter's stateless passport was valid until 23rd December 1984, given to her on the 24th September 1984 and signed by Lorna as an underage child herself, the journey out of the GDR allowed only until the 3rd October 1984, permit given for a single journey to the UK.

---

[3] Biedermeyer style; A decorative style, popular in Germany between 1815 and 1848.

Why I came back;

Due to the circumstances I found myself in 1984 there was no other way out. The authorities of the GDR demanded that I as a foreigner, now accepted as an English citizen living illegally in the GDR that I should not possess any property in Dresden. Also my daughter was only 10 years old at the time and there was the threat that eventually I would be forced to leave her behind if I did not do as the authorities demanded.

The missing possibility to continue working in my profession in the GDR, forced to live very isolated and withdrawn, the Stasi haunting us consistently, no work in Dresden and the only possibility to live from the little money I earned through my private pupils, this income from my freelance teaching was insufficient. For our own safety we stayed together because the Stasi were constantly after us, especially after my mother. I could not afford to take work in my profession outside Dresden.

A permanent place of work was made impossible due to the political situation.

I never received the sum for the Bahnhof Street. The piece of paper stating that I had received something was a false document to satisfy the GDR authorities.

As is known I was not allowed to take any East currency out with me out of the country. The sale of my property took place under an extreme anxious situation. I was scared that I would not be allowed to take my daughter with to England, that she would be taken away from me. She was only 10 years old at that time. I left the GDR 1984 and was forced to leave many things behind. I was forced to prove to the GDR authorities that I did not own anything anymore in Dresden.

The events of the years 1972 – 1976; if it would not have been for these events I would have had still work in my profession and our lives in the GDR would have been normal.

Life in the GDR could have been wonderful. If all good social laws had been kept and GDR citizens given more satisfaction, it could have been a happy place. One learned to live without certain things that were not really important. But Stasi intervention and control made life often difficult and stressful.

My daughter Lorna with her gran

Last photo of my mother..

4.

The Legacy

"In the capitalist world abroad you stand in the open opposite the enemy. Here, he is undercover, hidden, and often in a safe position. Because of this many innocent people become the victims". Quote from a letter Gretel wrote to the GDR authorities concerning the destruction of her artworks and victimisation from Stasi, approx 1973.

' Sonnenblumen.'

'Sie funkeln und strahlen im Sonnenschein,
Jeder eine Sonne fur sich allein.
Meine Sonnenblumen.

Die riesigen Köpfe sanken
Schwer geneigt zur braunen Mutter Erde.
Die großen herzförmigen Blätter geben
Schatten vielen kleinen summenden wesen.

Bienen hängen an den braunen Kissen,
Doch die gold gelben Blätter abfallen müssen.

Zu bald ist vorüber die sonnige Pracht,
Zulang der Winter,
Und zulang die Nacht'.

Translation

'Sun Flowers'

They glow and sparkle in sunshine,
Each a sun for it's own self.
My sun flowers.

Their huge heads sank
Heavily stooping down to mother earth.
The large heart formed leaves giving
Shadow to many small humming beings.

Bees hang on the brown cushions,
But the gold yellow leaves must fall.

Too soon has past the sunny splendour,
Too long the winter,
And too long the night'.

CHAPTER 15.

The Return to Britain 1984

The Legend, part 14.

The family of Berka von Duba is an old aristocratic gentry of noble birth in Bohemia and Mähren, a branch of the family lineage from the masters 'von Dauba'.

The Berka originate from an old Bohemian aristocratic family, the ' Horovitzer' that was last heard of in the fourteenth century.' This family was already mentioned in the year 1180. 1235 Peter Berka was the chief principle of the masters of the temple in Bohemia.

The founder of the lineage of Berka von Duba was Hynek (1219 – 1286). Towards end of the thirteenth century he became the principle master of Prague castle.

The Berka occupied and owned Hohnstein in the year 1353 and later bought an extensive property in the North of Bohemia.

The original family lineage branched into the Schwarzberger and Adersbacher family line. After the battle at Weißenberg in 1620 a part of their wealth was confiscated.

Most of the aristocratic lineage however remained faithful to the king. In 1637, a branch of the family was raised to a higher position.

The Bohemian lineage disappeared in 1706, after the death of the king's adviser Franz Anton Hovora, dukes Berka von Duba and Lipa. Nothing more is really heard of the Berka after the 19th century. The name Berka von Duba existed until 19th century in Sweden and Saxony.

My grandmother's maiden name was Tube; there was obviously no male lineage to continue the name. Tube was a variation of the name after many changes over the centuries from Duba, Tuba to Tube.

My eccentric uncle Hans told many tales about this ancestry, and the mountain property was his castle of the 'von Tuba's'. When my uncle Hans died, he left us a marquetry case, this last little bit of family heirloom now gone thanks to Stasi intervention. A parchment scroll was originally in this case that had been past down from family to family over the centuries. This scroll that was originally in the marquetry[1] case, had disappeared, but it must be still around somewhere then someone stole it. When my mother went to sort out the assets my uncle left behind, she took this scroll out of the case, looked at it and then put it back inside. The lid of this case was tightened with screws, so it is not easy to open. When we eventually took the case home, we found a large selection of very old photos from family members from the 19th century and a drama in four acts written by great granddad Theodor Tube. My uncle had also placed a copy of the history and legends he had found in a museum in Saxony, but this scroll that my mother discovered when opening the case when she first went to sort out my uncle's assets after he died were no longer there. Regrettably she did not take it with her the first time. Later, after the authorities had finally sorted out the complicated testament my uncle had made, this scroll was no longer inside.

My uncle had put the coat of arms design on the lid.

The very last male lineage of the Tubas most probably died out during the First World War. But there is no doubt that my grandmother, born a Tube, was a direct descendant of the ancestors 'von Duba'.

---

[1] Marquetry; is an art of making a 2D picture with very thin pieces of wood called veneer as used on and seen on old furniture. We have several works of art from my uncle made in this way.

1.The Last Week in Dresden.

Certain dates of events in your life can never to be forgotten, they include birthday dates, and dates of happy events, but also dates when something tragic happens, but nothing can be worse than a viciously purposely imposed event on a specific date.

The GDR authorities and Stasi made absolutely sure that we, my daughter and I, would never forget the date when we were ordered out of the country.

No one can even imagine how it was or even felt. It was my worse nightmare and I still shudder with despair and horror when I think back even today. In fact I had no time to think during those last days in Dresden, or even the first days back in Britain October 1984.

It is only now after over twenty years later that I am able to fully realise, understand and shed tears of pain and relief about that last week in Dresden.

Fourth of October was my daughter's birthday and I knew it might be her last one in Dresden. I wanted it to be special and had organized a birthday party with all her friends and a ride in a pony cart around the area.

Just a few houses away there lived a very friendly couple. They had a pony and occasionally gave local children a ride in the cart drawn by this handsome pony. He was a fine friendly little pony and we often went round chatting to the friendly owner who allowed us to stroke and feed the pony. It would have been wonderful to have this ride and to listen to the peaceful repetitive rhythmic trotting clatter of the pony's hooves on the pavement. The ride was supposed to go past the house where my uncle used to live, down to the river Elbe, a little way along it and back home. You could see our mountain property in the distance on the other side of the river.

We had been quite happy here, at last, living on the Bahnhof Street. It had been our happiest years in Dresden in spite of Stasi intervention and the neighbours were friendlier here.

Everything possible was already organized for our departure. I could do nothing more, just had to wait now, like many others having to leave for some reason or the other for that so-called 'run notice'. And it came, my 'run notice.'

From start to finish my application went under the title of 'a holiday trip' - but I knew it was not going to be a holiday. I had to go. I had no choice and decisions had to be made quickly and with utmost care. I was not willing to give up my British passport, especially after the events that lead to the death of my parents.

My mother had died in nineteen eighty-two, and I got out two years later.

We were ordered to leave East Germany third of October1984, the first day back in the UK to be the fourth of October, Lorna's birthday, she would then be eleven years old. They had done this purposely.

I found out some years later that it was custom and already a practice for the Stasi secret police to select a birthday date in the family. That was the day they chose to order you out, to hand out their ' run notices' with the demand to leave when someone in that family concerned had a birthday. No one, no family could leave the country on their own account; it had to be a particular date, they, the Stasi decided on. Only then when the so-called 'run notice' was given could final arrangements be made, if there was time!

I was extremely lucky; I was given one week's notice! That was a lot! Usually you were given only twenty-four hours notice! One day's notice given to leave the country was normal.

Many tragic stories can be told of families being torn apart, and tales of desperate people forced to leave for some reason. Whatever the motives, nothing can justify the horrendous stress and despair the Stasi caused with their cruel acts of vengeance because certain families wanted to be reunited with loved ones living in the West, or some one had made some ridiculous silly remark that the Stasi did not like.

Many were so unhappy and dissatisfied with life in the GDR, the lack of the most necessary things to buy in the shops that they forgot they need money to buy these things, and that was something they would not have once they were over in the West. They could look and see these things in the shops but no money in their pockets!

As I already mentioned, I was lucky to get one week, but that was due to help and protection from the British embassy. The Stasi had no alternative than to allow me one week, how lucky I was!

Most of my friends had already left. One friend was given only half a days notices. Their children had already left for school when their 'run notice came ordering them to leave at mid-day. They had to be fetched and rushed of to the railway station to catch the train as ordered by the Stasi. Can you imagine what that meant? Collecting the children from school out of their lessons, informing friends to sort out their belongings etc, organizing the train tickets and journey of into the unknown? They had only six hours notice. Luckily they had good friends to help with their belongings left behind and were able to get their possessions sent to them afterwards.

Their mother had left sometime earlier. She was ill and could only get the right medical help in the West. As only pensioners were allowed to visit the West, she used this possibility to get the right treatment. That last time she overstayed her visit and could not return. Her children wanted to be reunited with her.

This lady and my mother were very good friends. They had known each other a long time since their youth and had many mutual memories of the past.

Another friend's husband did not return from a business trip to the West. He used his business trip over to the West to defect leaving his family behind in Dresden. His wife left a short while later. This was a common practice and many families used such occasions to stay and move over to the West. She was given the usual twenty-four hours notice. Again she had luck with her friends helping her to save their belongings. I did not have that luck and lost what I left behind, thank goodness I took with what I could straight away and organized to send my luggage over myself.

What happened over in the West, how they managed is a story they have to tell. This is my story and my destiny lay in the hands of Stasi officials and the friendly British embassy.

I received my so-called 'Run Note' ordering me out at the end of that memorable week. That one-week alone is a story in itself. The traumatic experiences of that week would make a moving film alone, hard to believe and even harder to accept that something like this happened in the 1980's.

The moment my 'run notice' came, I knew, that was it, no turning back. I had to be brave for my daughter's sake. Everything was packed. My first concern was my daughter's safety and my mother's artworks. My two pianos that I was going to take with had to be packed in wooden boxes, and I needed a wooden container for the transport of our little dog ' Lux'. He was coming with, although I had no idea how I was going to pay for things at the other end!

Payment for transport of luggage was possible only in East German currency within the GDR. Once it left the GDR it had to be paid in West currency.

But I had found out and made sure that the fee payable would also included transport onto the boat. I had enough GDR money to pay for this part. I would have to pay the rest; journey from boat to London and to my new place of residency in England as well as kennel fees for Lux our little dog in English money. How? I had no idea, but I had to trust hope and luck!

The GDR authorities were keen to obtain as much west money as possible. My GDR money had no value beyond the GDR border. I had said from the start of this adventure, that I would not leave my daughter, my mother's artworks or my little dog behind. For the kennel fees for Lux, I would have six months time to sort this out, then he had to go into quarantine, as was the law in the UK!

I cannot remember the name of the friend who helped me that week. I think his name was Christian. I had organized sometime ago that when the time came he would get my car, our trabant.[2] As well as the money he gave me for the car he would help me with making the boxes for transport. I did not have much time. My poor little child was mostly left alone at home, going to school was no longer necessary that last week. I had no one to trust.

Christian worked at the cemetery and my first journey was to his place of work.

On arrival I met his workmates. They knew what was going on and I only needed to say; "Please tell Christian, S. O. S."

Luckily I already had the material needed for the boxes. He came straight away, although it was his son's birthday! I don't know how he managed to get off work. This friend worked the whole night through, hammering away, building those boxes, my pianos were packed, ready for transport and the wooden container for Lux ready that next morning. I was not going to leave anything to chance; my mother's artworks were already packed some weeks earlier, but I still needed those containers for the pianos and a transport cage for Lux our dog. If you ask yourself why would I want to take the pianos with? Remember, once I am in England, I will be penniless and unable to buy myself something like that for a very long time. As a musician I needed my instruments! East German money would be of no use. In fact I still have one of those pianos today.

I had two pianos that time, one in the downstairs apartment that I had used for teaching, and one that my uncle gave me upstairs.

None of the neighbours complained about the noise that night, the hammering, nailing and sawing continued till very late, actually till early morning and usually in Germany there were strict rules about noise at certain times.

It was Christian's son's birthday that day, but he came to help me and I am forever in debt to him for his help.

I worked that week from early morning hours until very late night with hardly any sleep. In between the journeys I had to do I continued to pack. I practically threw things out of the cupboards, looking for any more important bits and pieces. There was no time for tidying. Contact with Mrs H who was supposed to be a friend and to whom I had given my mountain hut property in care, was that week non-existent.

I had many important journeys that week, it was a week I will never forget and it will be forever imprinted in my memory.

I cannot remember exactly in what order I did the necessary things. There was no time to think. I had to act quickly and concentrate on the most essential needs for the journey ahead on which I was about to venture.

There were phone calls to make and I had no own phone. I had to inform my friends over in England that at the end of that week I would be there. I had to make two important journeys to Berlin, one to the British Embassy and one to the airport to send our dog Lux of! I do not know how I managed everything.

The British Embassy in Berlin was great and very supportive. Lorna's permission to enter the UK as a stateless person was granted without any problems, then she was not allowed to leave East Germany as a GDR citizen. One of the first things I did when I arrived back in the UK was to sort out my daughter's British nationality. I did not want her to go through life as a stateless person!

That journey done, now what was next to do? Lux, our little wired haired fox terrier, now I had his wooden box for transport I had to contact the airport to arrange his journey of into the unknown! Poor little fellow, how was I to explain things to him?

---

[2] Trabant; was a type of car available in the GDR

We took him to the airport, presented the certificate that allowed us to take him with us, gave him a last little cuddle, said our farewells, and then we saw how he was transported in his box onto the plane. Luckily he held his tail bent instead of straight, so I was given the permission to take him with. If he had held his tail straighter, I would have had to leave him behind! I had made sure that the kennel people would collect him at the other end, but how was I going to pay for it? When we did see him at last, quite some time latter he was so pleased to see us, but his fir was all matted and had grown too long.

How much time did I have to rest or think that week! None. It was an endless constant running around, but I must not forget that I was very lucky, I had one week and was given the opportunity to sort things out myself. I was very fortunate!
Next problem; the luggage, my mother's artworks!
I had to contact Deutrans, the transport firm to come to collect the boxes. There were eighty boxes, mostly containing my mother's sculptures and pictures. And so I managed to save the rest of the sculptures we had and managed to bring them back. Many had been left behind in Prague and Maidenhead, this time I was not going to leave any artworks behind.

I had all papers and certificates needed. Everything was now certified and permission given to take my luggage with me. I believe the transport men came a couple of days before we had to leave. They were a rough looking lot, those men and were grinning in a sort of arrogant way. One of the men dropped one of the boxes and I feared that something inside might have broken. It was not one of the sculptures, just something else that broke, a lamp from our mountain hut property. Those men were quite careless, but everything arrived safely except the contents of that one box. Of course I had to present my certificates allowing me to take my luggage with!
In between times I continued to pack as much as possible into the cases I was taking with me. The rooms were beginning to show more and more telltale signs of a hurried departure. Clothing, belongings and personal effects that I had to leave behind were thrown out of the cupboards, there was no time for tidiness, only time to pile things up in the corners of the rooms. I also had to take care of my little girl! How I did it, I do not know. There was no one there to help me.

Before I left Mrs. H persuaded me to rent one of the rooms on the ground floor of our house to a young man she knew. At that time I still believed in her help, although I was beginning to be suspicious. I agreed, and this young man seemed to be all right, but on the last day some things I wanted to take with disappeared. True, it was only small unimportant things but still it would have been nice to bring that new camera with I had bought! Mrs. H seemed to want some one she knew always present. I had to make many phone calls to try to organize my arrival in the UK as letters took too long.
I had put a pile of belongings on one side for Mrs. H to send over to us, but she never did. Instead, she sent us old clothing and baby toys that I then threw away. It was not what I had left behind to send over to us. It was useless stuff.

My feelings about this lady, that I should not trust her began to increase as my time to leave came nearer, something did not quite add up, but I had no choice and was forced to do certain things that under normal circumstances I would not have done. Her attitude to me changed gradually as soon as I had sorted out the mountain property with the East German authorities that I was forced to 'pretend sell' to her. Everything was chaos. Especially during that during that last week in Dresden, October 1984, when I so urgently needed a friend, Mrs. H was not there. She was not available that week! Conveniently she said she was on holiday, but that she would send a colleague round to me the last evening before we were to leave to collect keys and all East German money I still had in my possession, because anyone leaving was not allowed to take any currency or valuable assets out of the country.

So, on our last day in Dresden she sent this stranger round to our house to collect these things. I was forced to give this woman I had never seen before, all left over East German money and hope that she would then pass it on to Mrs. H. I was very upset that she sent this stranger round to our house. I gave her what I had left of my East German money; remember, I was not allowed to take East German currency with. I never heard from her afterwards and I never received a receipt, so with Mrs H could never prove I gave it to her. Mrs H said she would put this money I had left behind on an account for me. I never ever saw this account; it is questionable if she ever did this. It was all lies.
Mrs H never informed me what happened to all my left behind assets. I never found out what happened to all my left behind possessions.
 This woman, whom I had trusted because she was a friend of my parents, kept away from certain talks and meetings, she was supposedly not around and not available, like the last day before we left, she was supposedly on a trip to Moscow, but later I was told that she was on a convalescent trip to the Baltic coast, and then I was told that she appeared on the day after we left at our house to sort things out that I had to leave behind.
On the day after our departure she appeared and looked through my belongings that I was not allowed to take with.
In principle the people who said they would help me, like Mrs. H made use of my misfortune to gain for themselves. Did this lady want to avoid any uncomfortable questioning from the authorities, or was she ordered to do things for the Stasi?
Later I was told, that this woman asked for money out front from a lady and her son who wanted to move into a smaller flat and had hope they might get help from her because of her position.

Any previous SED member would admit, that, as in my case, any member who gives up their party membership as a demonstration, as a protest, as we did, then usually any personal connection to this person, now known as an enemy of the party, of the state, that all connections to that person should be discontinued.
Although Mrs. H put her function as a Brigade team leader by the folk's solidarity job in danger, she did not discontinue her connections with me. In contrast she showed her connections to us in all openness and so called support for me, until the mountain property was 'pretend sold' to her. It is now clear that she was only thinking for herself and for the property.
She had shown too much so-called friendliness, suspicious especially as she had a leading position in her job. She helped clear out the rest of my household property, and was obviously put in to sort out other household assets left by other illegal and legal citizens leaving the GDR. Some time later, someone informed me that she was even given an honouree of a journey to Leningrad.

There were several last visits I needed to make; one of them was a visit to my mother's grave. It was painful to remember the hardship and suffering she had to experience and I planted a little miniature rose bush and placed a last bunch of flowers on her grave, not knowing when I would be able to visit her again. I paid a larger sum of money for the upkeep of the grave for many years and I made sure that each year on her birthday flowers would be laid in remembrance. If I had given this money to Mrs. H, she would never have used it for this. In fact, Mrs. H was surprised I did not leave more money for her!

We paid a last visit to our mountain property, looking over Dresden into the distance, the river Elbe flowing beneath us like a glittering silver ribbon in the sun. We went to see Mrs. G, that friendly lady who came to visit us after that so-called nerve doctor accompanied by those two nurses had forced their way into our flat.

I had to go to the railway station, to sort out our journey and to make sure that I could take all those extra cases with as well as our bikes. For travel luggage we had an enormous amount, about twelve extra cases that had to go in the luggage carriage. It had to travel with us on the same train. It might have been more; I cannot remember the exact amount. Those extra cases had to be delivered to the station the day before we left. I cannot remember how I did it all.

I must not forget to mention our beautiful tortoise shell cat we had. We called her Krümel, meaning in English, little crumb. How could I take her with as well? The couple that were going to live in our house promised to take care of her, but no one ever told us how she was. We gave her a last cuddle; a last feed and hoped that she would be all right.

Lorna never forgave me for not taking her beloved rocking horse with when we had to leave Dresden, so when we managed to visit Dresden for the first time again, about two years later, (East Germany was still GDR) we took it with us back home to Britain. Good I did, then by the next time when we went to visit Dresden, the GDR no longer existed and contact to Mrs H as well as to the mother, her daughter and boy friend who was living in our house no longer existed. It would have been lost like all other assets left behind.

We saw Krümel, our beautiful tortoise shell cat once more a few years later when we went to fetch Lorna's rocking horse. She hurried past us, not even looking up at us as we entered the property. Cats are more independent creatures than dogs and we knew now at last that she was all right!

That last evening arrived and I had quite a few visitors, I am still not sure today who were friends, who were so-called friends and who came round out of curiosity!

There was that lady and her daughter who now had our house. There was that young man to whom Mrs H had persuaded me to rent out that room on the ground floor. That stranger came round to whom I was told to give all the rest money I had left over. Gertrud came round, she was a very friendly helpful lady, and she gave me a small bottle of Champaign to drink when I left so that I could drink it on the train after leaving GDR. She and her partner were very helpful some years later and I am forever grateful for their help. I can't remember who else came, but they did not stay long and soon left.

Once they had all left I was alone and exhausted, drained and frightened. What did the future have in store for me? What was going to happen? Why was history repeating itself? My parents had to flee from Nazi Germany 1933, now 1984 I fled with my daughter, from what? I was confused and scared. I was about to leave the home I had for the past twenty-four years, my lovely house, and the mountain property. I cannot describe my despair that last evening in Dresden. We had our last meal in our house that evening, gave Krümel our cat her evening meal, I put my little girl to bed and then I was even more alone. The night was clear and the stars shone brightly high in the sky as if to say farewell. Heavy hearted and sad I went to bed. Somehow it was extremely hard to believe what was happening, the fridge was still full of food then a couple of days earlier I had bought some things and as Gertrud commented asking me why I had bought so much when we were about to leave?

The torment of my feelings that last evening and my anguish was great.

Most probably things would have been easier for me if I had not been alone, especially that last week and then over here in England. It was a hard time.

It is extremely seldom that you remember a dream you had decades later, and also can tell the date when you dreamt it. I was worn out and my fear for the undecided future controlled me. My eyes were filled with tears of despair. That night, 2nd of October 1984 I remember I dreamt of a peaceful place, and I saw a blue room bright and sparkling clean and looking out of the window into a green pleasant garden. It was a peaceful dream. I woke up the next morning with courage in my heart and ready to face the next steps into the unknown. Although my flight was no way near the disastrous events my dear parents had to face, way back 1933, I could feel and understand how they must have felt. Why was history repeating itself?

The last day had now arrived, 3rd of October, our luggage packed, and in each room were piles of belongings, clothing and various other things I had to leave behind, as there was no more room in our cases. Everything that last week was done in a rush, there was no time left for tidying. You could see we were fleeing, from what? The place alone told the tale of what we were experiencing! It looked like someone leaving in a hurry.

In a last effort to find anything worth saving I had searched in as many cupboards and drawers as possible.

We had each two instruments, one strapped to our backs, the other placed on top of our luggage carrier. We each had a trolley to pull the two cases fastened on it and we both had a large rucksack. How my little daughter managed I do not know, she never complained, she was so good and brave, her behaviour, way above her age.

My daughter was ten years old when she left Dresden and she arrived here in Britain on her eleventh birthday. Her first words about the British school children were, 'the children are so childish here'. That was in 1984. She cannot remember saying this today.

My mother had twenty pounds left from the money she took over with 1960 and I was allowed to take that with as well as those seventy-five Swiss francs from my friend's husband, so I smuggled that out in my pocket as well. Another friend, a kind lady who often came round for flowers and roses, then our garden was full of them, suggested I could take some jewellery with me, and perhaps I could then sell it over in England for money. As I was not allowed to take any currency with me out of East Germany I thought this a good idea. All valuable jewellery had to be worn and seen, had to be visible. It was not allowed to pack anything of this sort away in bags and cases.

Never before in my life or since have I ever wore so much jewellery on my person. I had a lovely expensive necklace round my neck, a few rings on my fingers and brooches! Why? Because I could take no money with, and at the other end I would be penniless!

How did we get to the station? I cannot remember. Did we take a taxi? Or did someone take us there? I cannot remember. It must have been a sight, to see how we were packed. I remember vaguely sitting in that train with my daughter looking out of the window a last glaze to Dresden that had been my home the last twenty-four years and I remembered how we had arrived here 1960, at midnight and my uncle Hans was there to meet us on that holiday of no return, a twenty-four year long holiday.

And so I left from East Germany with my ten-year-old daughter, with as much luggage as we could take, thinking that at least something of our unmovable assets was safe for my child, for some time in the distant future. I thought I had a good friend whom I could trust as she had known my mother, and her husband's parents had also been émigrés fleeing from Nazi Germany like my parents.

We came back with 12 cases, 1 sack, 2 bicycles, 3 instruments, school satchel, rucksack, cloth case, 2 travel bags, and 3 other bags. This is the luggage we took with us on the train. The rest had been sent with the luggage transport.

We waved goodbye, and the train took me away from Dresden, away from the birthplace of my dear mother, my grandparents and ancestors who had lived in Saxony for centuries. My uncle Hans had told us many romantic tales and legends of the ancestors 'Birken von Tuba' who had lived since the middle ages in Bohemia in Saxon Switzerland, also known as the

Elbe Sandstone Mountains which covers about 368 km of Saxony and about 300 km of Bohemia in the Czech Republic.

The journey was eventless and we past the border without problems. Somewhere in West Germany we had to change trains. I cannot remember where. My little daughter looked tired but inquisitive. Perhaps it was more of an adventure for her as it had been for me 1960! We were supposed to meet my friend at this station, but the train timetable was not quite correct and I was concerned not to lose my luggage that travelled with us on the same train. I was dreadfully disappointed, I could not find her; she had left Dresden I think six months earlier. She was given the usual twenty-four hours time to leave. We missed each other, and perhaps, who knows it might have been a different story if I had decided to stay in the West, but my luggage was sent over to Britain! I did not want to miss the boat. When we got to the ferry, I think at Ostende we had to stay seated outside, then we had too much luggage to move around and I had no money to buy a drink or food.

I had no choice where to go in Britain, but received help from a friend who lived in Loughborough. She was the daughter of Jewish émigré friends from my parents. I wanted to go back home to Maidenhead.

I cannot remember the time when we arrived in London St Pancras station. It was now the 4th of October, Lorna's birthday. We did not see our friends from Loughborough straight away and I was concerned that my luggage had arrived as well. No problems, all my cases and the bikes were there.

I was so thirsty and was dying for an English cup of tea, but we had a cold drink instead. I am grateful and thankful to this lady who helped us that time, but she did not quite understand why I should have bought so many cases with. She thought I needed only a small case and would come by plane!! Why bring all those boxes?

When I at last returned to the UK with Lorna, the only person who helped to return was this kind lady, the daughter of Jewish friends from my parents.

2. What Next?

So I ended up back home in Britain1984 together with my daughter and all remaining artworks. I had no idea how I was going to pay for the transport of our luggage, over - eighty boxes, no furniture, just my mother's paintings and sculptures, my instruments, clothing and other smaller things needed for daily use. I had my daughter with me and our little dog was safe in the kennels. I was allowed to pay for the transport of my luggage onto the ship, but as the East German Mark had no value here in Britain I would have to pay the rest in British pounds.

My first impressions coming back to Britain were strange feelings. Suddenly overnight I was transferred back into a capitalist society, of computers, homeless people, profit makers, casinos, and prostitution. It was a different world to what I had left 1960. I felt that the capitalist world had reached a different level.

During my first weeks back in Britain, 1984, walking through the town, Loughborough was for me a strange place. My longing to return home to Maidenhead Berkshire where I was born and grew up was unbearable. I knew only the family of the lady who helped me at that time. She was the daughter of Jewish emigrant friends from my parents. I remember looking at the colorful shops and casinos, in fact I felt so insecure and very unhappy and also guilt that I had been forced to leave the GDR. If I had been allowed to come for a visit I might have stayed in Dresden.

Back home in Britain did not feel like home. For one thing I was now in a strange place I had never seen, with no contacts other than the lady who had helped me. I longed to return

home to Maidenhead. The train from London took me in the wrong direction! It was bad enough having to cope with such an enormous change and Britain was not the country I had left 1960. We stayed a few days with this lady and I am grateful for her assistance.
During my first days back, when walking through Loughborough with this lady who had helped me that time, on passing the police station I asked her;
"Haven't I got to go there into that police station and let them know I am here?"
This lady was so surprised at my query, then that that was the sort of thing one was used to do in the GDR.

I received a council flat I think at the end of that week. All the while I was concerned how am I going to pay for the transport of my luggage when it arrived. I was told by a certain group of people that I had only been allowed back to Britain if I go twice to church on Sunday and visit bible study sessions in the week. They said it was compulsory for me to do this! This disturbed me greatly and did nothing to help me settle into my new life back home in England! None of my old acquaintances from Maidenhead were around. I knew no one except that lady who helped me back. This group of people were so fanatic in their religious belief it dominated all else. They meant it friendly and wanted to be helpful.

I seemed to have been transported from one nightmare world to another strange world, and I was so homesick for the place where I grew up.

We moved into this small flat and my new friends bought some old second hand stuff round that was sufficient to keep me going for the moment. I had been used to good furniture, and after my uncle died we had wonderful antic furniture. In Dresden, our problems were of a different kind; here I was transported into a world dictated by money and profit. Which world was worse? It seemed both, although this one was different, it was just as bad. I had left Britain as a seventeen year old, a teenager with dreams and positive wishes for the future.

My luggage arrived, eighty boxes and two pianos! How was I going to pay for it here…? I had luck, all the way luck. The transport people were very sympathetic and supportive.

They said; "Oh, we'll sort all that out from Rostock to Cleveland, you have left money behind? Well, then they must pay the rest of the transport from that money that you have left back in Dresden."

The GDR authorities were left with no choice but to allow the outstanding balance to be paid from the rest of the money I had left behind. I only had to pay for the transport from London to Loughborough. That day, when my luggage arrived I worked till late to get things into safety. The large boxes were placed outside in the yard behind the flats. Luckily, there was a yard where they could be placed then the transport men did not carry everything up into the flat. Moving one of the pianos up those narrow stairs was enough, the other piano had to be taken back to their storehouse. Even then, the transport people were kind and eventually sold my second piano for me. The weather was in our favour; fortunately no rain fell, so at least I was able to carry everything up in the dry. Those large boxes had to be emptied one by one and I carried my mother's sculptures up to safety There was no one to help us. We were on our own. Strangely, there were no inquisitive eyes watching me emptying those boxes and carrying them up those stairs, one sculpture after the other, and folders containing Gretel's paintings were now safe.

Luckily I had just received my social security money. It seemed I was doomed to continue a restless existence. That past week, and also the past year was still in my mind and I longed for peace. This money came just in time to pay for the transport from London to Loughborough. I had just about eight pounds left to use, to live on for the rest of that week and the week had only just begun.

My very religious friend was very concerned that I attend the Baptist church services on Sunday and attend the bible studies during the week. My wish to see Maidenhead was great and at last, one day I decided to travel down to Maidenhead not know where I would stay. We just decided to take a train and go. My extreme fanatic Baptists friends said 'God had spoken to me' when I made this head over heals decision, and they made me stay after the 'compulsory' Sunday morning church service to pray an extra thank you. I was confused, why I should do this.

I had found a cheap place to stay, a B+B for homeless people and met Dorothy, an old school friend. She took me by car to Hareshoots and I saw the house we had lived in from outside one last time. I tried to find a possibility to move back home but Maidenhead, but the authorities said there was no place for me and that I should go back to Loughborough. Dorothy asks if Lindy is some comfort to me, if I have contact with her! I saw Dorothy once more a few years later, but have now lost contact

My cousin Hannelore lived in London, she had moved over to the UK from Düsseldorf years earlier already when we still lived in Maidenhead. She used to come down to visit us, but now that I was 'home' again she never bothered and I never saw her again. My aunty Dinah lived in London and I was longing to see her at last. We had spoken to each other on the phone and arranged to meet up on our way back to Loughborough. My aunty was to meet us at the station. This was my first visit to London since we came back. We got out of the train at Stratford, walked out onto the street and up to the zebra crossing. There she was on the other side waving to us. We hurried over the road to her and she hurried over the road to us. There, on the middle of that crossing we embraced each other in joy at seeing each other again at last. The traffic just had to stop and wait. This memorable meeting on middle of that road will be forever in my memory. That night, we talked till early morning.

It was with great difficulties that I managed to overcome all bureaucracy and red tape to save my mother's artworks, and to get them back here to Britain where I hope they will receive a permanent and loving home.

Many German people were pleased when the Berlin Wall came down. Looking to the West, they thought; "Oh, now you can get anything you like, and you can buy anything you want, you are free to go anywhere in the world where ever you want."

They forgot completely you need money to do these things.

We arrived in Britain 1984 penniless with no home and had to begin completely from new. So much was left behind. The guilt I felt with leaving the GDR, my parents, 'dream world' that they had hoped for now gone. This world, the GDR as it was 1984 could not last forever. I had no choice, and although there was supposed to be no unemployment in the GDR I was practically unemployed. My daughter was only 11 years old; the first day in Britain was her 11th birthday, a forced departure from the Stasi. She coped with the change, so-called socialist GDR, over to capitalist Britain, yet my sister, 13 years old, back in 1960 could not cope with the change; capitalist Britain over to so-called socialist GDR!

3. The first months back in Britain.

Back in England after twenty-four years absence was very strange. It was bizarre coming back to a place I had left as a seventeen and a half year old teenager; -full of plans and dreams for the future. We went to Dresden 1960 to visit my uncle Hans and to see Dresden, my mother's hometown and her place of birth. It turned out to be a twenty-four yearlong holiday. Back in England after such a long absence created an uncanny sense of something unusual. I was on a different 'planet'. I returned from a different world. The world I returned to was full of strangers. I knew no one. I saw teenagers with red coloured hair and black painted lips, queues of unemployed, bright coloured shops with absolutely everything in them, computers, something you never saw in East Germany, immensely rich people, and immensely poor and homeless.

Back in Dresden in my house in the garden, I suppose the snowdrops and crocuses were beginning to poke their heads through the earth into the world. I was longing to look out of the window of our little mountain weekend house to observe that wonderful view over Dresden, reaching over the city, far into the distant mountains. Perhaps the deer have come down from the surrounding woods to feed out the feeding box my uncle had built? Everything was beginning to become green after the long cold winter, and the catkins on the branches of the willow trees waving in the fresh spring winds.

I wondered if the woodpecker was still there by the old oak tree? Why did I leave Dresden? Why was it possible to leave those wonderful things behind? Why have I never felt at home and at peace over there, behind the iron curtain? Would I be able to find peace back here in England, in this world of unemployed, red coloured haired, black painted lipped teenagers and computers? Will they give me, and my child the chance to begin anew, the chance I so desperately needed.

I smelt spring in the air. The snow had disappeared and I could only think of spring in Dresden. My heart hurt, I felt pain when thinking of those past years.

I remember the last things I did, before leaving Dresden, a last visit my mountain hut property outside Dresden where we had been so happy, and had spent so many happy hours. I visited every single place; that oak tree, that lime tree, I looked for the last time down to Dresden, saw the river Elbe winding through the City, saw the mountains in the distance, breathed that wonderful mountain air for the last time! The sun was shining and everything looked so peaceful.

I remember my last visit to the graveyard where my mother was laid to rest nearly two years ago. I stood once more by her grave. It was like a pretty little garden. I had planted rose bushes on it and flowers. ' Farewell mum, I loved you so much'.

I was fleeing, away from the past into something new and I was dreadfully afraid of it. In fact terrified. But I had courage, my child, my little dog and my mother's artworks.
No one can imagine how I felt walking through Loughborough, a strange small town, looking at the shops loaded with goods and the game casinos. Although I had new friends, they did not understand me.

Farewell our lovely house on the
Bahnhof Street in Dresden.

Farewell mountain hut property
on the Wachwitz Heights outside Dresden.

How I felt coming back, no one can image. I knew no one. 1960 I left my childhood behind for a new adventure. That time I was curious, yes even excited about the new world about which I had heard good and bad. Coming back was different. There was nothing there anymore of the world I had left 1960. I felt alone and deserted. I had left behind a beautiful place, a beautiful city with wonderful surroundings, for what?

The despair I felt was incredible. No one understood or even wanted to know what had happened in Dresden. There was no one to talk to.

If anyone thinks I did everything to come back because I wanted to come back, this was not quite the case. I had no choice. The unnatural death of my mother, Stasi involvement and refusal to allow me to work in my profession made me extremely vulnerable. Yes, I was homesick and politically very confused. My coming back was not of my own free will. The Stasi forced it upon my daughter and myself. Our visit to the British embassy three weeks before my mother died set everything in rolling. Until the very last minute, my application was for a visit to England, to Maidenhead only, and I wanted to keep my newly regained British nationality. I was practically thrown out of the GDR because I now had a valid British passport and had been told that I was now living illegally in the GDR!

From Deutrans Rostock, Mrs K who now had my house on the Bahnhof Street received the bill to pay for my luggage. It is not to forget that I never received the full amount for my house. It was practically 'given away'. The GDR authorities had forced me to do certain things. How the bill was finally sorted out I do not know exactly. Mrs. K and Mrs. H were not able to pay the bill from Deutrans for the transport of my luggage to England straight away. The GDR authorities refused to accept East money. They wanted west currency. A short while later I received a court order from Dresden threatened to take me to court because I had not paid in West before hand. How it was sorted out in the end I do not know. But I know that there was still a certain amount of my left behind money available after paying this bill. I had also given Mrs. K a key to one of the huts from the mountain property. But Mrs. H took the key away from her.

I had planned to ask various 'so-called' friends to look after my mountain hut property together as I thought it would be safer and make it easier if several people were up there. But Mrs. H did not agree. There was a right squabble over my assets that I had left behind. Back here in England my 'new friends were trying hard to force us to become fanatic religious with the opinion that all I needed was 'four walls and a bible'!

I had put Mrs H in as administrator for my mountain hut property that I so wanted to keep, but I was forced to say to the authorities that I had sold it to her. Some years later, after the fall of the Berlin wall, my application for compensation for lack and loss of job and forced sale was refused. They wrote that I had no real reason. It was acknowledged I had to sell, was forced but refused to recognize my loss of job possibilities. If I had been put in prison that would have been another matter, but as it was just not getting a job because of the political situation, this was not enough.

My first Christmas back in the UK was bizarre, living in strange surroundings, not knowing anyone; I was a stranger, on my own, was I now back home? Luckily, a very friendly family, vegetarians invited us round for Christmas. They were members of the CND[3]. They were very nice people and I was so grateful to be asked to spend that first Christmas with them. In the GDR, where you could not get sufficient vegetables it was hardly possible to become a

---

[3] CND; Campaign for Nuclear Disarmament.

vegetarian. If I had known I would never get back to Maidenhead, I would have wanted to stay in Dresden, but then, I had no choice, the Stasi forced me out.

I must not forget to report about how our little dog was coping and how he suffered. At last we managed to arrange to visit Lux. He had been already some time in that kennel near Peterborough and we had to make our way by train. It was a long walk from the railway station to the kennels and he was so pleased to see us. His tail would not stop wagging he was so thrilled. I was a little surprised that it seemed that he was not given proper care as his fur was so matted. I wished I had been able to visit him earlier, but I had arrived in the UK penniless not knowing how I was going to pay for anything.

At last the required quarantine time came to an end. I cannot remember how I managed to pay the bill. I remember that I had phoned up the kennel asking if they would agree to my paying the bill a little later, but they refused saying he would have to stay there until I paid. That would have meant paying an even larger bill!

Somehow I scraped the money together and off we went to fetch him. He was in a right state, his fur even more matted and dirty. That kennel was only interested in profit and not really concerned with the requirements of English law to prevent rabies or other illnesses.

By this time we had already moved to another larger council house. The neighbourhood was quite rough and we were not used to this.

We were also subject to racial harassment and had to move again soon afterwards. Over in Dresden my daughter had been called, 'dirty English girl!' now we were called, ' German, Hitler, Nazi!' Luckily we managed to move again for the fourth time fleeing away from that area, but regrettably not far away enough.

As soon as we arrived home I trimmed his fur, gave him a wash and brushed him. It was good to have him back, but he never quite got over this quarantine. It seemed he blamed any stranger for the separation, then he never trusted anyone else. He was a very faithful little chap and we were so glad that we brought him back as well.

'Lux von Hellerberg' our little dog brought over from Dresden

4. Back home, 1984 – 1985

After my mother died, a friend I thought I had helped Mrs H clear out my house. She was working in Mrs H team, but a short time later she was thrown out. We found out that Mrs H did this with others as well. Did she want to get rid of any witnesses to her critical behaviour?

Any receipts I gave her were fake, were false ones to try to prove to the GDR authorities that I had sold my property as required by their laws. I had been forced to do this. Mrs H was supposed to keep our left behind assets for us. She never did. She never put the East German money I had to leave behind into an account as she promised. What if I had left my mother's artwork behind in her care? I would never have seen them again. They would have been lost forever.

When the Berlin wall came down 1989 I had hoped that I would meet up with Mrs H and that we could sort out personally the mountain hut property I had left behind, as I thought in her care. 'The mountain' this weekend home was part of the heritage my mother left behind for us, for my daughter. As long as the Berlin wall was reality, letters from Mrs H arrived on my doorstep confirming, I thought, the security of my daughter's assets.
Something did not add up. Mrs H was never clear in her letters about my left behind belongings. She never sent me things that I would have liked to keep, instead she sent me packages of old clothing and useless things.

It was only after the Berlin wall came down that the reality of the situation became clear. One day I received the message from a friend that Mrs H had sold my beloved 'Mountain' property. I had entrusted it to her in good faith. I wrote to her, "Please do not sell. It belongs to my daughter, wait till I can come to visit Dresden". Then came an angry phone call from Mrs H, requesting me to tell her who was it who told me this. A short time later the letters stopped, contact broke off completely.

The permission for any GDR citizen leaving the country at the time when we left Dresden 1984 for whatever reason was only granted and made dependent on selling any private property they might have. This was practice and although there was no written law about this, as I had lived in the GDR for 24 years I was treated like all GDR citizens.
I found on my return to Britain, although you might have insufficient income here, that the food was richer, better and more interesting. Although the average person living in the GDR generally had far more money available than over here in Britain, the shops over there were empty.
We managed to go back for a short holiday; I think it was about 1986 at Easter. After living again back here in Britain for about two years we were already quite spoilt with the abundance of offer in the shops and it was quite an experience to see queues for cucumbers. It was great to see Dresden again, but sadly we did not like the thought of wanting to live there once more. Today is a different matter and I often wonder what it would be like to return.

A short while some months after my return, I received a letter from the German Embassy informing me that my father 1961 had received a 'Heimatschein'[4] for himself and his family. We never knew about this. At that time when we were already living in the GDR this fact was not in our favour, but when I had to return 1984 this turned out to be helpful as I was concerned to get the British nationality for my daughter.
Now I was 'back home', but it did not feel like it. Loughborough was a strange town. I had no connection with this place. No one can imagine how I felt.

---

[4] Heimatschein; My father obviously applied for this 'Home Note' during his stay with his sisters in
Düsseldorf before coming over to us in Dresden. This Heimatschein was obviously necessary for regaining
the German nationality then my parents were living in England as stateless persons.

5. A Last Message from my Sister Lindy.

I loved my little sister and wish so much to have her back. But this will never happen. What happened to her? Where is she? I wrote to my cousin Hannelore and informed her that I had written already several letters and that I believed it to be important that we talk, that we see each other at long last. I wrote that there were so many things Lindy does not know and that we are now strangers to each other. One point is certain; the previous GDR government should be bought before a court and we both should get compensation for what they did to our family. I wished so much to see her again.

As I knew my cousin had contact with my sister, I wrote and asked her to tell my sister that I invite her over to visit us, and please tell her to come on her own. I wrote that I was just as much afraid as she is. I asked her to inform Lindy that I had found out that we both had been living in East Germany 1960 to 1984 with illegal papers, that our German documents were not valid. Lindy could have easily without any trouble have returned to Britain long ago just through her birth certificate and that I gave the British consulate 1984 a paper for Lindy and asked them if they would have helped her. I had no contact with her and also no real contact with my cousin. I wrote we should be strong enough to overcome our fear.

One day 1992, as I was at work giving violin lessons at a school in Nottinghamshire I suddenly had strange thoughts about my sister and her son. There was no reason why I should have had these thoughts. Whilst giving lessons I had a strange feeling, something was wrong and I thought of my sister. Whilst driving home one evening I had again these thoughts, this time they were so strong I had to pull over by the roadside and calm down.

A few weeks later I decided to contact the Red Cross service through the Salvation Army to ask for advice to search for my sister. I hoped that this would put my mind at rest.

A short while later a letter arrived from Dresden. My heart started to beat wildly when I opened it and saw that my sister's name was under it. But the signature was different, unrecognisable. It was not my sister's handwriting.

The letter was type written and informing me about the tragic death of her son Frank. He had been killed in an accident. He was only 21 years old, had just started his own business; he was 8000 marks in debt. According to the information in this letter, his parents could not afford to pay the debt. According to German law, this was to be passed on to the next of kin. I was now to inherit his assets, which supposedly consisted only of these debts.

The information in the letter stated that the German law would only pay off the debt after the state had sold all of Frank's belongings and that all other relatives had to go to a notary to refuse this inheritance that consisted only of debts. My sister's husband's mother, sister and brother, and all relatives had to do this. Now it was my turn to receive this notice from the German courts that I was to inherit these assets, whatever they were.

The letter was intended to warn me about the message I was about to receive from the courts in Dresden. It stated that I only needed to go to a public notary for a signature confirming my refusal of this inheritance as advised in this letter. This was not so easy to do here in England. I had to go to a lawyer. My daughter then received the same message and I again had to ask for legal assistance from a lawyer. Copies of declaration that we both were not going to accept this so-called debt inheritance, had to be written in German and English and signed by witnesses.

My sister, if it was her who wrote this letter, which I doubt, began by stating that she assumed I would tear it up, and that I should read it first. Why should I tear up this letter? I was longing so much to find out something about her. For months, before I received this letter, I had these strong feelings and strange thoughts came into my head about my sister as the days passed.

I would suddenly think of her, for no reason. During my lessons while teaching, I would suddenly feel a strange sensation of someone, a boy asking for help, Frank?

My request for help through the Salvation Army was negative. They said they had found her, but she did not want any contact with me. About the same time as this happened I received this letter about her son. It was a most confusing time and I had great problems finding out exactly what I should do as I could not contact her. What exactly had happened? What are the laws? Did Frank really have debts? Why should I inherit debts? Why didn't the parents take more care of him? There were so many unanswered questions.

I contacted an MP and made many enquiries through the German embassy in London, but no one could advise me. I found out from a friend, who had been informed from another person that Frank had lived alone, presumably in the old flat. His parents had moved out and left him behind. Frank had been killed, either accidentally or had committed suicide. He had either shot himself in his flat, or his gun went off whilst cleaning it, killing him. Why did he have a gun in his flat? What had he been up to? I was given different information from different sources. Friends from Dresden told me one story, my cousin Hannelore from London told me another tale. What was I to believe? If my sister did not want anything to do with me, why send a letter to warn me?

One tale informing me to believe he had committed suicide because of his debts, the other tale that his gun went off whilst cleaning it and my sister's letter, if it was from her, just mentioned he had died. If I were to inherit his assets would I not have the right to know exactly what had happened instead of leaving it as a mystery?

As much as I still feel for my sister's loss concerning the death of her son, as much as I am so sad at her grief I cannot really understand what happened, as I have never been able to talk to her personally.

My cousin who lived in London gave my sister my address.
I have not seen my cousin again since 1960 when I left Maidenhead for that memorable 'long' holiday. Although I had exchanged letters and phone calls we never saw each other again.

After this letter I never received any more messages from my cousin and we lost contact completely. Some months ago I received a message from a cousin from Düsseldorf that Hannelore had moved to Wales and has now died. I have never been invited to see my cousin and she never made any effort to see me. This cousin from Düsseldorf is the only vague contact I have and we only exchange Christmas and new years greetings. I have never ever seen her.

I went many times to London to visit my adopted aunt, but my cousin was not interested to meet up with me. What was I to think when I received this mysterious message? This was the first and only letter I ever received from Dresden concerning my sister. I was so happy, so pleased to hear from her. According to this letter, I was to be informed that Frank did not have a lot of money and that I was to inherit his debts! The person who wrote this letter also stated that she did not know, quote;

"If your German is still so perfect that you understand Amtsdeutsch", (official German). She had heard from a friend that I was on a 'downhill path' and that Mrs H had cheated me out of "your garden in Niedersedlitz". She thought I had swapped my house for a ring, and she hoped that after all these years I would realize that she;

"Did not do any damage to 'mummy's artist work" and "Did it never come into your head that it possible was the Stasi just sending some young careless fellows to control us – No one

306

could understand why we left England to come to such a wreaked country like East Germany".

These are my sister's exact words in her letter. Does she mean, wretched country?

A locked door was no hindrance to the East German secret service. Then the letter stated that she and her husband Peter had been, quote;

"Controlled a lot of times - we are not so stupid as not to notice that, but as Peter and I have nothing to hide, they left us in peace."

We also had nothing to hide and we certainly were not stupid either.

I believe to this day, that this letter was not from my sister, but written by some other person to inform me of the letter I was to receive from the Dresden authorities concerning the death of her son.

Strange facts about this letter;

1) The signature underneath it does not resemble my sister's handwriting in anyway. Maybe her handwriting has changed over the years, but I did not recognize her signature.

2) To write that I might not understand official German? I had lived there over twenty years and had studied at the music school. This statement was implausible. True, the official language used at such official places may be more complicated, but I was not a beginner with the German language.

3) To call our mountain property a garden was a false description. Anyone who had seen this property would never have called it a garden. It used to be a vineyard; it was a beautiful place with wonderful views over Dresden, reaching into the mountains in the distance.

Then there were these remarks she had from someone else about 'downhill path' and selling my house for a ring!!

4) She confirms that the Stasi were in our flat, but she had a key and only a family member could know about certain things; about certain newspaper cutting, about my very early composition attempts and her handwriting was everywhere. At the time of the disaster 1970-1972 my sister had made no attempt to get in touch with us, to try to correct any possible inaccurate allegations. Instead she stayed away as advised by the Stasi!

5) It seems that she, and particularly her husband, were manipulated and influenced by the Stasi secret police, then she writes, "they left us in peace", of course, because of Stasi involvement. I was told through a third party that my sister's husband was caught up working for the Stasi! Indeed his behaviour had been very suspicious.

"Young careless fellows to control us" as she wrote, would not have gone so far as to take pictures out of their frames, make certain changes, to put them back on the wall and to scribble certain marks on sketches and life drawings. 'Young careless fellows' would have left more 'visible' damage. Why should 'careless fellows' create damage to pictures in such a way and go to so much trouble to put them back in the frames again afterwards? Why mess around in folders with newspaper critics of the artworks and the various articles concerning them? Only family members knew what belonged to what.

There is no doubt that there was Stasi and individual involvement in the destruction of my mother's artworks at that time. To go to so much trouble to destroy my mother's artworks in this way, as was the case, was done by some individuals with vicious and revengeful thoughts in mind. The damage done was not of a careless nature. Of course the Stasi used this situation to spy on us and to mess around with our personal belongings. They tried hard to discredit my mother, to declare her of unstable mind.

I made an appointment to see an official person to ask for help. The night before my appointment I received a phone call from Miss S. H. from Dresden. She was on a visit in London and requested that I come down to London the next morning to talk to me about the property we once had.

307

Although, my sister, if this letter really was from her, reports that she took part in the demonstrations against the Stasi in 1989, and this was supposed to speak for her, could this confirm her innocence? Was she, or the person who wrote it, trying to free herself from any guilty feelings? Complete clarity would come by looking into the Stasi files.

To this day, I have not received anything to confirm this possibility; only my application to regain my British nationality is mentioned in the copies of the Stasi files that I have received, and something about my father's time as a 'red front fighter', but nothing about my mother.

To this day I do not know the actual facts about the death of my sister's son. I wrote several letters to her, obviously on a round about way;

"Dear Lindy,

I sincerely hope you will read this letter. For months now I have been thinking of you. My heart bleeds and I suffer with you for your loss earlier this year.

My anger how our family was pulled apart is great. I long to see you again. We both must overcome our fear of the past.

I cannot describe the shock I had when I read your letter. How glad I was to read your name at the end of it and how sad I was to read the contents."

The letter I then received from the Dresden courts that I was to inherit my sister's son's assets was very confusing. I had no idea or knowledge what is going on. I was told that I was to inherit my sister's son's debts! I had no contact with her now for over twenty years. The Dresden courts wanted to know if I had children, then if I were to refuse these debts they would be past on to next of kin! Of course these letter never mentioned debts, just assets, what were they? What was exactly going on here? I have never been given proof what it was I was supposed to inherit!

Fact; I have had no personal contact with either my sister Lindy or my cousin.

Although the Stasi no longer exist, these people are still alive, are still around.

At the court hearing for return of my mountain hut property I met several previous Stasi members; Mrs. H and her so-called friends to whom she sold the property. In order to sort this problem out I was told that I would have to go to a notary or to the German embassy. I was at loss what to do. No official person could tell me. I was told that it was not easy to refuse debt inheritance.

I was told that my refusal signature would have to be witnessed by a German consulate or witnessed by a notary public or by a commissioner for oaths. The legislation would have to be made by the foreign and commonwealth office in London. The same would apply for my daughter Lorna. The fact that I was not given any exact knowledge what was going on made things even worse, also no contact with my sister. I have now given up ever to see her again.

Most important of all was for me now to build up a new life, take care of my daughter, and my mother's legacy; her artwork.

View from mountain hut

The garden at Bahnhof Street.

6. Hoping to regain my mountain hut property.

After the Berlin Wall came down I tried to regain my mountain hut property and any left behind assets. My friend was going to help me. She wrote in one of her letters that she came to me with her two children so that they could have music lessons, violin and piano lessons. She wrote that my mother was a reserved, sensitive dainty and delicate woman and that we lived together in harmony with each other. We found escape and relaxation on the mountain property. The political and economical situation in the previous GDR, the general bad atmosphere, and personal bitter experience helped to make a decision to visit the English consulate in Berlin. With this an avalanche was set in motion. Her husband, during an official business trip to the West stayed there. I often went to visit her after my visits to Berlin to tell her what was going on, and to exchange advice etc. I had difficult ways and journeys to make. For the authorities, my bad German was a false misleading deception and that it would not be possible for me to visit England. She also confirms that I wanted to keep the mountain hut property and that Mrs. H was an old acquaintance of my mother's and that the sale of the property was made as a fake, that it was a pretend purchase. I thought my mountain hut property was still safe when I went to visit Dresden 1996-1997? East German money was useless. When the wall came down I tried to get my property back, we had believed that the mountain hut property was in safe hands. This turned out to be false.

I had never sold the mountain hut property. No sale contract was made. Mrs. H said I had refused to accept money. This is incorrect. She was only supposed to take care of it. The GDR government was only interested in a signature. If I did not comply, there was the danger that I would not be allowed to take my daughter with me back to England. Because of this, the so-called contract was invalid. I was misused from certain people in a scrupulous way.

Although Mrs. H knew she was not the rightful owner of the property she still sold it on to a Mrs. J The promise that Mrs. H would send me more details and an exact report about the money she had for me within the next days never happened. I never got this, I never heard from her.

Mrs. H had the position as a brigade leader, an important position taking care of older citizens. I trusted her, but my trust turned into mistrust as time progressed especially how she behaved when I returned to England. I never had the intention to sell the property. I was put under pressure to at least pretend to sell. Certain people used my position and situation I was in at the time. They thought I am now in England and would never come back. I was under extreme pressure from the authorities.

The sales contract for the mountain hut property was false, was done just to satisfy the GDR authorities. At first I tried to organize to rent out the huts to a couple a people I knew. I thought this would not only help Mrs. H to keep it for us, but also be a safe guard for a possible return later. But Mrs. H was concerned to keep things for herself. She wanted mountain hut property all for herself. I had sorted out two possible friends and already given them the keys to the huts concerned. Mrs. H was to take care of the main hut with the rest of our assets but she took away the keys from my two friends.

I wanted to keep the mountain hut property so much, but Mrs. H was not prepared to share the property with others, as I originally wanted. She was supposed to keep our assets until a return to Dresden was possible but she kept things for herself and her own use. She persuaded me not to include another friend who would have been willing to help to safe keep the mountain property. Mr. D was a friend from another friend who had previously left Dresden some months earlier and he was taking care of their left behind assets.

I strongly suspect that Mrs. H used my critical situation 1984. I gave her complete trust. Finally when all was sorted out at last to her satisfaction she suggested that a lady, working under her as carer, should be put in as an authorized person to care for things. Mrs. H then stayed away from me the last weeks I spent in the GDR with the excuse that she was away on holiday. I was very disappointed then I had trusted her. As soon as the wall came down the contact with Mrs. H broke of.

I had never given her permission to sell. I never wanted strangers on the property. I found out from a friend that she had sold it. I was supposed to stay in suspense and lack of knowledge. I had given her addresses of friends to help her care for the property but she regarded the property now as her own.

My uncle and grandfather, as well as my parents, my daughter and myself had spent many happy and peaceful times up there, on this land with the wonderful view over the river Elbe and Dresden, reaching far into the Ore Mountains and the Saxonian Swiss mountains in the distance. 'The mountain' as we called this weekend home because of the exceptional beautiful view, had a special place in my heart with many wonderful cherished memories and this was the 'unmovable assets' I intended to keep it for my daughter.

I do not know what happened to the belongings left behind, and the valuable antic furniture. What did Mrs. H do with it?

During my visit to Dresden 1994, Mrs. P who now had my house on the Bahnhof Street said she had given the 7000 DM still owing to me already to Mrs. H, but I never received anything. I do not know what happened to the rest money from our Bahnhof Street property.

Officially I sold our house on the 3rd September 1984, but the entry in the property books took place only much later on the 9th May 1985. Why so late? Mrs. P obviously changed her partner. His entry into the books happened much quicker. It is highly likely that her mother's husband who was a jurist had his hand in this game.

So many people were after our house including a friend who wanted to give me a violin as payment.

Watercolour; Old oak trees.

Farewell mountain hut

CHAPTER 16.

Artistic Recognition for Gretel.

'Unsere Städte.'

'Du, Bruder im Westen, reich uns die Hand,
Wir waren und sind ein und das selbe Land.
Wir sind und werden es immer bleiben,
Auch wenn sie mit List dich von uns treiben.

Für dich auch, ist es das den Frieden wir bauen,
Nur mußt du auf unsere Macht vertrauen.
Für unsere Stadt Schutz, Wohlstand und Ruh,
Für deine Stadt Bruder, das selbe willst du.'

Translation

'Our Cities.'
'You, brother in the West, reach us your hands,
We were and still are the same lands.
We are and will always be,
Even if they with slyness drive you away from us.

For you also, we build up peace,
But you must trust our power.
For our city safety, wealth and peace,
For your city brother, we want the same.'

1. The years from 1993.

I feel I am pining for what we have lost due to the Stalinist involvement.
When I go to visit and stay with Lorna's father, looking back, he, his family, and others like
him, were better off in the GDR then they are today.
Some of my friends over in Dresden do not want to know anything of socialism, but others
think back on the good things, jobs for all, no unemployment and wish the clock of time could
be turn back, the mistakes and Stasi dictatorship removed and make way for a real socialist
peaceful society. The class divide today is wider. The gap between rich and poor is worsening
and many have to move home several times to smaller apartments. Under the GDR Stalinist
government, their so-called socialist society, we were, (except those at the top) more or less
on the same level; equal. Although there was a lack of many necessary things during the
GDR time, many forget the dictatorship we had there.
   The incredible pain I still feel when I remember and think about what happened in the
previous GDR is something no one else can understand. For me, coming back to Britain was
inevitable. There was no choice. People today are still too keen to regard me as German. If I
were, I would have stayed, and because of this attitude, I don't know where I belong.

Does anyone understand how it feels? Here I am regarded as German. In Germany I am regarded as English. What am I?

I speak and write German only as a foreigner, but I had the wonderful opportunity to study in Dresden, my dream to become a professional violinist became reality. My mother and I stood up for the truth and I was not willing to give way to Stasi endeavors to manipulate and discredit my mother and her artwork.

My daughter 1984, came better to terms with the change, moving from Dresden, a society that was dictated by Stasi, over to Loughborough, a small town in a capitalist society, than my sister Lindy 1960, from Maidenhead, a town in a capitalist country, over to Dresden, a town in a supposedly so-called socialist society.

During my first years back, we were often subject to racist bullying from ignorant mindless neighbours, colleagues at work and school. My plea to the police to help combat the racist behaviour from senseless neighbours was useless. They were unable to help.

But on the other hand, eventually on my return here, I was able to pick up a decent job, as a peripatetic instrumental teacher, although not straight away, I completed an MA and even a PhD in music composition in spite of being made redundant three times, due to cutbacks in the education service. This would have not been possible in the GDR. My job as an orchestra musician as mentioned earlier, was sabotaged due to Stasi intervention.

2.Situation today.

Today, the situation over there in the previous GDR has worsened. East Germans now have to come to terms with living in a capitalist society.

When we arrived in the GDR 1960 it was a different world. The train, full of drunken Russian soldiers, and those very hard wooden benches tainted my first impressions of the GDR on arrival at the border. The food was different and most of people were very small-minded, prejudiced, looking at cosmetic things like clothing, if it was different to what everyone else wore. Everyone had to fit in one sort of life style dictated from the government. If you were different they regarded you critically. This can be seen in the creative arts, in music and artworks, each had to be of a similar style. Individuality and criticism was not wanted.

Letters from friends confirmed that by my departure from Dresden I had to undergo an enormous, inhuman and ruthless pressure from the GDR authorities. If they had their way, my daughter would have had to stay behind. They did not want to allow me to take her with. I tried without success to make an application for compensation. It is a fact that certain people, in order to gain for their own good used the enormous strain and forced position on me by my departure from Dresden. Obviously certain people in Dresden, including neighbours and so-called friends have made use of my assets and property left behind, and made money out of it. I never got the compensation that should have been payable to me, loss of job, threat to lose Lorna, my daughter. And concerning the unnatural circumstances surrounding the death of my parents, this has never been solved.

Certain people, for their own gains, were very keen that my application to visit Britain would be turned into a permanent leave. They were after my house on the Bahnhof Street and the mountain hut property. When we left, they helped themselves to our left behind belongings.

My application for compensation for the injustice and wrongs that had happened to us in Dresden was not accepted and was refused. It was decided that no compensation was due to me, that my forced sale of the two properties was not true, not realistic.

Fact; if I had been the daughter of Nazi fascists, a previous Nazi sympathiser, or someone who had fled the GDR in the sixties, or early seventies who had fled East Germany and had their properties confiscated, then I would have been given compensation. But as the circumstances were different, they wrote my reasons for application for compensation were unfounded and groundless.

Fact; Due to the circumstances I found myself in 1984 there was no other way out. The authorities of the GDR demanded that I, now living as a foreigner, as an English citizen living illegally in the GDR that I did not possess any property in Dresden. My parents experienced something similar when they applied for compensation from the West German authorities I think in the 1950's. This was also refused and not accepted.

One day I received a telephone call that Mrs H's daughter was in London. She wanted to talk to me. Mrs H was the lady I thought I could trust with the mountain hut property that I wanted to keep for later for a possible return. I was very surprised to hear from her so suddenly. Luckily I could not go down to London that weekend. A little later a friend informed me that Mrs H had sold our mountain hut property without our consent to a stranger. When I tried to ask Mrs H in a letter that a friend had informed me that she had sold the property I received a very angry phone call from her demanding me to inform her who it was.

Another strange fact; I left the GDR on the 3rd October 1984, one day before Lorna's birthday. But the GDR authorities put 12th December 1984 on the papers as the date when I was supposed to have sold the property. I found out that Mrs H was friends and acquainted with many of those in authority.

3. Stasi papers.

I managed to apply to look into Stasi papers. Not all Stasi files[1] are available. Many files have been destroyed with the fall of the Berlin wall. I received various copies of these documents. One Stasi document dated 23rd June 1983; in this document there are no remarks about files and registration papers concerning permission to live to GDR 1960, also the remarks that the marriage of my parents broke of, divorced in England is wrong. They divorced in Dresden short time after my father arrived.

The Stasi, according to files they kept on me, seemed to express disappointment that they could not find any signs of unlawful activity, that I had tried to leave the GDR illegally. They write; no unlawful activity and unlawful visits to Britain have been attempted and that no unauthorized attempts have been made to leave the GDR.

All extra examinations and searches that I had done something illegal of this kind remained unsuccessful. They mention that my parents were 'supposed' to have been recognized VDN. This was in itself strange, then my parents were recognized as VDN. Nothing is mentioned in the files about my double nationality that I had obtained due to my visit to Berlin to the British embassy. They wrote that I, as well as my parents have always been GDR citizens.

The next copy of a document is dated 28th June 1983. This was the date I was ordered by the police authorities to come to their office for a 'talk' because of my application for a visit to England. They wrote that I was extremely obstinate and stubborn and that I already had the

---

[1]. Stasi files; The East German secret police kept files on everyone living in the GDR

British nationality. They mention that I had presented a British passport to them, that I had received in May that year.

They got something wrong in their documents, writing that I had applied for it after the death of my mother in November 1982. Fact; I went with my mother to the British embassy in November three weeks before she died.

They only found out the fact that I had, or was to get a British passport later on. Enquiries were made why our British passports had been taken from us 1960. They were asked what had happened to these passports.

They wrote, that I made an unsocial, antisocial and mentally weak impression, that I was an idiot!

They wrote, that I lived as a self employed music teacher giving private lessons. They then mention that I was informed that it was against the law to obtain and keep connection with the British embassy and that I counted as a GDR citizen. With this meeting their business is complete, but it is to be expected that I would continue to try to obtain a permit to visit Britain, that I would continue to be active to leave the GDR. This document then states that they took certain safety precautions for further elucidation and clarification to my person in regulation with the department 'k'. They also had copies of letters I wrote to England. The Stasi even mentioned that the copies they made were sufficient for translation. They could send the original letters over to England. The Stasi obviously opened all letters, even if they were sent registered. Nothing was safe from the Stasi. They even knew that Lorna's dad had paid his maintenance money, they knew on what account he paid it in, and when the account was dissolved. They knew everything, every little move I made. How could I feel at home, and safe in such a collapsing ill society?

They mention that my parents had died. Many sentences and even pages of the copies I received have been blacked out, especially sentences that obviously concerned my sister.

They did not like my double nationality, GDR, British. They wrote that I only came over1961 to the GDR on my mother's request, that it was her wish. Facts were wrong and they changed things according to what they wanted.

They also mentioned that I had no connection with my sister since 1972 and they even knew that my sister was not at my mother's funeral.

The British embassy sorted everything out; all I now needed was permission to leave the GDR.

The Stasi must have been very busy, then on each document seems to be a different date, and different time, sometimes very day. They wrote that I was living as a normal citizen in the community and they had obviously made many enquiries about me from neighbours, so much that the locals and Lorna's school must have thought I must be a person with a criminal record.

The result of their enquiries was not as negative as they had obviously hoped. They wrote that I was a friendly decent, quiet and reserved woman, not married and living in an old family house. It seems they were trying very hard to find something bad about me, asking some informant person how the inside of our house looked like, and what kind of clothing we wore, even what sort of things we bought when shopping. They were so keen, at least to write something bad in their report, that I made an untidy impression and that there were often problems with my daughter at her school because she made a supposedly dirty impression. I have never been ordered to my daughter's school because of her looks.
Who ever wrote or reported this must have said things to make an impression on the Stasi, to get in their 'good books'.

About this time, I was also buying new clothing for my daughter, but this person wrote that my daughter often wore second hand old clothing to go to school. This statement was completely wrong. They also wrote that I often went wandering. They knew when I was out.

They could not find out anything about friends and acquaintances. They also wrote that I did not have connections with any negative unstable people. There were no parties or orgies held in my house. My financial situation was considered normal.

They knew that I was a professional orchestra musician, that I gave private music lessons and sold flowers that I grew in our garden.

Not much could be said about my political opinion. My whole character was considered to be very reserved, that I lived for myself and that I had not made any political comments in public openly. Politically, nothing was really known of my opinions and that I lived very isolated for myself. Negative statements and actions were not known, but they knew I had connection with the British embassy.

The dates of these documents are 1983 – 1984. As is to be seen from all these notes the Stasi had been extremely busy making all sorts of enquiries and involving all sorts of people and neighbours to spy on us.

It is to be noted that with all these comments in these Stasi files, nothing is said about my mother, nothing has been found about her, no comments about what happened 1972- 1973, not one word is mentioned about her. I received something concerning my uncle's court case when he came over to England, illegally to visit us, I received something about my father's activities in the resistance, but nothing from either my parents or my uncle during the time we lived in the GDR. When my father died, my sister was so concerned to take that certain package away from his cupboard without showing me what it was, yet all old letters and his diary were left available for me. She was not bothered about these documents.

No wonder life was for us so hard, especially for my daughter. She was only 9 years old at the time and often came home complaining that the other children were teasing her, calling her 'dirty English girl'. She could not even speak one word English! I had to apply to get her into another local school. That was something very unusual for the GDR to apply for your child to be relocated to another school. Also, 1984 many of my friends had already left the GDR. What sort of future did this offer us? And what about the future of my mother's artworks?

4. January 2004 and May 2005.

In January 2004 we tried to recover some of the assets we left behind, especially our mountain hut property. I had arranged to meet up with friends that year, to try to sort something out. It is inevitable that on each visit to Dresden the ghosts of the past beginning to appear and memories begin to gather in my mind of past times.

No visit to Dresden goes by without a visit to my mother's last resting place and my eyes fill with tears when I think of the pain and suffering she went through. Now she is at rest. The Trinitatis cemetery where she lays was covered in snow and unlike the English graveyards each plot is like a small carefully kept garden. Even now in winter the heather showed through the snow and the first shoots of spring flowers could be seen. It is unbelievable what changes have been made since 1989; many ruins were newly rebuilt; the Semper Opera House and the Frauen Kirche[2] are just two of them.

To this day I have no idea where what went of my moveable assets that I left behind. I am so glad that I managed to save my mother's sculptures, and some personal belongings, as well

---

[2] . Frauen Kirche'; Cathedral in Dresden destroyed by the bombing of Dresden, now rebuilt.

as our little dog that we managed to bring with under great difficulty and above all my daughter.

When at last we saw our beloved mountain property again, May 2005, it was very emotional and upsetting. There was nothing there any more of the place I left behind 1984, leaving it hopefully in the care of Mrs H. for my daughter later when the time was ripe for a possible return if we wanted.

The huts were all neglected. The once upon a time wonderful view over Dresden and the mountains in the far distance were no longer visible. Everything was over grown. The mountain property was in an extremely bad state, yet they, Mrs H. and her daughter, Family J. to whom Mrs H. had sold the mountain property to, without my knowledge, and also some other individuals were still squabbling over it and now demanding me to pay for all sorts of things.

The greed of certain people was so obvious, the memories of those last years in Dresden becoming more and more dominant.

When we open the door of the main hut that had been my uncle's pride and joy, our amazed eyes saw only an empty stripped bare hut, nothing there any more. Even the outside had been changed. Where was all that fine antic furniture, those deer antlers that were once above the door and what had happened to the little tower that my uncle had built up on the roof. It was gone.

The deer-feeding box was no longer there. It used to be a special experience to observe the deer feeding regularly from the back window of the mountain hut. In fact my beloved mountain hut property existed no longer, it was now only a broken empty shell.

My dream for a place in Dresden for holidays or perhaps to make a possible return if we wanted was ruined and destroyed. The value of the property had disintegrated and ruined through the vicious and constant threats and squabbles from strangers.
My heart bled when I saw it again. There were huge piles of rubbish piled up everywhere.
There was nothing left of that wonderful place I had left behind. The two visits to Dresden January 2004 and May 2005 to try to regain our property, for at least as a place for holidays, was destroyed forever. If I ever thought of returning to Dresden, the sight of this once upon a time beautiful property, now in ruins, was made impossible.

I can never forgive the Stasi and the previous GDR authority to what they did to my parents, especially my mother, my daughter and myself. I am completely aware that the Stasi most likely put my sister under pressure to spy on us, as was custom because we came over from the UK, but that is no excuse to destroy my mother's work, her reputation and to want to create a situation to try to label her as an unstable person.

The Stasi made Lorna write her own reasons why she would want to come back with me. They asked my daughter, "why do you want to accompany your mother back to the UK?" There is no doubt why I had to leave such a beautiful place, a city like Dresden. There are still too many neo-nazis around.

I had the choice, if you could call it one, 1972 – 1973, either I do what the Stasi wanted and also my sister, to do the same and discredit my mother, accept that the Stasi told me that my mother damaged her own work, or I stand up to the truth, help, protect and support her.

5. Artistic recognition.

The GDR authority refused to acknowledge and accept my mother's artworks. They did not want to give her recognition as an artist. Only one year before she died, was she accepted as a member of the 'Dresden Artists Union' after a very successful exhibition of her artwork at the Gallery Comenius Dresden.

She had to suffer the theft and destruction of her artwork first before she was accepted. I managed to organize a follow up exhibition 1987 at the John Denham, Gallery in London. These two substantial exhibitions of her work have secured her a place in today's art world. Two galleries in Germany possess a couple of her sculptures, Halle Moritzburg and Berlin. It is important to mention this as the Stasi tried so hard without success to discredit her and her artwork.

I grew up surrounded by artworks, sculptures and paintings. As small children my sister and I used to play among the wood chips my mother created when carving her sculptures. My daughter also spent the first nine years of her life watching her grandmother create her artworks.

During the GDR time, artworks created had to be of a positive nature, no criticism was wanted. Anything other was regarded suspiciously. There were hardly differences in styles, and hardly any individuality, no freedom of style. All creative art had to be of a positive nature and show how good working conditions were.

Most of Gretel's artworks made in the Czech Republic were left behind when she had to flee from the approaching Nazi troops. But they should be around somewhere still. Hopefully they may be found one day again.

The Stasi, and those who tried so hard to destroy and damaged my mother's artworks 1972, also messed around with papers, newspaper cuttings and purposely-changed dates in the albums destroying certain documents. But they did not succeed to damage her reputation although at the time the damage done was severe.

Gretel sculpted so many figures of pain and suffering as well as several crucifixions. I think two on the Isle of Man during her internment as well as a couple in Prague. One lovely small sculpture was given as a present to a doctor's wife in Dresden about 1965. We have two at home of a different kind; 'Crucified Prisoner in Concentration Camp' and 'Crucified Mulatto'.

Today I understand why she did this, why she sculpted so many works of pain and suffering. Many people do not understand this. Why did certain people treat each other so badly, the main reason being ignorance and greed?

It is with great delight that I found her biography in the book; 'The dictionary of artists in Britain since1945' from David Buckman lately in London. A new edition has been published 2006. Here, not only British artists, but also foreign artists of importance are mentioned.

Gretel's time spent in Prague was the happiest time in her life, artistic wise, she had recognition, took part in exhibitions, was a member of the Oska Kokoschka league, had study opportunities, and work in the stone yard.

So many questions are unanswered. What happened to my little sister? Where is she today? Fresh copies of Stasi file papers would prove they knew even more than already realized, they knew everything and were everywhere. They even knew my address after I had moved back to Britain. All letters and all calls to Dresden were noted and the mystery about my sister deepens with passing years.

One fact that comes out clearly from copies of latest Stasi file papers sent to me; because we came over from the UK, we were always regarded as spies. It is partly the British authorities fault that Gretel went back 1960 to Dresden and eventually stayed there as the

GDR authorities wanted, and did nothing more to try to return to the UK. If my parents had been treated here in Britain differently, not as aliens, as outsiders, my mother might not have gone over in the first place and perhaps waited until a little later.

A similar problem exists still now even today. My daughter and myself, although we both have now spent most of our lives in England, I was even born here, grew up here, we are still regarded by some people as Germans. This is so wrong. Over there, in Germany we are regarded as English because we have spent most of our lives here.

Most probably there are many others in the same position. Often I do not know where I belong? What are we?

Socialism could work in spite of my experiences. There were many contradictions in the GDR. Both my parents should have had a happier life there, but that was not the case, and both died as a result of neglect, wrong treatment and possible elimination.

My parents were not given the respect and honour due to them. Instead they were treated as unwanted persons.

On my return I felt stuck and cornered. This was a resulted of a psychological wall being built around me because of the GDR experience. It seemed that my struggle to write music again was a psychological Berlin Wall, but with the fall of the Berlin Wall, I started to compose music again, at first slowly, but now I have written many pieces and cannot stop writing. My daughter Lorna has also inherited this urge and love to create art and now she is an artist.

Perhaps I should not have returned, but I had no choice. I now have an MA and PhD in composition and have recognition as a composer. My carrier as a violinist and recognition as a professional orchestra musician was stolen by the Stasi.

On receiving further copies of Stasi papers it becomes more and more clearer how the Stasi intervened in personal affairs, spying on every aspect of private life. No wonder I left for return to Britain. How could I have continued to live in such an ill-fated sick society where everyone spied on everyone? And so I returned to Britain of into the unknown. At least as my dear mother said; "Here in the UK we can speak open."

I want to end my story on a happy and positive note. I hope that my mother's artworks will continue to find recognition, that there will be many more exhibitions of her works.

Three sculptures were sold to a Mrs.Thompkins in Bristol. It is unknown where they are today. Several artworks were sold to private collectors 1987 as a result of the exhibition at the John Denham Gallery in London. There was an exhibition, 'Art in Exile in Great Britain, 1933 – 45', at the Camden Arts Centre 1986.

Dr Gert Gruber, in Germany has a wide range of graphics, watercolours and Linocuts. He organizes regularly exhibitions of anti-fascist artists. He has and will include works from my mother that he has in his collection in the following exhibitions;

2002. Verfemt, verfolgt – nicht vergessen, art and resistance against fascism in Dessau. 2008. Exhibition in Germany, Aufbruch in die Moderne.

2011, Wittenberg; large exhibition for anti-fascist art; 'entartet' verfemten Kunst der Jahre 1933 – 1945.

The latest inclusion of two of her works in an exhibition took place in, Leicester; New Walk Museum, Great Britain; 2009, October – 2010 May, 'Journey Out of Darkness.'

I hope my book will help to contribute to further exhibitions and artistic recognition.

Although our return to the UK 1984 was far from easy and there were many difficulties to overcome, I will mention a few positive events. Two of my compositions were performed by the Vienna Modern Masters series in the Czech republic. These two concerts organized by VMM were very special and wonderful. One event to mention, we decided to visit a castle outside the town Olomouc where the events took place. It was to our surprise that we found a sign outside the castle; 'von Duba'. Ah, so here lived our ancestors many centuries ago!

I completed an MA degree in composition followed by a PHD degree at the Birmingham conservatoire. The ceremony on completion of my doctor's degree for music composition was successful with an award for my composition work and a performance of one of my compositions. My daughter has now an MA degree in fine art, sculpture and exhibitions of her work.

What connection have these events got to do with the life of my mother? It is thanks to her, to her encouragement and support that my daughter and I are where we are today. This is a story that has to be told, her life, her struggles and optimistic views an example for us all.

I miss the good sides of socialism, the friendship we had without the technology of today's world, visiting friends, as was custom at Christmas time. I miss our mountain hut property and the wonderful countryside around Dresden. I miss our regular wanderings in the rocky sandstone mountains of Saxon Switzerland. Above all I miss the positive optimistic views we had of a future socialist world, a world of peace and equality, without unemployment and where everyone could be happy and caring for each other. My mother's artworks, her legacy, should have a permanent place in her hometown, Dresden, but I had to bring them back to Britain in order to save these artworks from Stasi hands. To find a permanent home for the future for this artistic legacy is something I have to do and I hope that this story will contribute to the keeping and safeguarding of this legacy.

Large woodcarving; 'Crucified prisoner in concentration camp'

Exhibition at John Denham Gallery 1987

John Denham Gallery
50 Mill Lane, West Hampstead London NW6 1NJ 01-794 2635

Margarete Klopfleisch (1911 – 1982)

An Exhibition of Sculpture and
Works on Paper
December 7th – 24th 1987

Open Weekdays and Sundays 11.00 – 5.00. Closed Saturdays.

Epilogue

My personal experiences I had with Stasi intervention and the unnatural death of my parents has affected my political views. I was very confused and I am still looking and searching for reasons why all this happened and I have many unanswered questions.

I hope the future will learn from past mistakes so that it may never happen again. Only a one sided history is reported. When there is talk about Germany and the Second World War, you hear very little or nothing of the resistance within Germany and the many German antifascists who risked their lives in their fight against Nazi terror. Hardly ever is anything mentioned about the part my parents and other antifascists played in it.

1960 it was possible for my mother to see her brother at long last, but I will never see my little sister ever again. I have tried.

Today we have different problems but they are just as devastating for many. My mother said decades ago, here one can speak openly. The power for profit making and money greed, the growing class divide between rich and poor, credit crunch, profit making banks and ailing health services, unemployment and homeless people do not give the impression that this world is better. This is a story that has to be told. Lessons need to be learned. I believe we can live all peaceful together, but there is a long way to go. I owe it to my parents and to all those who have a similar story to tell, but due to circumstances stays untold.

Socialism could have worked but Stasi intervention and old Nazis under cover disguised as socialists destroyed it.

No one can even imagine how I felt coming back to Britain, leaving a dream behind of a better world, the dream my parents had of a socialist society. No one can imagine the guilt I felt coming back. It was as if I had betrayed my parents. But then, my mother was so adamant to take me to the British embassy three weeks before she died. It was as if she knew way in advance the fall of the Berlin wall. Today, looking back it is clear I had no choice. Destiny made that for me. What were my thoughts when the wall came down? Some one said I should be glad and happy! But that was not the case, just unbelievable sadness. We were so happy the first ten years in spite of certain hardships as reported in my story. But the mistrust and refusal from the GDR authorities, my parents experienced to return to the GDR in the ninety- fifties without any explanation given never left them. Life in the GDR could have been wonderful, but the Stasi made that impossible. There were many good genuine achievements made; free education, no unemployment, no homeless people, less crime on the streets, equal rights for women, free health service, no payment required for dental care, great cultural events and cheap, religious freedom, cheap travel fares, the list is endless. Also people were friendlier, helpful and more social, until Stasi started to increase their interference in daily lives. What can we learn from this? I so hope that my story of my mother, her experience as an antifascist, as an émigré, her life in England, her return and life in the GDR, as well as her legacy, her artwork can help in some way to understand what happened, to improve our understanding of a possible future happier and positive society.

Note; Woodcarving; 'Peaceful world family'. 1969

FAMILY TREE

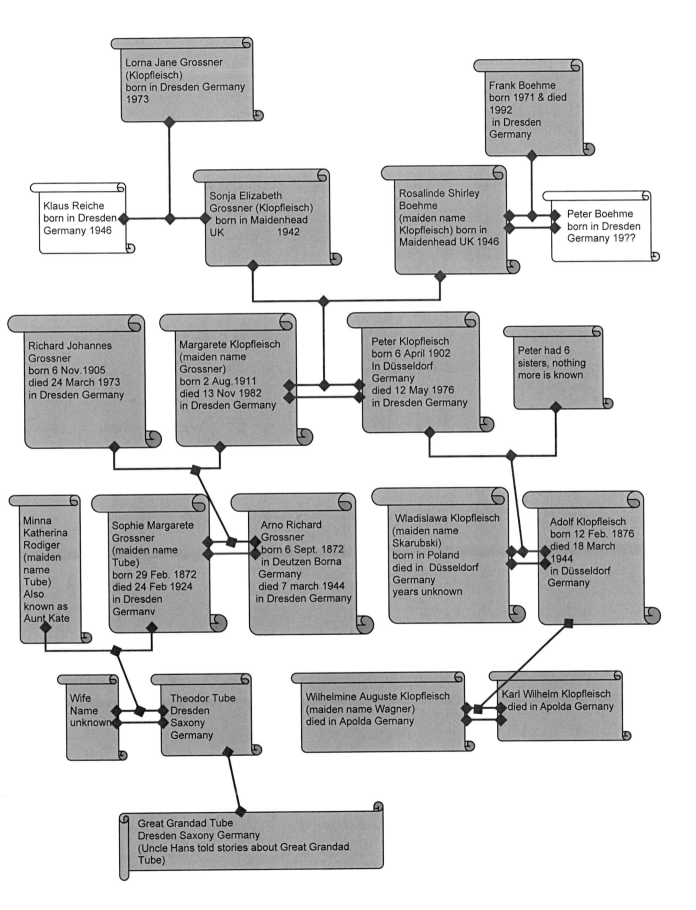

Lorna Jane Grossner (Klopfleisch) born in Dresden Germany 1973

Frank Boehme born 1971 & died 1992 in Dresden Germany

Klaus Reiche born in Dresden Germany 1946

Sonja Elizabeth Grossner (Klopfleisch) born in Maidenhead UK 1942

Rosalinde Shirley Boehme (maiden name Klopfleisch) born in Maidenhead UK 1946

Peter Boehme born in Dresden Germany 19??

Richard Johannes Grossner born 6 Nov.1905 died 24 March 1973 in Dresden Germany

Margarete Klopfleisch (maiden name Grossner) born 2 Aug.1911 died 13 Nov 1982 in Dresden Germany

Peter Klopfleisch born 6 April 1902 In Düsseldorf Germany died 12 May 1976 in Dresden Germany

Peter had 6 sisters, nothing more is known

Minna Katherina Rodiger (maiden name Tube) Also known as Aunt Kate

Sophie Margarete Grossner (maiden name Tube) born 29 Feb. 1872 died 24 Feb 1924 in Dresden Germany

Arno Richard Grossner born 6 Sept. 1872 in Deutzen Borna Germany died 7 march 1944 in Dresden Germany

Wladislawa Klopfleisch (maiden name Skarubski) born in Poland died in Düsseldorf Germany years unknown

Adolf Klopfleisch born 12 Feb. 1876 died 18 March 1944 in Düsseldorf Germany

Wife Name unknown

Theodor Tube Dresden Saxony Germany

Wilhelmine Auguste Klopfleisch (maiden name Wagner) died in Apolda Gernany

Karl Wilhelm Klopfleisch died in Apolda Gernany

Great Grandad Tube Dresden Saxony Germany (Uncle Hans told stories about Great Grandad Tube)

ANCESTRY TIME

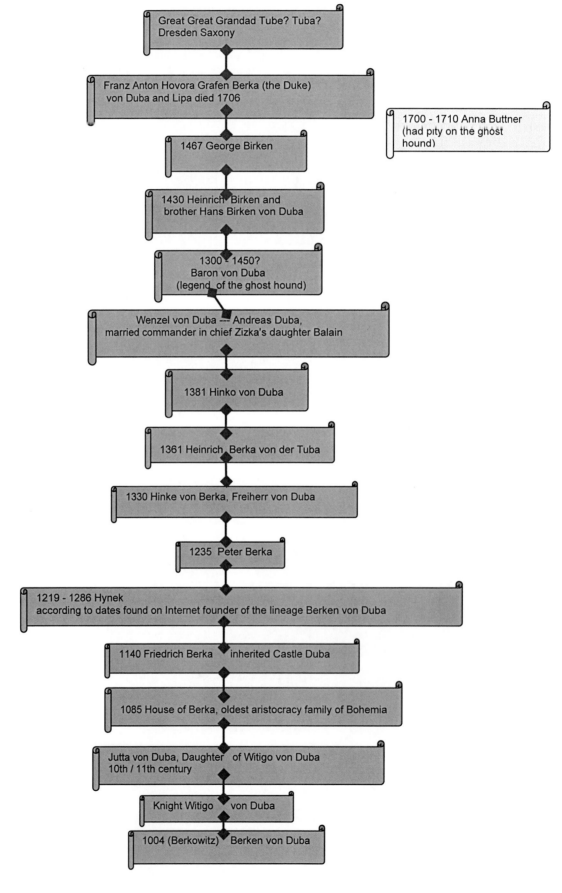

Great Great Grandad Tube? Tuba?
Dresden Saxony

Franz Anton Hovora Grafen Berka (the Duke)
von Duba and Lipa died 1706

1700 - 1710 Anna Buttner
(had pity on the ghost
hound)

1467 George Birken

1430 Heinrich Birken and
brother Hans Birken von Duba

1300 - 1450?
Baron von Duba
(legend of the ghost hound)

Wenzel von Duba --- Andreas Duba,
married commander in chief Zizka's daughter Balain

1381 Hinko von Duba

1361 Heinrich Berka von der Tuba

1330 Hinke von Berka, Freiherr von Duba

1235 Peter Berka

1219 - 1286 Hynek
according to dates found on Internet founder of the lineage Berken von Duba

1140 Friedrich Berka inherited Castle Duba

1085 House of Berka, oldest aristocracy family of Bohemia

Jutta von Duba, Daughter of Witigo von Duba
10th / 11th century

Knight Witigo von Duba

1004 (Berkowitz) Berken von Duba

Notes about life in the GDR.

The history of Germany is full of struggles and extreme changes;
-The German monarchy, that was denounced 1918.
-Republic under Ebert who was an SPD[1] man, (more right wing).
-The inflation years that ended 1923.
-1933 Hitler fascism until 1945.

The differences between socialists and communists before 1933 contributed to the weakening of the position for all those on the left. These are important facts to understand the development of the later SED[2] in the GDR.

German socialists and communists had to learn the hard way, through their mutual experiences in concentration camps, emigration and in the resistance to unite in their fight against fascism under these difficult conditions of Nazi terror.
1946 the KPD[3] and SPD united and formed the SED, the party as it was then known in the GDR.
After the war, 1945 Germany was a split country. The new beginning began under difficult conditions.
What sort of material and what sort of people were available at this point to build a new socialist Germany?
Not only were towns destroyed and in ruins, but normal German working class people themselves were physiologically in ruins, and torn from the lessons of the fascistic holocaust. Not only had the Jews suffered a dreadful fate, but also antifascists, communists and socialists had either been in concentration camps, had emigrated, or had died. The few anti-fascists who managed to come back straight away were in bad health and exhausted from their traumatic experiences. What was left?
The GDR was founded 1949. It was the previous part of Germany occupied from the Soviet Union. The previous GDR was the smaller part of Germany. When the republic was founded it had to put up with less. The West had the better factories, the necessary industry, and the better economy. The GDR in 1949 had a harder fight for its existence.
The beginnings, 1945 – 1949 were honest and good. People were generally more helpful and social to each other in spite of starvation, need and shortage of everything. They learned from past lessons and many older GDR citizens were proud of their achievements.

SED members were a mixture of people from different backgrounds, a united party of; Socialists and communists from the time before 1945, veterans from 1946 – 1949, younger members, grandchildren from Germans born before 1945, and many careerists.
As the SED was formed 1946 a certain amount of the normal population joined the party. These people had never been politically active before 1945 and had learned from the war experiences.
At this time, former soldiers also joined the party and even some previous Nazis themselves; some of whom had been sent to schooling camps in the Soviet Union. It was said that these people had changed, and that you can't get rid of every Nazi.

---

[1] SPD – Socialist party from Germany.
[2] SED – Socialist United party from East Germany.
[3] KPD – Communist party from Germany.

These veterans from 1946 – 49 received special attention 1971 – 72. They received certificates, medals and special mentions in newspapers for their work 1945 – 50 in the building up of the new socialist Germany.

Some of these veterans who had joined the party 1945 – 49, had never changed. They were still the same Nazis. The SED had allowed them to join, no matter what they had been before!

Main differences of life in the GDR were;

It was a completely different life in the GDR compared with the world this side. I still even now have the feeling that I have lived in an upside down world.

Generally people had sufficient money to buy necessary products, but often the shops were empty and it was difficult to obtain certain essential products. It was a case of being at the right place, at the right time, in that particular shop when delivery came. If a person had any West connection and West currency then usually you could get anything you wanted behind the counter.

There were many cultural activities of all sorts in the GDR, plenty of theatre performances, operas, operetta, musicals, symphony concerts and pop music. There were no violent or horror films shown in the cinemas. Prices were cheap and affordable for every one and there were often long queues for these cultural events.

There were many galleries and exhibitions of artworks. Usually the works on display were all of a similar style, hardly individuality shown. Avant-garde and contemporary style artworks of a decadent nature unavailable to be seen.

The freedom to travel anywhere you wanted in the world was an unfulfilled dream for the majority of GDR citizens.

Generally you applied for a holiday place in December to January. There were long queues, and even a simple camping place had to be applied for, and booked well in advance. A trip abroad for a tourist holiday could only be booked at the one travel agency that existed in Dresden on a special day in January at a certain time and you had to expect a long wait for endless hours. Many people queued up a whole night to get a holiday place. Only visits to certain other socialist countries were possible, no visits to the West and other capitalist countries. But as with many things there were ways around this problem, if you had the money, west connections, or a job that sometimes allowed you to take a business trip to the West.

Pensioners were allowed to visit the West, but were not allowed to take any East German money with them, relying financially completely on relatives that were living in the West.

Everything was state controlled and everyone had to carry a personal document around with them at all times. The police had to be notified at once of any change of address.

The GDR was completely dependant on foreign hard currency from the West to exist.

Many good aspects of life in the GDR included complete equal rights for women earning the same amount as men.

The health service was free for everyone; medication and dental care also free.

Travel within the GDR on trains and tram was extremely cheap. For example; for twenty pfennig [4] you could go anywhere on the tram in Dresden.

Anyone visiting the GDR as a tourist in a group, saw only one side of life there; great cultural activities, newly built buildings, new factories, large blocks of newly built flats and a beautiful countryside, great for holidays. There were achievements, and many elements of socialism over there.

---

[4] Pfennig – East German penny.

Schools; Each year the state published schoolbooks that were used for the whole of the GDR and there were new revised editions regularly. The same material was used everywhere. The standard of teaching and quality was high. The standard expected from each pupil was very high. This had great results for the children and students, but everything was closely controlled.

This also had the effect, that, because of the high demand on pupils, they were trained in a sort of 'short knowledge' way, with exams nearly each month that counted towards the results at the end of the school year. This pressure meant that the pupils easily forgot what they had just learnt for one exam to make way for the next. No time was given for newly gained knowledge to sink in.

From the first school year onwards each child had a tremendous amount of homework. Parents were expected to work and help.

There were many specialist schools of different grades; plenty for those talented children that the GDR government thought could be of special use for their policies. But also many normal children were in danger of being put in special schools for backward children and being labelled as unintelligent if they for some reason stayed behind in their schoolwork.

Children with learning disabilities, such as dyslexia and autism, had hardly any chances whatsoever. These disabilities were not recognized.

The brother of one of my friends is severely autistic. It was only through the endless support from his dedicated mother that he was able to learn. He was labelled as stupid and placed in a school for severely physically handicapped children. Today he is an engineer.

There were no computers or calculators used. In fact, no one had a computer; there were enough jobs, enough training and employment for everyone. The choices varied each year according to the situation in industries and amount of places available in the universities.

Some GDR people thought and believed that we were living in a socialist society, wanting to believe it, to believe in the good things, the positive achievements and success stories in spite of many rumours and beginning restlessness under the population.

Shopping; Goods were unequally shared out. One town received more than other towns. Berlin, Potsdam for example had the advantage of being served first. Reason; it was the capital. The GDR was a very poor country living and existing on hard currency. When we arrived in the GDR 1960 things were not quite so bad. But the situation worsened in later years. In order to obtain more and more West currency, the best products from the industries were sold to the West. The GDR population got what was left over. This was then unequally shared out and specially privileged people, like the police were able go to their own special shops and buy goods like bananas, tomatoes, cucumbers etc, whilst normal shops stayed empty. But prices of goods were the same everywhere in all shops. Fresh goods were seldom available, depending on the time of the year, and if there were, then that created long queues. The message that something special was available at that shop down the road pasted quickly from mouth to mouth and people dropped what they were doing to rush down and join the queue in the hope that those special goods were still available and not sold out by the time you got there.

In late summer certain products like cucumbers became available to public because there were enough grown locally.

Buying a new car was a great problem. There were very long waiting lists of approx ten years or more. Second hand cars were often more expensive than new ones and if your car was in need of repair it often took weeks or even months before getting the part you needed. This situation created a black market.

There were so-called inter-shops where nearly everything could be bought with foreign hard currency. These products were not seen in normal shops. People who received West money from well-off West relatives could change West currency for vouchers at a bank and purchase specials things in these inter-shops. The offer in these inter-shops ranged from chocolates, bananas, even things like baths, toilets and kitchen sinks. It also was even possible to buy trades people on the black market for West currency.

It was a great advantage to have West relatives. Often it was difficult to get the required material needed for necessary repairs. Even cement was a luxury and often sold on the black market for West money. Some trades people even refused to work without getting West currency.

Votes and elections; There were no genuine opposition parties. The names of candidates were sorted out, long before the elections and their success from the start guaranteed. Those who disagreed with the elections just did not go. Those who refused to vote were noted on a special list and visits were made to speak with them. Nothing really could alter the decision that had been made long before in Berlin.

Studying; With the foundation of the GDR various good and social laws were made. One of them, giving children from working class parents, especially children from Nazi victims first priority to receive a place of study at universities and high schools. So, these children from poorer parents who had little, or no opportunity to study, either before or during the war, were now given the wonderful chance to study.

Law; Working- class children were given first priority to study

	A	**B**
First Generation; 1) Before 1945	Nazi's, Intellectuals; Teachers, Doctors, Professors; Engineers, etc	Nazi victims, Working-class; Factory workers; Unskilled labourers,
Second Generation; 2) After 1945 –1960 1965	Their children were given little or no chance to study; Factory workers. Unskilled labourers,	Their children now given priority to study, Teachers, Doctors, Professors, Engineers, etc. now become intellectuals;
Third Generation: 3) From approx 1965 -1976	Their children, (grandchildren from Nazis) now given first priority to study: Teachers, Doctors, Professors Engineers, etc	Now given second priority as these children now have intellectual parents (Grandchildren from Nazi victims). Factory workers, Unskilled labourers.

The standard of the courses at universities were very high and thorough with great demands and expectations from each student.

Children from intellect parents who had studied during, or before the Nazi time were given little or no chance. This law worked out quite well after the war enabling these children from poorer background to study at Universities and High Schools. But this law never changed, was never updated. So then 1970, 1976, in the third generation you found grandchildren from previous Nazis and Nazi intellects now given first priority to study, because their parents were now considered as working- class, or as unskilled labourers, although their standard of living in the GDR was by no means so hard as the previous generation under the capitalists.

The grandchildren from Nazi victims and working-class were now given only second priority because their parents were now intellectuals.
This was also the generation of children and youth who spoke with two tongues.

Double Tongued; A typical feature of life in East Germany was this 'double-tongue' speaking. This was a particularly distressing fact when children were involved. They learned to speak;
   -What was requested in schools or at work.
   -What was said at home in their own four walls.

Not every child had a background that fitted into the required norm, and very few German children had grandparents of that sort, like my own parents who were socialists and anti-fascists. It must not be forgotten that the majority of anti-fascists, socialists, communists and anyone that was against the Nazi regime had fled or had died in the concentration camps.

Television; There were only two channels. All programmes were carefully censored. It was possible to see West programs in some areas of the GDR. It was a fact, that in areas where GDR citizens were able to see West TV in full, they were less inclined to apply for permission to leave the country. Dresden and surroundings had the highest amount of people wanting to leave. It was an area where many previous Nazis had gathered. GDR citizens tended to let themselves be blinded from the 'colourful West'.

Social laws; There were a variety of good social laws. If they had been kept, life in the GDR would have been fine. Everyone had work. There was no such thing as unemployment. There were laws for protection for mother and child. A pregnant woman could not lose her job. She got about four months off with full pay before birth, also two or three months again full paid leave after birth. I cannot remember exactly the amount of time she was given. If she could not find a nursery place for her child, her job had to be kept open and paid in full for up to two years. Mothers with children, under, and of the age of three were supposed to have special protection and could not lose their jobs. Nearly all children went to Kindergarten.

Leaving the GDR; Circumstances and situation for each citizen leaving the GDR was differently dealt with. It was, in most cases a most difficult and stressful time, involving years of waiting. The reasons for leaving varied personally from;
-Split family, GDR – West Germany. This was I believe the main reason for many leaving. The after war years, creating two Germanys left many families split, unable to see each other for years and years.
-People, who were not given enough chances in their career to succeed, or to change jobs for some reason or the other, took any opportunity to leave the GDR, hoping to get a better position in the West.

-Unwanted persons; people who had said something that was uncomfortable, offensive, and that the GDR authorities did not like.

-People who were blinded from the products on offer in the West, colourful shops for example. (They forgot they needed money for these things).

Conclusion; Life in the GDR could have worked. There were many good aspects and achievements made. There were elements of socialism. This is one point not to be forgotten. Why did it go wrong? That is one question still open and there are many lessons to be learned from the experience of living in the GDR. It was a life in a community that was completely different to the life in a capitalist state. It was not perfect and condemned to fail due to Stalinist dictatorship.

Terracotta; Relief, 'Prisoner'

Work in Public and private Collections;

Early sculptures mentioned in catalogue, 'Kunst im Exil'1938;

'Mother with child',
'Fairy story teller',
'Comedian',
'Gypsy Children'.

These sculptures were sold to a woman doctor, art historian in Prague 1939 before my mother left the Czech republic for Britain. Her name is regrettably unknown to me, but this private collection may still be around.

Several artworks were sold to private collectors 1987 as a result of the exhibition at the John Denham Gallery in London.

Four sculptures sold to Mrs Thompkins in Bristol, unknown where they are today.

Dr Gert Gruber, Germany has a wide range of graphics, watercolours and Linocuts.

Several artworks were sold to private collectors 1987 as a result of the exhibition at the John Denham Gallery in London.

'Hand with Dove of Peace' 1960 terracotta; Polish Peace Committee Warshaw.

'Mother with child', approx 1943 – 1948. woodcarving;
    Halle Moritzburg Gallery 1965.

'Prisoner' and **'Man from Concentration camp'.**
 Woodcarvings, approx 1940 – 1943? Museum for German History, Berlin 1971.

Note; All dates of when artworks were made are approx. only.

Exhibitions;
Early exhibitions;
Prague 1937 – Oska Kokoschka League.
2 Art Festivals in emigrants hostel Strasnice.
Exhibitions organized through the Free German League of Culture in Great Britain.
Exhibition in Internment Camp Isle of Man; 1940-41.
Exhibition; 1946 in London; Free German League.
Exhibitions with Maidenhead and Cookham art clubs,
1946 –1960, a variety of exhibitions in Cookham; took place nearly every other year.
(Exhibited together with Stanley Spencer).
Exhibitions with the Artists International Association; April 1951.
London Hampstead Festival; 1950 and also 1957.
Exhibitions in Reading, and Eaton College; 1951.
Slough Arts Festival; 1958.

Exhibitions in GDR;
Kunstausstellung Kühl, Dresden 1967, exhibited together with the Dresdener artist Otto Schubert.
1970; Exhibition together with Prof Dr Erich Drechsler.
Further exhibitions organized by Gallery Kühl; 1970,1971, 1972 and 1973.
Exhibitions organized by Dr Gert Gruber, from his collection, as mentioned in catalogues from Neubrandenburg, 1978.
Wittenberg 1983; Kunst Gegen Faschismus in VEB Chemische Werke Buna.
Small exhibitions in various clubhouses; Putjatkin Haus Schachwitz in Dresden, 1980.
1967; exhibited some works in the Leonbaad museum, Dresden.
Worked as a stage artist; Bühnen Bildner, Dresden Staats Theater, 1960-1961.
Last exhibition in Dresden; Gallerie Comenius Orbis Pictus 27, 1981 Kulturbund der DDR Stadtleitung Dresden, Dr Diether Schmidt.

From Dr Gerd Gruber's collection;
1982, 'International Graphik seit 1945.' Haus der Kultur und Bildung, Neubrandenburg, Germany.
1983, 'Sie haben eine Welt zu gewinnen', exhibition of graphics, Lutherstadt Wittenberg.

Further exhibitions;
1986; Camden Arts Centre, Arkwright Rd London,
    'Art in Exile in Great Britain', 1933 – 1945.
1987; Exhibition at the John Denham Gallery in London.
Further exhibitions organized by Dr Gerd Gruber from his collection;
2002; 'Verfemt, verfolgt – nicht vergessen', art and resistance against fascism,
    Dessau, Germany.
2008; 'Aufbruch in die Moderne'.
2011; Large exhibition for anti-fascist art;
    'Entartet' verfemten Kunst der Jahre 1933 – 1945'.
2009; October – 2010 May, Great Britain, Leicester, New Walk Museum,
    'Journey Out of Darkness.' Leicester's collection of German expressionist art.

Literature;
Kleine Sammlung 1946; FDKB Bücherie; Page 38. Published by the 'Free German League of culture' in Great Britain.

Fundus- Bücher; 'In Letzter Stunde', Künstlerschiften, 1933 bis 1945 by Dr Diether Schmidt.VEB VERLAG der Kunst Dresden, 1964; Pages 251 and 266.

'Dresdner Monats Blätter'. Zeitschriften der Dresdener Heimatfreunde in West Germany....18 Jahrgang, August 1967; Folge 8, page 1e.
Catalogue; 'Kunst gegen den Fashismus', 21 Ausstellung in VEB Chemische Werke Buna 1969; Pages 37 and 70.

Catalogue; 'Antifaschismus-unser stil'. Exhibition in Haus der Kultur und Bildung Neubrandenburg, April-May 1978' Gert Gruber; Pages 19 and 20.

Hansjörg Schneider; 'Exhiltheater in der Tschechoslowakei 1933-1938, Deutches Theater im Exil'. Henschverlag Berlin, 1979; Pages 61.

Reclam; 'Exhil in der Tschechoslowakei in Grossbritannien, Skandinavien und Palastina. Kunst und Literatur im antifaschistischen Exhil 1933-1945'. Verlag Philipp Reclam jun. Leipzig 1980; Page 129.

Catalogue; 'Deutsche Geschischte', 1917- 1945,
    Museum für Deutsche Geschischte; Page 74.

Catalogue; Gert Gruber, 'Internationale Graphik seit 1945',
    Auststellung 1982 Haus der Kultur und Bildung Neubrandenburg.

Catalogue; Galerie Comenius Orbis Pictus 27; November,1981.
    'Margarete Klopfleisch; Sculpture and Watercolours'.

Catalogue from exhibition; 'Kunst im Aufbruch, Dresden 1918-1933',
    Staatliche Kunstsammlungen Gemäldergalerie Neue Meister,
    30 September1980 to 25 February 1981; Page 28.

Catalogue; Camden Arts Centre, 'Exile Art in Great Britain 1933-45'.
    August 1986, London, Zuleika Dobson.

Catalogue; 'Kunst in Exil in Grossbritannien'
    1933-45. Frölich & Kaufmann; Page 138.

2002; Germany, Dessau; Orangerie des Schlosses Georgium, 9 feb – 17 March.
    'Verfemt, verfolgt – nicht vergessen,' art and resistance against fascism, Dessau,
    (Dr Gerd Gruber's collection). Published by Anhaltischer Kunstverein Dessau E.V.

'The dictionary of artists in Britain since1945' by David Buckman; London. First
    published 1998 by Art Dictionary ltd; Pages 15, 706 -707.
    A new edition has been published 2006.

Latest discovery of literature ;
Andreas Schätzke; ' Rückkehr Aus dem Exil'
Bildende Künstler und Architekten in der SBZ und früheren DDR.-
REIMER VERLAG. Page 76.
Erhard Frommhold; -' Ein unerschöpfliches Thema'
Texte zur Kunst und Kulturgeschichte Sachsens.
Herausgegeben von Hildtrud Ebert. Page 94, 2009 Lucas Verlag.

Woodcarving; 'Mother with child', approx 1975?

Historical Events

1.8.1914	Out break of world war one.
1.1.1916	Foundation of the Spartacus group (Karl Liebknecht and Rosa Luxemburg).
Oct. 1917	October Revolution in Russia.
4.11.1918	Sailors revolt in Keil.
9.11.1918	Declaration of the German republic, (Kings resignation)
31.12.1918	Foundation of the KPD (communist party of Germany).
Jan.1919	January fights in Berlin 'workers and soldiers' Republic in Bremen, Strikes and armed fights in Ruhr territory, 'Workers and soldier' Republic in Munchen.
28.6.1919	The Versailler Peace contract was signed.
11.8.1919	Acceptance of Weimarer constitution.
Nov.1919/23	November revolution,
Mar.1920	Capp. -Putsch, General strikes in whole of Germany. Fights in Ruhr territory (Red Ruhr army)
Jan. 1923	French occupation in Ruhr territory, economical and political crisis in Germany
Aug.1923	General strikes, overthrow of the Cuno Government.
Autumn 1923	Revolutionary crisis. Highest point of inflation. Entry of Reichswehr (Empire army) in Sachen and Thuringen
Oct.1923	Revolt of the Hamburger workers
Nov.1923	Unsuccessful Hitler - Putsch
29.9.1938	KPD is prohibited.
1929 / 33	World commercial crisis; constantly growing unemployment, governing through emergency laws (Bruning). Increased class struggle and a strong growth of the fascist movement.
1933 / 45	Fascist dictatorship.
February 1933	Beginning of Reichs Tag. The beginning of fascist terror. Erection of concentration camps.
1936	Occupation of the first military zone in Rhineland.
1938	Occupation of Austria from the fascist troops.
-In October 1938	Parts of the Czech republic are occupied,
- March 1939	The rest of the Czech republic occupied.
1.9.1939	Begin of the Second World War with attack on Poland.
May 1945	End of the Second World War.
August 1945	Hiroshima and Nagasaki destroyed by atomic bomb.
Post 1945	Division of Germany.
July 1945	Formation of the 'Iron Curtain'.
7th October 1949	Foundation of East Germany.
1961	Berlin wall erected.
1989	Fall of Berlin wall.

A report of an exhibition in Düsseldorf about the resistance 1933 – 1945.

Amongst my father's papers I found a report of an exhibition in Düsseldorf about the Düsseldorfer resistance 1933 –1945. I do not know the dates of this exhibition. It reports of the underground fight against Hitler, the opposition and the growing fascist terror. This exhibition was put together following months of long hard work and research from active Düsseldorf antifascists.

'Exhibit 1)
The result of the vote 6.11.1932 in Düsseldorf was 31 % for Hitler and 65 % against Hitler. From this result, the question arises how come Hitler was able to be put in as representative from a minority and for him to become Rechskanzler.
The strong interest of the money givers of the NSDAP were the responsible ones. The Hitler opposition were not united, so that in the end the Weimar Republic was not avoidable.

Exhibit 2)
Events from the year 1933 and the illegal opposition, illegal fight consistent only of explanations; posters, leaflets and newspapers.
By the end of 1933 as a result of the beginning Nazi terror 13 Düsseldorfer were killed, 49 given 136 years imprisonment and ten condemned and given the death sentence.
About 600 Düsseldorfer were given 'so-called' 'Schutzhaft' (safety imprisonment) on the 'Ulm' and in the Moor camp by Paperburg.
These Düsseldorfer were given these so-called lighter sentences without process.

Exhibit 3)
The amount of posters and newspapers against Hitler were not insignificant. By the process in Solingen - Ohlip 261.000 and in Koln 55.000 pieces of antifascist writings were printed and found their way to places for further distribution.
In 27 cases, in the year 1934 many resistant groups, about 423 antifascists, stood accused before the judges and at least the same amount found their way into the concentration camps.

Exhibit 4)
The next board pictures the justice building on Königsplatz at the Oberland courts.
11 am on the 8th March 1935 over 3 resistant groups were taken before the judges and over 69 accused were given 210 years imprisonment.
Four well-known antifascists stood out in this process. From the 69 accused 13 were imprisoned and died before 1945.

Exhibit 5)
This exhibit starts with the Second World War, beginning in Spain. Düsseldorfer anti-fascists fight on the side of the republic again the fascist dictatorship and have losses by the defence of Madrid.
The process list for this year is long. 26 anti fascists groups had to take 600 years imprisonment and the amount of years of imprisonment given grew to 2000.

Exhibit 6)
Driven to death; this exhibit report tells of the story of the Düsseldorfer nature friend Moritz Ludwig and his heroic death.
This exhibit, 1937, also reports of the fate of the director of the town, the major Dr Walter Hensel, how near death, under continuous bodily and physical torture he tried twice to escape the dreadful humiliation.
We read in the chronics how more and more social democrats, bible experts and priests, religious people were treated as dangerous opposition were arrested, imprisoned and condemned.

Special exhibit 7)
Youth in the fight against Hitler, Kaplan Dr Rossaint and a young communist Berta Karg
were the leading heads for the united fight of the youth against fascism. One was given 12 the
other 15 years imprisonment.
A large photo shows how the young communist threw self made hand notes and lino prints
out of the windows of the shopping centre Tietz down onto the Theodor Körner Street below.
Exhibit 8)
München Agreement gives Hitler free hand. This exhibit shows a burning synagogue on the
Kasernen Street. The III Reich is documented from anger confirming these connections.
Exhibit 9) explains the position shortly before the II World War begins. Here, April 1939,
according to the reports that were sent to the central place in Berlin from 61 Gestapo head
quarter's 300.000 Germans were imprisoned, sent to concentration camps, and prisons. The
exact amount of Düsseldorfer is not known.
Exhibit 10)
Europe under the 'Hakenkreuz', (Nazi cross). This exhibit has the most impressive photos
under the net of occupied Europe. This exhibit shows new evidence of the anti-fascist fight in
Düsseldorf and shows exact figure, times and amount of the transported Jewish citizens from
Düsseldorf.
The final action is shown. Names and death notices of Düsseldorf victims of Nazi terror.
Exhibit 11)
This exhibit shows a picture of Hitler troops marching into Paris, also of the resistance in
Paris. This exhibit also showed a photo of Düsseldorf in ruins after the heavy bombing. Also a
small exhibit in shown of the resistance group in the year 1942; Kowalke – kaps – Fuchs with
the help of the painter Peter Ludwig.
In May 1942 a conference from Hitler opposition in Niederheim took place and the
population was called out for anti-war work. The amount of victims from active Düsseldorfer
Hitler opposition grew during the years 1942 and 1943.
Exhibit 12) shows the real criminals but also the resistance fighting to the very last minute.
Anti-war activists were captured and a Captain Schweitzer helped with the transport of
political prisoners successfully. This captain helped to save these two transports of political
prisoners to escape their liquidation through the Solinger and Wuppentaler Gestapo out of the
top-security prison Lüttringhausen.
The memorial honouring of 71 shot victims in the Wenzel mine by Langenfield concludes this
picture exhibition.
This exhibition showed the damage done to us all and thoroughly condemns the thesis opinion
of the 'collective guilt of the German folk.'

   I believe it important to mention this exhibition as it shows the growing resistance, hardship,
the destruction of life and the damage done to the German folk, especially the last sentence
concerning the so-called 'collective guilt'. Many people, to this day, when talking about
Germany associate the German people with Hitler and Nazis. They hardly talk about the
resistance, the underground movement and antifascist fight.